THE PRICE OF COMMAND

A BIOGRAPHY OF GENERAL GUY SIMONDS

DOMINICK GRAHAM

First published in 1993 by
Stoddart Publishing Co. Limited
34 Lesmill Road
Toronto, Canada
M3B 2T6
(416) 445-3333

Canadian Cataloguing in Publication Data

Graham, Dominick
The price of command: a biography of General Guy Simonds

Includes index.
ISBN 0-7737-2692-6

1. Simonds, Guy Granville, 1903-1974. 2. Canada. Canadian Army - Biography. 3. World War II, 1939-1945 - Biography. 4. Generals - Canada - Biography. I. Title.

FC611.S44G73 1993   355.3'31'092   C92-095634-3
F1034.3.S44G73 1993

COVER DESIGN: Brant Cowie/ArtPlus
Printed and bound in Canada

All maps used in this book are courtesy of the Department of National Defence, Directorate of History.

Grateful acknowledgement is made to Faber and Faber Ltd. for permission to reprint two quotations from T. S. Eliot's *Little Gidding.*

Stoddart Publishing gratefully acknowledges the support of the Canada Council, Ontario Ministry of Culture, Tourism, and Recreation, Ontario Arts Council, and Ontario Publishing Centre in the development of writing and publishing in Canada.

We few, we happy few, we band of brothers; for he today
that sheds his blood with me shall be my friend . . .

— *Henry V*, act 4, scene 3

*Je crois que dans l'Armée canadienne outremer nous avons
trouvé un esprit vraiment canadien dans lequel le service
pour le Canada a pris la première place. Si nous pouvons
ramener avec nous, au Canada, cet esprit, nous aurons,
alors, remporté une double victoire en Europe.*

— General H. D. G. Crerar, Commander First
Canadian Army. Message at the Armistice,
May 1945

Contents

....

Foreword

....

IT IS A PRIVILEGE to write a foreword to this magnificent, long overdue biography of Lieutenant General Guy Granville Simonds. He was a giant in Canadian history, and it is significant that the biography is published on the fiftieth anniversary of the 1943 invasion of Sicily which, discounting the minor landing in France in 1940 and the disastrous Dieppe raid of 1942, was the first major successful Canadian operation of the Second World War. Guy Simonds, of course, commanded the Canadian contingent of that invasion.

The Royal Canadian Artillery Association has been committed to the publication of this biography for a number of years. Guy Simonds was a gunner but is best known as a brilliant senior commander. As a divisional commander in Sicily and Italy, a corps commander in Italy and Northwest Europe, and an acting army commander in Northwest Europe, he was the exemplification of military professionalism. His subsequent career in the United Kingdom, as chief of the General Staff in Canada, and in retirement are part of the history of this country and the story of this man.

I am indebted to the Simonds Biography Committee of the Royal Canadian Artillery Association for making the publication of this book possible. I am also indebted to the donors who contributed to the funding of the project. My special thanks are due to Lieutenant General W. A. B. Anderson, O.B.E., C.D., and Colonel C. Malim Harding (now deceased), who were the driving forces behind the creation of the biography committee in 1989. The members of the

Simonds Biography Committee include Lieutenant Colonel J. D. Gibson, C.D., A.D.C. (chairman); Lieutenant General W. A. B. Anderson, O.B.E., C.D. (colonel commandant 1989-91); Colonel R. A. Jacobson, C.D. (colonel commandant 1991-); and Lieutenant Colonel B. G. Brulé, C.D. (secretary-treasurer RCAA). Other members are Colonel B. S. MacDonald, C.D., and Colonel J. C. McKenna, C.D.

Benefactors of the Simonds biography project are the Canadian Corps of Commissionaires; the Forty-ninth Field Regiment Royal Canadian Artillery; the Henry N. R. Jackman Foundation; Colonel Donald Maclaren; Colonel the Honourable Mr. Justice John R. Matheson, C.D., LL.D.; Lieutenant Colonel M. D. McKay, C.D.; Nationale-Nederlanden Canada Holdings Limited; the Royal Military College Club Foundation, Inc.; the Royal Regiment of Canada Association; Major R. W. Sears, C.D.; Lieutenant Colonel W. E. Sills, C.D.; Mrs. Dorothy F. Simonds; Colonel James H. Turnbull, O.M.M., C.D.; and Captain S. H. Usborne.

Sponsors of the project are Colonel J. Howard Coleman, M.B.E., E.D.; Colonel W. R. Dawes, C.D.; Lieutenant Colonel J. E. de Hart, M.C., C.D.; Brigadier General R. G. Heitshu, C.D.; the Lawson Foundation; Lieutenant Colonel R. W. Lockhart, C.D.; Colonel A. G. Lynch-Staunton, C.D.; Colonel Brian S. MacDonald, C.D.; G. A. Martin; Brigadier General S. T. McDonald, C.D.; Lieutenant Colonel E. C. Scott, E.D.; and Lieutenant Colonel D. A. Wynn, C.D.

Supporters of the project include Major Stuart A. Beare; Brigadier General R. P. Beaudry, C.D.; Lieutenant Colonel J. C. Berezowski, C.D.; Colonel D. Berry, C.D.; David Black; Colonel T. Bond; Lieutenant Colonel B. G. Brulé, C.D.; Major C. Chaplin; Colonel H. D. Chapman, C.D.; Major M. F. Doan; Colonel S. H. Dobell; Captain Walter E. Doede; Major R. R. Doyon, O.M.M., C.D.; Noel K. Flemington; Colonel D. H. Gunter, C.D.; Colonel H. M. Hague, D.S.O., E.D.; the Hamilton Artillery Association; Colonel C. F. Harrington, C.D.; Captain A. H. Hoole, C.D.; D. A. Houghton; Lieutenant P. S. Irwin; Lieutenant Colonel J. P. Jeffries, C.D.; Colonel M. D. Kearney, C.D.; Captain A. S. Keator; Major General J. A. MacInnis, C.D.; Colonel D. B. McGibbon, C.D.; Gordon W. Mepham; Major G. D. Mitchell, M.C., C.D.; His Worship B. P. Morin; Kelly Mothersell; Major A. B. Pennie; Colonel N. W. Reilander; Lieutenant Colonel R. A. Rodgers; Colonel E. H. Rowe, O.M.M., C.D.; W. K. G. Savage, M.C.; Captain W. T. Seed, M.B.E., C.D.; Colonel A. E. Sherwin, C.D.; Major S. Steinke; Major H. P. Stickley, C.D.; Lieutenant Colonel William Tyndale, E.D.; Lieutenant Colonel H. T. Vergette, C.D.; Lieutenant Colonel C. E. Wallen, C.D.; S. Witt; Lieutenant C. E. Wright; and Captain J. O. Young.

Finally I must pay tribute to our author Dominick (Toby) Graham, M.C. He has performed a masterful feat. A gunner himself, he is widely known as a historian and professor, and the RCAA has been very fortunate to have him perform this invaluable contribution to the artillery and to Canada.

JOHN D. GIBSON
LIEUTENANT COLONEL
President, Royal Canadian Artillery
Association

Acknowledgements

THE WRITING OF THIS BIOGRAPHY of Guy Simonds
has been a team effort. That is appropriate
because Simonds was a team player. Bill Anderson was the motive
force as colonel commandant of the regiment. Without his energy
the project would have dribbled on forever without an outcome.
Around him he gathered a committee: John Gibson as secretary
and eventually chairman, an invaluable anchorman; Bernie Brulé
as treasurer; and after Malim Harding's sad death, Jack McClelland
as contact man with the publisher. These were unfailingly supportive. Most important of all, a biography cannot be written without
the active support of the family of the subject. All of them have
consented to be interviewed and have given friendly advice.
Dorothy Simonds, the general's widow, graciously endowed the
project, and his children, Charles and Ruth, contributed valuable
additions to the drafts.

Simonds's contemporaries were friendly and helpful. Bill
Anderson had been an active participant in some of the events
recounted in the book, and he knew so many of the actors that he
was always the source of last resort for checking facts and finding
new witnesses. I only wish it had been possible to talk to all those
whose names were put into my hand. As it was, many sent letters,
which even if their contents have not been directly inserted in the
text, added to my knowledge of Guy Simonds.

A few who were centrally involved and had much to contribute
must be mentioned first. They helped unstintingly, spending long

hours reading drafts, cudgelling their brains, and searching for documents. They gave the book its content and me much pleasure. George Kitching wrote many pages of comments and gave me hours of his time in Victoria. Elliot Rodger became almost an alter ego as he produced names and lobbied support, besides lending me his diary and talking to me about events at Second Corps headquarters. He helped sort out the story of John Bennett and the amendments at Ford Manor, and Bennett wrote a letter about Guy Simonds as a hunter. Bob Moncel encouraged me every time he returned key corrections to drafts. Bruce Matthews, who died recently, produced a staff officer's commentary on artillery practice, beautifully presented and answering all my tiresome tactical questions. He talked to me at length on two occasions, although in poor health. Another senior officer who must be thanked is Fin Clark. Quite apart from the interview he gave me, I also listened to the extensive tapes of his talks with Professor Reginald Roy in Victoria. Geoffrey Walsh, another central character, filled in many details from his extensive memories of Guy Simonds. Pat Bogert and his wife in England entertained me, and I enjoyed his stories and lively memory for detail.

Among the more "junior" witnesses, Michael Kearney gave me two long interviews about his time as ADC, and Bob Kingstone, who saw much of the workings of the Chiefs of Staff Committee from the inside, read drafts and added greatly to my knowledge. Stuart Graham gave me a long interview with interesting sidelights on his time as ADC in Sicily and in postwar posts. Douglas Harkness, a fellow gunner and later minister of defence, was an entertaining informant. Ab Knight, here in Fredericton, explained much of the staff work for Husky and for the repatriation scheme in 1945, apart from providing miscellaneous details about Second Corps administration under Darrel Laing. Sparky Sparling and Stan Todd gave time and wrote reports, the former sending me some useful documents and the latter giving me a charming and sensitive interview — his memory is, indeed, remarkable. Robert Rothschild travelled to Ottawa to give me information that is in the book. Trumbull Warren read drafts and wrote useful comments. I regret not having reached him in Toronto, for which, mea culpa. Mr. Justice John Matheson, a longtime admirer of Guy Simonds, has been generous with papers, information, and encouragement. Philip Fisher collected printed articles and books on Simonds and handed them over impeccably bound. Mary Plow gave me lunch and charmed me with her energy and her conversation about wartime England. Bob Rayment gave me two interviews and papers on the activities of the Chiefs of Staff Committee.

Historians whom I thank for reading chapters are John English, Bill McAndrew, Marc Milner, and Reginald Roy. Bill McAndrew has taken trouble over the years to direct me towards useful documents, and on this occasion to argue patiently about points on which we shall never agree. Reg Roy offered me the use of his interview tapes, of which the Marshal Stearns and Fin Clark tapes were particularly useful. My friend and colleague Shelford Bidwell applied his skills as an editor, tactfully as ever. I have long since learned that he is usually right.

Simonds's retirement years have not been as thoroughly covered as some readers would have liked. However, it seemed that another chapter would have slowed the pace of the book and diverted its theme. The linkages have been made, I hope. Marshal Stearns and his family, Tony Griffin, J. E. McNelly, and the Holland and the Roell families, who generously contributed to the writing of this book, were important influences. But several others have received only a brief mention at best. For that I apologize.

I end by thanking the following who contributed by writing to me or by giving an interview: Ted Beament, John Bourne, Ben Cunningham, Dick Danby, Larry Dunlap, Philip Fisher, Tony German, Willis Hague, Bob Heitshu, Christopher Hull, W. A. Joyce, Allan S. Joyner, Oscar Lange, Brian Lees, Robert MacNeil, John Marteinson, J. S. McMahon, Frank Miller, Marc Milner, G. Duff Mitchell, Robert Mitchell, Brigadier and Mrs. Morres, Robert Noble, Jack Orton, John Page, Frank Saunders, Norman Shaddock, Bill Simcock, Jamie Stewart, R. A. Ryder, C. E. Vickers, Brigadier and Mrs. Wattsford, Denis Whitaker, and W. S. Ziegler.

I fear that this list of helpers may not be complete, and I apologize if that is so. As well, there are those who, if they had been consulted, might have corrected my errors in the text. I apologize for not contacting them and for the errors that may have resulted. I am entirely responsible for the text.

DOMINICK GRAHAM
Fredericton
June 1992

What we call the beginning is often the end
And to make an end is to make a beginning.
The end is where we start from.

T. S. ELIOT, *Little Gidding*

Prologue

....

"WE SEND YOU our warmest and most affectionate greetings," the telegram read. "We
understand you are fighting a great battle and all of us wish we could
be close to you now. Your inspiration to gunners is immeasurable
and everlasting. From your many gunner friends."[1] This communication was sent to Lieutenant General Guy Granville Simonds, C.C.,
C.B., C.B.E., D.S.O., C.D., from the Conference of Defence
Associations on February 1, 1974. He was fighting lung cancer.

Simonds died on Wednesday, May 15, 1974, aged seventy-one.
After the service in Toronto's Grace Church-on-the-Hill that
Saturday, the coffin, draped with the flag and bearing the general's
sword and decorations, was taken on a gun carriage through sunlit
streets to Mount Pleasant Cemetery. Veterans ten-deep lined the
streets. There were thousands of flags and banners. A four-
hundred-man guard of honour was led by Lieutenant Governor
Pauline McGibbon and General Jacques Dextraze, the chief of the
Defence Staff. The ambassador of the Netherlands was present, but
neither the minister of defence nor any other representative of the
Canadian government attended. A body of distinguished soldiers
who had served with the general followed to the beat of muffled
drums and solemn music. The booms of a fifteen-gun salute
marked the progress of the cortege, and riflemen fired a volley at
the graveside. The Reverend M. C. Evans spoke the final, quiet
words of committal, a trumpeter sounded "The Last Post," and a
moment later the mourners left deep in thought about the man

who had been Canada's greatest Second World War soldier and an outstanding chief of the General Staff (CGS) during the early days of the cold war.

They remembered a man, seemingly cold and remote, a perfectionist who had succeeded in every step of his military career from its beginning in 1925, when he passed out of the Royal Military College (RMC) with the Sword of Honour and second in the order of merit, to its summit as professional head of the army. In success he showed no spice of devilment and humour that would have endeared him to soldiers, particularly those of a nation of pioneers organized on the militia principle. Those traits were foreign to him, for he lacked a sense of humour. He was driven by ambition, but it was not motivated by a desire for personal success; rather, it was for high professional standards in himself and his Canadians. So he was a ruthless weeder-out of the inefficient, even of trusted subordinates who erred only once.

Yet he was not Canadian-born but an English immigrant with the drive and determination of the typical immigrant reinforced, in his case, by insecurity in youth. From his mother he imbibed the ideals of an earlier England, but he was always torn between them and those of his adopted country, of which he could never quite be a part. But for all that his colleagues were proud of him because he brought honour to Canadian arms. That he became a gentler man after his retirement, praised and liked for his patience and kindness instead of being respected for his ruthlessness, shows him to have had a far more complex character than may appear thus far.

Like many successful generals, as he ascended the ladder of promotion, Simonds took with him a group of trusted officers, proved in operations, beginning with those who had worn "the old Red Patch" of the First Canadian Infantry Division. He brought some of them from the First Division to Second Canadian Corps, and they stayed with him from the Battle of Normandy to the final surrender on May 7, 1945. They were his "military family," but others could be found in HQ First Canadian Army, which made for friendly cooperation, and some later worked under Simonds when he became chief of the General Staff.

It is when the varying perceptions of Simonds's closest associates are canvassed that complexities in his character emerge. None claimed to have been a close friend of Simonds. For instance, few men could have known him better than General George Kitching, who said of him, "Guy kept all his subordinates at arm's length." Kitching was one of the best general staff officers in the army. He had been Simonds's chief operations officer in the First Division and commanded the Eleventh Infantry Brigade in the Fifth Armoured Division in Italy, which Simonds commanded briefly. When Simonds left Italy to command the Second Corps in the United Kingdom, Kitching followed him to be promoted to major general on taking command of the Fourth Armoured Division, only to be sacked by Simonds in Normandy. Some who knew the facts felt Simonds had been unfair. However, Kitching himself never bore a grudge against the man he considered the finest soldier Canada has produced.

Yet we see a very different and warmer relation with Bruce Matthews, a member of the Nonpermanent Militia, a prominent Torontonian, businessman, and Liberal. Matthews rose to be Simonds's Commander Royal Artillery (CRA) in the First Division, then filled the more senior post of Commander Corps Royal Artillery (CCRA) in the Second Corps and finally commanded the Second Infantry Division. It took a very smart militia gunner to satisfy Simonds, who had been a gunnery instructor in the Permanent Force himself. The two men respected and liked each other. Matthews, already a successful man in civil life, easily applied his talents to running Simonds's artillery. Their enduring relationship until his death demonstrated Guy's liking for men who could talk to him on many subjects besides war, and those who took burdens off his shoulders. Bruce Matthews could always be trusted to give a candid opinion on a subject rather than the answer calculated to please his chief.

Geoffrey Walsh, a Permanent Force engineer, was Simonds's Commander Royal Engineers (CRE) in the First Division and, like Matthews, later joined him in the Second Corps. By the time Simonds commanded the First Canadian Army in the Scheldt battle in October 1944, Walsh had become chief engineer there. In 1951 Walsh commanded the Twenty-seventh Brigade, which was Canada's first contribution to the North Atlantic Treaty Organization (NATO). Fiery, caustic, a bit of a bully, he was energetic and always on the spot when trouble occurred. It was at the bridging sites, the minefield breaches, the approach roads where the field squadrons were working under fire that Walsh was usually found, not at the desk in his caravan. Like not a few Canadian soldiers, he liked his dram, but kept off it when Guy was his commander. After the war, he was known to have thrown his brigade major across a room. And he fell out with troublesome prelates, particularly with a senior chaplain and a mission that descended on his brigade in Germany and unwarrantably criticized not only the brigade's morale but its discipline, as well. Simonds defended him from the criticism that appeared in the press, looking beyond its questionable basis to

Walsh's ability as an engineer. And Guy was no prude when it came to judging eccentric individuals. It was dishonesty, lack of energy, and mistakes that cost men's lives that he never forgave. Walsh had never failed in those respects and eventually became chief of the General Staff.

Elliot Rodger had not yet served in a theatre of war when Simonds chose him as his brigadier general staff (BGS) in the Second Corps. Rodger certainly had the qualities universally recognized as desirable in a BGS, but he might not have suited Simonds. At the top of Rodger's qualities was a modest and equable personality. He created an oasis of calm when all others around him were losing their heads. The calm was based on competence. One thinks of levelheaded mothers of large families who manage to direct their offspring towards their duties without friction and without doing everything themselves. Rodger had a knack for anticipating and preventing trouble, smoothing down irritated senior officers, always telling the truth, and never guessing what he did not know. These are qualities a commander looks for in his staff officer. Above all Rodger made a close and affectionate study of his boss in all his moods. He knew when and how to introduce potentially explosive subjects and could divert and amuse him in mess after a trying day.

Darrell Laing, the head of the administrative staff in the Second Corps, was also a master at lowering the temperature and providing perquisites that raised the well-being of the staff. In General Sir Harold Alexander's mess in Italy shoptalk was taboo. Instead, art and the activities of the English countryside were discussed entertainingly and knowledgeably. This practice was sought in Simonds's mess, too. A sense of proportion was an essential quality for team members. Simonds was fortunate to find that quality in both Elliot Rodger and Darrell Laing.

General Findlay Clark, the chief signals officer in the Second Corps, survived Simonds's slaughter of the old and bold incumbents of Second Corps HQ when he arrived in January 1944. Clark had been a technical instructor at the RMC with Simonds just before the war, but they had not served together since then. A perfectionist who was as energetic and innovative as Simonds himself, he was intense and did not suffer fools gladly, but he made the Second Corps Signals the best in the Twenty-first Army Group. His relations with the Americans and with industry paid off. For instance, Canadian Signals procured, through Philips of Eindhoven, special communications equipment far superior to anything the British had. Fin Clark's technical skill set an example all the way down the line. His mischievous streak was revealed when he pulled the leg of First Army staff by demonstrating that the "secure" phones forced on him by General Henry Duncan Graham Crerar, the army commander, were quite insecure.

Commanders have often been considered a different breed from staff officers, and to an extent that is true. It is essential for all commanders to know how to handle staff, and in their appointments Matthews, Walsh, and Clark were commanders and effective staff officers. Soldiers who rise to the higher echelons of their profession, men like Alan Brooke, must be masters of command and staff functions. Simonds was not an exception to that rule. However, a few of Simonds's contemporaries with whom he had close relations were not so versatile.

Chris Vokes, a diamond in the rough, commanded the Second Infantry Brigade in the First Canadian Division before taking the divisional command when Simonds moved on to the Fifth Armoured Division. A Permanent Force officer, Vokes was a classmate of Simonds at the RMC, and Guy had long known his limitations. He nursed Vokes even as a brigade commander, knowing full well that divisional commander was his absolute limit and that the man was a poor staff officer. This was Simonds as a patient manager, not a role for which he was usually given credit. Howard Graham, another brigade commander in the First Division, was sacked by Simonds but reprieved when General Bernard Montgomery advised Simonds to give him another chance. Graham was too slow as a commander but made a good staff officer, and Simonds recommended him to be the next CGS when he retired in 1955. General Charles Foulkes, who was a subordinate divisional commander in the Second Corps, went on to command the First Corps in Italy and was made CGS after the war in preference to Simonds. The junior staff referred to him as "Foxy Granpa." Simonds did not regard him highly as a commander, and there was some antipathy between the two men because Foulkes was widely known as a political soldier, a type Simonds disliked. Foulkes satisfied Brooke Claxton, the minister whom he served both as CGS and chairman of the Chiefs of Staff Committee, but did not please the army then or later when he supported unification and seemed to have no sympathy for its traditions or spirit. The same could not be said of Simonds, who was unwilling to compromise with politicians when, in his opinion, they put party in front of country. Graham and Foulkes were less emphatic and opinionated than he. Indeed, they were not what politicians regarded as typical military officers.

So far we have a vicarious preview of Simonds's character as a soldier. His qualities as a human being outside his office and not in uniform are less easy to sketch, for he was a very private person who did not share his closest feelings with his military friends. Marshal Stearns, who became aide-de-camp (ADC) Operations at the conclusion of the Sicily campaign, was an exception, for he bridged the civilian and military sides of Simonds's life.

Stearns was the only man who could claim to have been his close friend, at least after the war. An American by birth from Massachusetts and a graduate of Harvard, he had become a Canadian and a Forty-eighth Highlander in the First Brigade of the First Division and fought with that battalion in Sicily. Like others in Guy's military family, he was in awe of him and even surprised to have been selected to serve so close to him. The two men were companions, father and son perhaps, albeit within the parameters decided by Guy, who never allowed himself to be familiar with those on whom he depended.

Stearns stayed with Simonds until the end of the war. They were regular correspondents in the disturbed years immediately afterwards when Simonds was bitter at not being selected for the post of CGS, was considering joining the British army or becoming a civilian in Canada, and was trying to maintain his first marriage to Katherine "K" Simonds. Later Marsh and his wife, Helen, provided a haven for Simonds when he was going through the loneliness of separation and a form of divorce, and after Simonds's retirement, Marsh helped him to enter the world of Toronto business. Marsh and his family were accepted as friends by the Anderson family in England during and after the war. Guy had found solace and relaxation in Mona Anderson during the war years and afterwards, and that relationship was the immediate cause of his divorce from K.

In peacetime the army frowns on affairs. During the war, they were common enough in England, and in Canada, too. Separation was a severe strain on both sides of the Atlantic, and the many wives who spent long periods in the United Kingdom in many different jobs served to strengthen their marriages by their presence. But most affairs were discreetly managed, and at first the personalities in this study, outside the family, properly denied any knowledge of Mona Anderson. Nevertheless, there were some in the small community of the Permanent Force who felt that K had been badly treated. Friends of both parties naturally refused to take sides, or were sympathetic to both.

That is the biographer's view, as well, and not from necessity. However, it was universally agreed that Simonds mellowed when he married Dorothy Sinclair, the widow of Gus Sinclair, who had been killed at Dieppe, and the sister of C. Malim Harding, who had been operations staff officer in the First Division after Simonds left. Indeed, in the last years of his life Guy Simonds was a happy man, something he had not been in earlier days.

1

Family Affairs

Guy Simonds, born in England in 1903, was the descendant of a line of soldiers devoted to the service of the British Empire. His great-grandfather had been an officer in the army of the Honourable East India Company, his grandfather had retired from the Imperial Indian Army as a major general, and his father, Cecil Simonds, had been commissioned in the Royal Artillery and had served in the South African War. Later Cecil worked in West Africa as a surveyor on the Anglo-French Boundary Commission between Nigeria and Chad. He was, in 1911, a major and General Staff officer in the intelligence branch of the War Office in London. He had married Eleanor "Nellie" Easton, the daughter of William, a wealthy Virginian breeder and trainer of racehorses who had immigrated to England and settled in Suffolk near Bury Saint Edmunds. There he had rented Ixworth Abbey, a stately and historic house conveniently near the great racing centre of Newmarket.

Cecil Simonds was regarded as a promising officer, but in the spring of 1911 was convalescent and expected to be boarded and placed on half pay. Well-known to Lord Roberts of Kandahar, at that time working hard to persuade the government to adopt conscription, he was upset by the division of the army into pro-Roberts and pro-Haldane factions. The latter was clearly winning the day. Through Roberts Simonds obtained an interview with the agent-general for British Columbia, who told him that he would be able to establish himself there as a surveyor, for which he had qualified in the army. But the agent-general's information proved to be only half the truth.

In the fall of 1911 he resigned his commission and emigrated with Eleanor and their offspring, consisting of Cicely, Guy, Peter, and Eric, to start a new life and a new profession in Victoria, British Columbia. Guy was then eight years old. Cecil found work on the survey of a new railway planned on Vancouver Island, but his hope of setting up his own firm of surveyors was dashed by professional regulations demanding that he first take British Columbia examinations. The pay was inadequate. He had discounted or ignored the disruption of his family's life if war were to occur and he were recalled to the colours, which happened in 1914. He left his family in Canada and did not return until he was demobilized in 1919 with a good record. Cecil had been wounded in 1918 and had attained the rank of full colonel.[1]

Cecil Simonds's retirement from the regular army and emigration were obviously ill-timed. In 1911, from his position in the War Office, he had seen England and France nearly go to war with Germany over Morocco, and it was commonly believed thereafter that war with Germany was inevitable sooner or later. War meant immediate promotion and employment on the staff. If he left the army, he would be recalled as a reservist, initially to serve in a less senior appointment. Be that as it may, the effects of his early retirement and his absence from home throughout the war affected Guy Simonds, whose eleventh through to his sixteenth years were spent without a father, and he left home in 1919 soon after his father's return. Until then his mother had been the predominant influence in his life, and it was his mother's influence on his complaisant father that had been the main reason why Cecil Simonds had left the British army.[2]

Guy Simonds regretted his father's decision to leave the army and regarded it as a mistake, although he enjoyed much of his early life in Victoria, which was a result of it. The Simondses were an army family, and Guy's conviction that his father had broken the mould by retiring stoked his burning ambition to restore the family's record of service by reaching the summit of the military profession. He respected and loved his father, but his relations with his mother were more complex. He found unconvincing explanations for his father's retirement that omitted her influence: Cecil's frequent foreign assignments, separations from his family, a period of ill health when Cecil suffered ptomaine poisoning in South Africa, and the reorganization of the British army in the Haldane Reforms of 1906 and subsequent years. The latter, in fact, increased Cecil's chances of serving in England, for it reduced the percentage of the army service overseas.

Richard Haldane actually initiated a period of intense professionalism. Those who left the army just before the First World War usually had private means, estates or a business to manage, or perhaps were disenchanted with the reorientation of the army towards a professional body with an efficient staff corps. Simonds had no estates or business, and if he was a dedicated soldier, even discounting the state of international relations, 1911 was not the year for him to become a civilian. Guy Simonds blurred the real reason for his father's retirement, namely his mother's influence and personality.

Nellie Simonds came from a wealthy family. On their arrival from the United States William Easton settled them into Ixworth Abbey, and the large, rambling, rented house served as home for his five daughters, three of whom had married army officers with private means. Besides Cecil Simonds, the others were Cyril Curteis and John Mather who, like Cecil, served abroad for long periods. In 1907 the lease on Ixworth ran out and the family moved to Skryne Castle in county Meath, Ireland. In 1909 William Easton died and his wife sold his racing Thoroughbreds from which a share in an inheritance came to Nellie. There was one son, but since the family had rented houses, there were no bricks-and-mortar roots to hold them together after William Easton died. Nellie and her army sisters, with their children, had spent much of their lives in their parents' houses in Suffolk and Meath, although Nellie had lived with Cecil's father for periods at Windsor. It was time, Nellie thought, to establish a home in one place and to bring an end to her husband's army peregrinations.

Much the same thought has gone through the minds of generations of army wives. But Nellie's motives were not singular by any means. She was ambitious for her husband and took the almost unforgivable step of interceding on his behalf with Major General Grierson, who in 1906 was director of Military Operations. She was politely told that her husband was one of the more highly thought of officers in the army, that he was the youngest major in the army at the time, and that she should be patient.[3] Cecil, on the other hand, was taken to one side and told to control his wife, who in truth was behaving like the new Lady Astor, another Virginian.

Nellie was a spoiled, high-spirited, and very attractive woman, and Cecil could not control her. She and her family enjoyed the social life of her class in Edwardian England and had toured the Continent in the style of the time. Her father had bailed her out when her extravagance ran through both her husband's pay and her own allowance. She never learned to accept no for an answer and continued to believe throughout her life that other people owed her favours. She assumed that country house living, nannies to look after the children, good food, and a host of inside and outside servants were her birthright, as did her contemporaries.

The Eastons were well connected, and the Simonds clan added significantly to that, for they were related to the Maxse family, of which Ivor Maxse was shortly to make a name for himself in the coming war, and the Milners, of whom Lord Milner of South African fame was to be a prominent wartime politician. Race meetings, theatres, and presentations at court were what Nellie was used to. Guy vaguely remembered that side of his early life through a rosy haze from which incidents later emerged from his memory, probably because he had often been told of them even if he did not remember them himself. There were visits to Windsor, where his paternal grandfather lived among old service friends who had been made "Windsor Knights." And there were many other memories: riding ponies in Windsor Great Park with Cicely and encountering the Prince and Princess of Wales; staying with his Uncle Cyril Curteis at Aldershot and saluting the glamorous but sadly veiled Empress Eugenie as she passed; and greeting in regular Guards fashion the future King George and Queen Mary when they visited and, astoundingly, having his salute returned with a smile.

Among these recollections the best of all, perhaps, was country-life living at Ixworth and, later, in Ireland where there were ponies and grooms and gamekeepers and poachers and all kinds of boyish adventures with fish and water and various animals. There, also, he experienced the discipline of grooming his own pony after riding it, tying on flies before fishing, and learning how guns should be handled. All this left a lasting impression that coloured his ambitious dream, later, to earn all these things for himself one day and to see his own children enjoying them, too. It was a long time before he realized that earning them might leave him little time for their enjoyment.

The social and cultural side of English life, his mother's side as he came to see it, was to be described to him with embellishment by Nellie as he grew up in Victoria. It seemed that she had been deprived of that life through no fault of her own. It was Cecil not she who had been determined to move to Victoria. The elder Simonds had a different view, but it was not expressed, for he left for the war when Guy was eleven and only returned when his son was sixteen.

The breakup of the Easton family, as far as Cecil was concerned, had meant that his means, added to those of Nellie, would not enable him to go on living at the pace to which she was used. In fact, it meant that he could not afford to live in England at all, because Nellie would continue to be extravagant.

There were two solutions. One was to rusticate in Ireland where it was possible to have servants, a large house, and the pleasures of country life on a lower income. That was the Mather solution. But Cecil's means, less than either Mather's or Curteis's, were insufficient to allow him to retire from the army without work, and there was nothing suitable in Ireland. Besides, he was adventurous. He had enjoyed South Africa and Nigeria and fancied playing the role of colonist. Furthermore, he had reached a point in his career, common among army officers in mid-career, when he was restless and bored with army life.

So Cecil was disinclined to resist his wife's insistence that he leave the army. Unaware how tough civilian life could be, particularly in a new country where he would have few contacts, he chose to go to British Columbia, still a frontier province where money could be made, and his young family could have the country life they enjoyed. No doubt he believed he could curb his wife's extravagance in Canada.

Cyril Curteis, his wife, and their son, Guy's young cousin Hugh, also moved to British Columbia. Nellie's mother and her youngest daughter, Vera, bought a farm at Duncan on Vancouver Island, while the Simonds family rented a four-bedroom frame house at 612 Battery Street in Victoria. They were joining the immigration surge of 1911, a year of economic recession in Britain. It was also a time of imperial pride: there was a new king on the throne, and no one would have believed that the sun was setting on a way of life when it seemed to be shining its brightest.

During the war years, after Cecil was called back into service, Guy's mother, his elder sister Cicely, and his Aunt Vera, affectionately known as Puggie, managed to hold the family together without the income that his father would have provided, although he must have sent them an army allowance. In those trying times, Simonds wrote in his auto-biography, Nellie's grit and single-mindedness came to the fore.

The true circumstances of those years have been partially revealed by his brother Peter's comments to Mr. Justice John Matheson, a longtime admirer of General Simonds. Pictures and other family treasures from England were sold to pay housekeeping expenses. But it appears that Aunt Puggie and Cicely were largely responsible for looking after the house and the younger children. Nellie was not a natural housekeeper, having taken remarkably little interest in such matters in England. At Guy's birth she made no special arrange-ments but left them to her Mather sister; indeed, she attended a race meeting at Newmarket the day before he was born.

Nellie was from a class whose children were brought down by a nanny at teatime but were otherwise relegated to the nursery.

Children should be seen occasionally but if possible never heard. Later they were taught by governesses or tutors until they departed to a boarding school. Extraordinary though this detached selfishness may seem today, it was commonplace at the time. Nevertheless, mothers of Nellie's class were seriously concerned with the education of their children and whom they married, and with their sons' careers. Guy was well taught by governesses in England from an early age.

In the war years in Victoria Nellie continued to be as extravagant as she had been in England and, when crossed, lacked a sense of proportion. No doubt the sales of pictures were to provide as much for her as for her family. But she was a charming woman and able to manipulate other men besides her own husband. According to Peter, she was often absent from home, but for what purpose is not clear. However, she educated her children, formed their characters, and maintained English ways of thinking. She read to them often and in a wonderfully expressive voice. Indeed she might have been an actress. Guy had learned to read from governesses in England at an early age. Now his mother introduced him to classical literature, to architecture and the fine arts. She encouraged his Englishness so that the feeling of being set apart from his friends grew in him. Having read much more than they, he had no difficulty in passing school exams. His general knowledge picked up from conversation at home was much wider than that of his peers. He particularly shone in mathematics and he wrote well.

At this time Guy was a slim, strikingly good-looking, dark-haired boy — a trifle aloof perhaps, but with his ready smile not unfriendly. He was an excellent rifle shot, although his young brother Eric, who was a reserve for the Canadian Bisley team at age seventeen in 1925 and later won prizes at Bisley with the Royal Air Force, was better on the range. Guy excelled with a shotgun. He ran and, in fact, played all games well, without having to train for them particularly. There was almost no ice skating done in Victoria at that time, so he missed out on playing hockey. The games played were rugby union, soccer, and field hockey. Peter remembers a feeling of irritation that Guy could excel at almost everything without, apparently, having to try very hard. In particular Guy rode well and was already good at judging horses. He could usually pick winners at race meetings out of the paddock. Peter remembered his selecting Soldier of Verdun as a place winner at fifty to one in the Duke of Connaught's Cup when his mother, who liked a flutter, chose Princeps, the favourite, at short odds. Guy's second place earned him more than his mother's winner. Perhaps the name appealed as much as the horse to Guy.

None of this — shotguns, horses, and racing — seem to be marks of a deprived childhood. And yet Guy paid a price for shining at these activities. Much later, after the war, when Peter Simonds was having difficulty in holding jobs, he made out that Nellie had always favoured Guy at his expense. Everything had gone into Guy's education, he asserted. With some indignation Guy pointed out that he had, at fourteen, given up school for two years to work in an office and that the pittance he earned contributed to the household expenses. His mother was incapable of saving a penny, he pointed out. Peter had had his chance in school but did no work. None of this appears in Guy Simonds's autobiography. It seems that the family was divided in that Cicely and Guy were energetic and ambitious, whereas Peter and Eric were easygoing, more like their father. Eric became a fine pilot, though, and had good brains.

Guy was equivocal about his mother. He admired her relentless pursuit of influential people and believed, with her, in consorting with the talented and ambitious. Not, though, for what they could do for him, but because he preferred their company. Like his mother, he was marked by a fear of being penniless and by the same desire for success and wealth. He was rather a skinflint, unless spending money to maintain high standards, for instance in his personal appearance. And even as a small boy in Victoria his appearance was neat and he had the advantage of hair that was easy to keep orderly. Unlike his mother, though, he was prepared to work hard for everything that he received without taking any shortcuts, and he was completely honest with himself.

Here Guy's father's influence was obvious. Cecil was a gentleman and competent, too, but he lacked the steel in his makeup that his son seemed to have from an early age: steel honed by the wartime years of relative want and the responsibility of being the eldest male in the house. Furthermore, fatherlessness had made him a loner and thrown him back on his own resources. That had strengthened his character further but had made it difficult for others to approach him. He was closest to Eric, his youngest brother, and to Cicely, who had much to do with his upbringing.

After Cecil came back from the war, it was decided to send Peter and Guy to an eastern private school, Ashbury College. In order to make this possible there had to be some economies, and Nellie negotiated for special rates on the CPR train to Montreal and for reduced fees at Ashbury, charming all concerned. Guy Simonds had been a prominent member of the cadet corps at the Collegiate School in Victoria and, although his mother had at first tried to deter him, he was determined to follow his father's profession. So it was planned that after two years at Ashbury Guy would take the entrance examination for the Royal Military College in Kingston. In his autobiography Guy gives the impression that he was always single-minded about joining the army. As an illustration, he wrote:

> It is appropriate to end this chapter with the following quotation from one of the Victoria daily newspapers published in the autumn of 1912: "*Emblems of War.* Guy Granville Simonds of 612 Battery Street has been adjudged the winner of the prize of toy soldiers offered by Major Beale to the boy who could write the best essay on the subject of which these little soldiers were the symbols. These toy soldiers have been for some months familiar to the passersby in Douglas Street in the windows of the recruiting office for the new Victoria Regiment, and having fulfilled their function there, now pass on to amuse and educate a possible recruit for H.M. forces. The writer of the winning essay is nine years and five months old."[4]

Young Simonds joined Ashbury in the autumn of 1919. In his two years there he shone at all activities, and when the results of the entrance examination to the RMC were announced, he was second in the order of merit. At that time there was a single entrance exam open to candidates from all over Canada. The arrangement favoured entrants from private schools where special classes prepared boys for examinations. Later, places were allotted by provinces, which partly took care of educational disparity across the country.

When he entered the RMC, Guy joined male society after spending the previous five years in one dominated by women.

2

Building a Reputation

....

SIMONDS AND THREE OTHERS from Ashbury entered
the Royal Military College of Canada at Kingston
in the spring of 1921. They had all done well in the examinations,
but Simonds placed second in the national order of merit. His success destined him for an official appointment in his class, which
distinguished him from the ruck at the outset of his career.

The RMC that Simonds entered was, in educational terms, in a
state of flux. The military curriculum was based on the narrow and
outdated lessons of the Western Front, and discipline and leadership
were inculcated by a manic obsession with smartness and turnout.
With the aim of character-building the responsibility for discipline
was delegated to students nominated to be cadet officers and to the
senior class as a whole. Unfortunately this admirable idea, if unsu-
pervised, led to an unofficial system of brutal and systematic bullying by senior cadets condoned by the authorities. In fact, it was
regarded as an essential form of military indoctrination, a form of
the rites of passage.

Simonds's class was the last to be selected from a competitive
nationwide exam and the first after the war to enter a four-year
course. These circumstances gave it the opportunity to play a part in
shaping the postwar RMC and allowed Simonds to take a leading
role. The changeover from a three- to a four-year course created a
disturbance for the classes ahead of his. The seniors had entered in
1919 and were to graduate in 1922 after three years. Seniors who

failed their final year in 1922 repeated it and became the seniors of 1923. The 1920 entry did not graduate in 1923, as they had expected, but were made to serve a fourth year. The disappointment may have affected their performance when they became seniors in 1924, but as part of the old guard all of these classes accepted, uncritically, conceptions of their responsibilities and authority that were outdated. They were also influenced by the belief of their wartime antecedents that the subjects in the curriculum most worthy of serious attention were those immediately applicable on the Western Front. In short, they were insufficiently convinced that the aim of the RMC was to offer a broad professional education in the art and science of war and in the enlightened management of the men they were to command, because the majority did not intend to make a career in the Permanent Force.

The commandant was Major General Sir Archibald Cameron Macdonnell, K.C.B., C.M.G., D.S.O., who had been an outstanding commander of the First Canadian Division on the Western Front. His general mandate was to prepare a few cadets for a professional career in the Permanent Force and groom the majority for service as officers in the part-time militia, while providing a curriculum suitable to both. That required, in particular, that the academic standards of the RMC approach those of a first-class university. On the way to that goal he had to remove the public's impression that the RMC was an anti-intellectual, rednecked institution. That task was made no easier by a press and public that were sick of the army and everything to do with war and regarded the RMC as a haven of upper-class snobs who swaggered about in fancy uniforms and lorded it over others. Nor was it helped by a cadet body that, too frequently, invited public criticism.

The main target for press attacks was the harassing of first-year cadets by the senior class. Called "recruiting," it had become a practice of sadistic bullying that was completely out of control. Simonds, as a class leader by dint of his standing on entering the RMC, demonstrated his natural powers of leadership by playing an unheard of part in reforming the system. However, while he was still a recruit cadet himself, his authority and opportunity to change anything were limited. First, he had to learn to obey and to perform excellently under pressure. He had been advised to adopt Keep Smiling as his motto for the first months at the RMC while he and other recruits were shouted at, mocked, and chased on the double from pillar to post.

This advice was soon tested. Even as the taxi deposited Guy and four other new cadets outside the administrative building that first day, the future Allied general led the group up the steps, only to be confronted by Chicks Mundell, the formidable Cadet Battalion sergeant major or senior under officer (SUO) of the RMC, standing at the top. "Wipe that goddamn smile off your face!" the potentate ordered. "This first verbal introduction to 'recruiting' at the RMC," Simonds recalled, "was not as sharp a contradiction of the advice we had been given by Clyde Caldwell as appeared on the surface. If it had to be suppressed superficially, to 'Keep Smiling' inwardly was an excellent formula to contend with the rigours of our recruit year."[1]

Simonds's career at the RMC provides an extraordinary example of inherent leadership. He went through no painful apprenticeship, but appeared to have been born mature. At Ashbury he was nick-named "Count," always neat and tidy, unlike a schoolboy, and always in control of himself and the situation. He was not popular, nor did he seek popularity. At the RMC, as class senior this aloof, superefficient youth became a role model for his contemporaries, excelling without apparent effort.

Simonds's second asset, associated with his personal competence, was that he organized his time and effort economically and proved a shrewd manager of the system as he found it. His power base was his own class, and he tackled its problems before essaying into more dangerous fields where the power was in other hands. In the war years cheating to avoid failure in written exams was tolerated. Passing was quite sufficient and gaining a high place in the order of merit seemed unimportant. Indeed, practice mattered much more than military theory and, as everyone knew, some of the best young officers were not good on paper. So it could be said that it was in the common interest that they be given the chance to lead in the field.

After the war, some members of the staff made stealing exam papers easier by carelessly leaving them on their desks instead of under lock and key. As class senior, Simonds put an end to the stealing and selling of exam questions. At a class meeting called to discuss cheating he met head-on those who grumbled that he, himself, had a vested interest because he passed all exams without difficulty. When he proposed to post guards on the cadet dormitory flats between lights-out and reveille during the weeks of the exams, only a few protested. Put into effect, the scheme prevented would-be thieves from leaving their bedrooms at night. One of the motives for stealing was removed when no one could obtain an unfair advantage.

Simonds became class senior two weeks into his first term and held the post for three years. It was Chicks Mundell who called for him and told him that complaints about his class were widespread. They were late for parades, there were unreported absentees, and saluting and dress were sloppy. In general the class was a disgrace, and Guy was to take over and smarten it up. Simonds did correct the shortcomings of his class and remained its leader until the class "mutiny" against recruiting, in which he played a leading part in his third year, denied him the position in his senior year.

Fagging was part of the recruiting system. Its rationale was that the duties of seniors left them little time to tidy their rooms, clean their kit, and study their books. If a cadet failed his fourth year, he could not repeat it but had to leave the college. Fags relieved seniors of some of the pressure on them. Although fagging was occasionally abused, there was little objection to it within the college. Outsiders with democratic ideas argued that fagging was degrading for young men of school-leaving age. It might be acceptable at a prep school, they said, but many of the recruits entering the RMC had been prefects or the equivalent or had captained their school teams, and it was wrong to return them to the status of "fags."

Simonds considered this argument hypocritical. As a high percentage of the recruits came from "privileged" middle-class private schools, in any other context the press would have argued that they were spoiled brats who should be taken down a peg. A more reasoned argument against fagging was that it imposed a strain on recruits and increased their failure rate, already high. Simonds had a happy experience with his own fag master and found that most seniors felt a responsibility to see that their fag recruit passed his year. Those who failed, he argued, would have done so, anyway.

It was the abuse of recruiting that led to reform. Some collective punishments had become excuses for bullying. For example, it might be decided that the whole class lacked moral fibre or that a particular shortcoming had become a general weakness. The class was then hazed by a general caning called "arse fanning." Individuals and sections of the class might also be disciplined by this means. Less extreme was "flat PT," an exaggerated and exhausting form of physical training given without staff supervision by a senior in the dormitory or on the track outside, where recruits were made to run several laps at an acceptably brisk pace. A particularly unpleasant punishment was the "shit meeting," for which the recruits of a company or a platoon were herded into a confined space in one of the dormitories. There they had to stand at attention, their fingers stretched down, while their seniors shrieked verbal abuse at them in degrading terms. Simonds's Fort Frederick dormitory held their meetings in the furnace room where recruits stood at attention on the edges of the coal piles in a low-ceilinged, fumy, badly ventilated room.

Even these recruiting practices might have been considered character-building had they not descended to mere bullying. Simonds remarked that a beneficial result was that it developed in the recruit a standard of personal cleanliness, smartness of turnout, physical deportment, and obedience quicker than could have been achieved by any other means. On the moral side it impressed upon individuals the important lesson that there were things in life that mattered a great deal more than self. College, class, company, and platoon all came before oneself, Simonds asserted. Lifelong friendships were cemented in sharing the trials and tribulations of recruiting. Nevertheless, there were seniors quite incapable of exercising their power reasonably. To them retribution was meted out post facto at the end of term. The morning after the June Ball they were "arse fanned" and thrown into Lake Ontario in full ceremonials. Such an ending to their career at the RMC was a disgrace difficult to live down.

It was the debit side of all this that concerned Simonds. Recruiting was unofficial even within the RMC; beyond its gates, in either the army or civil life, it was an unacceptable system, one that was outside military or civil law and had no checks and balances to restrain it. The commandant who was responsible to higher authorities could not and did not condone it and, indeed, gave explicit directions to the senior class in Simonds's third year that it was unacceptable. Yet most members of the faculty knew that it continued and that it was actively encouraged by ex-cadets who formed a pressure group to ensure that the "hard discipline" of their time at the RMC continued. Thus recruiting created a double standard that perpetuated itself until the system was openly examined, its beneficial and controlled elements were recognized and confirmed, and the rest was thrown out. This examination came after a series of scandals over runaways and injuries sustained by recruits culminated in the Arnold affair.

Arnold was a recruit during Simonds's third year. He had run away, making a hazardous crossing of the ice of Lake Ontario to Cape Vincent on the American shore. Thence he joined relatives in New York City. In New York he was interviewed by the press, and soon the Canadian newspapers took up his case, which was that he had been unmercifully and illegally bullied at the RMC. The commandant placed the whole senior term under arrest and promoted Simonds and Jack McMahon, his deputy and another Ashbury boy, to take battalion parades.

Harried by the press, General Macdonnell made a public statement in which he denied the principal accusations made against the RMC by Arnold. That made his action against the senior term seem too drastic. The view of Simonds's class was that the staff was aware of what was going on and therefore should have taken responsibility for the events and not blamed everything on the seniors. The principle of responsibility was at stake. A class meeting decided that Simonds and McMahon ought to interview the staff adjutant and ask him to communicate the view of the class to the commandant.

In his autobiography Simonds wrote:

> So we went to see Major Eric Greenwood, the then staff adjutant, in his office and stated our view of the situation. He went scarlet in the face, said, "Wait here," got up from his chair, and strode into the commandant's office next door. Within minutes Eric Greenwood reappeared, and we were marched into the commandant's office to face Sir Archie Macdonnell. Eric said, "Simonds and McMahon here accuse me of knowing everything that has been going on." Sir Archie's opening words were: "I have seen mutiny on the high seas, and it's mutiny I read in the eyes of you two." But he then went on to tell us why the senior class were being severely disciplined. When the case had first broken, he had called upon the senior class, whom he trusted, to tell him exactly what had happened to cause Arnold to run away. The seniors had not told him the truth or the whole truth. His, the commandant's, statement to the press was based upon the information given to him by the seniors. Arnold and his father had been able to refute details of this statement, which had placed him in a most difficult position and was very damaging to the RMC in the eyes of the public.[2]

The situation was unfortunate for Arnold in that his own class sided with the seniors, which made it impossible for him to return even had he wished to do so. The outcome was that the senior term was deprived of its authority and the staff supervised the dormitories, which made recruiting impossible. Clearly, though, the staff had known what was going on and had shielded the commandant from the knowledge. Simonds and McMahon, as the bearers of bad news, suffered accordingly. At the end of term, when appointments were made in Simonds's class for their senior year, he and McMahon, who were expected to be senior under officer and senior company commander respectively, were passed over to the extent that, instead, they were appointed senior company commander and senior platoon commander.

The Arnold affair cleared the air once the new seniors showed that they could be trusted to administer the new recruit entry sensibly. Nevertheless, some of the staff harboured residual distrust of all seniors because no one wanted more bad press. Simonds's company commander, new to the staff and not an ex-cadet himself, bent over backwards to take the side of the recruits, even when they needed disciplining. He adhered, too strictly in Simonds's opinion, to standing orders that needed amendment and were a guide not a rule book, and his decisions gradually cooled his relations with his young cadet company commander. Finally a dispute arose on the occasion of his inspection of quarters when he found the room of a junior NCO and a classmate not up to standard and instructed Simonds to place him on a formal charge.

Simonds protested. He knew the cadet's academic standing was precarious and that the young man was already studying until the early hours. To saddle him with defaulter's parade would ensure his failure. It was a convention that during exams standards of tidiness were relaxed. He told the company commander that he intended to speak to the cadet because he thought the young man was overdoing his swotting but that any further action would be counterproductive. In reply he was admonished that the NCO should set an example and that as standing orders had been contravened he was bound to punish the cadet. Simonds recalled:

> I retorted rather hotly, "And how many great leaders have stuck rigidly to regulations regardless of human factors?" Without hesitation he replied, "But, damn it, Simonds, I'm not a great leader." We both burst out laughing. He agreed to let me handle the case in the way I had proposed, and we got along famously from then onwards.[3]

The important point that Simonds had struggled to make with his company commander underlay the whole issue of recruiting. It was that the RMC was supposed to prepare young men for positions of authority, and recruiting as practised taught a bad lesson. Men were best led by example, and when they erred, by equitable and proportionate punishment. On the other hand, battle was an unreasonable and unfair environment and men had to be trained to expect hard knocks, not only from an enemy that visited pain upon them but from weather, hunger, and physical exhaustion. Potential officers ought to suffer these things before visiting them upon their men. However, they should also be prepared to explain them and ensure that such measures were proportionate to their purpose. Here recruiting had failed to achieve its intended purpose and had become an end in itself.

A minor scandal occurred towards the end of Simonds's senior year when a visiting American girl persuaded the SUO, whose guest she was at a dance, to let her dress in a cadet's uniform and parade with Simonds's company the next morning. She changed in the company dormitory. Simonds was away temporarily, but when he returned, the incident was reported to him by the duty officer, who allowed time for investigation before reporting the matter. The SUO was reprimanded and the story appeared in a corner of the *Whig-Standard* but drew little attention.

Perhaps the chief result may have been that the recipient of the Sword of Honour at passing out was not the SUO, as was customary, but Simonds. Most people thought justice had been done since Simonds had been unfairly treated over the Arnold affair. Simonds also received the Victor Van der Smissen Award, given to the cadet adjudged the best all-rounder, morally and physically, by secret ballot of the cadets. The SUO was not eligible for that award. Placed second in the academic order of merit, Simonds received the Governor General's Silver Medal and various other smaller prizes, including the artillery prize. Although generally considered the best horseman in the class, he had not carried off the "spur and crown" because of a bad performance in the final competition.

The quality of the academic programme satisfied Simonds at the time, but on reflection in the following years he revised his opinion. He had affection and respect for the academic staff but felt that there had been too little written work, insufficient study of world affairs and government, and proportionally too much time spent on engineering subjects. Time was wasted on military triviality so that the course could have been completed in three years rather than four. On the other hand, the military curriculum gave cadets a balanced foundation in artillery, engineering, signals and supply, and cavalry and infantry tactics. The course was more than twice the length of the British Royal Military Academy, Woolwich, and Royal Military College, Sandhurst, and had a broader scope. After he attended the Staff College in 1936 and 1937 and visited the British academies, Simonds returned as an instructor to the RMC in the year before the war. There he developed and modified these ideas further, but he always regarded his four years at the RMC, with his tours at the Staff College at Camberley and the Long Gunnery Staff Course, as the foundations of his military career.

A cadet could spend his vacations in any profitable and mind-broadening manner he wished. Simonds spent them with a survey company in Nova Scotia where he was given responsibility for a squad of men. No doubt his father advised him that having a second string to his bow, particularly one related to the military profession, was wise.

In 1925 it was commonly believed that an ambitious professional should enter the British rather than the Canadian army, for it was larger and offered far more scope. The majority, though, took a militia commission on leaving the RMC and entered business or a civilian profession, particularly engineering. A few joined the Royal Canadian Air Force or the RAF. Simonds was unusual in being determined, even at Ashbury, to become a professional soldier, and it was on studying the role of the Canadian Corps in the Great War that he decided to serve in the Canadian not the British army. He was commissioned in the Royal Canadian Artillery (RCA) and was duly appointed to a Royal Canadian Horse Artillery (RCHA) battery in which to begin his service.

Simonds joined a small service of a few thousand officers and men with no field formations. Its function was to train the militia, which in war, if it were necessary to raise another expeditionary force, would provide its manpower. Training, sports largely associated with horses, which still provided the power to draw field guns, and lively social events in garrison towns like Winnipeg, Kingston, and Halifax were the foci of military life. However, the lack of opportunity to serve in operational theatres and the small size of the army strained the enthusiasm of all ranks. Promotion was slow and staff appointments were largely in static headquarters.

Before joining his horse artillery battery Simonds was interviewed by Lieutenant Colonel C. F. Constantine, the commander of the Royal Canadian Horse Artillery Brigade (later Regiment), who gave him the advice that his chief function was the support of other arms, which depended largely on the care of the horses in the gun teams, which could not speak for themselves. A much-respected officer with a fine record in the recent war, "Consie" was about to be appointed to succeed Macdonnell as commandant of the RMC. In 1943, about halfway through the Sicily campaign, where Simonds was commanding the First Canadian Division, he received a strange-looking parcel, which contained a fly switch and a note from Consie. Fly switches seemed to be de rigueur, Consie had written. He had seen a photograph of Monty holding one and thought that Simonds should have one, too. The switch enclosed had been made from the tail of his favourite charger during World War I, and he hoped Simonds would find it useful.

Simonds's career until 1939 fell into three phases. In the dozen years between 1925 and 1936, when he went to the Staff College at Camberley in England, he learned to be an exemplary regimental officer. His time was about equally spent in training horses and training men. Musical rides occupied much of his time. They are a dangerous form of entertainment that require split-second timing, discipline, self-control, and attention to detail. Equipment failures may cause serious accidents, and undisciplined competition between teams makes them take unnecessary risks. The injury of horses, quite apart from time-wasting courts of inquiry, may cause a valuable horse to suffer and even to be destroyed. The rewards were less obvious perhaps. The army in general and the regiment in particular gained public esteem — very important when defence was low on the agendas of politicians. Also battery morale was raised at a time when low wages made it difficult for soldiers to afford other recreation and interests apart from the bottle. As important, the boring routine of daily stables parades and equipment maintenance and repair was given more point when horses were being trained for a specific purpose and occasion.

In this activity, and in polo, Simonds excelled. Much of the rest of his time was spent training the militia at practice camps, in drill halls, and in classrooms. The Canadian army never received the new generation of guns that only appeared in the British army just before the outbreak of war in 1939, and mechanization was slow in coming. But most of the practices that had to be taught were the same whatever the equipment, and Simonds gained the reputation for being a patient and thorough teacher. This was particularly so in the year after he returned from the Long Gunnery Staff Course and served at the School of Artillery, Kingston, as a qualified instructor in gunnery. Even commanding officers listened with respect to what young Captain Simonds, wearing his Herbert Johnson hat with the red band of an instructor gunnery (IG), had to say about the strengths and weaknesses of their regiments. Junior officers remembered the way he settled the butterflies in their stomachs when they were called forward and told to land rounds in a small area in front of their observation post "splinterproof," while their critical fellows looked on. What he lacked was warmth and bonhomie, a fund of stories to be told around the bar afterwards. These weekend volunteers found him markedly deficient in that respect.

In these years he established himself as a gunner and gained a firm military foundation in his own arm of the service. It was the Staff College that made him think more broadly in terms of the balance of all the arms and services and the respective roles of commanders and their staffs. Good though he had been at the regimental level, most were to agree that the more senior he became the better he performed. He shone at the Staff College and credited any success he attained later as a senior commander and staff officer to its instructors and the enlightened two-year curriculum they conducted. Almost as important was that he met there, either as directing staff (DS) or fellow students, many of the men with whom he was to be associated in the coming war and afterwards.

The British staff college system was intended "not to indoctrinate officers with preconceived theories, but to make them think and come up with their own solutions to the problems of war." Each section of the course was introduced by a general lecture, followed by a demonstration in the form of a playlet in which humour brought out the points without too much labour. The laboratory of the Staff College was the syndicate of ten students supervised by a member of the directing staff who could be from any arm of the service. All questions were thrashed out in this forum where the DS was not the chairman so much as the impresario. When the syndicate moved out onto the ground, each member had an appointment, usually as a member of a divisional or brigade staff. Every study culminated in the writing of an order, appreciation, or directive, a verbal presentation that was expected to be submitted in faultless style against the pressure of time, or an exercise without troops, often conducted as a telephone battle. In addition individual papers had to be written on subjects revealed only when each student found one in his box at 9:00 a.m. with instructions to deliver the paper completed by noon.

After dealing with each phase of battle at the divisional level — defence, attack, advance and pursuit, and withdrawal — the first year ended with interservice exercises that included moving expeditionary forces overseas, assault landings, the defence of airfields, and tactical air support.

The second year, termed the senior year, was concerned with the theory of war and with political questions, particularly those involving the defence of the empire and relations with the dominions. Here there was more essay writing and the focus was less specifically operational. Winston Churchill once referred to the Staff College as "the most exclusive institution in the British Empire." Entry was by competitive exam or nomination, the latter to ensure that outstanding officers who lacked the time to prepare for the exam, or who had proved themselves in practice, could enter. The two provenances probably contributed about equally, although Simonds stated that in the opinion of the DS, nominated officers performed better on average. The competition to enter the Staff College was intense, for of about four hundred qualifiers each year only a hundred and twenty could be accepted. Hundreds more failed the qualifying exam annually. Once at the Staff College there were few failures and the story is apocryphal that a cavalry officer, about to be returned to his unit as unsatisfactory and asked by the commandant whether he had anything to say in his own defence, answered, "Yes, sir! I must say that I shall hardly be able to recommend this place to my friends."

The output from the Staff College proved too small to provide for the army when it expanded in 1939, and the course was reduced to one year just before the war. Except for the war years it has remained a one-year course since. In 1936 two Canadians joined the course. Each had passed the exam and had attended a prestaff course in Canada. With his Long Gunnery Course behind him Simonds would have been well prepared to contribute as an artillery member of syndicates, and his Canadian prestaff course had given him a good foundation in divisional staff duties. However, his fellow officers and even the gunners in his troop testified to the lights burning in his rooms late into the night in Winnipeg and Kingston as he studied wider questions of imperial defence and strategy. Over the years, by assiduous reading, he had acquired far more knowledge than the average staff officer. His excellent memory for facts enabled him to shine in syndicate, as did his talent for clear thinking, his ability to organize "staff" projects, and his leadership skills when it came to presenting plans clearly to large gatherings of the whole student body. Gradually he emerged as one of a small handful evidently destined for high appointments.

Some think of military officers in terms of stereotypes, but in the profession, as in any other, there is room for thinkers and doers, sceptics, Young Turks, backroom boys, and the rest. In Simonds's time the directing staff reflected this variation, and the "pink" briefs from which they worked as guides were written after intense arguments in committee that anticipated those that were to take place in the student syndicates. Major General Lord Gort, V.C., commander of the British Expeditionary Force (BEF) in 1940 and defender of Malta later in the war, was the commandant in Simonds's first year. He was replaced by Major General Sir Ronald Adam, later to become the distinguished adjutant general for much of the Second World War. Lieutenant Colonel Bill Slim, destined to be commander of the Fourteenth Army in Burma and arguably Britain's greatest soldier of the war, was a DS. Francis de Guingand, Windy Gale, and Gerald Templer were among the students.

Prolonged discussions distilled into schools of thought among students and DS as the course progressed. The curriculum and how it was taught came in for much criticism. Some argued against so much paperwork, for instance, written appreciations and orders, arguing that in a mechanized battle events would move too fast to allow much paper to be distributed. Orders would be sent out by radio.

Simonds, among the moderates in this, agreed with the premise but not the conclusion. He argued that the written orders and appreciations in exercises assured that their subjects were tackled systematically: only from orderly and standard reviews of military facts could sound conclusions be reached. The written work at the Staff College was a method of training the minds of commanders and staffs so that they could, if necessary, issue effective, brief, verbal orders face-to-face or over the radio. They did not disagree that orders should be as short as possible and follow a pro forma. But the skeleton of facts such as locations, codes, times, and phases had to be recorded in writing. Radio could be insecure and sometimes unreliable.

At the other extreme the First War custom of issuing orders from army headquarters that directed the movement of subunits and in consequence became voluminous, as well as inhibiting, was to be deprecated. Too much paper indicated unfamiliarity with the business of fighting. That was quite clear to Simonds when he joined the Eighth Army in July 1943 and found very little paper in contrast to the practice in the United Kingdom. Orders reached him verbally, face-to-face, through liaison officers, or over the radio. The Eighth Army had reached this doctrine mainly by improving its communications and by reducing tactical operations to drills that required no orders from above.

Staff College students supported their study of the operations of the First War from documents in the Staff College library. Simonds's appreciation of the problem of breaking through the Western Front was enlightened. It was more remarkable that he put his finger on the fact that battle conditions by 1936 had restored the balance between tactical and strategic mobility so that armies need no longer rely on attrition to break through prepared defences as they had earlier. Two factors had ensured this: airpower, already an important factor on the Western Front, was now decisive because of its increase in range and striking power; second, mechanical vehicles had markedly increased in speed, reliability, and cross-country capability. Airpower could isolate the battlefield and prevent the rapid reinforcement of the defence. It could also intervene crushingly on the battlefield itself by bombardment, vertical envelopment with airborne troops, and the resupply of isolated ground troops. Mechanized troops could move rapidly in the attack and retain the initiative over defenders brought forward by rail and road.

Theory was well advanced at the Staff College concerning air support and mechanized battle. Work on the practical details of the new scene involving aircraft and armoured troops was much less so. The technical and systematic foundations for coordinating tactical air support had been laid by 1918, although Simonds seems to have been unaware of it. Nor was he informed about the differences of opinion concerning priorities in the Royal Air Force (RAF). Some favoured defence by fighter plane, observer corps, and antiaircraft gun, while others supported attack by bombers. In any event, there was a widespread feeling that resources would not be directed towards army cooperation at this time, although the army knew that to be essential.

On the second point Simonds was concerned with the implications of the disparity between the increased speed over the country of modern tanks and the laden infantryman whose speed had not improved. The disparity led to two schools of thought. One argued that infantry was obsolete in mobile battle, of use only for holding ground. Armoured battles would be like naval battles at sea with the infantry defending the ports. Tanks would fight other tanks for which they required only armour-piercing capability.

That view ignored a couple of facts: first, the threat of antitank weapons as early as 1918 and their development since, and second, that towed and self-propelled antitank guns would probably remain superior to those carried on tanks. It followed that as villages in which antitank guns might be located had to be mopped up, infantry had to work with tanks and tanks would have to carry guns that fired high explosive as well as armour piercing shells to support the infantry. It also suggested a requirement for a slower, more heavily armoured tank to accompany the infantry, which was a retrogression, for it ran counter to the agreed doctrine that fast tanks must penetrate quickly to the full depth of the defences in order to deny the defence time to recover from the initial attack. Accompanying infantry, it was argued, would impede them. In concert with the latter doctrine, covering fire from the artillery should seek to neutralize, not destroy targets because the latter forfeited surprise. Here means had to be found to continue artillery support when the attack reached beyond range from the original gun line. An answer was self-propelled artillery such as that built in the late twenties for the experimental brigade on Salisbury Plain.

This complex subject was at the centre of tactical debates in Simonds's time at the Staff College. Solutions, however, could not be found until suitable equipment and formations were available to provide a flow of practical experience to test theory. Simonds continued to think about modern all-arms tactics when he returned to Canada.

Simonds was also concerned at the Staff College and afterwards with the operation, a central one for the British, of landing from ships on a hostile shore. His examination of the lessons of Gallipoli was one of his successes in his first year. In the second he was syndicate leader of a combined arms study of the landings planned in 1917 in conjunction with the Third Ypres campaign on the Belgian coast. He asked Admiral Bacon, who had been the naval commander concerned with putting General Rawlinson's Fourth Army ashore, to attend the syndicate presentation. The work entailed a visit to the ground during which they decided that the operation would have failed had it been attempted. Bacon did not agree.

Towards the end of the second year, in conjunction with the Royal Naval College at Greenwich and the RAF Staff College at Andover, Simonds led a combined syndicate to examine a projected attack on Hong Kong by the Japanese. Simonds's syndicate impersonated Japanese staff, with Simonds as the Japanese army commander responsible for the attack. The final work was done at Greenwich. One of the sticking points was Simonds's insistence, as the commander of the land force, on having a command ship properly equipped with communications on which to locate not only his army staff but also that of the flag officer commanding the fleet. The latter did not like that at all and insisted at first on being located on his own flagship. Simonds sought the support of the air force commander who had been neutral, being mainly concerned with obtaining air superiority over the landing area. Simonds persuaded him that a command ship would be a benefit to the air force as well as the army by providing the communications to control aircraft and organize air support. Outnumbered two to one the naval gentleman gave in, expostulating, "Well, I'll go on your damn ship, but I know no real admiral would."

By 1942 command ships had become unexceptionable, and Simonds and Sir Philip Vian managed the Canadian part in the Sicily assault in July 1943 from HMS *Hilary*. The syndicate also advocated the production of special assault shipping which, by displaying air photographs from the Yangtze, they demonstrated that the Japanese already possessed. So impressed were the DS and the commandant by the syndicate plan that the latter called Simonds over and detailed him to repeat his presentation on the last day of the exercise when the First Lord of the Admiralty, Duff Cooper, and the secretary of state for war, Hore Belisha, were to attend. Obviously the occasion was a personal success for Simonds.

The final joint exercise was with the RAF and the military attachés from the Continental capitals. The setting was the confrontation of an aggressive Germany and a peaceful Anglo-French alliance. The assumption, the current one in 1937, was that British land forces would not be involved and that the French would handle the Germans alone with help from the RAF. Simonds's syndicate deployed the French forces echeloned back from the western end of the Maginot Line with most of the armour concentrated in the centre ready to counter a move by the Germans against either flank. The "German" syndicate attacked through the Ardennes, which was General Rundstedt's plan in May 1940, while General Gamelin had the Allies rushing forward their left flank into Belgium. DS critics in 1937 said that a German advance through the Ardennes was not practicable. Ironically the "German" syndicate leader was killed in action in the campaign of 1940. Of interest is that Kenneth Strong, British military attaché in Berlin, and later Dwight Eisenhower's chief of intelligence in 1944-45, warned that the German army was built for offensive action solely and that they should disbelieve any statement from Hitler that he had no more territorial claims after his entry into the Rhineland.

All the students of Simonds's year came away certain that it was no longer a question of whether there was going to be a major war but of what incident would provoke it. They were amazed at the overt complacency of political leaders in the face of the evidence. The guests invited to speak at the various dinner clubs that students formed included politicians as diverse as Winston Churchill and Aneurin Bevan, as well as senior civil servants and industrialists. Dinner meetings broadened the students' view of the problems facing the country but also changed the opinion of their guests about the intelligence and knowledge of their hosts. They do not seem to have shaken the view of the student body that war would break out in the near future.

The years 1936 and 1937 were momentous. Germany entered the Rhineland, the civil war started in Spain, King George V died, Edward VIII abdicated, and George VI and Queen Elizabeth succeeded to the throne. Prince Henry, the duke of Gloucester, was a student in 1936 and performed ably as a professional whose greatest ambition was to command his regiment, the Tenth Hussars. The abdication denied him that honour by immersing him in extra royal duties. During the war, Prince Henry stayed with the Second Canadian Infantry Division for several days, living in A Mess. Simonds, then General Staff Officer I (GSO I), the senior operations staff officer, was astonished at the duke's stamina and at his knowledge of military matters. Simonds enjoyed a privileged position as a dominions officer at state occasions: for the funeral of George V he stayed with "Murch," Major Murchie, his best man, who was serving in the War Office, and he attended the coronation of George VI.

Before the end of term Simonds heard that he was to be posted to the RMC. On inquiring of Colonel Ken Stuart in Ottawa he learned that he was to teach tactics, strategy, and international affairs under the commandant, Brigadier Harry Crerar, who had been his battery commander in Kingston. He was not pleased at being shifted to a teaching job when he believed war to be imminent, but when he learned he would have the opportunity to take part in reorganizing the curriculum at the RMC, he accepted his fate with good grace.

Simonds's years at the RMC as an instructor included ceremonial occasions. President Franklin Roosevelt opened the International Thousand Islands Bridge just north of Kingston in August 1938, and Simonds had to lead the president's convoy to the bridge. Roosevelt was guarded by burly and heavily armed G-men who rode on the running boards of his armoured open tourer. They leaped off whenever the car stopped, and faced the onlookers threateningly. When Simonds reached the bridge, he gave a prearranged hand signal to start the saluting guns. As his hand fell, and a loud bang sounded from the number one gun in an adjacent field, the president and his bodyguards drove up. Simonds expected to be riddled by a nervous G-man whose hand on his weapon shook palpably. The other ceremonial occasion was the visit of the king and queen to the RMC in the early summer of 1939. The cadet body was drawn up on the square in fading light as the schedule was much in arrears. Although not intended in the original planning, the combination of half-light and floodlit scarlet tunics against a background of green fields created a magical scene.

Fresh from the heady and yet practical mood of the Staff College, Simonds attempted to have the plans for the RMC, in case of war, clarified. In fact, no decision had been made about what should happen to it. In 1914-18 it had remained open, and Crerar said that he thought that had been a mistake. He believed that all officers should be selected from the ranks and given the same training in officer training units. Simonds disagreed. He argued that a two-year course for cadets aged sixteen and holding a junior matriculation would offer them a good grounding in general education, mathematics, science, the humanities, and social sciences. When they came to military age at eighteen, they could be quickly trained as junior officers and provide an invaluable additional source of officers. After the war, they would be qualified to enter university. In any event, the RMC was closed in 1942 and potential officers went to officer cadet training units as Crerar wished. General Andrew George Latta McNaughton, who came out of retirement to command the Canadian contingent that went overseas, was appalled at the decision.

Simonds's final year at the RMC before the war gave him an opportunity to organize his ideas and to try them out on colleagues and the cadets. He published three articles in the *Canadian Defence Quarterly* in 1938 and 1939 in which he disputed with Major E. L. M. Burns, a sapper who had served in the war, passed Staff College in 1929, and was some years his senior, over the organization and employment of the infantry division.[4]

Simonds's writings about the infantry division summarize his opinion about the Advanced Tank School and the opposed Reactionary Infantry School current when he was at the Staff College. His reasoning and conclusions were rigorous and logical, and with the advantage of hindsight seem to have been correct. He asserted that if a Continental war broke out Britain would contribute only a token land force. It was the policy of the British government to hinge its defence policy on sea and air forces, not on the army. The overall Allied strategy would be to gain time for the British to mobilize their manpower if the French could not go over to the offensive against the Germans and win the war for themselves. In no circumstances would we fritter away the regular army and follow it with half-trained reserve units as we had in 1914. Nor would we repeat the mistake of adopting a continuous offensive that ensured, between 1915 and 1918, that we could never build a large enough striking force to launch a decisive offensive.

From this premise came Simonds's argument against Burns's articles in support of "a division that could attack" that included integral armoured units. First, he said, our role would be defensive and the division should be able to defend. Second, when it attacked, it would be part of a large-scale attack and its offensive capacity would be enhanced by additional units from an army reserve. It would be uneconomical to include those units in the permanent establishment of the division as Burns wished. Burns, he said, overestimated the capacity of British industry, which found it difficult to provide the tanks for an armoured division, let alone for infantry divisions. Extra artillery would have to be added to an infantry division to enable it to attack, as Burns admitted, and the same would apply to armour.

Simonds's visit to the United Kingdom had opened his eyes to the small scale of the British effort compared to that of the Continental powers. The Canadian contribution to an Allied effort would be substantially still smaller, and Burns was wrong to write as though the Canadians would be an independent force. He did not contribute to the idea, common at the time and held by Burns, that conscript armies were inferior by their nature to so-called professional volunteer ones. In no way could German divisions manned, as in 1914, by a proportion of conscripts who had served up to two years and trained with the unit with which they would go to war, be compared with the British conscripts of 1917 and 1918. The latter were enlisted after the cream had been taken for the earlier volunteer Kitchener armies and trained by men who were not, in most cases, capable. Continental conscripts included the cream of the crop and were a cross section of the population. Initially they would not be inferior to British regulars.

An advocate of tactics in which all arms cooperated, Simonds developed an argument that the main attack should be launched by tanks. An infantry platoon of twenty-five men could be said to have cost the country, by the time each was eighteen years old, $142,500. A platoon could develop slightly less firepower than a single tank with a crew of five men. A tank crew cost $28,500 and if, for the sake of argument the equipment cost another $114,000, bearing in mind the cost of infantry equipment, the tank was a more economical unit. But was it as effective? he asked.

Simonds then compared the tank in attack to the infantry platoon. The anti-infantry weapons of the defence, given the expected state of visibility on a battlefield, were more effective than the anti-tank weapons. The former could cover all approaches, even in mist, using fixed lines, whereas antitank guns must see their target. Indirect artillery of field calibre had little effect on tanks but was decisive against infantry in the open. The problem of the tank was that while it could enter an enemy position it could not easily evict infantry from houses with cellars and from woods. Nor could it come to grips with infantry protected by obstacles covered by fire. Infantry, which was tactically more mobile, was required for those tasks and they must appear on the scene quickly. Getting them there might require tracked or at least cross-country transport, which Simonds did not mention on this occasion but in Normandy answered by the provision of armoured personnel carriers (APCs). He did deal with artillery support.

A weakness in manuals was the statement that where the location of the enemy is not known the barrage is the most effective fire support. The tank can move almost in the barrage without suffering, but infantry must hang back, although keeping as close to it as possible. Where the enemy locations are known concentrations are preferred, the manuals stated, suggesting that that would be the normal form of support. Simonds objected, pointing out that very seldom will enemy weapons be located and therefore the concentrations will be ineffective in protecting the infantry, which will inevitably suffer heavy casualties as they did on the Western Front. He concluded that the barrage designed only to neutralize the enemy temporarily is to be preferred in most cases to concentrations and that tanks ought to make the main attack. However, "for the time being," he favoured the use of infantry tanks to work with the infantry in the second phase of the attack when enemy infantry is being winkled out of its positions.

Since these articles were about infantry divisions, cover much ground, and were intended to comment on current practice rather than to rewrite the manuals, several questions were left in the air, including whether or not there was a difference between the actions of armoured and infantry divisions in the attack. Simonds did not deal with deep penetration by the medium tanks nor with how the infantry was to keep up with the advance, which was one of the unsolved problems at the Staff College. But it seemed that his subject was an infantry division not intended to make deep penetrations and, in the context of his debate with Burns, was mainly a defensive formation required to mount counterattacks. What they do show are glimpses of his future methods as a divisional and corps commander, as well as of what was to become standard practice by 1943.

Simonds disagreed with his commandant, not for the last time, by taking a British and European view of tactics and strategy in his lectures and articles, contrary to the policy of the Canadian government, which had avoided committing itself to imperial strategies, let alone another land campaign in Continental Europe. Crerar was uncomfortable with officers who contradicted the manuals because it confused the cadets and created discord among the instructors.

3

On an Insecure Foundation

··

IT IS NECESSARY to return to 1929 to follow Guy
Simonds's family affairs. In that year Cecil and
Nellie Simonds separated. It was not an amicable parting, and she
insisted on a court order that was intended to provide money
from Cecil to pay for the education of Peter and Eric as well as her
own maintenance. Instead she spent the money on herself. Cecil
was not well-off, and the alimony drained his resources. Nellie
moved to Virginia and, habitually hard up, continued to demand
subsidies from her husband, and later from Guy. She remained a
time bomb in Guy's life and in that of her complaisant husband
until her death in 1959. Neither could turn his back on her, and
she continued to blackmail them. Much later, in 1950, Peter
Simonds wrote to his father of his mother's place in this earlier
part of their lives:

> Despite her faults — and they are many — Mummy is Guy's mother,
> and she did more for him than any other of her children. Being the
> eldest son, he was able to get safely launched on his career before
> Mummy went right off the deep end and broke up whatever home
> life Eric and I had previously, which wasn't much at that. Eric and I
> finished by living together in a boarding house with me in third-year
> and he in first-year high school, for which you paid the bills while she
> pocketed a separation allowance for herself, which a court order had
> allowed her for her own and our supports.[1]

When his parents separated, Guy Simonds had passed out of the RMC four years earlier and had served as a subaltern, first in B Battery, Royal Canadian Horse Artillery in Kingston, and then in C Battery in Winnipeg. There he won a reputation as an accomplished horseman and a polo player whom his wealthy friends welcomed as a team member and provided with ponies, which otherwise would have been beyond his means. He was a good-looking young man, and local society women set their caps for him as a likely husband for their daughters, although he had no private means. It was obvious enough that if anyone in the army was going to be successful, it was Guy Granville Simonds.

The girls, though, found him difficult, even intimidating. With a drink or two inside him he was amusing enough, but he had no small talk. You had to prime him. He could be fun when he was in the right mood, but he did not go out of his way to charm his companions. The girls thought him too taken up with his horses, guns, and men. What he needed was a bright, uninhibited woman with brains who was not overawed by him, someone to take him in hand and unbutton him. He took himself too seriously. So it was a surprise when he started to go about with Katherine Lockhart Taylor, a petite, attractive blonde who was not at all what many other people had in mind for him.

Katherine, who was known as "K," was the second daughter of Charles Taylor, a prominent Winnipeg businessman in the stockbroking firm of Osler, Hammond, and Nanton. K was the apple of her father's eye. No doubt she wished she had been a boy, as one or other of the girls in a family of girls usually does. A tomboy, the practical doer in the family rather than the delicate flower, her forceful mother resisted her adventurous spirit. It was K who learned to drive, looked after the family car, and was the family chauffeur. She also started to learn to fly, something she yearned to do at a time when barnstorming was all the rage and the northland was being opened up by relatively flimsy aircraft. But when it looked as though she would earn her licence, and had already flown solo, her mother stepped in and made Charles Taylor put his foot down. "Your poor mother will never have a quiet moment if you persist in your dangerous adventure" was his reluctant line of argument with K. To her regret K felt that she had to give way. Instead she took a course as a motor mechanic. Charles himself seldom kicked against the pricks at home. He came into his own when he entertained. Then he was the life and soul of the party. He was a short, jolly man whereas his wife was rather serious and tense. She admired her husband's ability to make a party really go, but otherwise kept him on a tight rein.

The attraction of two young people for each other can be seen more easily than it can be explained. Guy was good-looking, competent, and admired by all his contemporaries. Quite a few girls had eyed him speculatively. Although the Taylor family was fairly well united, K was not entirely happy at home. She felt that her sisters were favoured by her mother because, unlike her, they were not rebellious. What better way of establishing her independence than marrying an attractive man before her older sister, who was so admired for her looks and vivacity? And, besides, she was in love.

It is probable that she conceived, better than Guy, what their parts in the marriage would be. Guy was not a practical, build-your-own-house type of young Canadian, although he later became an accomplished cabinetmaker. K, on the other hand, was practical, dutiful, and motherly. She taught Guy to drive. No doubt she expected that, as he had demonstrated his ability to master anything he set his mind to, he would eventually be the perfect father and husband when they settled down and raised a family. She could not know that the service would always be his family, and that the lure of success and the excitement of war were to deny her what she wanted most. Service wives had to be especially tolerant and adaptable so as to face competing demands for selfless loyalty to the service itself and to their partners. They also had to be prepared for frequent moves and separations. K was not ready at all for what was to follow.

A subaltern could not marry without obtaining permission from his commanding officer. The reasoning was that he might get into debt, for he would not be entitled to either married quarters or a marriage allowance. And he would spend too much time with his wife and neglect his horses, guns, and men. The mess, too, would suffer from his absence. Subalterns were at the bottom of the regimental totem pole. In his senior term at the RMC he had been warned that the first claim on the gunner officer's loyalty and attention was the infantry or cavalry unit that he was assigned to support. Next came the guns with which he gave support, the horses that took the guns into action, and the men in the gun detachments. The battery and regiment embraced all these, and the private affairs or preferences of young subalterns were of no importance.

The young couple courted each other from 1930. Outings in the early thirties were frequently foursomes, for cars were often shared. Young officers were impecunious creatures, and still are, but as K always drove the family car, they were at an advantage. By Christmas

1930 Guy and K were heading towards marriage as soon as they could afford it, and when Guy could obtain permission to marry. Normally that could not be for over a year. On January 5, 1931, K wrote:

> Now that I have begun a letter I only want to sit and think about you, which wouldn't help you much, so I will write a letter. I am so glad you rang up last night. I wanted to tell you how much I love you only Mum was right by my elbow, and so I couldn't as she would make me blush and I couldn't hide a blush in a nightie. . . . I didn't think I'd begin to miss you for a few days because I often don't see you for ages, but my tummy drops every time the phone rings at meals and I keep waiting for you to ring up, so you see I loved you doing it last night and I went to sleep properly. . . .[2]

In June 1932 Simonds's application to get married was turned down on the grounds that he would not attain the age of thirty until April 1933, that it was detrimental to a junior officer's training to be permitted to marry and live out of mess and that, if he were married, he would not derive full benefit from the Long Gunnery Staff Course on which he was shortly to embark in England. From Practice Camp at Camp Hughes, Manitoba, Simonds formally appealed to Brigadier T. V. Anderson, the district officer commanding (DOC). He pointed out that the rule about age had not been universally applied and mentioned some officers who had married before they were thirty. Besides, he would attain thirty during the Long Gunnery Staff Course. Many Canadian officers attending the course in the past had been married, and he was confident that, having attained a "distinguished" grade in the Canadian artillery course, marriage would not interfere with his work in England.

His rank at this time was brevet captain, which entitled him to the rank but not the pay of a captain. It indicated that he was marked for accelerated promotion, for he would gain seniority when he was promoted to substantive rank at the age of thirty. His record obviously impressed Anderson, for on August 17, 1932, Guy and K were married in All Saints Church, Winnipeg. Geraldine, K's elder sister, was a bridesmaid. Major J. C. Murchie, "Murch," was Guy's best man and was to be a lifelong friend. Sadly the only Simonds representative at the wedding was Cicely, at that time married to Tim Matson of Victoria. Cicely was a bright, happy young woman and very fond of Guy, but her marriage was to break down in 1935, leaving her with a daughter, Mary.

The young couple disappeared to Detroit Lakes in Minnesota for a brief honeymoon and then took a train to Halifax, where they boarded the *Duchess of Bedford* on September 2, bound for England. The gunnery course started on the nineteenth. During that year, the Simondses lived near Shoeburyness, although Guy had to travel to various ranges and artillery schools. Before Guy left Canada Cecil Simonds wrote to brief him about his English relatives and apprised them of Guy's arrival. Guy was at once welcomed and entertained by the Maxses, Milners, and Mathers. As well, the British army authorities and the Canadian high commissioner endeavoured to make Canadian officers feel at home and on a par with British officers. Simonds was a guest at a dinner for dominion officers given by the British Council at the Cavalry Club. They were included in the invitations to court occasions. The service clubs, like the army, navy, and cavalry, accepted them as honorary members. Canada House and the high commissioner looked after their interests. All of it was warming and exciting for the young Canadian on his return to the land of his birth.

In June 1933 their daughter Ruth was born in a nursing home at Southend on Sea. K wrote from there to Guy, who was in Somerset:

> Such a nice letter from you Tuesday and thanks heaps. . . . I hope there is another scavenging party here and I can go on it, but you forgot to enclose the list. . . . I always thought tiny babies were handled gingerly, but you should see them heaving Ruth about, and I have to slap her face hard to wake her up . . . [the birth] was painful and I won't go into details. I could never hope to imagine anything worse, but I'll be doing it again for Charles. . . .[3]

The Simondses were back in Canada a year later, and Charles Simonds was duly born at Kingston in 1934. In the meantime Eric had joined the Royal Air Force. When Guy obtained one of the sought-after places on the Camberley Staff College course that began in January 1936 and lasted two years, the brothers saw quite a lot of each other and corresponded regularly. Eric was on the RAF Bisley team and on visits there stayed with Guy and K at Southernwood, their rented house on King's Ride, close to the Staff College.

Guy and Eric, the youngest of the Simonds family, had been close friends as children, but the youngest boy had been nominated for a dominion cadetship at the RAF College at Cranwell, and for some years the two had not met. On commissioning Eric was posted to the crack Forty-third Fighter Squadron at Tangmere, Sussex, which was responsible for the formation aerobatics display at Hendon and air shows on the Continent. After establishing his name as an outstanding pilot, he was posted in 1931 as an instructor to the Fourth Flying

Training School in Egypt and was still there when Guy attended the Long Gunnery Staff Course. At the end of his stint in Egypt in 1934 he was grounded in accordance with RAF regulations and decided to fill in a year before returning to flying duties by studying to be an interpreter in Russian. He attended Kings College, London University, for three months and spent the rest of 1935 with the Count and Countess Baranoff in Tallinn, the capital of Estonia. He then qualified as a Russian interpreter, first class.

On his return to England the RAF was reequipping with the first of the all-weather monoplane fighter aircraft. The early marks of the Hurricane and Spitfire, and training aircraft like the Miles Magister, were being tested at Martlesham Heath on the Suffolk coast. Eric was posted there as a test pilot. Guy visited him at Martlesham and was shown the latest aircraft. He thought Eric's fellow pilots as fine a group of young airmen as could be found anywhere. Those that survived were destined for high posts. Among them were Squadron Leader Frank Whittle, who was to invent the jet engine that first ran in the Gloster E in 1941. By 1937 most forward-looking officers in the services were convinced that a war with Germany was inevitable, and Eric and Guy were both mixing with highly motivated men, many of whom, like Guy, were to become famous.

In the summer of 1937, Guy's second (senior) year at the Staff College, he was enjoying an attachment to the Royal Navy, and on July 22 he was in the aircraft carrier HMS *Courageous*.[4] They were engaged in exercises in the English Channel when a telegram was handed to Guy: "Regret to inform you . . ." Evidently Eric was missing, believed drowned off the Suffolk coast. Guy was flown off the ship to Blackbush airfield on the flats above Camberley. From there he drove to Martlesham, where he learned that Eric had been putting a Miles Magister through spinning tests. He was over the sea when the aircraft failed to come out of a spin and Eric had to bail out. The wind caught his parachute and took him out to sea. For some reason there was a long delay before a boat took off to pick him up. It found no sign of him. Guy was flown up and down the coast for two days by Eric's fellow pilots, but they saw nothing. Later his body washed ashore still attached to the parachute.

Letters of regret and admiration for Eric arrived for Guy at the Staff College. An inquiry into why the rescue effort had been so tardy revealed that no station rescue facilities were in place. Simonds suggested in his autobiography that, as a result of the accident, the air-sea rescue service that saved the lives of many pilots during the Battle of Britain and in the cross-Channel operations that followed was equipped and formed. In fact, in 1940 the Germans still out-shone the RAF in rescuing pilots until pitched battles over them led to British MTBs and seaplanes being assigned to the rescue service.

Nellie was distraught over Eric's death. She and Guy correspond-ed, of course. Writing to him from Virginia, she said that she had heard from some friends of Eric's at Martlesham:

> *Please* don't let them think that I am a boor or ignoramus, that I have not replied — I simply *cannot*. . . . If any letters of mine were amongst Eric's possessions, should they have been disposed of don't worry. If not please keep one at least intact just as he left it. It is just the idea, although if anyone has them, it is not so bad that a brother officer should have them. . . . I received the package of beloved things . . . thanks for all the miserable trouble you have had to take, dear, but at its worst I don't think that anything could approach what I endured and am enduring. It is a shattering unhappiness which has left me finally broken. Nothing can atone for it, nothing alter it.[5]

Cicely and her daughter Mary were with Nellie in the United States at the time, Cicely still looking wan and unhappy after her separation from her husband. Peter was on his way down from Toronto, and some of Eric's things were to be passed on to him. Nellie observed snidely that it was not likely that *he* would ever require full evening dress. "He has *nothing* beyond the little I have struggled to provide him with." Peter was a permanent worry, unable to hold a job. He had refused to go into his father's business. Of all the family he alone seemed to lack the grit and determination to succeed.

Guy's years at the Staff College reinforced his love for England and strengthened the affection for its social milieu that his mother had implanted in him. The Staff College Drag, race meetings, invitations to country houses, salmon fishing, and many clever and amusing people to talk to attracted him powerfully. K did not enjoy the social life very much. That was sad as the Staff College was a happy place where wives as well as husbands made friends for life. She did not enjoy riding particularly, and two small children seemed to keep her too much at home. Perhaps she was too earnest, too much a martyr to her home to be able to relax and embrace the accepted English style, which was never to give the impression of taking work, play, or duties too seriously.

At the end of the second year it appeared that Guy had emerged as one of the outstanding men on the course and had he been a British officer would have been marked for accelerated promotion and a return to the college as a lieutenant colonel instructor, a member of the directing staff (DS), within a few years. When it was known that he was interested in joining the British service, it was suggested that he should apply. An inquiry by one of the DS elicited the information that he would normally have to enter with the seniority of the bottom of his age group, although an exception might be made. At the time he was informed by Lieutenant Colonel Kenneth Stuart in Ottawa that he was earmarked for a post as instructor at the Royal Military College, Kingston, with the rank of major. As we have seen, he decided to accept it.

On their departure in the *Duchess of York* from England bound for Halifax, Nova Scotia, Simonds received a telegram from the Canadian high commissioner, Vincent Massey: "To wish you and your family a pleasant crossing and success in your next appointment in Canada. My warmest congratulations also on your wonderful results at Camberley. You were a credit, indeed, to the service."[6]

War came the following year, and Simonds was posted as a General Staff officer to the First (Canadian) Division. He was soon in England. Cicely, like many other Canadian women, got herself to England, too. In 1941 she was secretary to Admiral King in the Admiralty. She had a flat with her daughter in Buckingham Gate and wrote long, newsy, typed aerogram letters, mainly to her father, with occasional reports about Guy, whom she saw from time to time when he was in London. She was busy and lived through the blitz in the cheerful and nonchalant manner of the time, admitting only occasionally how frightened she was. Somehow her flat had a charmed life.

In early June of 1944, while Guy was commanding the Second (Canadian) Corps and preparing for D-day, they would walk in the park during her lunch break when he was attending a conference in town. Soon after D-day the buzz bombs (V1s) started to fly over. This was the period when London came under bombardment by V1 and V2 missiles, no fewer than ninety-two hundred of the former and one thousand of the latter landing in the capital or falling short in southern England. When Guy was in Normandy, a V1 struck Cicely's flat, and she and her daughter were buried under the rubble. Peter, in London doing a signals staff job, was informed and hurried to the scene. Mary had been killed instantly. Cicely, according to the state of her body when it was recovered, had lived for as much as twenty hours under the rubble. There are no letters in Guy's papers about the incident, but after Eric's death this second loss was a dreadful shock.[7]

K remained with the children in Canada throughout the war, mainly in an apartment in Winnipeg. She wrote regularly to Guy, whose letters in reply were less regular, as one would expect. She was informed by newspaper articles as her husband rose to fame, and her father-in-law collected every article he could find about his son. But Guy could tell her very little about what he was doing, or was about to do, so when he took command of the First Division and was photographed wading ashore in Sicily, it was as much of a surprise to her as to her friends. It was an uncomfortable adjustment for her to have to share him with the nation. It would have eased the transition had he dashed off frequent little notes that showed he still loved her, and that she was on the inside track of his life. Surely, K felt, scribbling them would have taken up so little time. K, Cicely, and Cecil shared news of Guy, but K was unhappily aware that she and Guy were slipping apart. It was not uncommon that both partners were changed by the war, and after up to six years of separation, some marriages never recovered; in others the partners had to get to know each other all over again. On July 31, 1943, K wrote:

> Guy darlingest, yesterday I got such a nice photo of you from the *Free Press*. Coming ashore in Sicily in the water. I love it, darling, but it makes you feel so far away and another man. You have on a beret and it looks as if it would be becoming. I love looking at you as I know your arms so well and I can see they are really you. And your moll [sic] on your cheek too. Guy darling, I miss you so and I do hope you can come home and be an ordinary man again and not so famous and super. I don't know how I'd behave if you were too public for the rest of your life. . . .[8]

Here was the cloud on the horizon, no larger than a man's hand. Simonds went on to be the most prominent Canadian soldier. He had won the approval of no less than the exacting Montgomery and was liked and admired not only by his British colleagues but also by the Americans. By 1945 he had arrived and would be a public figure for the rest of his life. Nothing could recall the Guy of 1939. Public men have had wives who remained private women. They have fulfilled their bare duties, entertaining, doing charity work, but avoided the public responsibilities that others take on as part of their husbands' lives, often enjoying them. K could and would have fulfilled her minimum duties; indeed, she did so later in Kingston and Ottawa, even though she hated them. But marriages in which the wife dissociates herself from the public life of her famous husband have to have very secure foundations if they are to last. Indeed, if the wife enjoys the public life, the privileges, and the hard work of fame, it may hold the marriage together. It is a strain for the man if he knows that his wife is counting the days until he "retires," for he knows that as a prominent man he can seldom lay aside the duties that will continue to be placed on him for the rest of his life.

Guy had always been attracted to the lifestyle of prominent people, and while he was in England he had tasted it and wished for more. He had met Ian and Mona Anderson, and spent any time that he could spare at their country place, Old Surrey Hall. His diaries are dotted with references to leisurely weekends and snatched days spent there. Ian was a wealthy man. A member of the London Stock Exchange, a territorial commanding officer and veteran of the First War, and a high sheriff, he had a house on the Spey, Inverness, with a stretch of salmon fishing that Guy was invited to enjoy.

Mona was an attractive, intelligent, amusing woman, and Guy fell in love with her. They frequently met in London where the Andersons had a flat in Mayfair, and dined together at the Dorchester, a favourite spot, or in Soho. The Andersons were a sophisticated couple, and the relationship between Guy and Mona was discreet and civilized. In his role as coordinator of a welfare organization Ian visited Guy in Holland during the campaign and later when Guy was commanding Canadian forces in the Netherlands after the armistice. They were good friends. Colin, the Andersons' elder son, became Guy's ADC. Had Guy joined the British army his future with Mona might conceivably have been different. As it was, there was no likelihood of Mona leaving Ian for Guy. Yet the relationship continued. No doubt Ian was intelligent enough to realize that the affair could never mature further. However, it was to be the cause of Guy's divorce from K.

4

The Perfect
Staff Officer

....

FROM **O**TTAWA on December 7, 1939, Guy Simonds
wrote:

Dear Daddy:

I have been unable to write to you before partly because our appointments were supposed to be kept secret and partly because handing
over the old job and taking over a new one has kept me on the hop.

I have been appointed GSO II (Operations) 1 Canadian Division and
naturally am awfully pleased. Though I hate leaving K and the children
I know I would have felt very restless (to say the least) to stay in a routine job whilst the war was on. I arrived in Ottawa about two weeks ago
and have had a flying visit to Kingston since to see the family moved
into their new quarters — a very nice flat at 176 King Street, Kingston.

K had considered going to Winnipeg but later decided from every point
of view that it was better to stay in Kingston. Most of her friends are
there now. The move out West would be expensive and she is nearer to
Europe (should the chance of a visit come) by staying where she is.

Many thanks for your letters and the National. I will look up Judy
Milner in the near future and of course Cicely.

I am sorry this has to be so short but I have to get the odd letter written between odd jobs.

Love,
Guy[1]

Two days later the First Division staff, headed by its commander, Major General McNaughton, went on board the Cunarder *Aquitania* bound for the United Kingdom. The First Division moved into barracks in Aldershot vacated by British Expeditionary Force units, then in France and Belgium. It was a cold winter and the barracks and lecture halls were uninsulated. Small black fire grates and round cast-iron stoves ate up in vain what the division considered a miserable coal ration. Nevertheless, they received twice what the British were allocated. Wooden fences and trees, even wall panelling, disappeared into the stoves when the coal gave out. The British district headquarters staff remonstrated, but without much result, and colds and flu were rife.

A generation earlier the First Division had been in tented camps on Salisbury Plain in much worse conditions. Otherwise the state of things was the same in 1939 as in 1914. The division was no better trained or equipped, for its brigades had been assembled from opposite ends of the country and its ranks hurriedly filled with untrained volunteers "off the streets." It had to make do for months with impressed transport and lacked field and antitank guns, mortars, Bren gun carriers, and even its full complement of machine guns. Until these deficiencies were made good anything other than basic training was an exercise in ingenuity if not futility.

As GSO II, a major on the operations staff, Simonds organized divisional courses, procured training areas, maps, and range allotments, borrowed instructors for weapons and procedures that were new to the division, and studied local defence schemes and other divisional tasks. His opposite numbers in the Adjutant and Quartermaster General's branch also had their work cut out. The A staff attended to morale and discipline, and there were many misfits, unfits, elderly, and compassionate cases to be returned to Canada. Some skilled men who should never have been allowed to volunteer had to be persuaded to volunteer again — this time to return to Canada to help the industrial war effort. The Q staff was concerned with barrack services, military equipment, transport, fuel, and a hundred other items that had to be procured from the British.

The first weeks in the Aldershot area were frustrating, an anticlimax after the excitement of the departure from Canada. No doubt volunteers had imagined that active service would be action-packed. It was just as well they did not know they would wait between three and four years before meeting the enemy. First War veterans found living conditions quite familiar: the smell in the air of coal smoke, the burst pipes, the chilly rooms, English food in none-too-clean cafés, well-meaning promises by harassed British officials, friendly civilians eager to help, a mixture of the good and the exasperating, the strange and the familiar. Above all, everyone waited desperately for mail from home that was promised but did not arrive. There was a rising tide of homesickness. Aldershot was not the friendliest of towns, for the people were used to soldiers coming and going and expected the Canadians to be a self-sufficient community like the British. That these were Canadians far from home did not, at first, impress itself on them. The Royal Twenty-second Regiment, the Van Doos, of whom fifty percent spoke no English, were particularly left out in the cold. It was not until the spring of 1940 when the division moved briefly to the Midlands and then down into Sussex that the Canadians realized that most English people were friendly towards them.

Initially this was the lot of the Canadian Active Service Force or CASF. It embraced the Permanent Force, or PF, the Nonpermanent Active Militia, or NPAM, and those in the ranks who had been in neither. All were volunteers. That distinguished it not only from the wartime British army, which had drafted soldiers in April 1939, but also from the Americans, who started to arrive in 1942.

As senior Canadian, Andy McNaughton had two staffs: his divisional staff and the Canadian Military Headquarters Staff, CMHQ, headed by Brigadier Crerar, recently commandant of the RMC. CMHQ dealt with the British army, the British government, and army headquarters in Ottawa. It had a finger in every pie, and Crerar was promoted to major general in the new year by way of recognition.

Because of his prickliness about Canadian rights Andy McNaughton was not popular with the British. His GSO I, Lieutenant Colonel G. R. Turner, did not run a happy team or make friends easily outside the headquarters. One of Simonds's assets was that having spent three years of his service in England he had British friends in key places, and where he did not he made new ones. British officers found in him a kindred spirit, cooperative and efficient. In the divisional staff the junior officers came to him when they wanted a problem solved, and it was he who set staff procedures on the right lines, laying a foundation for the future.

The headquarters was a training school for higher appointments. There were three officers on the operations staff who rose to high positions: Churchill Mann, who became Crerar's chief of staff in the First Army; Pat Bogert, who later commanded the West Nova Scotia Regiment, was GSO I of the division and commanded the Second Brigade in Italy; and John Tweedsmuir, who succeeded his father, the governor general of Canada, as second Baron Tweedsmuir in 1940 and commanded the Hastings and Prince Edward Regiment in a famous action at Assoro in Sicily.

Lieutenant Colonel Turner seldom initiated action, and the junior staff looked to Simonds for leadership. An example was Turner's reaction to Bogert's handling of an instruction about dealing with parachute invasion that was marked "Not to be disclosed." Bogert, taking that to refer to the press, issued it to brigade commanders. Turner blew up and tore into him for disobeying orders. Simonds could see that the order was useless unless brigades were informed, so he told Turner, "I'd have done the same." Turner cooled down but was not pleased that Simonds had taken Bogert's side. To make matters worse, Turner became a joke after he sent out a strong warning about wasting gasoline and it was discovered that the work ticket of his own car showed irregularities. His driver had either sold gasoline or used the car for joyrides. The man denied it vehemently, but the two were known as Snow White and Dopey from then on.

John Tweedsmuir, as GSO III (Intelligence), was responsible for the war diary — not usually light reading. He had been a noted shot in the Colonial Service in Africa, so when the local zoo telephoned to say that they could no longer feed their elephant and wanted someone to shoot it, Tweedsmuir's name was suggested. Permission was granted by CMHQ, but Turner made it a condition that the entry in the war diary show that it was in response to a request. The sad deed was done. Later the war diary was found to have the bald entry under the date "Leatherhead, 1531 hours. The G 3 Intelligence shot an elephant."

The Chiefs of Staff Committee and the responsible politicians, including Winston Churchill, who was First Lord of the Admiralty, did not cover themselves with glory in the first year of the war. They underestimated the enemy's capacity and overestimated their own pitifully small resources. A series of muddled operations started with a project to send help to the Finns, then fighting for their lives against the Russians. Fortunately the gallant Finns gave up their unequal struggle before "help" could be sent. Next an attempt was made to prevent German iron ore freighters from using Norwegian coastal waters on their way from Narvik to Germany. On this mission Captain Philip Vian of the *Cossack* intercepted the *Altmark* and freed some British prisoners, which caused a stir because the German ship was sailing in territorial waters. But it was a bold and successful action that cheered the public. In July 1943 Vian, by then an admiral, covered the landings of the First

Division in Sicily from his command ship *Hilary*, in which Simonds sailed to war for the first time.

It will be recalled that from the declaration of war until April 1940 a virtual truce on land was observed by Germany, France, and Britain. This ended abruptly when the Germans invaded Denmark and Norway in April 1940, and Holland, Belgium, and France in May. The German invasion of Norway led to the first of three abortive Canadian operations. On April 16 a small force of eight companies of a hundred men each selected from the Second Infantry Brigade joined an army/navy group called Hammerforce, which was ordered to seize and man the forts covering the port of Trondheim. Two larger forces, Operation Sickle, landed at Namsos and Andalsnes, on the flanks, to intercept Germans advancing north-wards to seize Trondheim. The Canadian contingent was chosen from the Patricias and the Edmonton Regiment. Machine guns and mortars from the Saskatoon Light Infantry and divisional signals units and gunners were added to man the forts. The Canadian com-mander of the force was Colonel Ernest Sansom, deputizing for Brigadier George Pearkes, V.C., the brigade commander, who was sick. As there were men of Scandinavian descent in the Saskatoon Light Infantry, Sansom was asked to send two Norwegian linguists to join the King's Own Yorkshire Light Infantry (KOYLI) with which the Saskatoon Light Infantry was affiliated and who were part of Sickle. Privates A. Johannson and G. Hanson, selected for the job, proved to be the only Canadians to set foot in Norway. One of them remarked that they found the heavily accented English of the Norwegians easier to understand than KOYLI Yorkshire.

Simonds retrieved a captain from a staff course at Camberley to help with the Adjutant and Quartermaster (A and Q) side of the operation, and they worked through the night to finish the order. It was like a staff college exercise that started off with the instruction: "Your GSO I calls you in and says: 'Guy, the general has just phoned from corps headquarters where he has received orders to have three battalions ready to move at first light to X. . . . I want you to. . . .'" X was the point of embarkation to which the brigade moved on the eighteenth. Although the operation was cancelled on the twentieth, the force had been readied and moved to Dunfermline in Scotland in about seventy-two hours from scratch. It was a useful exercise, for there is nothing like the expectation of actually having to use weapons and equipment against the enemy to make men take their state of training seriously. Sleeping bags, winter clothing including heavy underwear, sheepskin coats, and leather jerkins, extra socks, and heavy lumbermen's boots had to be provided by the staff. Functioning on the spur-of-the-moment welded the divisional team together, for the staff of the other two brigades mucked in. McNaughton was not much use at such a fundamental level himself so, sensibly, he left Simonds, who had an excellent mind for detail and remarkable energy and drive, to play the key role. Noting his performance, McNaughton marked him for accelerated promotion from then onwards.[2]

Hammerforce began the role of the division as U.K. mobile reserve, for it was the only mobile and more or less fully equipped division left in Britain once the Norwegian expedition had left Scotland. Both parts of Sickle returned in bad shape, and even a force that captured Narvik and withdrew in good order in the first week of June came back without its heavy equipment and weapons.

By that time the British Expeditionary Force had returned from Dunkirk, temporarily demoralized and also without heavy equipment; indeed, many returned without personal weapons. For, on May 10, the Germans struck on the Continent. Within two weeks the BEF was being driven back on Dunkirk, Calais, and Boulogne by a panzer army that crashed through the Ardennes, crossed the Meuse, moved in on the right flank, and cut the BEF's lines of communication to the sea. While this drama was unfolding the Canadians were summoned again. The project was for the First Brigade, followed by the rest of the division, to reestablish road and rail communications between Calais and Dunkirk in case evacuation should be necessary.

On May 23 McNaughton and Turner were ordered to reconnoitre both places. On the twenty-fourth McNaughton started to shuttle between Calais, Dunkirk, Dover, and London in an effort first to discover what was happening on the ground and then to explain to the staff in London that it was organization, not troops, that was lacking. Based in Dover Castle, Simonds kept in radio touch with McNaughton and interpreted his recommendations to General Dewing, the director of Military Operations at the War Office. At the same time he superintended loading troops and two-pounder anti-tank guns into ships below in the harbour and liaised with the Royal Navy. His confidence in the operation was dampened when he observed explosive charges being laid against the cranes on the moles. It heightened the atmosphere of barely suppressed panic evident among naval officers who seemed to be expecting the Germans to invade at any moment.

Simonds was not surprised, after McNaughton had come back across the English Channel and hurried up to London to confer, that

General Ironside, the chief of the Imperial General Staff (CIGS), agreed that sending a brigade over at that late stage would be simply to lose it. So the troops were disembarked, packed into trains, and sent home disappointed. Back at Aldershot, peacetime modes of behaviour prevailed. Tweedsmuir had had to hand in all the maps of the Aldershot area, so when he returned he went to the engineers to retrieve them. "No, sir, I'm afraid not, sir. All maps handed in as no longer required are destroyed by fire, sir. Them's regs."

The whole affair had been a letdown, but no equipment was lost. The next operation, however, was a fiasco in which they lost a lot of it, as well as confidence in their British commanders. By this time Winston Churchill had become prime minister and was determined to demonstrate to the French that the fight was not over just because most of the BEF and survivors from the French northern army had been evacuated. So, while the French forces were still fighting south of the Somme, he ordered a so-called Second BEF sent to Brittany to advance eastwards and join hands with French forces south and west of the Seine. Lieutenant General Alan Brooke, who had commanded a corps in the BEF, was in command of this force of corps strength, of which the First Division was to be part. The Canadians were to be placed south and east of Rennes on the German flank from Saint-Nazaire through Le Mans. It was believed that the hilly, wooded country made the ground unsuitable for German panzer troops and that brigades could operate separately and on wide frontages.

The First Brigade again led the way with the Royal Canadian Regiment (RCR), the Hastings and Prince Edward, and the Forty-eighth Highlanders. The main party, having been seen off from Plymouth by Lady Astor, the Member for Plymouth, and her Women's Auxiliary, were displeased to find that the lifeboats on SS *el Mansour* and the *Ville d'Alger* were reserved for the crew and that the fixtures had been removed from the latrines, which were blocked. When they arrived at Brest, no instructions about this hastily improvised operation had reached Movement Control authorities in Brittany.

Movement Control, familiarly but occasionally unfairly known as Muddle and Chaos, was convinced that the Canadians were on a non-operational move up the lines of communication towards a front of which they knew nothing, and cared less provided it was far away. So they applied the procedures of 1939, when some units of the BEF entered the theatre through Brest. Vehicle parties were separated from rifle companies. The latter were put into trains "with the aid of much pushing and cursing" and not without the odd broken window. The platform was crowded with people, many of whom were trying to get rid of "huge quantities of French beer and bread" eagerly bought by all ranks. The train then departed with well-lubricated passengers on a magical mystery tour. Even the engine drivers had no idea where they were going. Trains were halted and turned around before they ran full tilt into the enemy, but by that time the railway staff were about to disappear to safety and a swelling crowd of desperate and smelly refugees were surging around the stations. The vehicle parties were much less organized, being assembled in batches, regardless of tactical units or whether there were officers and NCOs in charge. Friendly Bretons, eager to celebrate the arrival of the Canadians, plied them with drink en route, with some unfortunate effects on the drivers.[3]

Fortunately, when General Brooke found that the French had collapsed, he was able to signal the War Office and have the expedition turned back to the ports. Then came the not inconsiderable feat of reembarkation in which individual initiative counted most. Robert Moncel, carrier officer of the First RCR, managed to find a boat on his own and embark all his vehicles, although the port staff were almost tearfully insistent that they should be destroyed. The First RCHA also withstood pressure and got all but one of its guns assembled. The twenty-fourth was "found" by a limber gunner and all were loaded into a ship. The gun belonged to another regiment, of course, and a long battle ensued with Ordnance, which wanted to claim it. By one Fabian ploy after another the First RCHA kept the gun until after the war. All in all, the Second BEF was a depressing affair, particularly as more good vehicles and some equipment were lost just after the BEF had left most of its matériel at Dunkirk. It was fortunate that the Second and Third Brigades of the division were not embroiled.

In July 1940 Simonds was posted to command the First RCHA. There were some who expected him to be less effective in command of troops than as a staff officer, and even a few who hoped that he might fall flat on his face. He had not served with troops since leaving C Battery in Winnipeg, and he had acquired a reputation for being a clever, rather intellectual man without the common touch. Doubters were proved wrong. Taking over soon after the fiasco in Brittany, he found his regiment in need of encouragement, and gave it.

He brought in Robert Rothschild, command post officer of A Battery, to be his adjutant. Referred to as "Baron" in the regiment, Rothschild found Simonds a formidable but understanding master. The first order Simonds gave him was to prepare a regimental training programme, something Rothschild had never done before. He had to admit, after struggling with it for an hour, that he did not know how to begin. Simonds sat down beside him and showed Baron what to do. It was a revelation to Rothschild to watch Simonds sketch out the skeleton of the plan with hardly a pause for thought. The ideas seemed to come out in logical order, as though he had done the exercise many times before. Yet Simonds had never served in a regimental headquarters. Being a professional, though, he had often imagined taking over command of a regiment and anticipated what he would do when it happened. His training as an instructor in gunnery pointed him in the right direction, and the years in Kingston and Winnipeg had taught him how to think like a good battery commander, although he had never commanded a battery. The prolonged absences of the senior regimental officers trained the junior ones admirably to replace them. As a commanding officer, Simonds simply "thought two down," as the army saying goes, and envisaged what batteries and troops should be doing.

The First RCHA was moving to Beckenham when Simonds arrived. Everyone was in fear and trembling, but within a very short time they were swearing by him. He knew his gunnery and his tactics and was well informed about the war and how it was progressing. It was excellent for young officers to hear a senior officer expressing complex ideas clearly. He wrote well, too, and that rubbed off on subordinates. However, as was to be his practice, any subordinate without the qualifications to do his job, or not showing signs that he would quickly learn it, was packed off after a warning. As well, a few elderly officers unsuitable for fieldwork were told not to unpack their bags. The work was mainly basic training because the stage of practice camps had not arrived. There was little opportunity for regimental training because of interruptive moves in connection with defence against imminent German invasion and the shortage of vehicles, many of which were still impressed from civilian firms.

Rothschild must have satisfied Simonds, because in November 1940, when Simonds was named by McNaughton to be the commandant of the Canadian Junior War Staff Course, Rothschild was nominated as one of the students. The decision to build the army overseas to five divisions and two armoured brigades made it necessary to train more grade two and three staff officers, and British courses at Camberley could not accommodate them. CMHQ had grown, and so had army headquarters in Ottawa. Wherever you looked, good staff officers were in demand.

The Canadian Junior War Staff Course started at Ford Manor, Lingfield, Surrey, in January 1941 and lasted fourteen weeks. All the material in the first year of the Camberley peacetime course at the divisional junior staff level had been condensed at Camberley and was now included at Ford, so the pressure of work was intense. The traditional Camberley style of instruction was used: introductory lectures, indoor demonstrations and playlets, syndicate presentations and discussions, and outside exercises, in which the students played the roles of divisional and brigade staffs. Every piece of equipment and weapon in a division was demonstrated by the most efficient unit of its kind that Simonds could procure. He was very persuasive and requests were never refused. The course was divided into three terms after each of which students changed syndicates. Every student was reported on by three directing staff members during the course and was seen in action with three different syndicates of their fellows. Simonds sat in on syndicate discussions, summed up exercises, introduced visiting speakers, and wrote many of the instructional précis himself.

Churchill Mann from the First Division, R. H. Keefler, who finished the war commanding the Third Infantry Division, and J. F. A. Lister, who was a noted administrative staff officer and was Simonds's chief of staff after the war in Holland, were three of the directing staff. Camberley loaned Lieutenant Colonel "Baldy" Dowse, one of its star directing staff, who was invaluable to Simonds. Church Mann, an eccentric, brilliant, but not always orderly staff officer, is remembered for writing an operation order entirely in verse, which was in the staff college tradition of blending satire with humour.

Many bright young officers who crossed Simonds's path later were in the student body. Robert Moncel and Bob Kingstone were then only subalterns; the former commanded an armoured brigade from Normandy to the end of the war, and the latter became a brigade major in Sicily and served as secretary to the Chiefs of Staff Committee after the war. Captain W. P. Gilbride would soon be Simonds's assistant adjutant and quartermaster general (a lieutenant colonel AA and QMG) in the First Division. Gilbride has been called many names, some of them uncomplimentary, but mostly by people less successful at procuring scarce commodities for his division than he. Captain D. G. Cunningham eventually commanded a brigade in Normandy. Very few attained A or B grades, and a C qualified an officer to fill a staff appointment. B qualified the student to be a brigade major, DAAG or DAQMG (majors on the Adjutant and Quartermaster General's staff), while an AB qualified him to be an instructor with the Canadian Junior War Staff Course.

Andy McNaughton delivered an address to sixty students at the opening on January 3. He announced that there would be only one course in the United Kingdom. Future ones would be conducted in

Canada. It was arguable that that was a mistake because only in Britain could current weapons and new tactics be demonstrated to the students. The latest thinking would probably never be available in Canada, since methods changed so rapidly. The necessity for one of McNaughton's remarks might shock a modern Canadian:

> I want to say to you gentlemen that you have been selected on the basis of proved ability; that not one of you owes his presence here to political patronage against which the most implicit assurances have been given by the prime minister himself and all his ministers. We have guarded against personal favouritism in any form and the members of the Board of Selection both individually and collectively have been charged to reach their decisions on merit alone.[4]

McNaughton remembered only too well the way Sam Hughes had interfered in such matters in the First War, and Simonds, who particularly rejected the exercise of political pull in the army, was content that McNaughton had mentioned the point.

Judging by the unanimous praise for the way that it was run, the course was considered by the students to have been a huge success. Many particularly remembered the innovation of issuing motorcycles to every student as their only form of transport. Only one student was slightly injured, which was creditable when officers and men were routinely killed riding motorcycles. Piccadilly Circus was a rendezvous for students seeing something of London on their motorcycles on half days off. The students' intense desire to learn and succeed was sharpened by the knowledge that they would be posted to active service staffs at the end of the course. On the last morning there was one disgruntled lieutenant colonel left behind when his cheery friends were wishing each other farewell and hurrying to the station. He was sticking amendments into a manual, having not taken seriously Simonds's warning to students on arrival that no one would pass out until they had handed in a fully amended set of manuals. (Lieutenant Colonel John Bennett explains his case in chapter 18.)

In April 1941 General McNaughton wrote Simonds a note of thanks the day after the Canadian Junior War Staff Course closed: "I want to express to you my very deep appreciation for the way in which you handled the staff course, and in this I feel that you have made a very substantial contribution indeed and I thank you for it."[5] McNaughton's support in the next two years accounts for Simonds's meteoric rise in his profession.

Simonds had made many friends at Camberley and the Air Force and Naval Staff Colleges, as well as among commanding officers who contributed demonstrations to the course. These were to be useful contacts, and he extended them after the completion of the course when he was appointed GSO I (senior operations staff officer) of the Second Canadian Infantry Division under Victor Odlum, with whom he had made a short visit to the BEF in April 1940. The two men remained friends after Odlum was declared too old for field command and went to serve in China and other places. After Simonds served a short spell as GSO I, McNaughton made him acting BGS of the Canadian Corps, which was established when the Second Division arrived in the United Kingdom. Simonds held this post until November when McNaughton went on sick leave and then to Canada.

Major General Pearkes, V.C., the commander of the First Division, took over as locum of the Canadian Corps in the autumn of 1941. Crerar had relinquished his post as chief of staff CMHQ to be CGS in Ottawa. Now he returned to the United Kingdom to take command of the First Canadian Corps from a rather disgruntled Pearkes and acted as senior Canadian in the absence of McNaughton. The latter had been canvassing the idea of establishing a Canadian army of two corps while he was in Canada, and on April 6, 1942, the First Canadian Army headquarters nominally came into being and McNaughton returned as its commander. Simonds was confirmed in the rank of brigadier and stayed as BGS to Harry Crerar until mid-July 1942 when he became McNaughton's chief of staff in the First Army.

Legions of anecdotes have been told about McNaughton. One that illustrates his eccentricity and points to the reason why he was eventually removed from command concerns his obsession with bursting shells in the air as a means of ranging on targets, instead of the standard method of using ground bursts. One day he called in his CCRA, Jim Stewart. "Jim, I have this little airburst ranging problem I'd like solved." And he handed Stewart a sheet of paper. Stewart took it away but could make neither head nor tail of it. So he handed it to the CRA of the First Division. The CRA thought it made no sense, either. Eventually the problem gravitated down to one of the battery commanders, who was an instructor in gunnery, but since he was unable to manage it, gave it to Teddy McNaughton, one of his gun position officers (GPOs). Young McNaughton, naturally, thought he should take it to his father and get it settled right away. And he did, and it was. But Stewart was hauled over the coals the next day.

In spite of his remarkable gifts and self-assurance Simonds took care to maintain correct relations with his two very different chiefs.

McNaughton was an eccentric who was unable to pursue a line of thought persistently. As head of the National Research Council before the war, he had done wonders to develop communications, radio and aerial, in Canada's North. But he was more interested in the science of war than in its applied tactics and strategy. On the other hand, his political influence in Ottawa was considerable. So he allowed Simonds to follow his own course in activities in which he had little interest himself, something that could be seen in the preparation of Hammerforce, as well as large-scale exercises that were held as soon as the danger of invasion ended in 1941. McNaughton's refusal to buckle down to "training for war" worried Simonds throughout their relationship. In 1969 he wrote to Trumbull Warren, later Montgomery's liaison officer:

> From the very beginning, I had a running argument with Andy . . . to make 1 Div, then 1 Cdn Corps, then Cdn Army, *fighting* headquarters, and do his other roles through CMHQ which was established for that purpose. He simply would not listen and matters finally came to a head after "Spartan" . . . the fiasco which resulted . . . was clearly *all* his own doing. . . . Following "Spartan," I went to see Andy privately. I told him I would serve him in any capacity he wished, except that I would not remain as chief of staff at Army HQ unless he would accept my advice on the matter of organizing Army headquarters to fight a battle and concentrating on the training and operational aspects. . . . He kicked me out of his office and within 48 hours I left on attachment to 8th Army. In all fairness I must add that he never held that interview against me.[6]

With Crerar Simonds's basic difficulty was the former's jealousy. Crerar did not understand how to use a staff, in the sense of having it implement his ideas and wishes. He was not an original thinker himself, so he expected it to provide both the ideas and the means of implementing them as well as ensuring that the staff machine worked smoothly. He spent much of his time on trivialities and in writing improving tracts to his subordinates in the most general terms. If his chief of staff did not think imaginatively, no one else in the Crerar regime would do so. In the Second Corps the commander and his chief of staff were certainly not made for each other.

Crerar could hardly restrain his brilliant subordinate from doing his job as he thought fit, but he may have been conscious of being overshadowed. Who was actually running the corps was plain to external observers, including the exacting General Montgomery, director of Exercise Tiger, who congratulated Crerar on the performance of his corps, but singled out his BGS for praise. It was on Tiger that members of the press corps noticed Simonds's ability to explain operations clearly and without notes. His relations with the press continued to be good as long as the war lasted. This, too, rankled Crerar, who was a dull and uninspired speaker. Simonds was at his best with a small group when the clarity of his mind and ability to deal with detail were most effective. However, neither he nor Crerar had the common touch that inspired a body of men. Officers, though, admired Simonds because he could approach them on an intellectual level.

Simonds has left very little in his papers about his time with Crerar. As we shall see from the confrontation between the two men in Italy, Simonds was aware that Crerar had not chosen him as BGS and wanted to replace him. He believed that Crerar was not loyal to McNaughton and considered that he pulled strings to undermine McNaughton's position. Crerar was after McNaughton's job and was certain to get it if McNaughton, for some reason, lost the confidence of the British as a commander of the First Canadian Army in the field.[7] Simonds may also have realized that, as a young commander, he would be the loser if Crerar replaced a simpatico McNaughton as senior Canadian.

The Dieppe fiasco in August 1942 was to leave an ineradicable mark on the relations of the two men, and Simonds never trusted Crerar again. The events of the Dieppe raid, in which the Second Canadian Infantry Division under Major General J. H. Roberts made the main contribution, are well enough known. The circumstances in which it was planned, then cancelled, and finally remounted are less so and have only recently been unravelled, if not fully explained, by the Canadian historian Brian Villa.[8]

Charles P. Stacey, who was responsible for the fine series of official Second World War army histories, investigated the planning of Dieppe thoroughly, and his assistant historians examined the actions of officers at Admiral Lord Louis Mountbatten's Combined Operations Headquarters (COHQ) and recorded their findings in a series of papers now at the Directorate of History and the National Archives in Ottawa.[9] Simonds's own part in the operation was peripheral, but as his views on Crerar's actions were so strong, this author considered it necessary to deal with them here.

Stacey laid out the story in two books, of which *The Canadian Army, 1939-1945* contained the original version in 1948. At that time Simonds was at the Imperial Defence College (IDC) and was not entering into any controversies about the war, for instance over reinforcements and conscription, expecting time to evaporate the issue, although he felt strongly that the story had not been squarely presented by Stacey, either. It was not until February 10, 1969, fourteen years after he had retired, that he sent Stacey the information about the Dieppe raid that he had acquired firsthand in 1942 as BGS to Crerar in the First Canadian Corps and as chief of staff to McNaughton in the First Army. He was convinced that Crerar was a major influence in restoring the Dieppe operation in August 1942 after it was cancelled by Montgomery in July.

The occasion for the correspondence was Simonds's perception of the "statements made about the Dieppe operation in the draft chapters of the proposed 'policy' volume of the Canadian official history of World War II." When Stacey pointed out that they were merely a rehash of what he had said in 1948, Simonds replied that he thought that Stacey had it wrong the first time. It was important that Stacey see the minutes of COHQ meetings at which Crerar had been present, which Simonds expected to be in the National Archives. Stacey told him that the minutes there did not explain Crerar's part in making the plan. Relying on earlier evidence, Stacey concluded that the Canadians were not responsible for the plan at all. In particular they had not initiated the controversial frontal assault on Dieppe town or asked for the cancellation of the bombing of the town, which had also caused controversy. In fact, he said, the Canadians had been brought into the operation after the nature of the outline plan had determined its method of execution. However, he avoided Simonds's main point, which is the chief question still unanswered to this day: who was responsible for restoring the July operation as Jubilee in August and what was Crerar's part in it? Stacey assumed it was the responsibility of the Chiefs of Staff, precisely the assumption that Simonds wanted clarified from the documents.[10]

In *Unauthorized Action: Mountbatten and the Dieppe Raid* Villa points out that Mountbatten mounted Operation Jubilee without authority from either the Chiefs of Staff Committee or Winston Churchill. He argues that Mountbatten wanted it and relied on a number of factors to excuse his carrying it out after Montgomery cancelled its predecessor, Operation Rutter, in July. Some of the factors were the known desire of the Canadians to get into action, Churchill's wish to mollify the Russians over the Second Front and, of course, the need to gain experience about landing on a defended shore.

Villa's case is circumstantial and relies on the absence of evidence to dispute it. That is, of necessity, how historical cases are often built.

Simonds argued when he was at the IDC in 1947, and did so again in February 1969, that there was nothing in Stacey's account "that did not accord with fact, insofar as fact could be gleaned from documentary record." His points, well-known to investigative historians, are that not everything that is relevant to a story is recorded in writing, and that when only documented evidence is used the whole truth will not emerge. Furthermore, the procedures followed in planning and carrying out a military operation must not only be understood by the writer but be used as a guide to lead him to the gaps in the documents. Simonds felt that Stacey had restricted himself in these directions and had not pursued "the most likely course" to its logical, if uncomfortable conclusion: that the Canadians, led by Crerar, were originally responsible not only for their part in the operation that was cancelled in July 1942 but also for its resumption in August. As senior Canadian, Crerar was responsible if Canadians took part in a badly planned operation and he, of all people, was capable of objecting to it if he thought the plan was inadequate.

Like Villa's, Simonds's evidence is circumstantial in part. He was BGS when the original Operation Rutter was planned, but it was cancelled at about the time he left First Corps HQ. He was working for McNaughton again when Jubilee was mounted in August. I have included Simonds's paper in the appendices of this biography, not with the object of entering the debate between Brian Villa and Philip Ziegler, who was Mountbatten's biographer,[11] but because Simonds felt strongly that Stacey ought not to have allowed Crerar to escape all responsibility for Jubilee.[12] Stacey believed Simonds was petty in pursuing this issue so long after the war, and perhaps he was. However, over the years Crerar had shown an ability to avoid responsibility to the extent that Simonds considered him a passenger in the war years.

In July 1942 Simonds was chosen by McNaughton to be his BGS in the First Army, which was to be engaged in assisting in the formation of the Second Canadian Corps in August. At this time there was a stir over the demand of the Russians for a "Second Front Now." Churchill was about to leave for Moscow where he had the unpalatable task of telling the Russians that the Arctic convoys would be stopped for three months because of the losses from attacks by German aircraft and submarines based in northern Norway. He also had to tell them that he could not guarantee a Second Front in 1943, although Franklin Roosevelt had given the Russians a different impression. As a sop, Churchill told them that Operation Jupiter would be undertaken against northern Norway to enable convoys to be restarted and that a study was under way. But since he knew that his chiefs of staff were opposed to it, he had also said that action would depend on agreement between Britain, Canada, and Russia.

In order to give the scheme the best chance of acceptance by the sceptical chiefs, Churchill invited McNaughton to prepare an appreciation of Operation Jupiter and earmarked him to travel to Moscow to explain it, although Prime Minister Mackenzie King was against the trip, as, indeed, he was against most schemes that involved Canadian troops in actual fighting. McNaughton ordered Simonds to write the appreciation, assisted by Major Dan Spry, one of his operations staff who was to be a distinguished member of the First Division and later commander of the Third Infantry Division. Working against time, they completed the job and issued their report on August 4. Despite Churchill's buttering-up of McNaughton, the team found against Jupiter. Brigadier L. C. Hollis, secretary of the Chiefs of Staff Committee, reported to McNaughton: "The Chiefs entirely endorse your conclusions. They expressed the opinion that this was one of the clearest and most ably worked-out appreciations which they had ever had before them."[13]

5

In Command of the Old Red Patch

....

IN THE SUMMER of 1940 the German invasion was to be met on the beaches. The original conception was a single line and, as soon as the manpower could be scraped together, a strong one in the style of General Falkenhayn in 1915. As recent fighting on the Continent had shown that lines could be penetrated, the next stage was to form a mobile reserve to deal with penetrations. The Canadians were employed in that role in 1941. The fighting in Russia and the entry of the Americans into the war in 1941 changed the purpose and methods of the armies in the United Kingdom again because invasion was no longer credible. Whereas the "enemy" in exercises had been depicted as breaking out of its bridgehead on the coast and "our" forces as trying to throw them back, from then onwards the enemy was now defending and "we" were breaking out of a bridgehead. This change of emphasis was the catalyst for revolutionary changes in the army.

Montgomery had always preached that the secret of defence was to maintain the initiative by movement and counterattacks. Now he taught that the same offensive tactics were to be used to serve a strategic offensive on the Continent. The transformation sounded easy, but it did not prove easy in practice. Although the primacy of the offensive was accepted in principle, the British had never mastered offensive tactics. With the German example in 1940 before him Montgomery set out to teach them, first as a corps commander and then as the commander of the Southeast Army in which the

Canadian Corps was serving in autumn 1941. As a means to that end, he demanded fit, hard soldiers who could fight a battle lasting several days and, thereby, he became the scourge of any veteran of the First War still serving in battalions. The older men found battle drill particularly testing. Pioneered in the Forty-seventh London Division and developed in the Canadian army by the Calgary Highlanders, it was practised at Barnard Castle battle school from which the School of Infantry sprang later. When Montgomery extended his drive for youth and fitness from line units to staff officers and even brigade and divisional commanders, he brought several Canadians in those categories into his sights. Equally he was on the lookout for rising younger men deserving promotion.

As acting BGS to McNaughton in 1941, Simonds helped his general through Exercise Bumper, the largest anti-invasion exercise to date, which was also designed to look at the problems of invading the Continent. The chief umpire was Montgomery. As we have seen, in the autumn McNaughton was sick and handed over the Canadian Corps to Pearkes as locum. While Pearkes was commanding, in November, just before Montgomery took command of the Southeast Army, Simonds wrote a corps training instruction that dealt with many of the ideas Montgomery was about to emphasize — physical fitness, progressive training, intensive fighting through the whole twenty-four hours, and Tactical Exercises without Troops (TEWTs) for officers. In the previous two months Simonds had the headquarters staff well drilled, starting each day with 0830 "morning prayers." William Hutchinson is correct in writing in his thesis that Simonds did not need to "ape" Montgomery because the training ideas of the two men were alike before they came into close contact. As Simonds was widely known to have earned an "outstanding" grade at the Staff College, Camberley, and at the School of Artillery, he was just the type of young staff officer in a senior post whom Montgomery intended to sponsor.[1]

One of the first directives that Montgomery issued was for all officers to attend certain courses. Simonds grasped at once that the Canadians had been stuffed with courses ever since they arrived and what they needed was practice — practice in managing formations and units, and managing men. It was not a time for theory. What happened next has been improved in the telling, but Simonds went to Montgomery and told him what he thought was required. Monty, he of the "quizzical, slanting eyes," met the "compelling, slaty gaze of the younger man." Monty listened. "Quite right!" he agreed. "Perfectly right! Go ahead. Do it your way. Of course. Quite right!"[2]

In December 1941 Crerar relinquished his post as CGS in Ottawa and replaced Pearkes as corps commander. Pearkes was disappointed, for he did not consider himself too old for the job. A man capable of commanding a platoon or a battalion, and who had built a sound foundation for the First Division, Pearkes was very different from his successor. Pearkes had little time for Crerar. The story of the exercise held during the hand-over to Crerar has been told with variations, but is not apocryphal. Pearkes nominated the CO of the Saskatoon Light Infantry to explain the points being brought out. "Make it simple," he directed. "Imagine you are explaining to a man who has never commanded anything."

Crerar had a good record as an artilleryman in the First War, but he had never commanded a regiment, brigade, or division. In fact, he was of the generation that the Montgomery "training typhoon" was designed to sweep away. Had he been in the British army his talents would have been used in an administrative post at the War Office rather than in an operational command. As a Canadian, however, given a first-class staff, his political and administrative role as senior Canadian might keep him protected even in a corps command. With Simonds as his BGS that seemed likely. After catching Montgomery's eye on Exercise Bumper, Simonds did so again on Exercise Tiger from May 19 to 30, 1942. After the exercise, Montgomery told Crerar, "You have a first-class BGS in Simmonds [sic]. I would like you to tell him I thought he was very good."[3]

After McNaughton assigned Simonds to write the Jupiter appreciation in August 1942, the former appointed him to command the First Brigade where he served under Harry Salmon, commander of the First Canadian Infantry Division. Salmon was a hard-driving stickler for detail with a fetish for night operations. Simonds brought in a new brigade major, instituted his 0830 "morning prayers," and spent a large part of every day with the units. He had a weekly commanding officers' conference at which he explained his wishes and also gathered their ideas. In the last weeks of December the brigade went to Inveraray for combined operations training. It was a place that he was to know intimately in 1943. In the new year his short tour of command ended with McNaughton calling for him again as his BGS in the First Canadian Army.

Simonds's successor as commander of the First Brigade, Brigadier Howard Graham, complained sourly in his autobiography that Simonds departed without handing over properly.[4] Clearly he thought this rising, arrogant Permanent Force officer, five years younger than himself, had not behaved politely. Graham, a prosperous lawyer from

Ontario, was to serve under Simonds in the First Division where they crossed swords again. Whatever the facts of the matter, Simonds was unwise not to cover his rear. The Canadian army was a small military family in which personal idiosyncrasies became well-known. Passed by word of mouth such stories built an adverse and self-fulfilling reputation. Simonds relied too much on his high professional reputation among his peers and the fine service he gave his superiors to carry him through. His attitude was: "They say? Let them say!"

This was hazardous. He probably acquired from McNaughton some political wisdom but very little knowledge about command in the field. From Crerar he could learn nothing about field operations, either. So it was to his British superiors, who had field experience, that he looked for models. In particular they could show him what to expect realistically from subordinates and their soldiers in the field, particularly what was acceptable and what was not. Simonds's own standards were punishingly high. The question was whether they were unrealistic. An answer had to be found to his own and his subordinates' satisfaction. In the process of finding it his reputation for ruthless efficiency might make him unacceptably unpopular. His English accent and wide acceptance in the British army might alienate him from Canadians who were older than he but no more senior in rank.

The serious lack of operational experience right through the Canadian army also had dangers for McNaughton and Crerar. The latter had sought to correct it by advocating Canadian participation in major raids, including Jupiter and the Dieppe operation. But if one Canadian divisional commander gained battle experience under British command, he might become the leader of a younger officer group in Monty-style and leave the First War veterans on the shelf.

McNaughton had taken Simonds from the First Brigade to make him chief of staff in the First Army in January 1943. In Exercise Spartan, in March, the First Corps under Crerar, the new and unprepared Second Corps under Major General Sansom, and the Twelfth Corps under Lieutenant General Monty Stopford went into the field in a Home Forces exercise. McNaughton obviously did not impress the umpires, although towards the end the Canadians began to perform effectively. Nevertheless, Spartan was widely believed to be McNaughton's undoing as a potential field commander.

In April Simonds was given the opportunity to see something of the fighting in Tunisia firsthand. He visited Eighth Army headquarters and the corps commanded by Lieutenant Generals Horrocks and Leese. Simonds also met Montgomery's chief of staff, Major General Francis de Guingand, who reported that his staff was impressed with the rapidly rising Canadian. A stream of visitors had come showing little or no awareness of practical problems in the field and having, apparently, made no effort to prepare themselves. In marked contrast to them Simonds had studied the campaign's development and was on their "wavelength" from the moment he arrived. He asked all the questions that they themselves considered important and proposed solutions.

After thirteen days, a signal from McNaughton recalled Simonds to the United Kingdom. While in the desert, on his way home and in the hurried days after his return to England, Simonds wrote a long report on his visit, which he delivered on April 29. Since some of the points that he made cropped up again later, it is appropriate to record them here.

Simonds disapproved of the use of tactical headquarters that separated commanders from their staffs for long periods and led to an overall growth in the size of headquarters. He agreed that the great distance between rear and main headquarters of the Eighth Army had made that division of the headquarters necessary, but modern communications and light aircraft made it unnecessary to have separate tactical and main headquarters in the forward area. He was struck, though, by the speed with which headquarters, formations, and units moved and with the way good and well-understood drills made paper unnecessary in many cases. Standard layouts of headquarters, like Roman camps, speeded up movement and reduced the time that it took to start functioning in a new location.

He returned from North Africa convinced that the day of blitzkrieg was over because of the strength of the defence — improved antitank weapons, mines and wire, and centralized mortar and artillery control. He predicted that there would be a shortage of infantry in the new era of defence ascendancy in which carefully prepared infantry attacks were required. With that in mind he had had discussions with the Eighth Army staff about divisional organizations. The shortage of infantry in armoured divisions suggested the need for a panzer grenadier type of division with a ratio of infantry to armour of two to one. In their turn infantry divisions would require the support of armoured brigades from time to time. That suggested a use for the army tank brigades. Armoured regiments ought to be standard in equipment and organization, whatever their role.

Simonds was surprised that air force and army headquarters were not side by side. The RAF insisted on their headquarters being close to airfields, which were too far back for army main headquarters. Given the superior communications between RAF headquarters and the airfields, Simonds was unimpressed with the reason, although the air support was good. The battle within the U.S. Army Air Force about the respective priority given to air superiority, interdiction, and close air support, in which the American air force was about to embrace Royal Air Force doctrine, was in full swing, and the location of Tactical Air Force headquarters reflected the priority placed by the RAF on the first two over the third task.

Immediately upon his return on April 20 McNaughton told Simonds that he was to replace J. H. Roberts, who had commanded the Second Division at Dieppe. On the twenty-fourth negotiations over the employment of Canadians in a theatre of war ended in the decision that the First Division would replace the Third British in Operation Husky, the invasion of Sicily. The change was appropriately called Operation Swift, and planning liaison began at once with Force 545, which was located in Cairo and was one of the headquarters responsible. Accordingly General Salmon, Rear Admiral Mack, the naval force commander, Lieutenant Colonel Chuck Finlay, the recently appointed divisional AA and QMG, and other staff flew off on the twenty-ninth in a Hudson aircraft on the first stage of their journey to Cairo. The aircraft crashed in Devonshire and all on board were killed. That afternoon McNaughton told Simonds that he was to replace Salmon.

During the next two days, the tragedy of the loss of Salmon and the others was almost forgotten in the press of events. A First Canadian Army team had been working in great secrecy at Norfolk House in London on a plan to retake Gibraltar were the Germans to seize it. After Husky was handed to his division, Salmon had taken over some members of the planning team and Husky continued to be planned from Norfolk House. It was there that Simonds arrived on the afternoon of April 29, soon after the crash.

The First Division, which Simonds was to command, was a lucky division. McNaughton had taken it overseas but in many respects was too much of a heavyweight as a divisional commander. But since he had the confidence of the politicians and a fairly free hand in Britain, he established the Canadian presence there. Then George Pearkes, a famous V.C., converted a willing but green division into one almost ready to meet the hazards of war. Harry Salmon had been a modern, up-to-date, nuts-and-bolts man. A stickler for detail, he had kept the division's nose to the grindstone. In two hectic months, packed with special training required for a landing on a defended coast, Simonds impressed his personality on the division.

Fortunately Lieutenant Colonel George Kitching, the GSO I, was not on the plane in which Salmon had died, and he had the operational plans, such as they were after only a few days of preparation, in his safe. The A and Q plans, on the contrary, had been lost in the Hudson. Simonds asked Major A. F. B. Knight, the DAQMG, if he could rewrite the plans that Finlay had taken with him. Knight had a photographic memory and said that not only could he do that but, more important, he could recall all the questions that Finlay wanted settled in Cairo. Simonds immediately ordered Ab Knight to join the members of the staff that would fly with him to Cairo shortly. Since Finlay had only been the AA and QMG for a few days, Knight was the continuity man.

On May 1 the new team took off in two four-engine Liberator aircraft with extra fuel and a flight path that took them well out into the Atlantic before they turned south and then east to make their landfall at Gibraltar. Travelling in one plane were Simonds; Rear Admiral Sir Philip Vian of *Cossack* fame, the new naval commander; Lieutenant Colonel Geoffrey Walsh, the CRE; and Ab Knight. In the other aircraft were Kitching; Lieutenant Colonel Eaman, the Commander Royal Signals (CRSigs); Brigadier Christopher Vokes, commander of the Second Infantry Brigade; Brigadier A. W. Beament, DAG at CMHQ, representing the A Staff; and Lieutenant Colonel D. K. Tow, who was to be the Canadian representative at Second Echelon, Mediterranean.[5]

Cicely wrote to her father in Vancouver, having seen her brother in London on April 20 on his return from Tunisia: "Isn't it marvellous? Everything has been wonderful and terribly interesting for him lately."[6] The press adored all the excitement over Simonds's recall and his appointment first to the Second and then to the First Division. With the news of the crash went the headline "'Boy General' To Succeed Dead Leader." The press learned that in a questionnaire for senior officers about his hobbies he had answered: "In normal times it includes riding, polo, writing. At present it is participating in beating the German army." A colleague had been quizzed about Simonds and told the press: "By the amount of work he gets through and the military study he does in his spare time, you might say Guy Simonds is a slave to his job were it not [for] the fact that the way he does it, it doesn't look like work. He enjoys every second." One journalist recalled having met him at Ford Manor in January 1941: "We said then, 'There's a real Guy. He's really on his toes, that chap.'" And he went on to record what colleagues had said about Simonds's work habits: "He reads through any memorandum put before him no matter how complicated, and at once has the whole thing summed up in his mind. Officers associated with him say it is a joy to work with such quick reactions, such a precise brain. There's never any humming and hawing."[7]

On May 19 a piece appeared in the *Winnipeg Free Press*:

Simonds is a tall, lean, hard-muscled man, a chap with the bronzed stamp of the Canadian outdoors and the African desert upon him. He has jet-black hair, without a trace of grey, that has a distinctive little wave at the temples. He wears a military moustache, like seventy-five percent of army men over here, and it's pointed up a bit at the ends.

It was said he was whisked back from Africa and told of his promotion before he had time to shave. "Actually, accommodation on the plane was excellent, and there was plenty of time to shave. Perhaps I was a little travel-stained, though," Simonds explained.

We asked him about the desert campaign. His grey-blue eyes, beneath bushy, black eyebrows were cool and steady. His long, lean fingers gripped only a silver cigarette lighter as he swung into the story. He spoke quietly to two or three of us for an hour and revealed himself as a master of tactical narrative. We'd heard him discuss the tactical setup before Exercise Spartan and gotten some appreciation of the clarity with which he sees and explains a military problem. When Simonds speaks, you imagine you're looking at a military map with all the features and problems thrown up into bold relief. You can get in the picture without need of a lot of coloured pins. The pins might help or they might get in the way because Simonds speaks in clipped, quick phrases . . . he's a marvellously keen observer who can put the picture into words without any need to write a long report about it.

That's the Montgomery style.

"I was impressed with the quickness with which all formations reacted to orders," said Major General Simonds. "The army commander's directive that there be no bellyaching provided the quickest reactions to instructions. All formations got on with the job!"[8]

The two planes on their way to Cairo came down in Gibraltar. One flew straight to Cairo while Simonds flew on to Algiers. There he was delayed by weather but was able to talk to General Sir Harold Alexander, who was to command the two armies in Husky — the Eighth under Montgomery and the Seventh U.S. under George Patton. Simonds learned that the Husky plan had not been finalized. On the fourth he arrived at Heliopolis airfield, a day behind Kitching and the others. Generals Dempsey, commander of Thirteenth Corps, and Leese of Thirtieth Corps were there to meet him. The party was taken to Shepherds Hotel where their escort collected keys and registered their names, apparently so that their Canadian accents would not be noticed. They had removed their divisional badges and were in anonymous khaki drill uniforms instead of distinctive Canadian battle dress.

Simonds would have less time to plan than other divisional commanders because the ships that carried his division and the First Canadian Tank Brigade from England would have to be tactically loaded weeks before the operation started. His plan could not be changed once he left Cairo on his way home. His Q staff had to ensure that all the special items of equipment such as saddlery for mule transport, mosquito nets, and mepacrine (malaria was endemic in Sicily and southern Italy) were obtainable in Britain or would be promptly supplied in the Mediterranean. Weaponry had to be standardized on Mediterranean scales, a point to which we shall return in the next chapter. These were a few of the details that had to be signalled to Britain from Cairo as soon as possible.

Admiral Vian and Simonds agreed to sail together in a command ship, merely a converted freighter. Since neither was satisfied with the intelligence about the beaches, they demanded a submarine recce as soon as possible. Its important report reached Simonds when the convoy was approaching the beaches. Vian, a senior and immensely experienced sailor, took Simonds under his wing, proving to be a very different type of man from the naval student at the Staff College in 1937 who had made such a fuss when Simonds insisted on raising his flag in a humble command ship. Since the Royal Navy was absolutely in command until the army stepped ashore, Simonds was content for their relationship to be like father and son.

The main briefing for Husky was given by Montgomery on a sand model in Kasr el Nil barracks. In his usual positive style he stated that his plan, not the original offered by Eisenhower's planners, was final. After that the floor was open for questions from corps and divisions. The First Division was to be under Leese, commanding the Thirtieth Corps. When it was Simonds's turn to speak, he shook the group by saying, "No, sir. I'm not going to do it that way." Instead of assaulting on a single brigade front he would go in with two brigades and four battalions. He explained that since he could not be certain of the depth of the water behind sandbanks offshore or the exits from his beaches, he did not intend to put all his eggs in one basket. Furthermore, he wanted to penetrate inland rapidly, which required a broader front. As was his custom when he trusted a subordinate, Montgomery agreed to Simonds's modification when he confirmed that the extra craft required could be provided. There remained for Simonds to tie things up with the Highland Division on his right flank and to obtain the help of a commando brigade on his left, which he had asked to be placed in the considerable gap between the Eighth Army's left and the American army's right.

After five days in Cairo, on the first of which he signalled his plan back to Britain and did not subsequently change it, Simonds and Knight flew back together. They were on their landing approach to "Plymouth" when Simonds turned to Knight and asked, "Do you recognize that place as Plymouth?"

"No," Knight answered.

Simonds went forward to the cockpit. A moment later the plane's engines roared and the aircraft banked to starboard. Simonds came back and sat down. "I thought that wasn't Plymouth. The bearing of the sun was all wrong. It was Cork." Had they landed they might have been interned. Finally they arrived at Lyneham without money or identification as a precaution against a crash in enemy territory and capture.[9]

The division had not been "mobilized" to combat scales before it was assigned to Husky. In other words, in the United Kingdom it was, in many respects, not completely manned and equipped as required to operate in the field. As well, the division's weapons and equipment were different in some respects from those being used by the Eighth Army. It would be futile to enter into all the details, but as a manning example, battalions had only three rifle companies, not the four that were required in Sicily. As there was not, at this time, a Canadian reinforcement and training unit in the United Kingdom to hold fully trained replacements destined for particular units and divisions, First Division units had to draw directly on other divisions to make up their numbers to war establishment. Inevitably sister units took the opportunity to rid themselves of a few undesirables as well as adventurous volunteers.

New and unfamiliar equipment entailed fresh training, of course. The last-minute introduction of the PIAT, the Projector Infantry Antitank, required special training in the final month. The Saskatoon Light Infantry, originally a machine gun battalion and now a support battalion, received the 4.2-inch mortar and the Oerlikon 20 mm automatic cannon. The six-pounder, which had been in service as an antitank gun in the Eighth Army since April 1942, replaced the two-pounder in infantry battalions, and the seventeen-pounder was hastily issued to the artillery antitank regiments. The First Canadian Armoured Brigade, which was to provide tank support for the division, had to adopt Sherman tanks armed with a 75 mm gun instead of the six-pounder Rams. The engineers had to learn how to lift and disarm the latest Italian and German mines, and samples of a wooden box mine were flown back from the Eighth Army. All of these equipment changes required last-minute training.[10]

In the next hectic weeks Simonds made frequent visits to the west of Scotland, where brigades rotated through combined operations, and returned to Norfolk House to make decisions about loading ships. The artillery staff saw to gun calibrations, and the Commander Royal Electrical and Mechanical Engineers (CREME) to waterproofing vehicles that had to be left until the last minute. At the same time Simonds had to get to know his command as its units moved to and from training areas. It was of utmost importance that he assess the character and capability of his senior staff, his brigadiers, and his battalions and regiments.

Naturally there were mishaps. The Second Brigade fell afoul of the duke of Argyll, who had kindly offered salmon fishing and deer stalking while they were in Scotland. Unfortunately some young Canadians, armed to the teeth, increased the kill inordinately with automatic weapons and Mills Bombs. The Seaforths of Canada had sickness in the ranks because they failed to hang their game properly. But all was forgiven, although the season had to be closed. On an earlier occasion the Second Brigade got into trouble when an A and Q staff officer "lost" exercise papers somewhere in Glasgow in a girlfriend's bedroom. As a result, it was not surprising that the brigade made no preparations for an exercise of which they had heard nothing, and there was a row with Simonds because of a subsequent cover-up.

The brigades did well in their combined operations and were regarded as star pupils. The training was tough and more arduous than the real thing. The final exercises at Dundonald near Troon were in poor weather, and men were soaking before they waded ashore. Captain A. T. Sesia, originally on the divisional staff, was suddenly made divisional historical officer for Husky, and his narrative offers a picture of the last three weeks before the division sailed. On May 22 he recorded:

At 0130 hrs this morning I witnessed the landing of troops from 2 Cdn Inf Bde Gp, who came ashore in LCAs [Landing Craft Assault] on the beach at Dundonald. This exercise, which in many ways is very similar to the actual landing that will take place in Sicily, has been made as realistic as possible. There were two powerful searchlights on the beach which picked out the craft as they came in, and it was quite interesting and informative to see how effective these searchlights are. . . . Watched the vehicles being brought in by landing craft. All these vehicles had been waterproofed and it was quite a sight to see them ploughing through some three to five feet of water. Jeeps waded through like nothing else on earth.

After breakfast, a squadron of Spitfires attacked the landing proceedings which were still going on. They fired live cannon shells and machine gun bullets into the water between the craft.[11]

In June embarkation leave was granted. Obviously everyone knew they had been preparing for an operation, but because they were not issued with khaki drill uniforms until they were on board, they did not know for certain that they were bound for warmer climates. There had been complaints from ordinary passengers that a train left Euston every night bound for Glasgow with sleeping cars that were unobtainable for civilians, and returned empty next day. This was the Ghost Train familiar to people living in houses along the railway line. Troops on the train were cheered by civilians leaning out of windows and over balconies who obviously knew that the soldiers were bound overseas.

What no one knew was that a complex deception plan had been in place for some time to conceal the destination and timing of Husky. Operations Barclay, Warehouse, and Withstand had been designed to plant in German minds the idea that a second front in the Mediterranean in Greece and Crete, with associated landings in the south of France, Corsica, and Sardinia, was about to be opened. Then came Mincemeat in which "Major Martin of the Royal Marines," alias the Man Who Never Was, had been procured as a cadaver from cold storage and floated off the Spanish coast from a submarine on April 30. In a briefcase attached to his body were some bogus military documents ingeniously crafted to confirm what the Germans had learned from the other deception operations — that Sicily was no more than a cover for the real destination of Husky, which was Greece.[12]

The ships in the fast troop convoy were loaded about two weeks before they sailed, which was eleven days after the slow convoy. In the last week final landing exercises were held at Troon, and there was a good deal of sailing up and down the Scottish coast for degaussing, an antimine procedure, which also helped to deceive any coast watchers. HMS *Hilary*, the command ship in which Admiral Vian flew his flag, was an old coal burner formerly employed in the Atlantic listening for U-boat signals. Accommodation in all ships was cramped, and the *Glengyle*, which carried the First Brigade headquarters and the Hastings and Prince Edward Regiment, was so crowded that it earned the sobriquet *Altmark II.* Staff trips between ships were often hazardous as passengers climbed down ladders and timed jumps onto launches that heaved vertically through ten feet. But the food was good and the drink cheap except in the *Circassia,* which did not fly the White Ensign and was dry. Whisky, at three pence for a double, was cheaper than mineral water and far less than beer at one shilling a half pint. If this was war, some said, let us have more of it.

Stymie, the last landing exercise, was in the early morning of June 18. Realism was added by high seas and rain so that everyone involved was soaked to the skin. By this time exercises caused little excitement, and it was felt that the real thing could hardly be worse. In this case the storm was a preview of the real thing, and the second Stymie exercise was cancelled because of it.

On June 28 it was piped that the last mail would go ashore at 1700 hours. In their cheerful letters home, which had to be censored, soldiers showed no foreboding, although they knew that a percentage on board would never see Scotland again. All assumed they would be among the lucky ones. One young man wrote to his English girl: "Did you play table tennis with that Canadian? Be careful of them — they are strong in the wrong places." Wardroom humour was of the usual abysmal standard. An item in the suggestions book read: "That the dangerous counterweights be removed from the lavatory seats owing to the number of big knobs on board."

On the morning of June 28 Simonds and the senior staff who had snatched leave at the end of the preparations came on board the *Hilary.* It was difficult to imagine how much had happened since April 29 when Guy Simonds first walked into the operations room in Norfolk House. Now he and the Old Red Patch were off to war together. Other than the Second Division at Dieppe his was the first Canadian formation in the Second World War to do so.

The Clyde was like glass as they weighed anchor at 2043 hours. The gap to shore widened imperceptibly. When they passed the antisubmarine boom, three naval officers in a launch saluted, standing at attention. Finally a naval signal station signalled "Goodbye and good luck."[13]

The next morning the convoy was off the northwest coast of Ireland. A naval signal to all ships read: "We are on our way to the Mediterranean to take part in the greatest combined operation that has yet been mounted. We shall be able to give further information later."[14]

6

The Old Red Patch Goes to War

EVERYONE WOULD LIKE to have relaxed in the sunshine as the convoy left the unreliable Scottish weather behind, but Simonds did not allow his division to lose its edge in idleness. All ranks knew they had been training for an assault landing, but where was their objective? Only the handful of senior ranks who had been privy to the planning at Norfolk House knew the answer. Now the secret could be revealed that they were bound for Sicily. The divisional plan could be explained and each man briefed on his specific part in it and how his tasks contributed to the whole operation.

By 1943 such elaborate briefings were common before exercises. They were a familiar preliminary to the procedure in an assault landing: forming up, going over the ship's side, getting into LCAs, and motoring several miles to shore, probably under shell fire and in a rough sea. But this time there was a new edge to the briefing and what was to follow. If things went wrong, the "exercise" would not simply be repeated; it would not be over in twenty-four hours with the units returning to barracks and hot showers. Willy-nilly the troops, once ashore, would fight for days or weeks without a break. Platoons had landed on the wrong beach in exercises, and the junior leaders understood that in real action it was their responsibility to make their own way to their objectives. This time the men in their sections studied the battalion beach, the defences guarding it, and their own objectives with equal interest, realizing that a few NCO casualties might make them leaders.

The artillery and engineers, too, had to apply months of training to this particular operation, but in their case the techniques they had learned were more to the fore. Communications between guns and forward observers were the worry of the gunners. If they worked, the guns could provide a first-class service; if they did not, the guns would be silent. The fleet bombardment forward observation officers would play a vital role in the early stages before field guns got ashore. The long range and heavy shells of the fleet were to be decisive in Husky and all subsequent landings. In fact, one of the Canadian observers, Captain G. D. Mitchell, earned the first Military Cross of the campaign. The gunners and sappers used intelligence reports and aerial photographs to locate enemy gun positions, targets, probable demolitions, and minefields, as well as provisional gun areas and movement axes for the division.

A division could not be expected to fight in all conditions without special preparation. For instance, the First Canadian Division had received time-consuming training with the Royal Navy and the RAF for its assault landing. Once that phase was over it would have to deal with a variety of predictable physical and tactical situations, some of them peculiar to Sicily, which training could not simulate. Sicily was dry, dusty, hot, malarial, and mountainous. Its roads were relatively few. Tracks and even dried streambeds would become unit highways. The Third Infantry Brigade had done some mountain training at Glenfeshie, but in the actual campaign it was the Second Brigade that had to make much use of mule transport, and the First that had to make an assault up almost vertical cliffs at Assoro.

It was not possible in England or Scotland to train men to exist on a gallon of water a day for several weeks at a time and in temperatures of ninety-five degrees Fahrenheit. Trudging great distances over Scottish bogs was tough, but not as tough as marching twenty miles in a broiling Sicilian sun after a sleepless night and then going straight into action, perhaps without a meal. Despite the most arduous and thoughtful training, the course of a division's first battle is seldom smooth. Divisions do not often shine at first; preferably they should be broken in gently. That the division successfully rose to the occasion of an assault landing followed by arduous fighting after nearly two weeks cooped up in ships on a long sea voyage is a remarkable testament to Canadian grit, planning, and training.

A complex cover plan protected the security of the destination of the division. The ultimate precaution was to make it known only to a handful of staff officers working in Norfolk House. Therefore, just before the convoy sailed, Simonds was shocked to find on a visit to the tank landing ship of Lieutenant Colonel Booth, the commanding officer of the Three Rivers Regiment, that he had already read his secret orders lodged in the ship's safe. They were intended to be opened at sea and only when ordered. Furious, Simonds left the ship and went back to the *Hilary* to talk over the implications with Kitching. It appeared that Booth had not divulged anything and that if he were removed from command of the Three Rivers Regiment and returned to Canada the security risk would theoretically be increased, as well as complicating operations and upsetting his unit's morale. Instead, Simonds gave him a dressing-down that he would never forget. Kitching described Booth's reaction when facing his general in the *Hilary* a little later:

> He was a small man physically — only about 5 feet in height — and although he later became suntanned and fit he was shaking like a leaf and quite pale as he staggered up our gang plank. I took him down to the general's cabin and went in with him. I had never seen Guy Simonds in a cold rage before. Everything was ice. For five minutes he told Booth exactly what he thought of his conduct. I was standing behind Booth and at one time thought I would have to support him physically as he wilted before the blast. . . . He told me a month later that his five minutes with Simonds had made him all the more deter-mined that he and his regiment would do well in Sicily. They did.[1]

Simonds's cold blue glare when angry became a byword. Booth proved an outstandingly brave leader in the Mediterranean and in Normandy, where he was killed in action commanding the Fourth Canadian Armoured Brigade.

In ships of the fast convoy the general briefing for the operation took place July 1, Dominion Day, when it was announced that the division was to be part of the Eighth Army. That news and a message of welcome from Montgomery were cheered. Next, the ship's bags were opened to reveal operation orders, maps, codes, intelligence summaries, air photographs, and all the details of the operation. These were distributed and assimilated so that briefings down to pla-toons and sections could begin. The First and Second Brigades learned that they were to assault beaches on the Costa Dell'Ambra on the southwest side of the Pachino peninsula. The Third Brigade was to follow up. The beaches were code-named Sugar and Roger and each was subdivided into Red, Amber, and Green for the six bat-talions of the assault brigades. The divisional frontage was eighty-three hundred yards. Behind the beaches was a limestone ridge, ten to fifteen feet high, and beyond some dunes lay a series of salt lakes, usually dry in high summer. Further inland were citrus orchards and grazing land cut by streambeds. Three miles inland was the airfield of Pachino, the first objective. Beyond lay the town of Ispica, the second.

Everyone was given a pamphlet about Sicily with simple Italian phrases, and lectures were held on how to behave towards the inhabitants. There were a few warnings. A mepacrine pill against malaria had to be swallowed daily. Only boiled or treated water was to be drunk, and the forty-eight-hour ration that each man carried had to last two days. It was not to be consumed in the first few hours ashore. Troops were told of the inevitable results of drinking wine as though it were Canadian beer and, after a few had suffered burns and a regimen begun of gradual exposure to the sun, a warning was issued that in future sunburn would be regarded as a self-inflicted wound. Briefing on the topography behind the beaches and discussion of the operation filled some part of each of the next days; physical training, shooting at targets in the sea, weapons inspections, and ammunition cleaning, most of the rest. In what spare time remained there were incessant games of cards, musical entertainment, smoking, and chat about what lay ahead.

The ships in both convoys were tactically loaded. Simonds and his staff knew precisely in which ship every weapon and item of equipment lay, and they had filed the manifest of each ship. Every morning they drew from a hat the names of three of the ninety-two ships carrying the Canadian contingent. Assuming they had been sunk, they made contingency plans for the loss of their cargoes. Kitching recalls in *Mud and Green Fields* that on July 3 they drew the *City of Venice*, the *St. Essylt*, and the *Devis* from the slow convoy. All the vehicles and equipment of divisional headquarters happened to have been divided between those particular ships. As the odds on all three being sunk were a million to one against, they assumed that divisional headquarters was safe from such an accident and dismissed the day's exercise. On the night of July 4 the convoy passed through the Strait of Gibraltar. At 9:00 and 10:00 p.m. the *City of Venice* and the *St. Essylt* were torpedoed in the slow convoy ahead. Large vessels, they carried, in addition to the divisional headquarters matériel, artillery pieces — six- and seventeen-pounder anti-tank guns and twenty-five-pounder field guns and their towers — and engineer stores and signals equipment. On the afternoon of the fifth the *Devis*, the commodore's ship in the slow convoy, was reported to be in a sinking condition. It carried the rest of the transport, signals, and office equipment for divisional headquarters.

On hearing this news and being ordered to pass Algiers at night, the fast convoy turned about, a drill that was achieved, miraculously in army eyes, without a collision. As the escorting sloops *Whimbrell* and *Cygnet* hurried to what had been the rear of the convoy, they surprised a shadowing U-boat. It dived, but their attempt to ram it forced it back to the surface and then into an emergency dive. A savage depth charge attack then sank it: all of this was clearly visible from the *Hilary*. On the seventh several slow convoys from the United States were passed and radar plots showed the seas around them thick with ships. On the eighth they were still heading eastwards as though for Tripoli, Crete, or Greece to conform with the deception plan, but in the night the convoy changed course hard to port and headed for Sicily. The next day the convoy found itself in the company of countless others. The division was to make the assault at 0245 hours on the tenth.

All ranks were conscious of being in a division that their fathers had made famous in the First War. It was a "new" First Division, but its members wore the Old Red Patch of the Canadian Expeditionary Force on their arms. Jake Eaman, the CRSigs, carried ashore the divisional signals flag from that war. In his prebattle message to all ranks Simonds reminded them of the past. The Eighth Army, which they were about to join, had a great fighting tradition, to be sure, but the First Canadian Division had inherited a tradition of success from the earlier war. Poised for their first action, the new First Division was better trained than any Canadian division previously. He was not telling them that, as a result, things would be easy, but that they would go into battle with a good plan, and if they remembered what they had been taught, they could be confident of success.

On shore the division expected to meet Italian coast defence and mobile troops at first. But German divisions would soon show themselves and, Simonds warned, the difference between Italian and German troops would be marked. Italians would defend static positions stubbornly, as they had in Tunisia, but when outflanked, or when Canadian infantry closed with them, they would probably surrender. The Germans, on the other hand, would fight even when surrounded and would have to be severely pummelled and harried.

The grand strategy pursued by the Western Allies in the Mediterranean had emerged as a compromise after heated debate. It was finally decided that the defeat of the Axis powers in Africa should be followed up by the invasion of Italy, beginning with Sicily. Initially the plan was for Lieutenant General Sir Miles Dempsey's Thirteenth Corps on the right to push up into the plain of Catania to enable the Tenth Corps under Lieutenant General Brian Horrocks to land on the Calabrian mainland of Italy and cut off the escape of the enemy. Airborne landings to capture key bridges and river crossings would help the Thirteenth Corps to play the main role in the campaign.

The dominating feature in Sicily was Mount Etna, a splendid active volcano that created a bottleneck at the northern part of the plain of Catania. West and southwest from the Etna massif ran a ridge of high ground dominated by hill towns of Norman origin that could not easily be bypassed. The Canadians were to fight on the left flank of the Eighth Army under Lieutenant General Sir Oliver Leese's Thirtieth Corps. They and the Americans, on their left again, would engage and hold opposite them any enemy formations they met but particularly the German Hermann Göring and the Fifteenth Panzer Grenadier Divisions, which were initially located in the west and centre of the island. For the Thirtieth Corps and the Americans the keys to the campaign were towns at road junctions, in particular Enna, in the centre of the island. Most Sicilian towns were built on high ground, not only to make them defensible but also to avoid malarial water courses.

While the Canadian convoy was still at sea, events affecting this scheme in general and the division's ability to carry out its part were occurring. The loss of ships from the slow convoy had deprived the division of guns and transport and Simonds's headquarters of radios. To a large extent this loss was overcome by improvisation in true Canadian spirit. Then, in the last twenty-four hours, a westerly storm cast doubt on the feasibility of the landings. The seas were so steep that Admiral Vian turned to Simonds's and asked him if he wanted to put his division ashore in such conditions. The division had endured rough seas in training and summer storms were rare in the Mediterranean, so the odds favoured an improvement in the weather. Simonds knew that a delay would affect other landings on beaches less exposed to westerlies than his. Surprise would be lost and the two German divisions would be given time to move eastwards to oppose the Thirteenth Corps. For his part Vian had to consider whether LCAs could cope with the seas, for it was his responsibility to get the soldiers ashore. When Simonds recommended going ahead, Vian agreed and said he had come to the same conclusion. They dismissed as nonsense a report that the sea area offshore was mined. Kitching records Vian's comment that Simonds would have made a good admiral.

The same storm, bad navigation, and antiaircraft fire from the fleet wreaked havoc in the airborne components of the operation. Parachutists and gliders were scattered around the island and many drowned when they were dropped into the sea. A few landed back in

Tunisia. Thinking that they were in Sicily, they started to fight air-field defenders of their own side. The scattering of part of the airborne force was but one factor in the failure of the Thirteenth Corps to progress in the plain of Catania beyond the Gornalunga-Simeto river system.

In turn the Tenth Corps's operation was cancelled. Hence the balance of Montgomery's plan was upset. Within the first few days he transferred his main blow from his right to his left, where the Thirtieth Corps was in action. General Sir Harold Alexander, commanding the Seventh U.S. and Eighth British Armies, reverted to an earlier plan to cut the island in two by a drive up the centre through Enna and to destroy the Axis forces in the two halves. The Canadians were consequently engaged in stiff and continuous fighting. Montgomery's new plan was to turn the western flank of the German positions on the slopes of Mount Etna on which hinged their Catania defences. At the same time Alexander released the Seventh U.S. Army to push up to Palermo in the northwest corner of the island while its Second Corps under Lieutenant General Omar Bradley fought for towns and road junctions en route to the east-west road between Palermo and Messina on the north coast.

The loss of transport, communications equipment and, to a lesser extent, guns from the slow convoy was a nagging factor throughout the long march from the south coast to the slopes of Mount Etna. Replacements for the losses were not expected until D plus forty-two days, which turned out to be after the division landed in Calabria in September. Lieutenant Colonel Gilbride, Findlay's successor as head of the A and Q staff, the Royal Canadian Electrical and Mechanical Engineers (RCEME) repair teams, and the Royal Canadian Army Service Corps (RCASC) drivers between them improvised logistical support. Kitching argued that deprivation made his divisional headquarters spare and more efficient. The infantry was adversely affected, however. In the first few days they marched in dust and high temperatures because not more than a battalion at a time could be lifted. Their hardship is not the point. What is important is that transport rushed over from North Africa might have enabled them to hustle Germans out of their positions or to occupy them first. The Americans were not affected similarly. Later the campaign demanded long marches because demolitions blocked the road or simply because the country was roadless. In most cases movement in contact with the enemy was across country where even jeeps, carriers, and gun towers could not follow.

In short, the campaign was largely fought on foot. It fell into three phases. The initial landings and exploitation lasted three days. After the change of plan on the fourteenth, which switched the main Eighth Army effort to the Thirtieth Corps on its left, came the division's first contact with the Germans. There followed a phase of vicious rear-guard actions by the Germans. These merged into a third phase in which the division fought a series of assaults along the mountainous ridge leading from Leonforte to the slopes of Mount Etna at Aderno on which lay the main German defences. There the Germans fought obstinately to hold the right flank of their positions in the plain of Catania, and the division suffered its heaviest casualties.

This lay ahead of Simonds and his division as the convoy's anchor chains rattled and eyes strained to see the loom of the Sicilian shore early on July 10. The assault phase was expected to be the most hazardous, but it proved easier than any other. Engineers had examined the sandbars off the beaches from a submarine in response to Simonds's request in Cairo. Howard Graham's First Brigade, which was to land on Roger Beach, had three days' warning that the LCAs could probably not pass over the bars and that the water inside varied between as much as nine feet and as little as four.

Only a few DUKWs, shallow-draught, wheeled, three-ton vehicles with a propeller screw, had arrived from the United States in anticipation of the problem and been carried in the convoy, so three Landing Craft Tanks (LCTs) and another twenty-four DUKWs were ordered to rendezvous with the convoy at the release point. Simonds ordered Graham to use the LCTs with DUKWs to motor and swim over the bar a company of the Hastings and Prince Edward Regiment and two companies of the Royal Canadian Regiment. Then, by naval signal on the seventh, Simonds instructed Graham that if the LCTs did not arrive by the planned release time, the units were to land from LCAs and risk their finding a hole or the flanks of the sandbar rather than delay the assault. As it turned out, the arrival of the LCTs was delayed beyond H-hour because the First Brigade's transports were out of position and could not be found in the dark. Subsequently there was a display of navy and army nerves on the *Hilary* when Graham and the senior naval landing officer (SNLO) in the *Glengyle*, Graham's headquarters ship, did not comply with their instruction to proceed.

Simonds knew that a delay in coming to grips with the enemy might prove fatal, but the SNLO sent two Hastings and Prince Edward assault companies away in LCAs only after Vian sent an irritable message to the *Glengyle*: "Will your assault ever start?"

When the LCTs eventually arrived, they were difficult to handle in the rough sea, but they each had seven DUKWs on board that drove up on the beach successfully, although a couple of hours behind schedule. The LCA companies had a wet time and some men, loaded down and fighting to keep afloat in the deep water of the lagoon, abandoned their equipment. By the time the soldiers reached the beach many of their weapons were full of sand and could not be fired.

In the Second Brigade, as had happened in rehearsals and was to occur in all assault landings, navigation errors by young midshipmen brought the Seaforth and the Patricias virtually to each other's beaches. That was considered par for the course on exercises and was sorted out when the battalions got ashore. But one Seaforth LCA got stuck on the bar and the doors jammed. Lieutenant Colonel Hoffmeister, the commanding officer, jumped on them and took an involuntary plunge into the sea as they suddenly opened under his weight.

All of this might have been disastrous had resistance been stiff on the beaches. Fortunately the prelanding bombardments had weakened Italian resolve, such as it was, and despite delays, difficulty over the bar, and landing on the wrong beaches, opposition was minimal if noisy. The forward companies pushed on to their immediate objectives while the follow-up companies and support troops landed and went to assembly areas, where they were sorted out by boatloads into their units and dispersed to their various tasks.

At first Simonds kept his operations staff on board the *Hilary* because of the loss of all their vehicles and most of the radios. He went ashore himself, with a jeep, and worked his radio back to the *Hilary*, which had good communications forward. The CRA, Brigadier Bruce Matthews, landed with only a typewriter and a clerk. The rest of divisional headquarters later set up in "a hovel twelve by sixteen feet inhabited by an old woman, eleven guinea pigs, four dogs, a goat, and four gallons of wine, all of which was quickly cleared out."[2] Lieutenant Colonel W. P. Gilbride's transport improvisation scheme was not aided when the navy, overzealously pursuing its own schedule, disappeared over the horizon still carrying some divisional drivers.

In the meantime the appearance on tracks and roads of requisitioned mules, donkeys, handcarts, and Italian trucks of all shapes and sizes, some of them towing captured guns, lent character to the division, as well as humour, when strange clothing of local provenance was worn by Canadian *muletieri*. The locals tried to thwart the requisition drive. Mules were found limping, with bandages on their legs, apparently unsuitable for military or any other tasks. Suspicious soldiers found disabling stones under the bandages.[3]

Montgomery, Leese, and Mountbatten appeared in a DUKW on one of the narrow roads on the first morning. A wag spread the story that as his DUKW approached the beach Monty tapped the driver on the shoulder and muttered, "Steer away from the troops. If they recognize me, they'll wonder why I'm not walking on the water."[4]

The first phase of marching, scattered engagements with Italians eager to surrender, as well as occasional sharp fights, ended when Montgomery ordered the division to rest for thirty-six hours on the thirteenth and recover its balance while he continued the advance towards Vizzini with the Highland Division on the Canadians' right. So ended a comparatively bloodless introduction to war. On the fourteenth the division was directed on Enna and Leonforte and met the Germans. From then on it was to be hard fighting all the way.

7

The Germans and the Mountains

O N THE EARLY MORNING of the fifteenth Howard Graham's First Brigade filed through Vizzini on Highway 124, their objective Grammichele, held by the formidable Hermann Göring Panzer Grenadier Division. The Germans had just been ejected from Vizzini by the Fifty-first Highland Division after a hard fight lasting twenty-four hours. In this second phase of the campaign the First Division led the advance. The plan was for the First Brigade to capture Grammichele as quickly as possible so as to secure space for the Second Brigade to advance on its flank while the Third followed.

The history of the campaign has been fully recounted in other works, but two episodes in particular illustrate Simonds's performance in his first experience of hard-fought and difficult operations. The first of these was at Grammichele and the second in the final phase when the Germans were holding the hilltop towns to the west of Mount Etna.

Simonds followed a strict daily routine which, by 1943, commanders maintained throughout the army. He received an early-morning briefing on events overnight, ate breakfast, and by 6:30 a.m. was on the road in a jeep with his ADC, Stuart Graham, his signaller, and his driver. He spent most of his day in front of brigade headquarters and travelling from one brigade area to another, and since the division fought most of the campaign with open flanks, he frequently came under shell fire. It is fruitless to try to maintain dignity facedown in a dusty ditch with a pile of other cowering bodies. The campaign was mainly a brigade, battalion, and company commanders' affair, but the divisional commander found it difficult to resist stepping in and taking over the brigade commanders' battles or even intervening in battalion battles. In short, contemporaries said that in his first campaign Simonds tended to breathe down the necks of his subordinates, none of whom had been in battle before.

The ideal commander is one determined to achieve his objectives but at the same time able to guide and encourage his subordinates when that is the right approach, as well as drive them remorselessly. To listen to their opinions or explanations and then quietly suggest a better course of action is often the more effective approach when they are fresh to combat conditions and nervous about making mistakes. Simonds himself had no battle experience at the lower levels of command; his system was the result of rigorous analysis, correct but as yet theoretical. The missing factor was sympathy. His silent and even menacing demeanour towards those he did not know was unnerving. Not many understood at once that he was a shy man and that silence did not mean disapproval. In fact, his silences could be as disturbing as his cold stare when he was angry.

Two of Simonds's brigade commanders had the advantage of knowing him for a long time. Vokes, the commander of the Second Brigade, had been Simonds's contemporary at the RMC and was a Permanent Force officer, what was known as a PFer. Vokes needed some guidance and occasionally had to be restrained because he was impulsive. Penhale of the Third Brigade had been a colleague when Simonds was an instructor at the RMC in 1938 and 1939. He was reliable but overcautious, overweight, and needed chasing occasionally. Howard Graham was the odd man out. He was five years older than Simonds and a militia officer, not a member of the Permanent Force.

According to Graham, Simonds's tense, clinical, and unfriendly manner towards him caused a clash outside Grammichele when the First Brigade was about to meet the Hermann Göring Division on July 15. Simonds first picked on him at Norfolk House when brigade plans for the landing were presented. Graham's was in two stages: in the first he established a bridgehead and only in the second did he seize his objective, Pachino airfield. Simonds told him sharply to get on to the objective at once and not waste time making a firm base. He would not listen when Graham pointed out that his was the orthodox procedure. Simonds was quite right, though, for a rapid move inland in the first hour of a landing is essential.

Graham took the rebuff personally, arguing that it was because he was not a Permanent Force officer. Coming a few months after what he thought had been Simonds's studied absence when he took over the First Brigade in January 1943, it seemed to confirm his impression that Simonds disliked him. Later, when the convoy anchored off the beaches, Graham wanted the new Hastings and Prince Edward battle flag, made on board the *Glengyle* by the naval sail maker, to be flown from the triatic stay. As this was a naval matter, the SNLO signalled the admiral for permission. Graham was angry when Simonds himself stuffily replied that he would not permit it since the flag had not been officially accepted by the army. Nevertheless, the flag was flown after a second signal from the SNLO elicited the reply from Vian: "Keep your shirt on. You have reached the age of discretion. Use it."

Witnesses to the incident outside Grammichele are Howard Graham himself; Stuart Graham, Simonds's ADC; George Kitching, his GSO I; and Major Bob Kingstone, who was Howard Graham's brigade major (BM). Each offered a slightly different version of what happened. In his account Howard Graham does not attempt to suggest that he could have been in any way to blame for what occurred. He tells us that Simonds tongue-lashed him by the roadside early in the morning of the fifteenth because he had not passed his brigade through the town of Vizzini on to Highway 124 rapidly enough after the Fifty-first Highland Division had cleared it.[1] Graham felt that this rebuke was undeserved and also, justifiably, that it was improper for Simonds to deliver it within the hearing of his driver and signaller. Graham asserted it was later that evening when he submitted his resignation after a divisional orders group because of the incident on the roadside that morning. Then he handed over to Lieutenant Colonel Ralph Crowe of the RCR and departed to corps headquarters, where Leese sent for him and heard his story.

Graham's account is not entirely credible. His procedure would have been culpable unless Simonds had sacked him and ordered him to hand over his brigade. He was not an employee of a business firm who could give notice if he was dissatisfied with his treatment; in fact, he was engaged in action with the enemy. Stuart Graham, on the other hand, remembers that Simonds did sack Howard Graham, but later for his handling of the battle at Grammichele:

> I told Simonds that First Brigade was very tired and that the orders given them would not work. In the event Graham did something other than that which Simonds had ordered. So he sent for Graham and asked him, "Why did you not carry out my orders?"

"Because it did not seem to be the right approach."

"I gave you an order. Now I have no option."

But later after Leese had suggested that Graham simply needed a rest, Simonds admitted his mistake. Monty told him to be more patient.[2]

Kingstone, Howard Graham's BM, said, "Graham was sacked because he was not aggressive enough. Graham simply said to me, 'Ralph Crowe will take over the brigade. I'm leaving.' Then he arrived back again. Guy felt uncomfortable about what had happened because later he sent Gilbride up to interview me as it was intended to put Graham up for a D.S.O."[3]

In *Mud and Green Fields* Kitching writes:

Early in the Sicily fighting, our 1st Brigade was in action at Grammichele, a sky-line town astride our main axis of advance. Unfortunately, the enemy was able to inflict a great deal of damage to our men and matériel in this our first action with the Germans. General Simonds was not satisfied with the performance of Brigadier Howard Graham who commanded the brigade so on his return to our headquarters at about six o'clock one evening he told me that I was to take command of the brigade at 7:00 a.m. the next morning. . . . When I saw General Simonds next morning at 6:00 a.m. he told me to wait at our headquarters until he sent for me. Shortly after leaving the headquarters he met General Leese, our corps commander, who was on his way forward to see how things were going. Simonds told him of his intention to replace Graham. Leese replied that whilst he had no intention of interfering in what was entirely a Canadian affair, he would be inclined to give Graham another chance. Simonds agreed to this and sent me a message to remain at headquarters and reduce myself to a lieutenant-colonel again. I was glad because Howard Graham was a good friend. The rest of this incident shows that Guy Simonds could forgive and be generous as well.

Only three days after the Grammichele fighting, the 1st Brigade were involved in two days of heavy fighting before capturing their objective, a town called Valguarnera. On the day we captured Valguarnera, General Simonds sent for Brig. Graham. The latter had had little sleep for two days and nights and when he arrived at our headquarters he was obviously very tired, a condition that was aggravated by the thick film of dust that covered us all. I saw Graham arrive in his jeep and walked over to the road to greet him. I congratulated him on the success . . . and took him over to the General. . . . After congratulating him for the capture of Valguarnera, Guy Simonds told him that he had recommended him for an immediate award of the Distinguished Service Order for his courageous leadership. Howard Graham was a different man when he left the headquarters. The weariness had left his face and I, for one, realized that Guy Simonds could be human after all.[4]

There are other angles to this affair. After Vizzini, it was clear to Simonds that resistance would stiffen now that his division had run into the Germans, so he and his brigadiers were rather tense before this first real test. The style and tempo of their daily life was going to change. For instance, brigade-scale battles were expected hereafter, and this required the general officer commanding (GOC) to intervene more closely than in the first three days of the campaign. He had to close up his brigades at a time when distances between brigades were considerable and the transport to lift them was scarce. Delays owing to movement were hard on the nerves. General Leese had told him to "get the whips out" and not allow the Germans to impose any more delays like that at Vizzini. He thought that Graham was dilatory and too lenient with his battalion commanders. Obviously he acted pre-cipitately in sacking him, but there was fault on the other side, too.

In response to the change in the tempo of the campaign the divi-sion's commanders and staff officers had to adopt a faster rhythm to cope with the distances and the pace of operations. The distances between brigades and battalions meant that the divisional staff under Kitching was frequently out of touch with brigades. Radio communications, particularly in the forward area, were unreliable; the essential flow of information was delayed and incomplete. As a result, brigadiers spent a lot of time with battalions to find out what was going on. At brigade headquarters the brigade major, the chief operations staff officer, often did not know where his brigadier could be found until he returned from battalions exhausted and very dusty at the end of the day. In search of information on which to base his plan and orders, Simonds spent his days forward with battalions where he could find the brigadiers.

Summer days of great heat and short nights squeezed sleeping time to three or four hours for days on end and made everyone short-tempered, red-eyed, dirty, and a trifle paranoid. In such cir-cumstances forbearance was needed, but commanders had to sense when the whip would serve better. The incident at Grammichele occurred when everyone was tired but had not yet adjusted to the strain. In such circumstances the brigadiers, who knew the capability and characteristics of their own battalions much better than Simonds, were still learning when to discuss operations with their battalion commanders and when to give them direct orders. Usually the brigadiers gave more latitude to their battalions than Simonds would allow them when he arrived at orders groups, looking as though he had just stepped out of a fashion magazine without a speck of dust on him.

When company and battalion commanders were experienced, it made sense to allow them to propose alternative methods to those ordered by the GOC or the brigadiers. This was the practice in the Eighth Army. It could obviously get out of hand but served in cases where divisional and brigade commanders had not commanded battalions in battle, were not familiar with the effects of their orders on companies and platoons, or did not know the current situation on a battalion front. The practice was not yet accepted in the First Division where everyone was still learning, senior officers were likely to treat their orders as orders rather than a basis for discussion, and officers at every level were wary of losing control over subordinates. A communal approach to tactical problems in which a soviet discussed what was the best solution had been common in the peacetime militia and the British territorial battalions, but it was discouraged for it admitted amateur rather than orthodox solutions and sometimes, when troops were tired, served to gentle them and even set up a tacit live-and-let-live arrangement with the enemy.

In these early days the difference between militia and the PF had not disappeared in the Canadian military as it had in the British army, although by the end of the Sicily campaign when both were veterans, it finally did. Howard Graham's relationship with his battalions, in Simonds's opinion, was along militia lines. He was too paternal, easygoing, and democratic. Graham, he thought, was making the mistake of becoming emotionally involved with his battalions. That was an error that experienced and hardened commanders sometimes made after many months of combat. At this stage Simonds was right to treat it as a weakness.

There was another factor at Grammichele of which Graham was not aware. Highway 124 leading west from Vizzini had been allocated to the Forty-fifth Division of the Second U.S. Corps. Since the Canadian advance west of Vizzini would pinch out the Forty-fifth, it was ordered to surrender the road to the Thirtieth Corps. That displeased Omar Bradley, the American corps commander, for he would lose time while he displaced the division to the west of his First Division. Instead of negotiating the timing of the hand-over, the Forty-fifth Division halted within sight of the road and allowed the Hermann Göring defenders of Vizzini to escape across their front and repeat their exploit at Grammichele. The Fifty-first Highland Division had taken longer to oust the Germans from Vizzini than Leese had expected and any further delay in using the road beyond the town, real or imagined, was irritating to both the Second Corps and the Thirtieth Corps. Had the corps commanders consulted each other the Second U.S. Corps might have cut the road behind Grammichele and cooperated in driving apart the Hermann Göring and the Fifteenth Panzer Grenadiers to the north and west.[5]

Montgomery informed Leese on the fifteenth that the Thirteenth Corps's advance on Catania was held up and that the Thirtieth Corps would have to drive hard for Enna. Leese passed on this information to Simonds that same evening in a note:

My dear Guy, many congratulations on your capture of Grammichele. I am glad that you have competed with their mines and demolitions. I believe that the Germans have blown the bridge over the Simeto facing 13 Corps. It is therefore all the more vital for us to get on quickly. I know you are doing this. I hear rumours that the Americans are in Caltagirone. If opportunity occurs, push a mobile mechanised force with tanks quickly through towards Enna. I will come up to see you tomorrow. All our experience in this island has been that if you are held up, put in a well-supported attack in strength. Best of luck and many congratulations on the long marching and good fighting of your Division in their first fight today.[6]

After this message, after a talk with Leese in the morning during which Monty's views on the Graham incident were passed to him, and with the prospect of a major task for the division ahead, Simonds looked at the Graham incident for what it was — a storm in a teacup. The two men worked well together thereafter. A letter from Montgomery on the seventeenth convinced him that he had been right. After congratulating him on the way the First Division had been fighting, he referred to the Graham incident:

I hear you have had a row with Graham. I have seen Graham at Corps H.Q. The Corps Commander will tell you my views about it, and my general views on the whole question of command in war. I want you to do the big thing and take Graham back, giving him a warning and a last chance. Difficult subordinates have to be led and not driven, and the higher commander has got to keep calm and collected and not be too ruthless. Good luck to you and once more I congratulate you on how you are handling your division and how they are fighting.[7]

Analysts of the campaign, which include some participants, have argued that Simonds imposed an artilleryman's mind-set on operations. Left to themselves, the kind of manoeuvre battles that brigades and battalions fought at Grammichele, Valguarnera, Leonforte, and Assoro, with simple and flexible fire plans, could have been fought as successfully later. The use of a large fire plan obstructed operations at Agira, it has been argued, and may even have caused heavier casualties, not fewer as intended.

This hypothesis deserves some attention. Simonds believed in using as much artillery support as he could muster, and that waiting a few hours for it might be advantageous. Most commanders agreed with that contention. The argument against Simonds is coloured by the prevalent belief today that in general the British allowed infantry and armour to be placed in a straitjacket by barrages and timed concentrations that restricted and slowed their movement. The course of the campaign in Normandy seems to bear out this belief, exposing an aspect of Simonds's role as a corps commander that will be examined later. However, conditions in Sicily were quite different from northwest Europe, and it would be an error to criticize his actions in the former in the light of those he, and others, used in the latter circumstances. Each case must obviously be treated on its merits. Examples make cases, and the example usually quoted against Simonds is the battle for Agira that followed the seizure of Assoro and Leonforte by the First and Second Brigades respectively.[8]

At Assoro the Hastings made a night march to a flank in order to assault the eastern and highest part of the fortress town. It was protected on that side by cliffs and a steep gully, which the Germans believed to be unscalable. Selecting an assault group of men from all companies as a vanguard, John Tweedsmuir, who had just taken over the battalion, led the rest through the night, virtually in single file. Silently they passed a boy slumbering in a cart as his mule took him home in the darkness. He awakened with a start and stared amazed at the silent, trudging men as they ghosted past. As dawn came up, they were climbing a steep couloir leading to a ruined castle at the highest point in the town. There they overcame an outpost and prepared to defend their vantage point, which overlooked the German positions. They were soon spotted from below and were shelled and mortared continually between determined attempts to oust them. The Hastings's battle on the heights, during which they penetrated the nearest houses of the town below them, lasted twenty-four hours. During it, they observed enemy batteries behind the town and used Canadian guns to silence them. In the end the Forty-eighth Highlanders attacked from the other side of the town and the enemy was subdued. The loss of Assoro made the enemy's position in Leonforte, farther west, untenable. Resistance continued there, but the result was not in doubt.

In battle Simonds needed seven hours of sleep each night. He used up a lot of nervous and physical energy in his jeep (in Italy and northwest Europe he used a Staghound) as he roared up and down dusty tracks, sometimes under fire, and had to recharge his batteries. Even divisional headquarters came under fire on occasion. He was generally asleep by 11:00 p.m. and was not woken until 6:00 a.m. In the night Lieutenant Colonel Kitching made decisions that did not require the GOC's attention. When the Second Brigade attacked Leonforte, the Edmonton Regiment led across the ravine approach and got into the town under heavy fire in darkness. There was confusion in the narrow streets, and the CO and about a hundred men holed up in a strong building where they decided to stay until daylight. They were unable to communicate with Brigadier Vokes or anyone else. Convinced by silence in the town that he had lost a battalion, for the shooting had died down, Vokes spoke to Kitching on the phone. Very upset, he asked whether he could speak to the GOC, or better still come down to talk to him. "I will wake the GOC and explain," Kitching told him, and later recounted:

> Chris arrived about ten minutes later — I went with him to Simonds's caravan. The latter listened as Chris told the story; and then to my surprise and delight Simonds spoke very quietly to Chris and told him that in his opinion the battalion was probably holed up somewhere in the town and conserving its ammunition as they assumed there would be no re-supply until daylight. He encouraged Chris to think on the bright side and make a plan to get support across the ravine as soon as the bridge across it was completed.[9]

Vokes had had a difficult twelve hours. Battalion headquarters of the Seaforth had been shelled by Canadian artillery, and his brigade major, Dick Malone, had been severely wounded and evacuated. "Simonds appreciated Vokes's problem," Kitching recalled, "and was very human in dealing with him . . . Chris Vokes was grateful. Simonds told me I had been correct in waking him."[10]

So fell two of the mountain towns, Leonforte and Assoro. The Hastings adventure is appealing and in marked contrast to the sequel when the First Brigade continued the advance eastwards towards Mount Etna. The objective was Agira, a town on a conical mountain that stuck up on the horizon like a thumb. Agira was eight miles from Leonforte on Highway 121. The road rose to cross a series of small ridges just beyond the village of Nissoria, which lay in a dip. The enemy held the ridges with determination but evacuated Nissoria, which they could overlook. Simonds expected trouble beyond Nissoria and laid on as many as five field and two medium regiments to deal with it. It was the first time that such a large fire plan was arranged. As was usual when enemy locations had not been accurately determined, the fire plan took the form of a barrage (smoke on this occasion) and concentrations timed and on call, moving from feature to feature in front of the advance on likely targets. The danger of a barrage and timed concentrations of such length and duration was that it might leave the infantry behind. It also seemed excessive when the advance was led by a single battalion, the RCR, and the location of the enemy was not precisely known.

When the RCR was held up beyond Nissoria, Graham committed his battalions piecemeal. Before committing the Hastings, the second battalion, he asked to speak to Simonds but was told that the GOC could not be wakened and that he should proceed with the plan. When they were held up, he attacked with his third and last battalion and failed again. Finally the Second Brigade mounted an attack with heavy fire support, two battalions astride the road and a third executing a flank move to the right. It succeeded and the Second Brigade went on to take Agira without the need of a fresh attack.

Nissoria was a classic example of committing troops in penny packets, of reinforcing failure and, if Graham is believed, of a misguided fire plan. Communication failure also played a part, as it did in operations throughout the war. Graham blamed Simonds for this first defeat of a brigade-sized operation. On a closer examination of the details it appears that Graham himself was largely at fault.

When the two leading RCR companies attacked the German positions beyond Nissoria, four miles short of Agira, they were held up. The two reserve companies then moved around the enemy's left flank and found a way through to the rear of his position. The company on the right in the stalled attack then filtered around to join the other two. Unfortunately, as so often happens, the companies lost radio contact and could not notify battalion headquarters of their position until morning when a company sergeant major found his way back. In searching for his lost companies the battalion commander, Lieutenant Colonel Ralph Crowe, was killed.

In *Citizen and Soldier* Graham places the blame for what happened next on Simonds. When Kitching refused to awaken Simonds, Graham felt he had no option but to commit the Hastings against his better judgement. "Orders is orders," he said to himself. The battalion's plan was to swing right as the RCR had done earlier. Unfortunately John Tweedsmuir was badly wounded shortly after the leading company had bumped into the enemy and become involved in a firefight. Had he remained on his feet his intention was to steer the others clear of it to reinforce the RCR success. Instead, the whole battalion joined in the firefight. In the meantime the RCR companies had spent the night about two miles behind the German positions. They were not reinforced but instead were recalled by a carrier platoon next afternoon so that Graham's third battalion could attack down the road with artillery support. Happily the RCR withdrew without being spotted by the enemy.

Some postwar analysts have been justifiably critical of the way the battle was managed. The fire plan, described in the war diary of the RCR as "the complete Div Arty, plus ninety bombers, plus more than a hundred fighter bombers in close support . . . [for] a set-piece attack, with a timed arty programme, bells, train whistles, and all the trimmings,"[11] seemed excessive and proved ineffective. In general such fire plans are appropriate when a frontal assault is necessary but not if there is an open flank. Be that as it may, Graham agreed to the fire plan which, because of the number of artillery units employed, was managed by Brigadier Matthews, the CRA. However, the fire plan did not prevent the RCR from finding the German open flank or cause the Hastings to fail. Committing the Forty-eighth Highlanders, the brigade reserve, was Graham's choice. The battle was, indeed, an example of the brigade commander failing to recognize and exploit success, for he did not order the Hastings to capitalize on the Germans' open flank.

As William McAndrew, a historian at the Directorate of History, points out, the sad thing about the attack is that the RCR did precisely the right thing. They held the enemy with one company and got behind him with the other three, and that, also, was what Tweedsmuir intended the Hastings to achieve. Simonds deserves to be criticized for imposing a mind-set on Graham, namely that the artillery should play the major part in the battle for the first time in the campaign.

Possibly Simonds had curbed Graham's initiative, but Graham was never at his best when he had to make quick decisions in the middle of combat, and this was his first brigade-sized battle. The final point is that Simonds had a fourth brigade under command, a battalion of which had cut the road east of Agira. He calculated that if he hit him hard with artillery and aircraft the enemy would not stand in front of Agira with that threat behind him. Had the First Brigade attack been more competently handled the enemy might not have done so.

This First Brigade affair was the division's first setback. In the following ten days the division pushed the enemy back to Aderno, which it reached on August 6 after several notable actions. One of these was the model tank/infantry operation by the Second Brigade beyond the Troina River on August 5, conducted by Lieutenant Colonel Hoffmeister. When the Seventy-eighth British Division came up on its right, the division was squeezed out to prepare for the invasion of the mainland and passed into army reserve in a concentration area south of Catania. General McNaughton arrived there to visit the division. He had come to Malta earlier, hoping to be allowed to see "his" division in action. Montgomery, not wishing to have him disturb Simonds in his first campaign, had warded him off, and McNaughton returned to the United Kingdom until the Canadian part of the campaign ended. The meeting between McNaughton and his protégé, who had obviously pleased his British commanders, went very well.

Oliver Leese wrote to congratulate Simonds and his division. The Thirtieth Corps staff had nothing but praise for the way the Canadian operations staff under Kitching had performed, and the A and Q staffs were pronounced second to none. Leese wrote that he was sorry to lose the Canadians who were to fight in Dempsey's Thirteenth Corps in the approaching assault across the Strait of Messina. In fact, the Canadians received a good press, and McNaughton had good reason to be pleased with them. An Associated Press dispatch published Montgomery's remarks that the advance of the Canadians from Pachino to Etna was "simply wonderful — quite amazing." They had "travelled farther in Sicily, and fought longer, than any division of the Eighth Army . . . with the most frightful conditions and terrain to contend with. . . . We all knew that 1 Canadian Division would deliver the goods."[12] On August 20, a couple of days before McNaughton arrived, Montgomery visited the Canadians, some of whom had once booed him at the end of an exercise in Britain, and told them, "We shall soon be packing again, I expect. Wherever I go," he added, "I would like to have you with me."[13]

Despite the prospect of more fighting ahead and the satisfaction of having done so well in their first campaign, there was a sense of anticlimax in the concentration area. There is always a letdown after battle when troops return to the tighter discipline and routine of camp. This time it was worsened by outbreaks of dysentery, sandfly fever, and some malaria. There was a lot of work to do making up deficiencies, which meant many inspections and repairs. And, of course, the plan for Operation Baytown, the invasion across the Strait of Messina, had to be read and broken down into subunit tasks. The staffs from division down to battalions enjoyed none of the amenities of Norfolk House. Because of the sinkings before Husky there were not enough tents, office equipment, or telephones. Under canvas the heat was intense, particularly after dark in the blackout. Flies were persistent. Only the Third Brigade, which was responsible for the assault phase, was comfortable in a house on an estate owned by a Canadian, Lady Eaton. They even had light from a generator on the estate.

In units the familiar vehicle waterproofing was repeated. Towns were out-of-bounds, but the beaches beckoned. Reports of the recent fighting were written by A. T. Sesia, the divisional historian, who interviewed officers in the battalions to collect stories of the fighting. A consistent complaint was the U.S. Army Air Force's habit of dropping bombs on them. An example was their repeated bombing of Regalbuto when they intended to hit Troina. The Americans felt very badly about it and were not pleased when a story went around that a German prisoner smilingly told his Canadian captor: "When you bomb us, we take cover; when we bomb you, you take cover; but when the American airplanes come over, we all take cover."[14]

Sesia was in Regalbuto just after one such incident where several men were being dug out from under debris:

> While this was going on General Simonds came by in his jeep with Stu Graham, his ADC. Somehow we managed to push the jeep through and it did not stop. It was unfortunate that he should have passed just at this time, for the soldier who had been pulled out from the debris was lying on the ground waiting for the stretcher bearers, and as the GOC passed, apparently not noticing him, it brought forth a few caustic remarks from some of the troops standing nearby. I felt rather badly about this because I believe I am acquainted with General Simonds well enough to know that he is not heartless or without feeling. He is seldom away from the front line and if he were to stop and "play to the gallery" for every casualty that he passes by and not get on with the directing of his battles, we'd never get anywhere. Essentially a shy man and aloof by nature, he is definitely not the baby-kissing type, but he does inspire confidence and he does win battles — what more does a soldier want of his general?[15]

The bombing of Regalbuto had caused Simonds great irritation. A rather smart liaison staff from Bradley's Second Corps had joined Simonds. It had no less than eight scout cars, whereas the First Division's embassy to Bradley was mounted in one three-ton truck, so short was the division of transport. When Regalbuto was first bombed, a polite signal was sent off to the Second U.S. Corps via the American liaison staff. The very next day when the U.S. Army Air Force did it again the signal was not so polite. Simonds was assured that it would not happen again and that everyone was very sorry, et cetera. At 4:00 p.m., the next day, Regalbuto was bombed a third time just before Simonds himself was passing through the town. Simonds's third signal was quite rude but effective.

While brigades, battalions, and regiments were preparing for the next operation, Simonds had to deal with political questions concerning his position as senior Canadian officer in the theatre. McNaughton and the Canadian government guarded their control over the employment of Canadian formations. They had not authorized the use of the division or the armoured brigade in Italy, although Montgomery's plans for them were already laid.

Authority arrived for the division's participation in Baytown but only post facto and after Simonds pressed CMHQ for a decision. Even then CMHQ did not tell him whether the Canadians would winter in the Mediterranean, serve there indefinitely, or return to Britain as had been the intention initially. These matters intruded again when Simonds was commanding the Fifth Canadian Armoured Division in the autumn. In Sicily he was chiefly concerned with reinforcement and the repair and replacement of equipment. It rankled that, as senior Canadian in the theatre, he was not made privy to McNaughton's intentions and that, in consequence, he had no control over these matters. In the subsequent advance in Italy he had to signal General McNaughton on this subject:

My present directive authorizes employment of 1 Canadian Division in operations under 15 Army Group "from or based on North Africa," qualified by cable stating Canadian Government authorizes employment of 1 Canadian Division across Straits of Messina and in toe of Italy. Neither of above conditions now apply. May I therefore be given a further directive freeing my hands in respect to operations in this theatre or stating clearly what limitations will apply to operational employment of 1 Canadian Division . . . ? If we remain here for the winter highly desirable reinforcement base and all Canadian installations be moved from North Africa and Sicily to Italian mainland thus obviating unnecessary delays and wrong acclimatization of troops staging as reinforcements. Further essential I institute short leave system with appropriate arrangements for leave base if we winter here and probable duration of operational role here affects many other details such as recommendations and release of personnel for promotion to vacancies which may mean in England. I have discussed these problems with General Montgomery who has received no indication as to the future of 1 Canadian Division and has referred me to you. . . .[16]

None of this was resolved to Simonds's satisfaction. Instead the matter of control and its implications festered and lay at the root of a dispute with Crerar when the latter arrived in the Mediterranean with the First Canadian Corps later in the autumn.

Earlier Simonds had written to McNaughton on the matter of his replacement were he to become a casualty, which was a normal procedure. His memorandum evaluates his subordinates, whom he had discussed with Montgomery, Leese, and Dempsey. Penhale was his senior brigadier, but he did not recommend him for promotion because his "overcaution and hesitation in making operational decisions in face of apparent risks may well result in creating even greater risks." When Penhale was given the time to make decisions, they were sound, but quick decisions were not his forte. Consequently he failed to inspire in his subordinates that sense of urgency essential in mobile operations. Simonds concluded that Penhale was too old and physically unsuited for brigade or divisional command in the field. However, he would make a good senior staff officer and Simonds urged that a place be found for him in a static headquarters. "Pen" went to CMHQ where he served with credit. Vokes was an excellent brigade commander capable of driving an all-arms team. He was acceptable to Montgomery as a divisional commander and would replace Simonds were he to be a casualty. Of Graham, Simonds wrote that he was "a good brigade commander but in my opinion has reached his ceiling in that capacity."

Reporting procedures in the Canadian army followed the British system. In general the man who wrote the report read it over to its subject and gave him the opportunity to challenge it. The subject was expected to benefit from reading a description of his strengths and weaknesses, of which he may have been unaware. In most cases critical reports improved performances and the openness of the system was a check on the reporter himself. Furthermore, if the reporter customarily judged his subordinates too harshly, his superior could modify his judgement by way of personal comments. Simonds was in a powerful position at the end of his successful campaign to further the careers of his deserving subordinates, and in this case he recommended Lieutenant Colonels Hoffmeister, Kitching, Walsh, Bernatchez, and Bogert to command brigades. All were to make their mark.

We shall return to the subject of reporting and promotions in the next chapter when, on arriving in the theatre, Crerar raised the age-old question of promotion in the field versus promotion by seniority from inactive stations. He challenged patronage dispensed by successful field commanders like Simonds. Crerar was not yet in a position to influence promotion in the Mediterranean when he wrote a congratulatory letter to Simonds from the First Canadian Corps headquarters in England on August 10: "You can well imagine the consuming interest and intense pride of all ranks here in the reported exploits of your command." Because of the interest in Sicily the absent-without-leave rate had fallen fifty percent, and Crerar observed, "I should dearly love to see you and your command. Perhaps wishes may become facts."[17]

The events leading to the decision to send Dempsey's Thirteenth Corps, consisting of the Fifth British and First Canadian Divisions, across the Strait of Messina, are still confusing, even uncertain. The Germans' withdrawal of their divisions across the strait from the vicinity of Messina was masterly, but the Allied navies and air forces should not have allowed it. The earlier idea of landing the Tenth Corps on the Calabrian coast before the end of the Sicily campaign died, although when and why is unclear. One of its purposes had been to prevent that evacuation. It was sent to Salerno with the Fifth Army instead. The lack of decisiveness at the top levels of command so evident in the planning and conduct of Husky was repeated when Italy was invaded. Not until August 24 was it decided to cross the Strait of Messina (Baytown) on September 3 and to assault at Salerno (Avalanche) on September 8. Firm allocations of landing craft could not be made even then until the total of serviceable craft after their rough handling in Husky was known. In short, the allocation made eleven days before D-day for Baytown was still provisional.

The subsequent campaign of the Thirteenth Corps has been described variously as unnecessary, unnecessarily slow, and a failure because it had only a minimal effect on the fighting at Salerno. In the words of Mark Clark, the American who commanded the Fifth Army at Salerno, his own landings were a "near-run thing." The object of Baytown, which started with a stupendous bombardment against a fleeing Italian army and a slippery German rear guard, was never clear; Montgomery himself was never reconciled to it. It is difficult, in consequence, to pronounce on its success.

Originally the Thirteenth Corps was not intended to join up with Avalanche. Rather, the idea was to hold the Twenty-ninth Panzer Grenadier and the Twenty-sixth Panzer Divisions south of Salerno in Calabria so that they might be squeezed between the Fifth Army and the Thirteenth Corps. Since only elements of those divisions and the First Parachute Division from around Taranto, and of the Hermann Göring and the Third and Fifteenth Panzer Grenadiers north of Salerno, reached the Avalanche battle, the roughly six Allied divisions at Salerno had nothing to fear but their own timidity. Unfortunately they never recovered from the shock when, instead of the walkover they expected after the Italians announced their surrender the evening before the landing, they met the noisy, active, and aggressive Sixteenth Panzer Division and a hastily assembled battle group from the Hermann Göring Division.

The Canadian part in the long advance to Potenza from Calabria was physically demanding. Some of it was spent high in the thick mist and chilly rain of the Aspromonte — a great contrast to the heat of Sicily for which the division was still dressed. Persistent demolitions exploded almost in the faces of the forward troops so that supplies and munitions had to be man-packed. Jeeps and motorcycles were the only vehicles that could negotiate the tracks and mountain roads. As a result, the extended division fought in small columns that were fortunate to be lifted occasionally in captured trains and trucks. The Forty-eighth Highlanders covered a considerable distance on bicycles, but the battalions were more frequently on foot.

Simonds's relations with Dempsey were excellent. Notes from the latter were brief but encouraging and always friendly. The two men obviously liked each other. So when Simonds contracted the prevalent jaundice and was confined to bed on September 22, Dempsey sent him a note:

> My dear Guy, I am very sorry indeed that you have had to fall out for a short time — but glad that you are taking it so sensibly. It is the only way. I will see that your Div. does not get into trouble in your absence! If there is anything that you want, please let me know. Do not try to come back too soon: jaundice is a wretched business.
>
> A speedy recovery,
> Yours ever,
> Miles Dempsey[18]

With Simonds still under the weather on October 12 but thinking about going back to the division, which Chris Vokes was commanding in his stead while the Second Brigade was under Hoffmeister, Dempsey wrote again:

> I am very glad to hear that you are getting on well, and that you have sufficiently recovered to think about coming back.
>
> Before you do this, let me give you a piece of very strong advice: Do not come back to your division until you are quite certain that you are 100% fit. It is very damp and chilly up in these hills, and there have been a number of cases of people coming back from jaundice too early, getting complications, and then being laid up for weeks. . . . Your splendid division is fighting just as well as ever in most difficult conditions. . . .[19]

Simonds's work as commander was rewarded with the Distinguished Service Order, which he added to his C.B.E., earned after Jupiter. But he was not to return to the division. When Dempsey was writing his note, Operation Timberwolf had started. On October 17 Simonds received a personal and most secret signal from Lieutenant Colonel Tow in the Canadian cell at the Fifteenth Army Group. It said that Crerar was on his way from Britain with the First Canadian Corps headquarters and that Simonds was to take command of the Fifth Armoured Division, which was in the United Kingdom and was soon to embark for Italy.

8

Canadian Army Politics

....

GENERAL **A**RTHUR **C**URRIE'S struggle to maintain the integrity of the Canadian Corps in 1917 and 1918 made an indelible impression on senior Canadian officers of the Second World War. Andy McNaughton and Harry Crerar, both veterans of the old Canadian Expeditionary Force, suspected that the British had a set design to break up the Canadian Corps into separate divisions, and they opposed it even when it was sensible. British officers, some of the senior of whom had fought with Currie, Alan Brooke, for example, wondered what all the fuss was about. Brooke pointed out that from an early stage the plan for the invasion of Continental Europe included a Canadian army formation of two Canadian corps, which would have a British corps assigned to it. It was the first ever army-level formation with the label "Canadian." Nevertheless, it would be fleshed out with some British administrative, artillery, and probably engineer units because the Canadians could not provide them. Hence, rather than Canadians serving in British formations, the opposite would be the case.

The strain of maintaining an army headquarters and two Canadian corps instead of Currie's single corps re-created in exacerbated form Currie's problem in keeping Canadian units up to strength, even when the British contributed to divisional slices.[1] Conscription had been a divisive issue in the Great War. In World War II Mackenzie King's oracular statement that the government's policy was "not necessarily conscription but conscription if necessary" soothed Quebec, but it meant that only volunteers among conscripts could be sent overseas. If, then, the two corps suffered the heavy casualties that were expected when they invaded the Continent, the supply of volunteers and volunteer conscripts would be insufficient to keep them up to strength.

In the First War the Canadians were involved in stiff fighting from early 1915. It was not until August 1942, three years after hostilities began, that they saw any fighting in the second one. Then they lost the better part of two brigades at Dieppe in twelve hours of fighting. At that point the government was under fire for the inactivity of the Canadian army overseas; by the end of 1942 the army and anglophone Canadians were indignant that the "Johnny come lately" Americans were in action in North Africa while the Canadians lolled in England, waiting for an invasion that could not be launched until 1944. Morale suffered in the army overseas. Consequently the government pressed successfully for the First Division and the First Armoured Brigade to be included in Husky in place of the Third British Division (see the previous chapter).

Drafts to replace Husky and post-Baytown casualties in Italy were easily found from the pool of volunteers until June 1944. After six weeks of heavy casualties in the Second and Third Infantry Divisions in Normandy and in the First Infantry and the Fifth Armoured in Italy, the equivocal policy of the Mackenzie King government began to disintegrate when the pool of infantrymen almost dried up, as many had predicted. Nevertheless, King defended limited conscription with skill, subterfuge, and the connivance of the higher command until the final months of the war when conscripts who had not volunteered to go overseas, called Zombies, were sent to Europe.

Although the trained reserves to replace the First Division and the First Armoured Brigade casualties in the Mediterranean were still ample while the bulk of the Canadian army remained in the United Kingdom, Husky had breached the policy of keeping the Canadian divisions together in the First Canadian Army. That was not apparent immediately because both Husky formations were expected to return to Britain for the invasion of Europe, bringing valuable experience with them. But on October 7, after two months in the making, a further agreement was reached with the British-named Operation Timberwolf, which expanded the Canadian contingent in the Mediterranean by sending the Fifth Armoured Division and the First Corps headquarters from the United Kingdom. By reducing the First Canadian Army in Britain to its headquarters and a single corps, Timberwolf threatened Andy McNaughton's tenure of the First Army.

Although Andy McNaughton expected to command the First Army on the Continent, the British, and many Canadians, thought him neither suitable nor competent. First, he would be a difficult colleague for the army group commander. Obsessed by the myth that Sir Douglas Haig was always trying to break up the Canadian Corps in the First War, he would be legalistic about Canadian constitutional rights in the command arrangements. Second, although he had been president of the National Research Council and CGS from 1929 to 1935 and was undoubtedly clever and well rounded, as a field commander, he was too engrossed in the technical, scientific, and engineering rather than the strategic and tactical aspects of war. Neither of these objections was likely to be decisive or to convince the Canadian government. However, when Alan Brooke, the CIGS, insisted that, in future, army commanders had to have field experience in commanding divisions and corps in the present war and pointed out that McNaughton had had none, he denied McNaughton his legitimacy. In Timberwolf Brooke had a further argument that since the First Canadian Army had been reduced to a single Canadian corps, it was no longer predominantly a *Canadian* army formation. Therefore, McNaughton became persona non grata as the untried, elderly Canadian commander of an army that would contain two or more British corps.

In agreeing to Timberwolf Brooke had overridden the wishes of Sir Harold Alexander, the commander of Allied Armies in Italy (AAI), and also of General Montgomery into whose Eighth Army the First Canadian Corps would be inserted. They did not need another corps headquarters or any more armour in that mountainous country: it was infantry that they wanted badly. Furthermore, they thought that the Canadians could ill afford the luxury of a corps headquarters in Italy. They surmised, correctly, that by including the Fifth Armoured Division in Timberwolf the Canadians provided themselves with a pretext for foisting a corps headquarters on them and gave its commander, Lieutenant General Harry Crerar, an opportunity to gain the field experience he needed to qualify as a Canadian replacement for McNaughton. Alexander and Montgomery would have preferred Simonds to command the First Corps, if it were to be foisted on them — and possibly even to command the First Army later — but Crerar was the incumbent in Britain. They did not need to commit to paper the further argument that a Canadian corps would inflict on them more dominion politics of which the Eighth Army had had its fill, although successive Eighth Army commanders since 1941 had been delighted with the quality of its Australian, New Zealand, South African, and Indian divisions.

As far as Brooke was concerned, Timberwolf made McNaughton redundant. Once the First Corps was established in Italy there would be insufficient shipping to bring it back to northwest Europe. A British commander for the First Army would then be justified and might even be accepted by the Canadians, who would be left with a corps in each theatre. However, Brooke was friendly with Crerar, and having him command the First Army would be preferable to a row with the Canadian government. So he decided that the First Army should remain Canadian in name even if it had but one Canadian corps.

Conveniently McNaughton went home sick towards the end of 1943, clearing the way for Harry Crerar, commander of the First Corps, to replace him after gaining experience in Italy. The steady and tactful Kenneth Stuart, Simonds's old friend from RMC days in 1938, came from Ottawa, where he was CGS at army headquarters, to be chief of staff at Canadian military headquarters in London. From there he acted as locum at First Army headquarters, either until McNaughton returned, which was unlikely, or Crerar came back from Italy to replace him. No senior Canadian was willing to relinquish the First Army to a British officer.

British commanders-in-chief accepted that their senior dominion subordinates wore two hats. McNaughton arrived in the United Kingdom as the commander of the First Canadian Division in 1939, but he was also the senior Canadian overseas, a partially political appointment in which he had to look after Canadian army soldiers and their interests whether they were directly under his command or not.[2] McNaughton's task had two aspects. First, he was in the same position vis-à-vis the British as Sir John French had been with General Joffre in 1914 and 1915: he could appeal to Ottawa against orders that affected Canadian forces in Europe. When McNaughton commanded the Canadian corps in the United Kingdom earlier in the war, he objected, after an exercise was over, that British commanders had removed Canadian brigades from their divisions and assigned them to British formations. He pointed out that it was reminiscent of Sir Douglas Haig's attempt to divide Currie's corps during the German offensive of March 1918. Brooke accepted McNaughton's case, as he was bound to since it was based on an agreement between governments.

A more complex aspect of McNaughton's role was that concerned with personnel. Reinforcement, promotion, appointments, honours and awards, discipline and supply, Adjutant and Quartermaster General's branch matters were Canadian concerns, but not entirely outside the authority and responsibility of British superior commanders. It was in such overlapping responsibilities that British and Canadian commanders in the field had to be flexible. McNaughton's position allowed him to have a finger in the Italian pie, but he was not a good judge of the operational effect of Canadian policies, preferring to construe British operational arguments as excuses for absorbing Canadian formations and functions. For example, when McNaughton wanted to visit the Canadians during the Husky operations and was deterred by Montgomery, he chose to overlook Montgomery's operational reasons for not wanting him there while Simonds was in his first campaign.

In his capacity as senior Canadian in the Mediterranean Simonds had worked easily with the Eighth Army; CMHQ and McNaughton, on the other hand, had fallen down on the job, it seemed to him. In mid-October Simonds was as dissatisfied with Canadian arrangements for reinforcement and supply as he had been at the time of Baytown. Despite his earlier signals on the subject, his base was still back in North Africa, and McNaughton had not delegated authority to him to control its functions or its movements. Signalling McNaughton on this subject yet again, Simonds was surprised at the reply: "Army Group should by now be fully informed of Operation 'Timberwolf.'" This allusion meant nothing to Simonds, nor to Montgomery when he was told. Montgomery signalled McNaughton: "Have never heard of 'Timberwolf.'"[3]

Simonds was told about Timberwolf soon after McNaughton's signal, but as the Eighth Army, like Simonds, purported to have heard of it only at the last minute, although it had been in the making for two months, Montgomery was displeased that Crerar appeared posthaste immediately afterwards as commander of the First Corps.[4] Since his plans did not include an extra corps headquarters, he kept Crerar in Sicily for some weeks, in the waiting room as it were. Crerar himself arrived in an apprehensive but rather belligerent mood, for he knew that no one wanted him and that he was on trial. He was not quite sure whether Lieutenant General Kenneth Stuart at CMHQ would be able to keep his place warm as commander-designate of the First Army if Montgomery were dissatisfied with him. It must have crossed his mind that he might be confirmed only after an unpleasant political battle.

Simonds felt strongly that news of the First Corps HQ's imminent arrival and of his posting to command the Fifth Armoured Division should not have been imparted to him in a signal signed by a Canadian lieutenant colonel at HQ Allied Armies in Italy. That did not seem to him to be a proper way to communicate such important information, and he was justified in expecting McNaughton to have written to him personally. At first he thought he had been demoted. The First Division was the plum command in the Canadian army and the transfer suggested to him that his superiors were dissatisfied. Montgomery reassured him on that point, pointing out that experience in commanding an armoured division would qualify him to command a corps. But when he learned that the Fifth Armoured would take the equipment of the Seventh Armoured Division, the Desert Rats, which was about to return to the United Kingdom to prepare for Operation Overlord, the invasion of France, he was furious. From his logistical work as senior Canadian in the Mediterranean he knew that new equipment was almost unobtainable and that the Seventh Armoured Division's had been flogged to death in operations all the way from Alamein and before. Taking over dud equipment would be a bad start for his new division. He persuaded himself that the secrecy surrounding Timberwolf was to avoid his objections to the arrangement, and he was not at all mollified to learn that Timberwolf had been conditional upon the exchange of equipment to save shipping.[5]

When Crerar appeared, Simonds, feeling he had been treated in a cavalier fashion, was in a fit of pique. Crerar was relieving him as senior Canadian commander as well as serving as his military superior. It seemed to him that McNaughton, who treated his own role as senior Canadian so seriously, had ridden roughshod over Simonds's. The procedure illustrated to him the redundancy of the constitutional obsession of senior Canadians. He was certain that Canadian relations with the Eighth Army in Italy, which had been excellent, would be upset by the arrival of the First Corps headquarters. No one would welcome to the club a Canadian corps headquarters fresh from England that would probably fight a paper war U.K.-style and emphasize none of the things that were important.

The Eighth Army was informal and easygoing, but it was very efficient in all the things that really mattered, like communications, movement, and simple verbal orders. Paper was kept to a minimum. Commanders at all levels liked and understood one another and differences between nationalities were rare. Nearly all of Simonds's Canadian subordinates agreed with these sentiments. Recovering from jaundice, never fond of Crerar, and by now a complete Eighth Army man, Simonds was edgy and vulnerable. Knowing that no one would embrace Crerar and kiss him on both cheeks when he arrived, Simonds did not bother to hide his displeasure at the man's arrival. In taking this attitude Simonds was riding for a fall.

We have seen Simonds's affection for England and things English. He fitted into the British army in the field as well as he had into its social circle. He liked the Eighth Army's healthy tolerance for Canadian idiosyncrasies. It had given him the best of both worlds, for it was an international army and his own background conditioned him to match its imperial coloration perfectly. Monty liked "his Canadians," and often said so. The two Canadian formations, the First Infantry Division and the First Armoured Brigade, were proud to be in the Eighth Army and resented the suggestion that they were temporarily visiting and needed protection from the British. It was a young army, for commanders at all levels had risen in battle and the old and slow and bureaucratic had been weeded out and sent back to England, which was regarded as a museum. Being so relatively young themselves, Simonds and his commanders were at home in Italy. The comradeship between those who had been in battle together was close, and the ranks were inclined to close against newcomers, particularly if they tried to throw their weight around before they had proved themselves. In common with those around him that he respected, Simonds resented it when Harry Crerar started to do that immediately. Crerar seemed not to notice the generation gap and the void in his battle experience that divided him from the Canadians as well as the British in the Eighth Army.

For these reasons the atmosphere was at a flash point when Crerar and Simonds met. Unless each respected the other's sensitivities there was bound to be an explosion. The onus of avoiding it lay with the older and, presumably, wiser of the two. Unfortunately the intruding Crerar provoked the row with Simonds. In assessing responsibility for it, apart from McNaughton's handling of Timberwolf, we should consider that Guy Simonds had come out of a tense period of operations and a bout with hepatitis, which is known to leave its victims with lowered energy and morale, pessimistic and tetchy. Quite apart from that, Crerar faced a changed Guy Simonds. No longer the efficient, subordinate BGS who had served him so well at First Corps HQ, Simonds was now a divisional commander used to expressing his opinion when he received orders that he thought ought to be modified, and used to making decisions and giving rather than receiving orders. Battle had made explanations unnecessary in the Eighth Army and speeded decisions, which may have given the appearance of being impulsive to someone fresh from a desk in England where "the war" moved at a slower tempo. It took a more robust, a younger and more flexible man than Crerar to cope with the mood in a combat zone. Furthermore, the Eighth Army was an intellectual democracy that, while it did not tolerate bellyaching, accepted outspokenness. (And we saw how Simonds successfully challenged a detail in Monty's plan for Husky in Cairo.) It did not approve of officers hiding behind their rank or office but judged them by their deeds. Crerar was a bureaucrat and did not fit into the Eighth Army.

There were differences in age, in experience of war, and in personality between Crerar and Simonds, but they might have been bridged. A fundamental difference between the two men that could not be spanned was the fact that Crerar's roots were nourished by different soil from Simonds's. He was a good Canadian in the sense that Mackenzie King and McNaughton were good Canadians: they were members of the British family, independent and separate, yet part of it. Crerar was determined that the British should never assume his support. He wanted them to treat him like an equal and ally. Simonds, in Crerar's opinion, had become a Trojan horse, someone who was more English than Canadian, a man who did not separate Canadian from British interests. He emulsified them by looking at every question as an operational one. For that reason he was unsuited to higher command, for there he might give away too much. What Crerar could not accept was that Simonds's view of Canadian-British relations had become typical of Canadians in Italy. Younger officers in the field had adapted to the British army environment and were inclined to think that it was the old Crerar-McNaughton gang, still fighting the last war, who were out of step. In this respect Simonds seemed to be leading the Young Turks in the Canadian army.

Before we pursue the confrontation between Simonds and Crerar any further we must turn aside and look ahead to Crerar's involvement in the removal of his successor as commander of the First Corps, Lieutenant General E. L. M. Burns. The Burns episode is informative about Crerar's attitude to his British colleagues.[6]

Neither Crerar nor Burns, who succeeded Simonds in command of the Fifth Armoured Division before taking Crerar's place as commander of the First Corps, was a success in the Eighth Army. Personalities apart, they were in a weak position because the First Corps was unbalanced in having only an infantry, an armoured division, and an armoured brigade. Until its commander earned the trust of his superiors he would not be given other formations to command. Initially the Eighth Army had no desire to employ the

Canadian formations as a corps. Neither Canadian divisional commander, Vokes and Hoffmeister in Burns's time, liked working in the First Canadian Corps because they found it inexperienced and bureaucratic. When Crerar commanded, he was inclined to issue training memoranda and tactical advice that his more experienced divisional commanders considered inappropriate. His plodding emissions, studded with platitudes and generalities, were mainly inspired by experience on the Western Front a generation earlier. They were exasperating. In Britain, when that old war-horse General Pearkes, V.C., received such literature from Crerar, he consigned it straight to the trash can.[7] Burns was also inclined to lecture rather than command, and his subordinates reacted to him as they had to Crerar.

Burns survived one crisis of confidence in June 1944 and was sacked in a second in October. Crerar was involved in both as senior Canadian in Europe. After Burns's first battle, Diadem in the Liri Valley in May-June 1944, Leese, by then commanding the Eighth Army, wanted to get rid of him. Burns survived, thanks to Crerar, although his divisional commanders were not supportive of his headquarters, which was purged after the battle. In October, after the Gothic Line battle was over, Burns was under fire from General Richard McCreery, Leese's successor as commander of the Eighth Army, and was removed on November 5. In the inquiry into his performance his own Canadian senior officers spoke out against him. It says much for his successor, Charles Foulkes, not a popular officer by any means, that he fitted into both the Eighth Army and the First Corps. He was a younger officer, though, with sound political sense as well as battle experience as a divisional commander in Normandy and as the acting commander of the Second Corps in the Scheldt battles.[8]

When Burns was finally sacked, Crerar was commanding the First Army but on sick leave while Simonds fought the Battle of the Scheldt in the autumn of 1944. He rejected General McCreery's statement about Burns in which McCreery wrote:

> I find that he is indecisive and appears to lack that grasp of the whole situation which is essential in battle. In fact, he does not lead. Owing to the handicap of not having commanded units and lower formations in battle, he lacks that knowledge of the many factors which must be weighed up in any tactical problem. This prevents him ever making any constructive proposal and causes his opinion to change, and puts him at a great disadvantage with his subordinate commanders. . . . His manner is depressing, diffident and unenthusiastic and he must completely fail to inspire his subordinate commanders.[9]

Crerar might have thought "there but for the grace of God go I," for he fitted McCreery's description in some respects himself. Fortunately for him he had never taken the First Corps into battle in Italy. He blamed Burns's superiors for trying to break up the First Corps and to place a British officer at its head. Indeed, that had been the proposal made by General Harold Alexander in June, during the first crisis over Burns after Diadem, the battle in the Liri Valley. On that occasion Alexander wrote to the War Office concerning Burns:

> He is intelligent and easy to work with but he is sadly lacking in tactical sense and has very little personality and no, repeat, NO powers of command. . . . Burns's shortcomings as a corps commander place Leese in a very difficult position regarding the employment of the Canadian Corps since he must either give them a task beyond the powers of the commander or below the capacity of his troops. Moreover, a corps of one infantry and one armoured division is sadly unbalanced . . . still further upset for fighting . . . [because] it has so far proved impossible to produce a second infantry brigade for the armoured division.[10]

Crerar, in his capacity as senior Canadian, had refused to recommend an additional infantry brigade for the Fifth Canadian Armoured Division in June 1944 to conform with the other Eighth Army armoured divisions. His stated reason was that the views of the Eighth Army were ephemeral, that earlier it had favoured more armour not less and that it would change its opinion again. He appeared unaware of a trend under way since 1940 in the German army, and since the Desert Campaign in the British, to create armoured divisions with more infantry and infantry divisions with some armour. (Panzer grenadier divisions and the New Zealand division were examples.) Simonds had returned from his visit to the Eighth Army in April 1943 with that message. Either Crerar was not following the news from the battlefields or his real concern was that the Canadians might run short of infantry in Normandy and he placed their needs above those of the First Corps in Italy.[11]

We must grant the fact that Oliver Leese was not everyone's ideal commander, and he was to fall from grace in Burma by trying to sack General Bill Slim, commander of the Fourteenth Army, one of the outstanding soldiers of the war. Nevertheless, the Burns affair illustrated the unsurprising fact that the minute prewar Canadian army was incapable of providing a choice of sound corps or divisional commanders until younger men had risen through the ranks in battle.[12] On this point, and that the manpower for two corps headquarters, five divisions, and two tank brigades, as well as corps and army troops, were too much for the Canadians to support, Alexander wrote:

> As regards another corps commander, I know of no Canadian other than Guy Simonds in whom I should have confidence as a corps commander, but if you can suggest one and cable me his particulars, I will willingly consider him as a replacement for Burns. . . . [He went on to say that he would have thought that Canadian amour propre was already served by the First Canadian Army.] Esprit de corps, tradition and fame are essentially unit and divisional perquisites. . . . As to manpower, a corps HQ and corps troops for two divisions is very extravagant. Saving it might allow [them] to find the extra infantry brigade.[13]

Crerar reacted to this angrily, although not in a reply to Alexander. He felt that Alexander's view was "typically that God is an Englishman" and he confided to Ken Stuart at CMHQ:

> I do not doubt the honesty of the views held by Generals Alexander and Leese. Neither do I doubt, however, that such views are importantly influenced by two factors. The first is ingrained in most Englishmen and is, at times, a source of great strength, as well as being a weakness on other occasions. I refer to the Englishman's traditional belief in the superiority of the Englishman. The second is "the military inconvenience," if nothing else, of restrictions in the complete interchangeability of formations, units etc. under a higher commander.[14]

Crerar seems to have arrived in Italy with the intention of bringing Simonds to heel. As army commander, he was to try the same tactics in Normandy with Lieutenant General Sir John Crocker, commander of the First British Corps, then in the First Army, as his intended victim. Neither episode was a success for Crerar. The pretext for his dispute with Simonds in Italy was trivial. In their first meeting in Simonds's caravan Crerar asked if one of his RCEME staff could inspect the caravan, since he wanted one of the same design. Expecting to receive notice of the visit and that Crerar would arrange a convenient time with him, Simonds was angered when, on December 2, several weeks later, he returned from a field trip barely in time for a conference in his caravan with J. L. Ralston, the defence minister, to find an officer, Captain Kirk, and an assistant tramping around in the caravan with dirty boots and taking measurements. Giving them fifteen minutes to finish the work, he dismissed them sharply. Later he learned that a junior staff officer, temporarily at Fifth Division headquarters, had told Kirk to "carry on" when Kirk weightily informed him that he was there on the corps commander's orders. There were secret maps in the locked caravan, letters on the table, and personal belongings. The caravan had just arrived off the road, and Simonds's batman had been told to prepare it for the conference but had been prevented from doing so. Instead of clearing up the matter on the phone, when there might have been mutual apologies and new arrangements made if still necessary, Crerar listened only to Kirk's version of the story. He then wrote a sharp letter to Simonds:[15]

> Although this might be regarded as an unimportant incident, and one which I could afford to ignore, there are certain implications which disturb me sufficiently to cause this letter.
>
> The least important aspect, which I will discuss first, is that this intolerant treatment of a junior officer dispatched to you on my initiative was, in effect, an indirect act, on your part, of personal discourtesy to me. I cannot bring myself to believe that this was intentional because I am aware of no grounds for this attitude on your part and I know of a good many reasons, extending over a number of years, which should induce in you feelings, for me, of loyalty and appreciation. All the same, whatever your actual intentions, the result has been to convey to a number of personnel on [sic] your own headquarters and to a number at present directly under me, a very regrettable impression. The much more important effect of this episode is that it tends to indicate that your nerves are over-stretched and that impulse, rather than considered judgment, may begin to affect your decisions. Should this, indeed, be the situation, I would be extremely worried, for you are now reaching a position in the Army when balance is becoming even more important to your future than brilliance.
>
> I would not write you at this length, or in this manner, if I were not now, as in the past, sincerely interested in your career. I am fully aware of the heavy mental strain you have been under for the last six months. Although it is difficult, I would like you to undertake a self-examination, and give me a diagnosis of your own mental and physical condition. It is always possible for me better to influence or arrange the future if I know the condition of the present.[16]

When this storm in a teacup occurred, Simonds was sorting out his commanders in the Fifth Armoured Division, some of whom he considered unsatisfactory for one reason or another. They had survived in their appointments in the easier milieu of the United Kingdom. In that connection a practice that particularly incensed him was that of posting away an incompetent officer without an adverse report so that he was foisted on another unsuspecting unit where he was equally unsuccessful. This was bad enough anywhere. In a theatre of war, where men's lives might be lost through incompetence, it was unacceptable. Concealment of the real reason for an adverse report, for instance heavy drinking, was also a practice he deprecated. It not only obstructed treatment for alcoholism but concealed the fact that whatever his job the subject of the report was likely to fail for the same reason. In a case where a regimental commander's unit was unfit for war after he had commanded it for two years, Simonds insisted that as he alone was to blame he should be removed. If he had been dissatisfied with his subordinates, he should have removed them. If he had not done so, he became responsible for their incompetence.

This was Simonds's argument for removing the CRA of the Fifth Armoured Division, Brigadier Morton. Instead of stating the fact that one of his artillery regiments was inefficient, with chapter and verse, and drawing the correct conclusion, that the commanding officer was responsible and should be removed, Morton asked for his reassignment on medical grounds. Simonds concluded that the CRA was covering up his own tolerance of inefficiency over a long period. By not revealing the whole truth in several other adverse reports he placed Simonds, the divisional commander who had to review each case, in a false position when the officer under report appealed against the facts stated. The upshot was that Simonds decided that Morton had been dishonest and ought to be removed. In the particular case of the divisional artillery, Morton had been in command since January 1943 but had failed to clean house. In general Simonds strongly disagreed with Crerar's position that he was unjustified in removing the Fifth Division officers before they had been tested in battle. Simonds countered that had Timberwolf been properly mounted he could have returned to Britain to take over the division and sorted out its personnel. Montgomery had suggested it, but by October when both learned of Timberwolf, it was too late.[17]

In removing Morton and the others Simonds was treading on dangerous ground, for Crerar, the corps commander, ought to have sorted out his command in the United Kingdom. Furthermore, Simonds had told Crerar that he would await his agreement before removing Morton. Instead, having been told by Montgomery, in the meantime, that the Eleventh Infantry Brigade of his division was required in the field where it would be supported by the First

Canadian Tank Brigade until the Fifth Division's armour was ready, he arranged with Brigadier Brownfield, Crerar's gunner, to replace Morton immediately with Brigadier Sparling from Britain.

In his reply to Crerar over this affair and the caravan, Simonds pointed out that the only strain he had been under was owing to the handling of Timberwolf, and the uncertainties and muddle that it had created. On the linkage, in Crerar's mind, between Morton and the caravan, Simonds denied the absurd accusation that he had acted under impulse over either the caravan or the removal of officers:

> Though things may burst out suddenly, there has been a lot of very deep thought behind them. I believe my judgment both of personalities and things in general to be as sound as anyone's and I do not make decisions on impulse. I have also satisfied myself that I can keep a level head and still make sound decisions under considerable stress and I believe I could produce highly responsible witnesses to bear me out on that.

> Physically, I think I can claim with accuracy that since the outbreak of war I have had fewer days away from duty for sickness or rest (weekends, leaves etc.) than any commander in the Canadian Army. I have had more changes and sudden demands placed on my stamina than any other. I know you think I should carry more weight, but after all surely that is a matter of opinion? Some have prejudices for fat men and some for thin, but I honestly cannot see how that affects mental capacity or judgment — both kinds have it and both kinds haven't. . . . During the first evening's talk in my caravan you accused me of "thinking of nothing but myself" and "wanting to go home to bask in my newly won glory." I thought the remarks and the sense of others unjust and uncalled for. . . . The conversation left me with the impression that the principal purpose of your visit was to administer a rebuke to me — for what reason or purpose I did not, nor do I yet understand. . . . Your reference to "brilliance" I do not understand. I have made a point of paying no attention to press "bally-hoo" or the public statements of politicians. I think I can correctly assess the value of both. . . . I have been perfectly frank in telling you of my feelings about being kept in ignorance of "Timberwolf" and as a result of our first conversation [sic]. I would like to make it clear, however, that I have not allowed nor do I intend to allow personal feelings of mine to influence my judgment nor my attitude to my senior commander. It had nothing to do with the Kirk episode which arose solely from annoyance with a junior officer who, I consider, acted in a most impertinent manner.

I can assure you quite honestly also, that you can rely upon my loyalty in carrying out your policies. I have worked for senior officers whom I neither personally liked nor respected, but I have never had one complain of my loyalty, honesty or usefulness of the service rendered. . . .

I would welcome an opportunity for a perfectly frank talk with you. Your letter reinforces the feeling that you are looking for an opportunity to "take a crack" at me. . . . If you cannot express full confidence in my judgment and ability to handle my command in battle, I shall have to ask to be relieved.

Sincerely,
Guy Simonds[18]

Simonds also reminded Crerar of the principle that the divisional commander should not take into battle officers in whom he had no confidence. His knowledge of their roles and also of how they performed was necessarily better than that of some staff officer responsible for career management in the rear, or even that of Crerar himself. He did not believe in a system that allowed failures to be foisted on him so that they could have a second chance. However, he could judge and make allowances for officers who failed temporarily from fatigue or made an honest mistake. No doubt he had in mind the lesson of Howard Graham whom he had sacked in Italy and then recalled on Montgomery's advice.

Crerar answered that he agreed with Simonds's principles because they were his own, but in returning to the allusion to impulsive behaviour cast doubt on his divisional commander's judgement rather than the principle that he should be the judge. Hence he returned to the assertion that the caravan incident demonstrated that Simonds was not, at the moment, a fit judge. He added the point that justice to the individual *must* be assured by giving him a second chance after a "mistake." Guy's counterpoint was that men's lives and the efficiency and success of the unit mattered more than a regulation better suited to peace than to war. It was better to do injustice to one man than to allow several incompetents to remain in command. And if he, Guy Simonds, was a bad judge of men, he should be removed himself. His record showed that his selections had been sound. In the case of Morton there was the factor that part of the division was about to go into the line and training of the rest had to go ahead.[19]

At this stage Crerar took the extraordinary step of writing to Montgomery for support and calling in a psychiatrist and his own deputy director of medical services to judge whether Simonds was fit to command.[20] To Montgomery he wrote:

Dear Monty:

A number of actions and reactions on the part of Simonds since I arrived in this theater of operations, nearly two months ago, have given me serious cause to doubt his suitability for higher command. I have known him, fairly intimately, for over fifteen years. He first came to my notice when he was my junior subaltern when I commanded "B" Battery, RCHA, in 1927. Some ten years later he was my professor of tactics when I was Commandant at the RMC and, more recently, he was my BGS 1 Cdn Corps, during the first half of 1942. He has always been an excellent soldier with a first-class military mind. He has also always been high-strung and with a tendency to be introspective, rather than objective, when faced with acute problems. Up till now, I have always been able to handle Simonds successfully whenever I was faced by some tense situation arising out of an over-wrought condition on his part. When our military ranks were wider apart, this, of course, was an easier proposition. On a number of occasions I have prevented him from following a foolish course of action, or got him "on the rails" again and my advice seemed to be sought for by him and appreciated.

Since arriving out here, I have noticed that Simonds is not only very highly "tensed up" but also gives me the impression that he resents any control or direction on my part — a responsibility which is now mine concerning certain "Canadian business" and later, when the Canadian Corps is functioning operationally, in the widest possible manner.

This situation does not worry me from the personal angle because I believe that I can handle him, so much as if should anything happen to me, or should a situation arise, which would remove me from Canadian command in this theatre of operations, Simonds being my potential replacement. My present judgment is that while he has all the military brilliance for higher command in the field, with his tense mentality, under further strain through increased rank and responsibility, he might go "off the deep end" very disastrously indeed.

I am not going to retail, in this letter, the various incidents which have taken place during the last few weeks, and which have led up to what I have written. I can tell you about them when we next meet, except that I might mention that the latest was to remove his new CRA from command, ordering him off to Cdn Second Echelon, two days after he had written to me asking for my views before taking any such action and before the letter had actually been received by me. . . .[21]

Monty replied cheerfully in his clear, rather childish handwriting, making his point equally clearly:

I have your letter of 17 December. I have the highest opinion of Simonds. He tried to go off the rails once or twice when he first went into action with his Division, but I pulled him back again, and taught him his stuff. Briefly my views are that Simonds is a first class soldier. After a period with an armoured division he will be suitable for a corps. He will be a very valuable officer in the Canadian Forces as you have no one else with his experience; he must therefore be handled carefully, and be trained on. Vokes is not even in the same parish. I am trying hard to teach him but he will never be anything more than "a good plain cook." I do not, of course, know what has taken place between you and Simonds. He is directly under my command for training and so on, but of course would deal with you on purely Canadian matters. If you have been sending him any instructions or directions on training he might possibly ignore them! He gets that from me — verbally. I suggest you discuss it with me when you visit Eighth Army. Come whenever you like. Meanwhile: A Happy Xmas to you.

> Yrs ever,
> Monty.[22]

Montgomery had written to Simonds on this subject in November and advised that he should ignore Crerar if he attempted to order him about.[23] No doubt, since they were on such good terms, Monty gave him some friendly advice in December to butter up Crerar. So when Simonds next wrote to analyze the existing system for selecting, assessing, and promoting officers, on which he was quite entitled and qualified to speak, he was extremely respectful, although persistent with his arguments.[24]

The evidence of his doctor and psychiatrist hardly bore out Crerar's belief that Simonds was overwrought let alone incapable of command. In any case their evidence could hardly be taken in preference to Simonds's superiors in the Eighth Army. So Crerar compiled a file on their correspondence, together with the doctor's comments and his own, in which he denied the suggestion that he had been bullying or had provoked Simonds. Then he consigned the file to Stuart to CMHQ, telling him to keep it under lock and key:

I am sending you by safe hands the attached copies of communications and memoranda as I consider that you should be informed as to the present and potential problem of Simonds. I do not think this is an acute matter at present because if he is selected to command 2 Cdn Corps, as I recommend, he will be under superior Cdn Comd (I imagine) and thus can be controlled or, at least, the result of any impulsive actions on his part minimized. What I was worried about when I wrote Monty was the possibility of something happening to me, and Simonds, through necessity, taking on not only operational command of the forces here (which he will do well) but also the higher policy responsibilities of what virtually is an independent Cdn Comd, which he might conduct very disastrously indeed. Monty's reply did not really answer the questions which I raised, I regret to say, but that might have been intentional as Monty's primary interest is field command, not Canadian policies and business.

The egocentric state of mind which now obtains with Simonds worried me to the extent that I arranged a meeting, under most confidential arrangements, with Van Nostrand and my DDMS, McCusker, to obtain from the "medicals" their technical advice on the fitness of Simonds continuing in command, or of assuming still higher responsibilities, in view of his mental condition. Van Nostrand, after perusing the attached communications, stated that in spite of marked egocentricity, Simonds, in his opinion, could be relied upon to function effectively as a Senior Commander though very preferably *not* as an independent Cdn force comd. McCusker generally agreed, though a bit more worried about Simonds than Van Nostrand. With that advice to guide me, I have therefore, as you know, recommended Simonds as 2 Cdn Corps Commander . . . really a tragic situation because . . . I cannot see him going on and up the way and distance I had anticipated. As I said, this file, and all I have said, does not affect the present. Simonds is the only present "bet" for Corps Comd. It is "background" to be locked up now, but to be read over again at some possible future time when the further employment of this brilliant, and comparatively young, man comes up for consideration.[25]

This was character assassination, and it revealed a Crerar who was jealous of his authority but uncertain of it. In the shorter run it appears now that Crerar was looking ahead to when Simonds would be his Second Canadian Corps commander in northwest Europe and was establishing, or trying to establish, a position of authority over his brighter and potentially difficult subordinate. After the war, when Crerar retired, Simonds believed that Crerar was a hidden enemy. In the conversation in the caravan Simonds told Crerar that he had reliable evidence that Crerar had not wanted him as his BGS in the First Corps in 1942. Crerar denied it. Simonds did not tell Crerar that he was also convinced, as we have seen, that Crerar had had much to do with the disastrous mounting of Operation Jubilee, the restored Dieppe attack in August 1942. So there was an undertow in this December 1943 encounter that both men remembered the following summer in France.

Crerar had written a report on Burns and Simonds in which he repeated his view that Simonds was experienced and brilliant but not suitable for command of an independent corps, which meant the First Corps in Italy. Burns, he thought, looked further ahead, was steadier, and could be trusted with independent command, although as yet he lacked experience. As we have seen, Burns failed with the First Corps, while Simonds succeeded as commander of the Second.

On the surface, although the relations of the two men improved, they became more formal with each other. There was no purpose in Simonds quarrelling with Crerar, obviously, and Montgomery's letter made an impression on the latter. Furthermore, McNaughton's departure was by then confirmed, so Crerar's elevation was inevitable. In December 1943 Montgomery was appointed to command the Twenty-first Army Group. Simonds was called back to command the Second Corps in January, as Lieutenant General Sansom, its commander, had been recalled to Canada. So Simonds served under Montgomery again in the Twenty-first Army Group, which pleased both men. Montgomery had a low opinion of Crerar and ensured that he had as little responsibility in the early stages of the campaign in Normandy as possible.

9

The Allied Campaign in Normandy

IN JANUARY 1944 Simonds returned to England to command the Second Canadian Corps, which was to fight in the breakout phase of Overlord after the bridgehead was firmly established. The corps included the Second Infantry Division, the Fourth Armoured Division, and an artillery group (AGRA). The Third Canadian Division and the Second Armoured Brigade would join the corps after they had fought in the assault phase under Lieutenant General Sir John Crocker, the commander of the First British Corps. General Montgomery explained his plan for the assault and subsequent phases of Overlord to senior commanders at Saint Paul's School Hammersmith, Montgomery's old school, on April 7, 1944, at Exercise Thunderclap.

Battle plans, it has often been said, do not survive beyond the first cannon shot. That is true at the tactical level since soldiers have to modify their tactics continually to serve their operational plan. The survival of a commander's operational plan depends on his being able to keep the initiative, and he may have to change his tactics in the battle to retain it. If his enemy can take the initiative from him at the tactical level, he may go on to gain the operational initiative as well and then the commander's plan may collapse.

When comparing Montgomery's plan in April 1944 with its execution in June and July, the distinction between his operational plan and the changing tactical means he adopted to achieve it must be borne in mind. That distinction escaped Air Marshal Sir Arthur

Tedder. During the battle, Tedder asserted that Montgomery had changed his plan and would not admit it; he was floundering, his plan had failed, and he was losing the battle. He urged Eisenhower to replace him. Tedder was Eisenhower's deputy and his chief airman while Montgomery was the Allied commander-in-chief (C-in-C) in Normandy of the Anglo-American Twenty-first Army Group. It was intended that Montgomery remain commander-in-chief until Eisenhower chose to move his Supreme Headquarters Allied Expeditionary Force (SHAEF) from England to Normandy and take over as supreme commander (SCAEF). Eisenhower would then direct the Twelfth U.S. Army Group of the First and Third U.S. Armies under General Omar Bradley, and the Twenty-first of the Second British and First Canadian Armies under Montgomery.

Eisenhower was too good a politician to initiate the removal of Montgomery, and Brooke had no intention of acting on Tedder's suggestion, for it appeared to him that Eisenhower and Tedder had grasped neither the original plan nor its execution, although Montgomery might have taken more trouble to explain what he was attempting. So Montgomery remained, but so has the impression that he mismanaged the Normandy campaign.[1]

The Allied bridgehead in Normandy pivoted on its left or eastern flank where the Orne Canal joined the port of Caen to the sea. The Germans, too, were bound to base their defences on the eastern hinge since, if their front gave way, they would be compelled to pivot on it as they swung their line through ninety degrees to a new one on the right bank of the Seine, facing southwest. If their pivot gave way, withdrawal of their western divisions, on the outside of the arc, would be hazardous. These fundamentals gave Montgomery two options when he announced his plan in April 1944. The first was to try to break the German hinge as soon as he had established a bridgehead and had achieved the most favourable ratio of forces and enough space to employ them. That meant attacking the German front at its strongest point. The alternative was to seize a position from which he *threatened* to break out at the hinge, compelling the Germans to launch preemptive attacks against him. Weakened by artillery and air strikes and overextended by their attacks in the east, the Germans would be unable to prevent Montgomery's counterstroke on the western, American flank. An American breakthrough there would envelop the Germans' left flank and force them to withdraw to the Seine under unfavourable conditions. If they reached the east bank of the Seine in a condition to defend the river line, their open left or southern flank would be vulnerable to further envelopment.

Montgomery adopted the second of these plans, and the Germans were indeed destroyed west of the Seine. What went wrong then? And why all the fuss? The short answer is that the battle did not go according to plan tactically and Montgomery had to make changes to keep the initiative and his operational plan on the rails. It was these changes to which Tedder objected.

Montgomery intended to hinge his left flank on the important port, road, and rail centre of Caen. He hoped to seize it in the first day or two and then push southeastwards, threatening to break out towards Falaise and eastwards towards the Seine, as we have seen. That would provoke the phase of German counterattacks, referred to above, in comparatively open farmland interspersed with stone villages with good fields of fire. Montgomery would defend these villages and inflict heavy casualties on the attacking Germans with his dominant artillery and tactical air force. That did not occur because Caen did not fall until July. Montgomery's failure to take Caen in the first rush changed the tactical shape of the campaign. At the very beginning there was a possibility that the Germans might turn the tables by holding the hinge against the British and switching their reserves to the American front before the Americans had taken Cherbourg, the essential port the Allies needed and which lay behind the American front. Consequently it was the British and Canadians who had to attack all through July to hold the elite German panzer grenadier and panzer divisions on their front and to "write them down," as Montgomery described it.

The consequent British and Canadian attacks, first to take Caen and then to expand the bridgehead beyond it, had two intended and related effects. They gained space in the bridgehead for manoeuvre while extending the length of the German defence line and, by reducing the German infantry divisions to a condition in which they were unable to hold the front, they made the German commanders commit their armoured divisions to the line. In consequence those elite divisions were used up as local reserves, not as a mobile reserve to launch a counterstroke against the bridgehead or stabilize the front after a major Allied breakout. In short, they prevented the Germans from concentrating against the Americans.

In this fashion Montgomery kept the Germans off balance by attacking them not, as he had planned in April, by compelling them to attack him. The tactical shape of the battle changed; the strategic design did not alter. The price for retaining the initiative was paid by his infantry divisions. They, not the Germans, had to attack an enemy armed with superior weapons in country that favoured the defence. They suffered heavy losses.

This explanation of the course of the Normandy campaign was not, by any means, universally accepted by the American senior commanders after the battle, nor has it been accepted by writers critical of Montgomery on the British side.[2] Eisenhower himself judged the progress of a battle by the territory won, as was the custom in measuring the success of operations on the Western Front in 1914-18. It seemed to him that Montgomery's progress was so slow that he was going to be there into the winter. Confusing the tactical with the strategic plan, he was convinced that Montgomery intended to break out at the hinge and was failing to do so. Tedder also refused to perceive that Montgomery's aim was to keep the initiative and attract and keep the German armour engaged on the British sector. All he could see was an enormous effort by the ground and air forces resulting in little territorial gain.

One aim of Montgomery's April plan had been to gain space in the bridgehead for airfields south of Caen.[3] Tedder complained when they were not obtained, although air support was not lacking because of it. On that issue Tedder was displeased when Montgomery's July offensive, Goodwood, made comparatively small territorial gains, despite help from the strategic air forces, when he had given the impression that he expected a breakout towards Falaise. Although Goodwood kept the initiative and pinned down the German armoured divisions on the British front, Tedder complained that either Montgomery was failing or he was deceiving his superiors about his intentions and expectations. Brooke had to warn Montgomery, not for the first or last time, to take Eisenhower and his staff more into his confidence so that they did not stir up trouble for both of them.[4]

Tedder and Eisenhower were both deceived by the opportunistic element in Montgomery's plans, particularly that for Goodwood. Had the German defence collapsed in the first days after D-day Montgomery would certainly have thrust to Falaise and beyond and obtained Tedder's airfields for him. So it was that in the armoured battle of Goodwood, which so excited Tedder's ire, General Dempsey's appreciation considered a breakout to be possible. It did not happen, but he was right to be prepared for complete as well as limited success. Realistically, though, Montgomery and Dempsey had learned that with their generally superior tanks and infantry weapons the Germans had to be ground down by overwhelming firepower, a limitless supply of replacement tanks, and continual battle.

Such an inelegant procedure was too slow for Eisenhower and Tedder, neither of whom grasped the inferiority of Allied arms. The others believed that it was the surest way to victory in Normandy, where the ratio of troops and equipment to space was high. The defence had gained an advantage everywhere by 1943. It was not the case that German offensives were more successful than those of the Allies. In their huge armoured offensive in the summer of 1943 at Kursk, in the Soviet Union, and their comparatively small but concentrated offensive against the Anglo-Americans on the Anzio front in February 1944, the Germans had been as incapable of completing an offensive in the style of 1940 and 1941 as the Allies. By 1944 battles were usually decided by the attrition that preceded the encirclements and great advances that were the payoff.

Despite the ascendancy of the defence in situations where its flanks were not vulnerable, both the bitterness of the attrition phase in Normandy and the decisiveness of the resulting encirclement and pursuit surprised many senior officers in London and Washington. Since the war, there has been widespread unwillingness to recognize the effect on the Germans of the attrition and to question the way that it was conducted.

The experience of all the armies on the Western Front in the First World War conditioned people to dread the word *attrition* thereafter, for it suggested stalemate and a ratio of losses favourable to the defence, as it had from 1915 to 1917. The Canadian and British battles in Normandy may be described by that dread word. They were a grinding mill during which the Canadians may have suffered heavier casualties than the enemy, but in the end the balance was heavily in their favour. On the Western Front the payoff for attrition was not dramatic; indeed Sir Douglas Haig's claim in his last dispatch that there was one in 1918 is often denied. In Normandy, in contrast, the end came with the dramatic collapse of the enemy's front and the loss of virtually all his equipment and most of the men in his fighting divisions.

Why did the battle end quite differently from that on the Western Front a generation earlier? There were three main reasons. First, the ratio of troops to space in Normandy, high though it was, was more favourable to the attacking Allies than it had been on the Western Front. Second, flanks were created and exploited. And third, German communications were precarious in Normandy, making their movement and reinforcement difficult, whereas the railway system behind the German front in the First War served them well in defence and attack until the end. Attrition proceeded in both wars until the ratio of the number of German troops to the length of their front made their hold so tenuous that they could not prevent an Allied breakout. Nevertheless, the Allied strategy in Normandy was similar to that used on the Western Front from July until November 1918, namely to keep German reserves moving and their commanders off balance. But when the break came in 1944 German annihilation followed because of the speed with which modern divisions moved around the German flank and the vertical envelopment by the Allied air forces. Attrition paid in Normandy; it did not in 1915-18 because it was conducted over too long a period in adverse conditions and because the Allies could advance only at the pace of the infantryman when the German front gave way.

This was the setting for Simonds's four battles in Normandy: the first two attritional, the second two breakout battles in conjunction with the American breakthrough in the west. Montgomery's strategic plan was succeeding, but the tactical plan conceived in April 1944 had failed for a number of reasons, all of which affected Simonds's ability to win his battles. The elements in that failure must be identified because Simonds had to grapple with them as his divisions paid a heavy price in executing Montgomery's strategic plan. Was the price higher than it should have been? If it was higher, did Montgomery or Dempsey err in setting Simonds's battles? Did Simonds or his subordinate commanders make mistakes? Was the training of the troops faulty? The answer to these questions is bound up with the tactical failures of Allied arms in Normandy.

Initially two general points must be made. First, it must be restated that the Allies and the Germans were equally capable of making attackers pay a high price for attempting to penetrate a front without a vulnerable flank. Second, American casualties in Normandy were relatively heavier than British, Canadian, and Polish. The only safe deduction from the latter observation, bearing in mind that the Americans fought in closer country than the Canadians and against fewer panzer and panzer grenadier divisions, is the negative one that the Americans were no more successful than the Canadians up to the time when they broke the German front.

In the country south of Caen, where the Second Canadian Corps fought its bitterest battles, fields of fire were very long. At a range of two thousand yards, from well-sited positions, German 88 mm and special 75 mm guns in tanks or on wheels frequently destroyed half or more of the sixty tanks of an armoured regiment advancing against them before being engaged themselves. The 75 mm guns of the Allies' Shermans, and even the seventeen-pounders with which about twenty-five percent of the British and Canadian tanks were equipped, were outgunned in open country. Yet casualties to tank crews, even when a regiment's tanks were disabled on that scale, were surprisingly light. As Simonds had pointed out in his 1938 article, fewer men are lost in tank than in infantry attacks, a fact borne in mind by General Dempsey, commander of the Second Army, when he launched his Eighth Corps of three armoured divisions, armoured brigades leading, into the country south of Caen in Operation Goodwood. For the British could afford tank but not infantry casualties. Simultaneously Simonds was fighting his first battle, Operation Atlantic, on the Eighth Corps's right with infantry in a built-up area. His next battle was also fought with infantry over ground similar to the Goodwood battlefield. The Canadians suffered much heavier casualties than British troops. Advancing through cornfields towards a village a mile away, they were cut down, just as British infantry on July 14 and 15, 1916, were cut down on their way to High Wood and Delville Wood on the Somme.

Indeed, the country south of Caen is similar to the Somme. Church steeples rise from stone villages with outlying orchards that were often hull-down from the advancing Canadians. Germans were hidden but had good observation over the battlefield. They pinned down Canadian infantry outside the villages and gave them little chance of surviving the counterattacks of their panzer grenadiers supported by Panther tanks, which formed up and debouched from dead ground. The panzers and grenadiers were on top of the Canadians before their victims could do more than scratch shallow grooves into the chalky clay soil for shelter. Canadian tank support was usually neutralized and unable to reach the infantry over ground dominated by German antitank fire. The Germans' skillful use of tanks and infantry was not matched by the Canadians at this stage.

Why the Canadians were not better prepared for Normandy requires an explanation: in particular, why was tank/infantry cooperation at best patchy and at worst nonexistent? The deficiency was not peculiar to the Canadians but was common in the Second Army at the beginning in Normandy. What was the Second Armoured Brigade's experience with the Third Infantry Division in England? They worked with them for about five months. However, the brigade was literally changing over from six-pounder Rams to Sherman tanks, with one troop of seventeen-pounder Firefly Shermans in each squadron in May 1944. The high-explosive shell made all the difference to the employment of their tanks. They had not had time to work out a common drill to deal with the 88s and 75 mm specials on the German tanks. When the Second Canadian Division joined the battle, they had not trained with the Second Armoured Brigade at all and cooperation in battle was bound to creak. Inferior Allied tanks, weak handling of antitank weapons, and the inability of infantrymen to defend themselves against enemy tanks in open country because they had only one PIAT in each platoon and were often unaccompanied by guns from the battalion antitank platoon contributed to "tank fear" and "88 mm phobia." Their own supporting tanks were essential if they were to overcome this fear, but all too often the tanks were frightened off, as well.

The tactical imbalance between the two sides in Normandy, not entirely redressed by artillery and air superiority, raises the question whether commanders who knowingly placed their troops at a disadvantage were competent. The question hangs over not only Simonds's battles south of Caen in late July and August but all the battles fought by the Twenty-first Army Group's corps commanders in Normandy. Part of the answer is that none of the commanders brought back from theatres of war to the United Kingdom to fight in Normandy in January 1944 had enough time to correct the negligence of the incumbent British commanders. Furthermore, to the extent that the setting of Simonds's battles was decided by Montgomery's strategic plan, Simonds's initiative in fighting them was restricted. That was truer of Operation Spring, Simonds's second battle following Goodwood, than of his breakout battles. The circumstances of Spring in the last week of July were that the American breakout in the west had been delayed, compelling Montgomery to mount one more holding attack in the east using the Second Canadian Corps. Montgomery's intention was that Simonds should make a limited advance to provide a springboard for a breakout towards Falaise later, although he should seize an opportunity to break out.

Once clear of the built-up area of Caen (the scene of Simonds's first battle, Operation Atlantic), the ground favoured armoured rather than infantry divisions. Yet, in the battle for that ground, Operation Spring, Simonds's infantry lost heavily, and it may be asked why he did not give tanks the leading role instead of the infantry, as was done in the Eighth British Corps's Operation Goodwood, conducted simultaneously with Atlantic. Simonds has been criticized for his conduct of Spring on that account. While his choice of infantry in the leading role was understandable in view of the failure of tanks fighting without infantry in Goodwood, in Spring he did not use enough of the armour that was available to him. In fact, he was surprised by the failure of his tanks to support the infantry effectively. Ultimately, however, Simonds learned from his experience in Spring when he planned the breakout battles Totalize and Tractable two weeks later. Here armour, attacking at night, played the leading role, while the infantry was mounted in self-propelled 105 mm gun howitzer chassis whose guns had been removed in corps workshops. The battles were ground-breaking, and although they did not go according to plan, they ended in the complete defeat of the Germans compressed into the Falaise Pocket.

The events in this survey lay ahead of Simonds when he arrived back in England in January 1944 and took over his new command in February. He brought Marshal Stearns with him from Italy. Stearns was a Forty-eighth Highlander who had fought in Sicily with his battalion and was recommended by his commanding officer as a suitable candidate for military assistant to Simonds in Italy. Stearns acted more as a personal operations assistant than as an ADC. At the beginning neither he nor Simonds could determine precisely what their relationship would be. In the years after the war Marsh, as he was known, and his wife Helen were Simonds's closest friends, their house in Toronto a second home.

Marsh Stearns was an American by birth, a graduate of Harvard, a lawyer, and destined to be a prominent Toronto businessman. Simonds found him competent, well-read, a good conversationalist, and liked by his friends, the Andersons, and by other commanders. In the field, easily recognized by the Forty-eighth Highlander Glengarry that he wore, Stearns travelled with Simonds in his Staghound armoured car or jeep and kept his maps folded and marked in impeccable artillery style. He did not attempt to influence operations, but Simonds did ask his advice about handling individuals whom Marsh knew better than he. His eyes and ears were alert and his mouth shut when Simonds spoke to other commanders. He listened when Simonds wanted to unburden himself over a mug of whisky at the end of the day and he knew when to speak out and when to remain silent on those occasions. His competence was admired by the divisional staff, who considered him an asset in that he helped to keep up their commander's morale through sticky periods. He often spoke on the radio on behalf of his commander for security's sake because Simonds's English accent was easily identifiable to German signals intelligence.

Simonds believed that the promotion of young, efficient officers ought not to be blocked by their superiors who preferred to retain their services. After following Simonds from the First Division to the Fifth Armoured Division and hearing that Simonds was destined for Britain and command of the Second Corps, Marsh had to make a career choice. He could attend staff college, which would probably have taken him back to Canada but might have entitled him to promotion from captain to major on taking up a grade 2 staff appointment at the conclusion of the course, or follow Simonds to the Second Corps as a captain. He chose the latter and was the first of several officers from Italy to join Simonds as a member of his military family at Second Corps headquarters.

By this time Simonds had a fearsome reputation for ruthlessly high standards, and the incumbent staff members expected to be removed, holus-bolus. Several were not disappointed and at each breakfast the survivors were fewer. "Italians" replaced those who did not match Simonds's standards. Bruce Matthews, his CRA in the First Division, and Geoffrey Walsh, his CRE, came as CCRA and chief engineer respectively. Simonds chose the sapper Elliot Rodger as his brigadier chief of staff. Rodger had only recently taken command of the Tenth Infantry Brigade in the Fourth Armoured Division. The chief signals officer, Findlay Clark, remained from the original staff. Both men were outstanding PFers. Darrell Laing and his DAQMG Ab Knight, who had come from the First Division in Italy earlier, were head of the A and Q staff and chief of the supply staff respectively. Knight was the officer who had rewritten the administrative orders for Husky in April 1943. Laing was a militia officer who was a graduate of the Canadian Militia Staff Course and had done an attachment in Italy to learn the ropes. He ran a staff that was never at a loss. Bob Moncel, a graduate of the first staff course, remained as GSO I, Rodger's right-hand man on the operations staff. He also travelled with Simonds on his daily circuit around the battlefront and was responsible for the executive action that followed when Simonds returned to corps headquarters.

Simonds was part of Montgomery's new broom, which caused anguish to those with no recent war experience. A few were shipped out to Italy to acquire it. General Sansom, Simonds's predecessor, was considered too old for the hurly-burly of field command. Some of Simonds's subordinate commanders were replaced despite surviving the stress of training and administration in the United Kingdom with favourable reports. However, their experience in Britain was not the best preparation for weeks of fear, sleeplessness, and noise in battle. A commander may acquire expertise from books and exercises. He learns from them that his mistakes will cost lives, perhaps the lives of close friends, and that Hobson's choices will be his daily diet until he cracks, becomes hardened and detached, or simply suffers mentally as his wounded soldiers suffer physically. To experience these things, and never be able to forget them, is quite another thing. Nothing can condition a commander to their reality but battle itself.

Consequently a leaven of Mediterranean veterans was injected into units as well as staffs. George Kitching, recently the commander of the Eleventh Infantry Brigade in the Fifth Armoured Division, whom Simonds had asked for as his BGS, went instead to command the Fourth Armoured Division in place of General Worthington, a veteran Canadian tank soldier. Worthington was considered too old for divisional command, although not too old to serve his country further. Lieutenant Colonel Booth came back to command the armoured brigade of the Fourth Armoured Division and Jefferson replaced Rodger in command of the infantry brigade. These were a few of the command changes.

The Italian veterans' contribution in the weeks before Overlord came too late to change tactical ideas or to introduce new equipment. Simonds's purpose was to express, in general directives, the experience of the Eighth Army at that time. As a matter of course, he spent time meeting and assessing his divisions, brigades, and units. But his main concern was to improve the performance of his own headquarters — its procedures, communications, standard layout in the field, the speed with which it moved from position to position, and its staff duties. In short, it had to learn how to operate for twenty-four hours in the day economically and without exhausting its personnel. As a result of simplifying and improving staff drills, orders were passed with less paper. At Simonds's first conference on February 22 he made it clear that he would *command* and that the staff would enable him to do it by acting as his *staff.* By March 4 Rodger noted: "The coolness towards him is fast wearing off as they realise his ability and competence for his command." On April 11, after Montgomery's presentation at Saint Paul's School, Simonds gave verbal orders, which Rodger described as "a masterpiece of clarity: and Bob Moncel and I see why no written confirmations of his orders are necessary."[5]

The impression that Simonds made on a party of Canadian editors at this time was recorded in the *Winnipeg Free Press* on August 14. The interview took place in early February when Simonds was still "on the secret list." The editors were whirled to corps headquarters deep in the countryside by roads from which all signposts had been removed. Most of the questions were about Italy, and Simonds praised the performance of his German opponents, saying that they would make the next phase just as tough:

What remains the outstanding impression of the interview was the general's modesty and self-possession. He sat on a low bench in front of a fireplace and dealt with each question in turn simply and clearly.

When he did not know the answer he said so. More remarkable was his assumption that he could speak freely and in confidence and his answers were not larded with solemn injunctions that this or that was not to be repeated. . . . This composure is a quality to be envied. It is hard to imagine General Simonds losing his head, just as it is easy to imagine that he will instil into the men under his command great confidence in the sanity and self-control of their Corps commander.[6]

Unlike many commanders who were better staff officers than commanders, he allowed his selected staff to get on with the job, and if they did not satisfy, he sacked them. Elliot Rodger and Fin Clark were key men in the retraining of the headquarters. Fin Clark was closely involved as "chief communicator." They both found that Simonds backed them up in straightening out procedures, some of which Clark would have liked to have tackled earlier. Simonds did not try to do their job for them, nor was he disinterested, extremes that were not uncommon in commanders. As for Matthews, Walsh, and Knight, they had served with Simonds, knew what he wanted, and discerned what was needed. Without disturbing the incumbents unnecessarily they saw to the training of artillery, engineers and the supply staffs to suit the role the corps had been given in Overlord. That included assault crossings of rivers to the east of the bridge-head, including the Seine, and the supply and artillery support of a breakout and advance.

A general weakness in the preparation of the Second British and First Canadian Armies for Overlord was that in the final six months too much attention was paid to the amphibious assault phase and too little to the dogfight and breakout phases that would follow. In explaining this omission it must be pointed out that by far the most difficult part of Overlord was thought to be the assault. Once safely ashore and with the bridgehead staked out in the first few days, it was not expected that the rest required special training. Follow-up divisions were not indoctrinated in the demands of grinding battles, described by Field Marshal Lord Wavell as "mobile battle at the halt," nor in the means to avoid them by persistent infiltration.

The avoidance of stalemate brings us back to the subject of cooperative tactics between infantry, tanks, and artillery, which is very difficult to practise realistically in training. At the time of Simonds's departure from Italy the Seventh was the only British armoured division in the Eighth Army that had been employed in the desert. The First Canadian Armoured Brigade had worked successfully with the First Canadian Division and with the Seventy-eighth British Infantry

Division at Termoli. However, the experience of the tank brigade had not been institutionalized and the Seventh Armoured Division was still fighting as a lorried infantry brigade and an armoured brigade, which did not encourage close cooperation between infantry and armour at all levels from armoured regiment and infantry battalion downwards through squadron/company and troop/platoon. It was not until after Operation Diadem (the battle in the Liri Valley for Rome) in May 1944 that permanent groupings of the same regiments and battalions began in Italy, and the experience did not fully mature in the Fifth Armoured Division until Operation Olive (the battle for the Gothic Line on the east coast) in late August and September 1944. (The First British Armoured Division still fought in separate brigades in the autumn of 1944, when it was broken up.) In June and much of July 1944 the armoured divisions in Normandy were still operating in separate brigades, and they seem to have found their way subsequently to what, by then, had become the normal way of operating in Italy — in four groups each of an infantry battalion and an armoured regiment or in ad hoc infantry/tank groupings — without guidance from above in the form of *Lessons from Theatres of War* or some other policy circular.

It is not surprising, therefore, that when the Fourth Armoured Division went into action for the first time in Operation Totalize, it was still fighting as two brigades, one predominantly infantry and the other armoured, their roles respectively infantry and armoured. Later, the roles and composition of the brigades of an armoured division were interchangeable. In general the Second Independent Armoured Brigade was reserved for fighting with infantry in separate units; it never fought as a whole brigade. However, although infantry divisions normally fought in more enclosed country than armoured divisions, and the tanks of the Second Armoured Brigade were less exposed to the long range of German guns, in open country they were at the same disadvantage from German tanks and antitank guns. In order to avoid antitank fire the Shermans of the Second and Fourth Armoured Brigades had to choose routes to their objectives separate from infantry companies, which often followed straight barrage lines and moved much slower than they did. Both faced the staff college problem of 1936-37 of how to coordinate the movement of infantry and tanks moving at different speeds on different routes and preferring different terrain. Simonds's solution in 1938 had been to base the attack on the tanks, but the problem of getting the infantry forward quickly was unsolved until Totalize introduced the armoured personnel carrier (APC) to the Canadian and British armies.

Simonds's APC idea certainly stemmed from his prewar conception of the problem, but it was the infantry's bitter experience in Operation Spring that taught him that the solution was to carry them forward in APCs. And it was the tanks' casualties that persuaded him to use them at night for protection against antitank guns. General O'Connor, hero of the victory over the Italians in 1940-41 and commander of the Eighth Corps in Goodwood, had considered the same solution then. The idea was not revolutionary, of course, for the Americans had some integral armoured infantry carried forward in half-tracks, and so had the Germans. The single, so-called motor battalion in Canadian armoured divisions, although not as well protected, was intended to serve the same purpose. Simonds advanced the conception of armoured infantry a stage further in Totalize.

10

A Mammoth Canvas

A T NOON ON JUNE **29, 1944**, the tactical headquarters of Simonds's Second Canadian Corps opened at Camilly. Crerar's headquarters was down the road at Amblie, while Montgomery's was at Creully in the same area. Montgomery's tactical plan had been modified. At that moment the First U.S. Army faced only six German infantry divisions and one battle group of the Second Panzer Division on a fifty-five-mile front; the Second Army's thirty-three miles absorbed seven and a half panzer and six infantry divisions. That part of Montgomery's plan was working. However, Caen had not been taken in the first days and was still holding out. So the Second Army was directed to fight through the city and beyond and, by continuing to hold a disproportionate weight of German divisions opposite them, enable the Americans to reorganize after capturing Cherbourg, and then to seize Saint-Lô and break out in the west.[1]

Crerar was told that his First Army headquarters was not at present required in the line.[2] Operation Axehead, the advance to the Seine and beyond, for which the First Army had prepared, was cancelled. Instead the Canadian Second Corps was to join the Second Army in the Caen sector with the Eighth Corps on its left and the First Corps on its right. As infantry casualties had been heavy and armour had not been performing well, the Second Infantry Division would come over at once and the Fourth Armoured Division would remain in Britain a little longer.[3] By July 9 the Second Division and the Second Canadian Army Group Royal Artillery had arrived and were near Ryes, four miles northeast of Bayeux. The Third Infantry Division and the Second Armoured Brigade would join the Second Corps as soon as Caen was cleared to the Orne River. Simonds's task was then to cross the Orne and clear the city's industrial suburbs with his left and the Orne Valley south and southwest of the city with his right.

While all this was being decided Crerar sent his private Anson aircraft to fetch Simonds and Rodger from West Hampnett near Portsmouth on June 25. He briefed them on their arrival at Amblie. On the decision not to commit First Army headquarters Rodger commented in his diary:

> To what extent political or constitutional reasons have or should enter I do not know. It is a position several rungs down the ladder from that which Gen. McN had in mind when he conceived and gave birth to and brought up to at least adolescence our First Canadian Army of five divisions and two armoured brigades. Crerar will see that Canada is "done right by" as far as is humanly possible.[4]

On the morning of the twenty-sixth Simonds talked first to Montgomery and then to Dempsey about his task. Rodger glimpsed Dempsey as he drove forward in his jeep after the meeting, "wearing raincoat and red hat. Nonchalant considering his big battle to turn Caen had started with 675 guns."

Lieutenant Colonel Bob Moncel remained in Normandy as Simonds's operations officer while Rodger returned to Dover to bring over the corps staff, which broke camp and moved to Tilbury on the night of July 1. For the trip to Normandy the personnel were divided between a British Liberty ship, the *Samnesse*, and an American one, the *John A. Sutter*. The former was clean and well run; the latter left much to be desired, and Walsh had occasion to "sort out" one or two members of the crew who he felt were not working for "our" side. The convoy sailed on the evening of the fourth and unloaded off Arromanches on the morning of the sixth. The staff moved to Camilly and was operational at 1500 hours on the eleventh. That night Brigadier Sherwood Lett's Fourth Brigade of Major General Charles Foulkes's Second Division moved into the line to relieve elements of the tired Third Division.

In the meantime Simonds had visited several headquarters and been briefed on the lessons they had learned so far. In a memorandum to all units on July 1 he pointed out that the effect of bombardments was ninety percent moral and designed to neutralize the enemy for a short time only. It was essential to close with the enemy before their effect wore off. This could only be done if advancing infantry "leaned on" the covering fire, even at the risk of casualties from their own artillery. The essence of German defence was the immediate counterattack. To lessen their chance of success it was essential that captured positions be quickly and thoroughly searched and the defenders killed or captured. The position had to be prepared for defence while patrols went forward to find the enemy, exploit the situation, and warn of counterattacks.

Tanks and antitank guns played a vital role in this procedure. The initial phase of an attack should aim at a penetration of four thousand yards so as to displace the enemy's mortar positions, which played an important part in his counterattacks. On the way to the objective troops should move steadily forward and not stop to fire, since it had proved very difficult to restore their momentum once they lay down. The objective should be a defensible position, but patrols should always work beyond it to locate the enemy and break up his counterattacks.

A remark of Simonds's that "nothing is more dangerous than to sit down in front of the Boche and not know what he is up to" must have been heard by every soldier in training many times. His other points were undoubtedly as familiar to trained units as they were difficult to put into effect. Simonds did not mention here that the start line of an attack had to be regarded as the first objective, thoroughly cleared and covered by two- or three-man posts to deter infiltration. Failure to do so caused trouble to the corps in its first battles, but the remedy was difficult to apply in Operation Atlantic in the built-up areas of industrial Caen, or in the darkness favoured by infantry attacking in the open country just south of it in Operation Spring.[5]

The author will not immerse the reader in the fate of individual battalions of the Second and Third Divisions and the Second Armoured Brigade and later of the Fourth Armoured Division in the four tough battles fought by Simonds in Normandy. Veterans of the first two, Atlantic, which cleared the southern part of Caen, pushed up the river Orne towards Saint-André-sur-Orne, and climbed the open slopes south of Caen to Ifs and beyond, and Spring, in which an attempt was made to extend the advance by seizing villages on and behind Verrières Ridge and Tilly-la-Campagne beyond Bourguebus, will remember neither battle with much satisfaction. Casualties were heavy among the infantry, well over twelve hundred in Spring, and the Royal Highlanders of Canada, the Black Watch, was virtually destroyed in the open terrain outside May-sur-Orne.

After the Germans were pushed out of the industrial suburbs of Caen south of the Orne in Atlantic, the pivot of their position was the twin villages of Saint-André-sur-Orne and Saint-Martin-de-Fontenay on their left, with May-sur-Orne as the backup. That triangle of villages was the strongest part of the German line. Its left flank was covered from German positions on high ground above the west bank of the Orne. As well, the Germans could infiltrate back into their positions after they were overrun through mine shafts with exits behind the British forward positions.[6]

Major General Foulkes's operations were dominated by his Second Division's failure to take this position as an anchor for the corps's right wing on the Orne. In their battle his battalions suffered not only from the twin disadvantages described but also from their commanders' tactical mistakes. In the centre of Foulkes's front an open convex swelling — Verrières Ridge, with the village of that name on its eastern side — invited a British armoured thrust, but its western flanks were covered from the "German Triangle" and its rear by the villages of Fontenay-le-Marmion and Roquancourt that lay hull-down to the south. Then, on the German right, ran the straight road from Caen to Falaise, the chosen axis of the Twenty-first Army Group's thrust towards Falaise and beyond. It rose in steps to Cintheaux from which the Germans overlooked the Spring battlefield and the British rear back to Caen. The ridge on which lay Bourguebus and Tilly-la-Campagne, east of the road and in the Third Division zone, was slightly higher than the road itself and had been the objective of the Eighth Corps in Goodwood, the battle that was occurring while the Canadians fought through the suburbs of Caen in Atlantic.

Bourguebus had been the high watermark of Goodwood, and when that battle was over, the Seventh Armoured and Guards Armoured Division, two of the divisions engaged, were given to Simonds for Spring to be used as a breakthrough corps if the opportunity offered. The Second Corps took over from the Eighth Corps the villages of Bras, Hubert-Folie, and Bourguebus from which they faced Germans in Tilly, Verrières, and Saint-Martin/Saint-André. The front line when the battle started in the early morning of July 25 was roughly along the road from Bourguebus on the Canadian left to Saint-André on the right. The line had advanced only marginally by the end of the battle.

The objective of Spring was the high ground on either side of the Caen-Falaise road about the crossroads west of Cramesnil. It was required as the springboard for a drive to Falaise in a potential double envelopment of the German divisions withdrawing from an American breakthrough in the west. Air support was declared to be a bonus for Spring, since most of it was going west to the Americans.

Some of the general tactical weaknesses of the Third Division and the Second Armoured Brigade, both experienced but tired formations, and the green Second Division and the Fourth Armoured, have been mentioned. None of the four divisional commanders, including Major General Maczec of the Polish Division, which joined the corps for the later battles, may be said to have directed their tactical battles sensitively. The crux of their difficulties was that they neither demanded, sought for themselves, nor received accurate and timely information on which to conduct their battles. In Spring Foulkes's brigades attacked with single battalions usually inadequately supported by armour, antitank guns, and other infantry; several were halted and attacked in the open by German tanks or were cut off without tank or antitank support on or near their objectives.

An extract from the historian's report on how the Black Watch, the Royal Highlanders of Canada (RHC), was destroyed illustrates both points. The historian explains that success in the centre, where Verrières had been taken by the Royal Hamilton Light Infantry (RHLI) of the Fourth Brigade under Lieutenant Colonel Rockingham in a model tank-infantry and antitank operation, made exploitation to take Roquancourt and the release of the Seventh Armoured Division seem imminent. It appeared necessary, the historian tells us, to protect the right flank of this centre attack by clearing May-sur-Orne and Fontenay-le-Marmion quickly. The Black Watch, directed on the latter by swinging left from Saint-Martin across the open western slopes of Verrières Ridge, was attacked from May on its right, which proved to be strongly held, and from the rear, where even Saint-Martin-de-Fontenay had not been cleared:

> At 0647 hours, H.Q. 5 Cdn Inf Bde gave the order by wireless: "Push on now: speed essential." Half an hour later Brigadier Megill ordered the battalion [the Black Watch] to open the attack on Fontenay-le-Marmion. As far as could be known at the time, it was reasonable to assume that Calgary Highlanders were sufficiently far forward to ensure that RHC's right flank would not be badly exposed. But accuracy of some of the reports received from the front and the confusion existing on both the right and left flanks were misleading. Thus, at 0715, it could appear at Lt-Gen Simonds' Tactical Headquarters that progress was generally "slow but steady," that the Calgary Highlanders were fighting in May-sur-Orne, completing the first

phase, and that on the left 9 Cdn Inf Bde was firmly holding Tilly-la-Campagne, although some mopping up remained to be done. On the ground, however, neither situation was so favourable.[7]

The RHC tragedy bears the marks of commanders who had not viewed the ground and had not gone forward to consult the battalion and company commanders before ordering an attack from the map. There were other marginally less tragic affairs in Spring that demonstrated the detachment of divisional and brigade commanders from tactical reality. Nevertheless, the account of the loss of the Black Watch by the minister of defence in 1946, while hardly mitigating this stark criticism, explains how it happened in terms of radios destroyed, commanding officers and company commanders killed, start lines infiltrated and under direct machine gun fire, and wishful thinking in the face of silence from units that had disappeared into the smoke and noise.[8]

The corps commander could not intervene directly in the muddle in the Second Division, where Saint-André was still not cleared, or in the Third Division, where Major General R. F. L. Keller performed no more surely than Foulkes. Tilly was lost by the Third Division and Verrières held by the Second Division, although under continual counterattack, thanks to tank support from the Seventh Armoured Division. One of the corps commander's functions was to decide where and when to commit his reserve, the two armoured divisions, to take the high ground around Cramesnil-Cintheaux. For two reasons Simonds declined to do more than commit the leading brigade group of the Seventh Armoured to support the Fourth Infantry Brigade in the centre during the forenoon of July 25. First, the Germans had been substantially reinforced and even the armour's start line would not have been secure. Second, the object of the battle, to draw German armoured divisions to his front while General Omar Bradley was remounting an attack in the west, had been achieved, even if the tactical objectives on the high ground had not. So, on the afternoon of the twenty-fifth, Simonds advised General Dempsey that pressing the attack towards the main objective would be useless. Dempsey agreed because Bradley's attack was under way and going well and he wanted to shift the armour of the Eighth Corps to the Caumont front to relieve American divisions of the Fifth U.S. Corps that Bradley required in his offensive.

The failure of Spring to make territorial gains was not a surprise, but Simonds was dissatisfied with the performance of some of his commanders, although he recognized that the tasks he had given them were difficult. On January 31, 1946, in his report of the attack of the Black Watch he wrote: "I considered at the time (and I have found no evidence since to change my view) that the objectives of May-sur-Orne and Tilly-la-Campagne were attainable, but in the event, the casualties of certain units were excessive. That we failed to capture and hold May-sur-Orne and Tilly-la-Campagne and . . . suffered . . . excessive casualties was due to a series of mistakes and errors of judgment in minor tactics."[9] Simonds then listed some of these errors: insecure start lines, failure to follow artillery support fire closely, unthorough mopping up, and lack of success in establishing a firm base to withstand counterattacks.

All of these points reflected on his divisional commanders, and Simonds was of two minds whether to sack Foulkes for the way he had handled his division. Dempsey and Crocker, under whom Keller had fought in the First Corps, were already unimpressed with the commander of the Third Division. Crerar had written to Keller about the sloppy appearance and attitude of many of his soldiers.[10] They had acquired an unenviable reputation for vandalism and looting, carried on under the cover of searching for snipers, and were, in Crerar's opinion, lowering the high standard expected of Canadians. They seemed to think they were owed a rest as veterans, an attitude that probably stemmed from Keller himself, who complained that under Crocker it had been all work and no praise.

Crocker reported that he found Keller jumpy after the landings and that his overcaution had spread to many of his units. He seemed to have lost his grip on the division and his staff were carrying him. In May 1943, when visiting Keller's division in the United Kingdom, Crerar had warned Keller that a senior British officer had shown him a letter from another senior officer "to the effect that it was too bad that Keller, who was an excellent commander, drank too much and made an objectionable fool of himself on social occasions." The adverse comments of Crocker and Dempsey were passed on to Simonds, but he was naturally reluctant to remove divisional commanders until he could make up his own mind after he commanded them in action. In his reply to Dempsey concerning Keller on July 27 he wrote:

The division has had some 5,500 casualties since D-day . . . the greater proportion of this number has been borne by the infantry and mostly in the strengths of rifle companies. The wastage and the fact that the division has been unable to get out of the line and re-organize properly has resulted in a deterioration of its fighting efficiency quite

The future general: Gentleman Cadet Guy Granville Simonds at the Royal Military College, Kingston, in 1924. (ROYAL MILITARY COLLEGE)

The well-dressed battery officer. Simonds as a subaltern in C Battery, Winnipeg, 1930. (DEPARTMENT OF NATIONAL DEFENCE)

Taylor family gathering, 1939: Sydney and Geraldine Stephens *(left)*, Beatrice Taylor, Ruth Taylor, Ruth Simonds, Guy Simonds, Katherine ("K") Taylor Simonds, Charles Simonds, and Charles Taylor.

K, Ruth, and Charles in the Taylors' Winnipeg garden at the beginning of World War II.

Simonds as GSO II, First Canadian Infantry Division, shaking hands with King George VI, 1940. (Department of National Defence)

Simonds *(left)*, with Generals Alan Brooke and Andrew McNaughton at the Canadian Junior War Staff Course in 1941. (Department of National Defence)

Lieutenant Colonel Simonds, CO of the First Field Regiment, Royal Canadian Horse Artillery, makes a point with a subordinate. (DEPARTMENT OF NATIONAL DEFENCE)

Brigadier Simonds watches his First Infantry Brigade march past, 1942.
(DEPARTMENT OF NATIONAL DEFENCE)

Invasion of Sicily: on board HMS *Hilary*, July 1943. Major General Simonds *(second from left)*, Admiral Philip Vian, and Lieutenant Colonel George Kitching.
(DEPARTMENT OF NATIONAL DEFENCE)

General Bernard Law Montgomery *(left)* and Simonds having a map conference under the olive trees in Sicily. (DEPARTMENT OF NATIONAL DEFENCE)

Off to war: Private Jack Bernard of the British Columbia Regiment says goodbye to his five-year-old son Warren in 1940 in New Westminster. Private Bernard would not see his family again for five years.
(NATIONAL ARCHIVES OF CANADA)

A First Brigade infantryman prepares to send a hand grenade into a sniper's hideout, Campochiaro, October 23, 1943.
(NATIONAL ARCHIVES OF CANADA)

King George VI inspects the Second Medium Regiment of the Royal Canadian Artillery in Italy, June 1944. (NATIONAL ARCHIVES OF CANADA)

A meeting of minds: General Montgomery *(left)*, Prime Minister William Lyon Mackenzie King, and General Crerar.
(DEPARTMENT OF NATIONAL DEFENCE)

Minister of Defence James Layton Ralston *(centre)* in the United Kingdom in October 1944, shortly before he resigned from the Cabinet. On the left is his son Stuart; on the right, Elliot Rodger. (DEPARTMENT OF NATIONAL DEFENCE)

A brief moment of levity in a grim undertaking: Churchill's visit to the front, December 1944. Alan Brooke *(left)*, Harry Crerar, the prime minister, Guy Simonds, Bernard Montgomery. (DEPARTMENT OF NATIONAL DEFENCE)

Hard decisions: Simonds *(left)* and Montgomery walk down a road in Italy. (Department of National Defence)

General Simonds receiving the Companion of the Order of the Bath from King George VI in 1944. (Department of National Defence)

Simonds looks out on the Etna Massif in Sicily. (Department of National Defence)

out of proportion to the actual losses themselves. Many sections and platoons are "sub-units" in name only. Losses among junior leaders have been heavy and sub-units lack the cohesion in battle characteristic of a trained battle team — the men hardly know one another or junior leaders their men and men their leaders. . . . Unit commanders and brigadiers are apprehensive about operations not through fear of becoming casualties themselves or of having casualties, but because they feel their units are unfitted in their present state of training to put up a good show.

Simonds concluded his letter:

I therefore consider that the individual qualities of Major-General Keller are unimportant at the moment in comparison with the bigger problem of maintaining the morale of 3 Canadian Division. The division has been under my command for sixteen days. In that time I have formed the impression that General Keller has not appreciated the vital importance of the moral aspects of higher command and the absolute necessity for the commander being a stabilizing influence in the give and take of active operations. . . . If I find, after considered evidence and judgment, that he is unfitted to the high responsibilities of the command of a Canadian division, I will at once recommend his removal.[11]

Ben Cunningham, a militia officer who commanded the Ninth Infantry Brigade in Keller's division, had received an adverse report from his commander earlier, and Simonds invited him for the night to talk things over. Cunningham told Simonds that he had not had the support and guidance he felt he deserved from Keller, and Simonds decided to leave his case in abeyance, too. However, after Spring he and the CO of the North Novas, Lieutenant Colonel Petch, following a board of inquiry on July 29, were relieved for their handling of the Tilly battle.[12] Lieutenant Colonel G. H. Christiansen, CO of the Stormont, Dundas, and Glengarry Highlanders, ordered to attack at Tilly to restore the situation after the North Novas under Petch failed, complained in writing to Keller that he had lost confidence "in . . . leadership and command that kept every unit . . . in action continuously in spite of severe casualties, and culminated in the launching of several worn-out and disorganized men . . . into the attack on Tilly-la-Campagne on July 25, 1944 . . . when it was apparent that the North Novas could be written off." And he added, "Under the above circumstances, or similar ones, I would have, and will, refuse to put the SD & G Highlanders in."

On receiving an adverse report on Christiansen from Keller, Simonds lamented that Christiansen "had the impression that battles can be fought on a 'limited liability' basis,"[13] and had him repatriated to Canada. As for Foulkes, Simonds spared him, for he could hardly give Keller a second chance and not Foulkes. But Simonds had spent the whole morning of July 25 at the Second Division command post in the basement of the distillery in Fleury-sur-Orne and had been dissatisfied with Foulkes's handling of his battle. In particular Foulkes had allowed Megill's Fifth and Young's Sixth Brigades to get in such a muddle that coordinated action was impossible.[14] Nevertheless, Simonds had persevered in the attempt on his right and centre to take Roquancourt and Fonteney-le-Marmion until late in the afternoon, long after he agreed with Dempsey to give up seizing his deeper objectives. And, in the opinion of John English, he could have done more to coordinate the Twelfth Corps's activities against the German positions west of the Orne to relieve the Second Division of some of the flanking fire. As to sacking Foulkes:

> One of the things "uppermost in . . . [his] mind on that day . . . [was to] get rid of General Charles Foulkes." For reasons possibly dating back to Atlantic or even before, Simonds had reached the conclusion that . . . [Foulkes] "did not have the right qualities to command . . . 2nd Division." On at least "three occasions," recalled Major-General Kitching, "Simonds confided in me that he was going to get rid of . . . Foulkes." But Simonds never would get rid of Foulkes. Protected by Crerar, he went on to command 1 Canadian Corps in Italy, replacing the dismissed Lieutenant-General E. L. M. Burns on 10 November. Indeed, through the continued patronage of Crerar, Foulkes was eventually chosen to head the Canadian Army [as CGS] before Simonds.[15]

Spring was the bloodiest single day for Canadian arms except Dieppe. A holding operation, which Spring was without any doubt, is thankless, for there is usually no compensatory gain in territory. However, the pill was sugared by Spring being represented as a holding operation with a chance of gaining the high ground around Cintheaux. There was but a slim chance of that when the Germans reinforced the sector from west of the Orne and the armoured brigades of the armoured divisions were not fully committed to help the infantry. For the outcome the commanders must take most of the blame, and their number must include Simonds himself. If Tilly was such an important objective, it was curious that Simonds permitted Keller's divisional attack to lead off with a single battalion when the experience of the division was that against broader fronts the Germans were unable to concentrate their counterattacks.

Foulkes attacked on a two-brigade front, but each brigade was in-depth. Units in-depth and on narrow fronts seemed to Simonds to offer greater penetration. What he did not appreciate was the muddle that would occur when units passed through each other while a battle was under way with German tanks milling about. Then it was a recipe for chaos. Furthermore, the Second Armoured Brigade was insufficient to support two divisions. There was plenty of spare armour, even if the integrity of the two armoured divisions earmarked for the breakthrough was held to be necessary. Dempsey's explanation of the way that he fought Goodwood emphasizes that infantry was in short supply and armour in abundance.[16]

When the Americans broke out on the Saint-Lô front, the Germans moved divisions westwards to close the breach, weakening their front opposite the Second Corps. The Fourth Canadian Armoured Division, Fourth British Armoured Brigade, Fifty-first Highland Division, Polish Armoured Division, and Thirty-third British Armoured Brigade joined the Second Corps for the next battle, Totalize, for which the corps came under command of the First Canadian Army. In the interval between Spring and Totalize Tilly was attacked again unsuccessfully. When a fifth attack failed on August 5, Montgomery signalled Simonds: "Congratulations, you've been kicked out of Tilly again." He meant that the corps was still "writing down" German units east of the Orne, but the ratio of loss was against the Canadians.

Simonds was determined to exercise more control over his subordinates in Totalize than he had in Spring. Totalize was designed to break through the German front, and he planned innovations to achieve it. To handicap the long range of German antitank guns he would use smoke or attack in darkness. To ensure that the infantry accompanied armour through the defences he mounted them in "defrocked Priests" — self-propelled 105 mm gun howitzer chassis with their guns removed — to carry them safely through fire belts of mortars and machine guns. Priests would provide tactical surprise as to method. To maintain the momentum of the attack he would use heavy bombers on the flanks of the leading troops as they "infiltrated through the [antitank] screen in bad visibility," and then medium bombers during the time that guns were moving forward to resume support of the advance.[17]

Montgomery ordered the attack for no later than August 8, the day of the Canadians' great victory in front of Amiens in 1918. The troops available were three infantry divisions, the Second and Third Canadian and the Fifty-first Highland; two armoured divisions, the Fourth Canadian and the Polish; two armoured brigades, the Second Canadian and Thirty-third British; and two AGRAs and troops from the Seventy-ninth Armoured Division (known as the "Funnies" because of the variety of its armoured vehicles for filling in ditches, detonating mines, and destroying pillboxes).[18] The general idea was to concentrate armour and Priests in the centre, using darkness to confuse the enemy armour and guns. Behind came marching infantry to mop up the villages bypassed by the armour and accompanying motorized infantry. A test, which satisfied Bomber Command's master bombers, was carried out in front of the First Corps with twenty-five-pounder red- and green-coloured smoke to mark targets. The model for Simonds's plan was the El Hamma advance of the Second (NZ) Division and the Eighth Armoured Brigade in April 1943. Behind a rapidly moving, thin barrage, a cab rank of Kittyhawk bombers overhead, the armour had moved without losing direction through dust and smoke that confused the enemy guns and tanks.[19]

Crerar later claimed to have laid down the principle of "Totalizor" (sic) in his directive of July 22, Simonds's innovation being the use of bombers and the Priests. But he was surely correct when he observed that the "idea . . . was far too prevalent that, without a colossal scale of artillery, or air support, continued advance of the infantry [was] impossible."[20] Of Crerar Montgomery unkindly observed that he was "desperately anxious" about fighting his first battle and seemed to have gained the idea "that all you want is a good initial fire plan, and then the Germans all run away!" He still had not realized, Montgomery continued, that "battles seldom go completely as planned."[21] The innovation was the use of armour at night. Elliot Rodger comments:

> I well recall his O Group before Totalize when the several div comds sat in a circle under the pine trees (all being much older than GGS and some with desert sand in their ears) to whom he opened, "Gentlemen, we will do this attack at night with armour." Their jaws dropped noticeably. Prior to then I believe that not I nor any of the Corps HQ Brigs knew of this plan. Perhaps he had some prior discussion with Clark (CSO) on the considerable plans needed to help the tanks and defrocked priests keep direction in the dark. But the whole plan poured forth complete and crystal clear.[22]

Of course, Simonds's RCEME staff was already at work removing guns from the SP 105 mm Priests and searching the beaches for armour plate with which to cover the apertures. And, as Rodger notes, Clark had been put to work on various devices to help the tanks keep direction. The radical element in the plan, though, was the idea of using tanks at night, let alone en masse. Tanks were used to harbouring at night and, no doubt, jaws dropped because that practice was being discarded.

Simonds was ill served by army intelligence, which was confused by the frequent moves of German divisions and their reduction to fighting groups of a single division appearing simultaneously on different fronts. As a result, Simonds overestimated German capacity. He was led to believe that the German second defence line would be tough to crack, for the Germans habitually kept their better troops in the second line from which they emerged to counterattack. For that phase of his attack Simonds retained heavy bombers of the U.S. Air Force to plaster the line in the fashion of Bradley's Cobra breakthrough.

On August 6, two days before Totalize was to open on the night of the eighth, Simonds learned that the enemy had withdrawn the First SS and Twelfth SS Panzer Divisions from his front line and replaced them with the untried Eighty-ninth and 272nd Infantries which, having been astride the Falaise road, were sidestepped to the east. Expecting that the SS divisions had both moved into the second line from about Bretteville-sur-Laize to Saint-Sylvain, he decided to exploit the numbing effect of the strategic bombing of the German second line by combining the second and third phases of the attack, namely, the break into and the subsequent breakout and advance through and beyond the second line. The weakness of the German first line led Simonds to try to maintain the momentum of the attack by ordering the infantry divisions in the first phase to be more aggressive, since the resistance of the Eighty-ninth German Infantry would be slight, and by launching the second phase on a *broader* front than at first intended. Simonds communicated this change of plan to Crerar:

> The probable thickening up of SS troops on the Bretteville-sur-Laize St-Sylvain position necessitates a widening of the frontage and increase in the weight of the attack in the second phase. It has, therefore, been decided to launch the Polish Armd Div simultaneously and parallel with 4 Cdn Armd Div and to direct these two divisions straight to their final objectives at phase three.[23]

The implications of the change were important. Parts of two infantry divisions, each with an armoured brigade, would advance rapidly through the forward German defences in Priests, leaving marching infantry to follow and capture the villages familiar from the Spring battle. This first phase of the battle was now believed to be less difficult than phase two against the second line. Then *two* armoured divisions (the Poles having originally been intended to enter the battle only in phase three), each weaker than an infantry division supported by an armoured brigade, would have to wait for the bombing before attacking the second line. They would be followed by the Third Canadian Infantry to mop up, just as the marching infantry of the Fifty-first Highland and Second Canadian had mopped up in phase one. The intention was that the armoured divisions would bypass resistance and press through to Falaise.

So far so good. But there were clouds on the horizon from the start. Necessarily the timing of the heavy strategic bombers had to be prearranged and could not be expected to be tailored at the last minute to the needs of the tactical situation, as could tactical air support. The bombing was to begin at 1226 hours on D plus 1 and end at 1335 hours when the armoured advance would start. The only flexibility possible in arrangements with the air force was to cancel the bombing if the armour could break into the second line "on the run," but that was a risk and the First Army considered it politically unwise after the difficulty in persuading the strategic air forces to operate in support of the ground forces at all. The second potential weakness in the plan was, despite Simonds's stated intention for a broader attack, the narrowness of the front, which allowed each armoured division one thousand yards and at one point only eight hundred yards. They needed more room for tactical manoeuvre, whether to avoid unexpected obstacles, which would cause bottlenecks, or enemy positions. The two-divisional advance made the inner boundaries particularly constrictive. This factor and the point about the bombing were put to Simonds by Major Generals Kitching and Maczec, but Simonds overruled them, perhaps because neither was an experienced armoured commander and Simonds preferred narrow fronts. In this case he believed that the cohesion of his armoured punch would be better maintained on a narrow front. The Cobra bombing on the American front had been decisive, and if the armoured divisions exploited the Totalize bombing swiftly, it would be worth waiting for.

On the morning of August 7 Simonds learned that elements of both SS panzer divisions were moving west to counter the advance of the Twelfth Corps, which had forced the Orne River on a three-mile front just north of Thury Harcourt on the sixth. Therefore, Totalize was advanced to 2300 hours that night, the seventh, when the bombing for phase one began, followed by the advance of the armour with seventy-two Priests and sixty M-14 half-tracks. Bofors guns fired down the axes to help the armour and Priests to keep direction. Searchlights near Ifs opened up at three degrees to illuminate the scene, but despite the moon, which rose soon after, a ground mist made movement difficult.

Smoke, fog, and dust caused chaos in parts of the armoured advance, but even so the first phase went well. Although the mopping up of the villages was only completed after hard fighting by the marching infantry at 1700 hours on the eighth, the forward advance was completed by 0800, leaving a gap of several hours before the bombing for phase two commenced on time. However, the move of the armoured divisions for phase two was delayed by the resistance of the villages, and it is questionable whether they were ready to start phase two much earlier than scheduled, although the forward units of phase one could have advanced beyond the start line had the bombing been cancelled.

With the committal of the armoured divisions, which passed through the Second Canadian and Fifty-first Highland Divisions at about 1345 hours on the eighth, controversy about the battle begins. The first points concern the bombing. On learning that the German divisions in the second line had been thinned out, should the bombing not have been cancelled? Kitching and Maczec proposed it on the seventh. Alternatively, since some armour and infantry were in position to move before the bombing began, should the bombing not have been cancelled on the eighth? Of Simonds's decision English wrote:

> That he should have been overruled is quite clear, but equally clearly it would have taken an army commander with the *coup d'oeil* and stature of a Dempsey or Patton to do it. Crerar simply did not know as much as Simonds, which in effect left the 2 Corps commander without any of the usual counsel, help, and coercion that he might have received from an army headquarters. He could not have been more alone.[24]

Firm bases, flank guards, gun lines, and sticking to a plan were central arches in the tactical buildings that all but a minority of British generals had constructed for themselves by this time. Simonds was from the same pattern. He thought like an infantryman; he worried about his own security before he sought to create and exploit insecurity for the enemy as a good armoured leader should. Not so their German opponents, who sought to create doubt in their enemy even if they could gain only time by doing so. But time was of the essence in this situation, as it is so often in battle. So the Kampfgruppe Krause, withdrawn from the Twelfth Corps front, hastened to Potigny in the neck between the Laison and Laize streams, a potential bottleneck for the armour. Kampfgruppe Waldmüller with two panzer grenadier battalions, one panzer battalion, and the Tenth Tigers under the redoubtable Captain Wittmann, who had destroyed the Seventh Armoured Division's advance against Villers Bocage early in the campaign, penetrated north to attack the high ground south of Saint-Aignan de Cramesnil at 11:30 a.m., even before the phase two bombing started.

English deduces from the Second Corps intelligence summary for the period ending 2000 hours on the eighth that the origin of this armour was unknown to Simonds's staff, and since Simonds was equally badly served by ground patrol intelligence, he was in doubt about the resistance to be expected and erred on the side of caution. The coming bombing plan frustrated any forward movement to obtain intelligence about the enemy for hours before the first bomb was dropped. Furthermore, the Waldmüller attack added to the congestion in the axes of the armoured divisions to the start line, already affected by the fighting in the phase one villages, and constricted the Polish division's advance for the rest of the day. It also brought the Germans within the bomb safety line. They were untouched when the bombs fell, although many other Second Corps units from Vaucelles to Cormelles were hit and sixty-five were killed and 250 wounded, including Major General Rod Keller.

The performance of the armoured divisions after H-hour was disappointing. The armour of Halpenny Force, on the right of the Fourth Armoured Division, lacked a sense of urgency. By nightfall Halpenny was hardly beyond Cintheaux, while the Tenth Infantry Group under Brigadier Jefferson had reached only Hautmesnil. Urged on by Simonds, Kitching ordered the division to press on during the night. Worthington Force was directed on Point 195 but surged ninety degrees off-line and fetched up on Point 140, southeast of Quesnay, where it was surrounded, attacked, and annihilated by Waldmüller, Krause, and Wunsche the next morning. Point 195 was later taken brilliantly and in silence by the Argyll and Sutherland Highlanders under Lieutenant Colonel J. D. Stewart. That marked the limit of the advance by the end of the ninth, a day and a half after phase two started. Quesnay and its wood remained in German hands. Totalize phase two had been a failure.

Of course, it is conjectured that had the armoured attack of phase one rolled on during the morning of August 8, it would have been successful, for the German reinforcements from west of the Orne would not have arrived. However, the Poles would still have been in a muddle, and the Fourth Armoured Brigade would, in all probability, have performed as lackadaisically when they eventually passed through the infantry divisions. In their first performances these two divisions made heavy weather against no more than sixty panzers and tank destroyers.

When that is said, armoured divisions need space for manoeuvre once their original dash has been blocked. That there was potential dash in the Fourth Division is indicated by the Worthington advance in darkness, spoiled by simply failing to read a map and compass correctly. More precisely, the advance of both armoured divisions might have been broadened early on and shifted eastwards. That would have required the intervention of Crerar, which was unlikely, even if he could have communicated with the armour through Simonds and the divisional commanders. The Fourth Armoured was not organized in infantry battalion/armoured regimental groups with artillery reps able to communicate to divisional headquarters, as was the fashion in the more experienced divisions by this time. Instead, the Tenth Infantry Brigade had one squadron of the British Columbia Regiment to support each battalion in a permanent affiliation, and a company of the Lake Superior Motor Battalion supported each of the other regiments of the Fourth Armoured Brigade. The commander of the armoured brigade lost control of his units and fell out of contact with his headquarters. Kitching had trouble reaching him but eventually found him fast asleep in his tank.

On August 11 Montgomery ordered the First Army to capture Falaise "quickly," and Operation Tractable was the result. South of Falaise, Argentan was to be secured by the Twelfth Army Group in order to close the pincers on the Germans by a short envelopment instead of a long one against the Seine as Montgomery preferred. Simonds briefed his subordinate commanders down to unit level on the twelfth and thirteenth. He demanded that they demonstrate more thrust, bypass minor opposition, and advance on wider fronts. That description in a draft of the official history is inadequate to describe how Simonds briefed his commanders. Major General Kitching remembers:

It was a very tough and unpleasant briefing of all armd regt C.O.s and bde comds on 13 Aug. Simonds blasted armoured regiments for their lack of support for infantry — he quoted the heavy infantry casualties of the past month compared to armour. He demanded much greater initiative from armd regts — drive on — get amongst the enemy etc. Forget about harbouring at night — keep driving on. Arrange your resupply accordingly. Don't rely on the infantry to do everything for you! It was a real blast and it shook everyone up. I was upset because apart from the Cdn Gren Gds ops and harbouring on the 8th August I felt our commanders of regiments did not deserve such treatment. Worthington had shown great dash on the night 8/9 and had captured one of the Polish Armd Div's objectives with the BCR and Algonquins . . . but it is important to remember that up to that occasion *none* of our armd regts had had to operate in the dark — it was policy to harbour and refuel etc.[25]

The attack began at 1200 hours on the fourteenth. However, as in Totalize, the start was still like the Grand National with smoke and dust, and when the horses found an unfordable Bechers Brook in front of them in the shape of the Laison River, which headquarters had said was fordable at almost all points, chaos ensued. Tanks bogged down or moved frantically along the river, looking for crossings. This major error delayed the advance for two hours until at least 1430 hours and cost the Second Corps a decisive battle, for Falaise was not reached until the eighteenth.

As if this were not enough, Brigadier Booth was killed on the first day, and it was not until 1900 hours that Lieutenant Colonel Scott was told by Kitching to replace him. Communications broke down, and there was no controlling hand in the Fourth Armoured Brigade for a few vital hours. Since Scott had a broken ankle, he called a halt to operations and was later replaced by Halpenny. A bombing error owing to the use of yellow smoke for the bomb safety line, which according to Bomber Command procedures was a target indicator, caused four hundred Canadian and Polish casualties, particularly in gun areas, and contributed to delays in getting guns forward.

As the fighting continued, the Poles, owing to a map-reading error, found themselves in the neck of the bottle from which the retreating Germans were struggling to escape the trap between the Americans and the Second Corps. The Second Panzer Corps was trying to hold open the passage from the outside, effectively surrounding the Poles. The Canadians then switched southeast towards Trun and Chambois where they met the Americans, who had halted their northern advance at Bradley's command. That unpredictable officer had initiated the envelopment himself, although when it came to the crunch, he was disinclined to help the Poles to dam the flood.

Totalize and Tractable, and the sharp fighting that followed them, completed the near-destruction of the German armies in Normandy. As John English points out, the Canadians had suffered graver casualties in Normandy than the others in the Twenty-first Army Group. There were 18,444 casualties, including 5,021 killed. The Third Division was followed by the Second Division at the top of the casualty list of the Twenty-first Army Group divisions, although the latter did not start fighting until Atlantic. Totalize and Tractable, up to August 21, accounted for 5,679 of the total casualties. In the opinion of English these figures indicate poor commanders, and he mentions Foulkes and Keller, although not Simonds among them. The author agrees that Simonds was not responsible for the high casualties caused by tactical errors, and the introduction of tank fighting at night and of the APC was bound to test the adaptability of inexperienced troops. However, the maintenance of the air plan, indeed the use of heavy bombers at all, was a mistake, for it prevented Simonds from adapting his plan to fresh circumstances and constricted the channel for the advance.

Other commanders were impressed by the novel introduction of Priests in Totalize. General O'Connor signalled his congratulations and said he wished he had had the nerve to try it in Goodwood. He sent a staff officer to find out how it had been done. General Hobart, the inventor of "Funnies," also expressed his pleasure in the experiment. Both considered it a success, for they were less critical than postwar historians blessed with all the facts.

German commanders have been interviewed extensively since 1945. Some have praised their erstwhile opponents; most have implied that if they had had the Allies' advantages in matériel and men, they would have done better. Since the German army became an ally in the cold war, British and American historians, by tending to agree, have downgraded their own side. Moreover, German criticism is blessed with hindsight and cannot, by the nature of the evidence, compare like with like. The Germans did not enjoy offensive successes themselves in the later stages of the war when the defence enjoyed a marked advantage. Nevertheless, the spoiling defence by the thin and exhausted battle groups that faced the Canadians and Poles in Totalize and Tractable excite our admiration and make us question the competence of the attackers. Yet, while the Twelfth SS Panzer Division was as green at the start of the campaign as the Third Canadian, they had veteran officers and NCOs to lead them, and that helped them to avoid making many tactical errors. In particular they anticipated the shape of battles. There were few veterans in the

Second Corps's armour, and the first battles of green formations are seldom scintillating.

The German view of the Canadians is instructive, nonetheless, so it seems useful to end this chapter by presenting the opinion of General Kurt Meyer, commander of the Twelfth SS Panzer Division, which had met the Canadians in battle many times. Had his division been less effective there can be no doubt that ninety percent rather than sixty percent of the Germans in the Falaise Pocket would have been killed or taken prisoner.

Kurt Meyer was imprisoned in Dorchester Penitentiary where he was interviewed on September 3, 1950, by Major James R. Millar, RC Chaplains Service. Later he advised the Canadian Armed Forces on a number of subjects, but on this occasion he commented on "the struggle on the Caen-Falaise road from Aug 7 to 16." First, he made some general comments, among which were the following:

> Every opening phase of a Canadian operation was a complete success and the staff work a mathematical masterpiece. The staff always succeeded in burying the enemy under several thousand tons of explosives and in transforming the defence positions into a cemetery. The Canadian Army never followed up their opening successes to reach a complete victory. Every one of the Canadian attacks lost its push and determination after a few miles. For example, in Totalize after gaining the first objective. British and Canadian planning was absolutely without risk; neither Army employed its armoured strength for which it was created. In both armies the tank was used, more or less, as an infantry support weapon. Armoured warfare is a matter of using given opportunities on the battlefield, therefore the divisional commander belongs in the leading combat group to see for himself, to save precious time, and to make lightning decisions from his moving tank. He, and no one else, must be the driving force of his division. I cannot assume that this principle was executed in "Totalize"; the development of this battle is against any such assumption. The British and Canadian forces executed the operation in an inflexible, time-wasting method. Never once did "speed," as the most powerful weapon of armoured warfare, appear.[26]

Meyer went on to comment on each phase of Totalize and Tractable. With some exaggeration he said that the Eighty-ninth Division was eliminated before the Canadian ground forces moved over the start line. The road to Falaise was undefended and open from midnight August 7 until noon August 8. By midday two battle groups of the Twelfth SS Panzer Division were in the line and moved, as we saw, in a way that avoided the bombing zone for phase two. There followed a gun battle between Tigers and Panthers on one side and Shermans on the other. The former were able to move back to Quesnay where they discovered the Worthington group on the high ground that they themselves had been ordered to occupy. With six Tigers and fifteen Panthers they destroyed every Canadian tank (forty-seven) without loss to themselves. The Shermans were all facing south but were attacked from east and west. The battle of the Falaise Pocket ended with the division having an infantry strength of not over three hundred men, a dozen tanks, four 88s, and two batteries of howitzers.

In his final remarks Meyer said he assumed that the Second Corps was convinced of the existence of a second German defence line that required the bombing attack on August 8 but that the bombing "stopped automatically the fluid movements of the Second and Fourth Canadian Divisions and acted in favour of the German defence." The time lost between dawn and midday on the eighth resulted in:

(a) Organization of the Laison River Defence

(b) Saving of much matériel and manpower of the armoured group "Eberbach"

(c) The rebuilding of the armoured divisions which were, a few months later, the main German forces in the Battle of the Bulge.[27]

Judgements (b) and (c) are harsh in that they place the whole responsibility for failing to close the pocket on the Second Corps. The decision to attempt a short envelopment and the order of Omar Bradley to halt his forces were as significant. No doubt the first deterred Crerar from directing the Second Corps farther east at an earlier stage to confront the German forces outside the pocket. Regarding the delay caused by the bombing, Meyer did not understand that an important imperative in Simonds's retention of the bombing was that from the Twenty-first Army Group downwards, the army had been at pains to acquire RAF support but was still having trouble with the procedures. The Eighty-third Group insisted on vetting all army requirements, and they took so long to do it that, in the words of Brigadier Churchill Mann, Crerar's chief of staff, "The situation as it stands at present makes it quite impossible to expect that there can be any heavy or effective air attacks within a matter of several hours, to say the least, which requires resources beyond those within the capacity of the Tactical Group supporting the army concerned."[28] Cancelling arrangements made after such a laborious procedure would have been a political error and would have mortgaged future air support.

11

Morale and Force Strength

....

IT HAD ALWAYS SEEMED improbable that the Canadian field force of three infantry divisions, two armoured divisions, and two armoured brigades, all volunteers, could be maintained at full strength in combat. High infantry casualties in the intense fighting in Normandy and Italy turned the improbability into impossibility. From high summer of 1944 until the end of the war the standard of training, performance, morale, and force strength of the Canadian Active Service Force suffered from lack of timely reinforcement.

If reinforcement policy in Europe was anyone's responsibility, it was Crerar's. Crerar was not only the First Army commander but also senior Canadian in Europe. If he was dissatisfied with the flow of reinforcements, his proper course was to inform J. L. Ralston, the responsible minister, of Canadian conditions and needs, either through the CGS or directly so that the minister could fight the army's case in the Cabinet. His failure there demonstrated lack of moral fibre. It also suggests that it was staff solidarity in concealing its errors and solidarity with the government of the day that guided his actions rather than responsibility to his men in the field.

It appeared to Simonds that Crerar persistently asserted his rights as senior Canadian against British incursions on them, as had McNaughton, but failed dismally when Canadian action was required. After the war, Simonds said that National Defence HQ (NDHQ) in Ottawa, Canadian Military HQ (CMHQ) in London, and Crerar in the First Army connived with the Liberal government to conceal the truth that the army had run short of trained infantrymen. Simonds and his close subordinates indignantly refuted insinuations that even as acting army commander in Crerar's absence in the fall, when Ralston visited the First Army on a fact-finding mission, he himself did not tell Ralston the truth. Ralston's rough notes on the subject are ambiguous perhaps, but it would have been completely out of character for Simonds to have kept silent. It is clear, moreover, that as corps commander he fulfilled his duty to point out to Crerar the effects of undermanning on unit efficiency and morale.

Crerar's attitude to his responsibility to the minister as senior Canadian and as army commander was the subject of letters to Ralston. Writing from Italy on November 29, 1943, about "a reapportionment of function and responsibility between the GOC-in-C and CMHQ"[1] if he were to become army commander, he said that CMHQ would be a forward extension of NDHQ and a rearward extension of the First Army. "GOC-in-C is consulted by his Government through the Minister in questions affecting his troops. To relieve him of much of the policy work CMHQ must be strengthened." On April 3, 1944, after he returned to Britain as army commander, he added: "The trouble only occurs when NDHQ thinks of CMHQ as exclusively its own forward link or agent and Army [treats CMHQ] as its agent with NDHQ."

Crerar seemed to be saying that CMHQ should not only facilitate direct communication between himself and the CGS and the minister in Ottawa, but make policy, as well. The CGS was not to treat CMHQ as a part of his staff. Then, on May 13, 1944, he wrote to Lieutenant General Stuart, chief of staff at CMHQ: "[I]n the future it will be necessary only to obtain his (the Army Commander's) views and directions in respect of matters directly or indirectly concerned with the field army." This ambiguous instruction seemed to mean that Stuart had to seek Crerar's agreement in all policy matters, since CMHQ's whole purpose was to serve the field army in Europe. Furthermore, CMHQ was Crerar's headquarters when he wore the hat of senior Canadian in Europe.

Finally a directive to Crerar from Ottawa on May 19 instructed him that "your channel of communication on all questions including matters of general policy will be to the Chief of the General Staff through the Chief of Staff at Canadian Military Headquarters, London." The purpose of this directive was to relieve Crerar, about to go into the field, of communications from Ottawa that had no direct policy implications for the First Army, and, no doubt, it merely confirmed an arrangement already agreed to with CGS at NDHQ. It was not intended to remove power and responsibility from Crerar and hand it to Stuart as though he were Crerar's superior.

Henceforward, Stuart acted as Crerar's major general of administration, and CMHQ became the First Army's rear headquarters. Stuart became a filter between Crerar and NDHQ, rightly saving Crerar from administrative chores. Wrongly he shielded Crerar from taking the politically hazardous but necessary initiative to fettle the reinforcement system.[2] At the same time Crerar continued to treat the CGS and NDHQ in Ottawa, as had McNaughton, as a superior commander treats a staff appointed to serve him and the overseas army, of which he was C-in-C. It was the minister, not the CGS, whom he regarded as his immediate superior.

This attitude was a throwback to the practice in the First World War when Haig and Pershing treated their chiefs of the General Staff in London and Washington as inferiors. As unchallenged professional heads of their respective armies in the Second World War, the words of Generals George Marshall and Alan Brooke were law: Marshall and Brooke were, in fact, commanders as well as chiefs of the General Staff. In Ottawa Major General Murchie, chief of the General Staff, was not a commander and, unfortunately for the Canadian army overseas, Crerar shirked his responsibilities as a commander but liked the power of his position. Between them, McNaughton and Crerar, Murchie and Stuart, spun a web of ambiguity around themselves within which everyone was a staff officer and no one a commander. Everyone avoided responsibility for the reinforcement crisis, just as Crerar had done in the Dieppe disaster.

A starting point in this disgraceful story is a signal on April 3, 1944, from Murchie to Stuart about NDHQ plans to increase the flow of volunteers to Europe:

1. We propose to inaugurate shortly, on the initiative of the Army itself, a campaign to increase the number of volunteers for overseas service from both the general public and the NRMA. [National Resources Mobilization Act soldiers had not volunteered to go overseas. Those in the Canadian Active Service Force, CASF, whether originally in the NRMA, NPAM, Nonpermanent Active Militia, or the Permanent Force or regular army, were all volunteers.]

2. The campaign will be based on the premise that the Canadian Army in Canada and overseas takes pride in the fact that its overseas

army is entirely a Volunteer Army and desires to maintain this status with its inherent advantages.

3. Consider that it would lend great weight to this campaign if the army commander could say something, not as a prepared statement but if possible during an address to troops which would be reported by press in Canada to emphasize the foregoing.

4. Care would have to be taken not to overemphasize the point but we feel that expression of overseas viewpoint along these lines would be fundamental in building up campaign here.[3]

Consulted by Stuart, Crerar commented that he did not think that a majority of the overseas army wanted a volunteer army. Obviously he favoured more volunteers coming overseas, but he did not intend to intervene in a political issue or involve himself in an acrimonious debate. Stuart passed this message on to Murchie, adding that Crerar might give a statement in *general* rather than *specific* terms to help recruiting.

It may be concluded from this exchange that more volunteers were required, that there were not enough in April for the coming struggle on the Continent, but that Crerar was not prepared to make a statement that admitted as much. Yet in May CMHQ had to remuster francophone men not currently in French units to provide reinforcements for the three francophone battalions of the Second and Third Divisions. Francophones in other arms and services were then remustered to infantry and earmarked as first reserves. Maintaining the strength of francophone infantry units was an anxiety from that time. CMHQ and army HQ staffs both resorted to questionable improvisations based on underestimated casualty projections, overestimates of the number of replacements from Canada, and on remustering to make up the difference. Remustering was not only a onetime measure but an offence to those who had volunteered to serve in a particular arm of the service with personal friends and found themselves pitchforked from a trade for which they were trained into the infantry for which they were not. It was widely understood that such shifts and stratagems could not ward off a crisis, in October at the latest, when income and expenditure would be hopelessly out of balance. Yet neither Crerar nor Stuart shared responsibility for correcting the situation with Ottawa, and when Murchie gave him the opening in April, Crerar sidestepped it.

The related problems of apportioning to the army the appropriate categories of men from the national pool, training them adequately and providing them in sufficient numbers and in time to replace casualties, were assiduously separated from each other by Stuart and Crerar; Murchie and Ralston found it convenient to follow the same line in Ottawa. Deliberately or not, a historian's report from the field to Colonel Stacey at CMHQ at the end of August, when units were desperately understrength, tiptoed around the issue, as well:

> The charge that reinforcements were not fully trained deserves some analysis. There appears to be little documentary support for such a sweeping statement, but some substantiation can be found. There was foundation for the implication in the remustering of excess personnel from other arms and services to the Infantry Corps for which authorization had been previously provided [on May 1, 1944]. For on the 28th April, at a conference for discussing reinforcements, it was agreed that if it became necessary to send forward personnel who had not completed their training in full that the standard reached should be appropriately indicated, in order that commanding officers should be made aware of the necessity of bringing them up to the standard required. . . . It was thought that no serious repercussions would arise from this policy since in the case of infantry reinforcements, battalions would have the required facilities to bring personnel up to the required standard of training. Some departures might temporarily have to be accepted in other corps.[4]

It was laughable that in May staffs should envisage battalion commanders training reinforcements in the middle of a battle. In the event, battalions were so short of men that reinforcements were sent straight off the ships into action in July.

As early as the first week in August, between Operations Spring and Totalize, anglophone as well as francophone reinforcements were drying up. Crerar signalled CMHQ on August 4:

> Am concerned about infantry general duty deficiencies which approximate 1900. Our ability to continue severe fighting or to exploit a break-through would be severely restricted through lack of replacement personnel. After forwarding all available rfts from 2 CBRG [a base reinforcement unit in Normandy] deficiencies exceeding five percent of unit strengths are: RHC — 370, R de Mais — 245, Essex Scots — 171, Fus Mr — 130, Camerons of C — 100, Q OR of C — 99, R Regt of C 91, S Sask R — 87, SD and G Hldrs — 78, Calg Hldrs — 78, Regina R — 72, N Shore R — 68, RHLI — 54, Tor Scot R (MG) — 52, R de Chaud — 47.

I consider this the most serious problem of Cdn Army at the moment and to require most energetic handling.[5]

Simonds briefed Crerar verbally on the situation in the Second Corps and on the seventh reported that the Second Division alone was deficient 1,910 infantry other ranks and would probably be 2,500 short by the end of Totalize. He continued:

> No definite information is available to this headquarters concerning further arrivals of infantry general duty reinforcements and it is felt that for one reason or another, the system for the supply of reinforcements to this theatre is not functioning satisfactorily and that reinforcements in sufficient quantities to take care of actual and probable losses are not immediately available.[6]

The next day Simonds reported that reinforcements were taken off ships and sent straight into battle. On another occasion a draft advertised as 1,600 strong arrived two days behind schedule and consisted of 690 infantry and 160 for other arms. "I feel," Simonds commented, "that field units should be relieved of any anxiety concerning the availability of reinforcements when an operation is required to be undertaken . . . nor does there appear to be any reasonable assurance of an improvement in the situation."[7]

In the meantime Stuart's reply to Crerar's signal of August 4 reassessed the situation up to October 15 and offered figures of reinforcements in the pipeline from arrival in the United Kingdom through training to delivery in France. He proposed remustering artillery, service corps, and armoured corps men into the infantry to satisfy eighty percent of the First Army's demands. Stuart could expedite the flow if Crerar would accept those who had not completed their training. Asserting that he was using Twenty-first Army Group casualty forecasts, he stated that the figures he offered were "in excess of requirements by approximately 1,500 Canadian Infantry Corps, this without taking into account any personnel obtainable from extension training . . . or recoverable cas[ualties] which should come in progressively from late September onwards."[8]

Stuart offered Crerar a choice between running short or accepting the semitrained. Furthermore, he seems to have used out-of-date Twenty-first Army Group casualty scales based on Western Desert fighting. They had been replaced in February in the light of fighting in Italy and had been discarded by the British staff (see note 25). Not surprisingly, Crerar did not accept Stuart's figures. He answered that the promised replacements would do no more than cover the short-fall in infantry as of August 2. "As the wastage rate has averaged nine Other Ranks [OR] per battalion per day," he replied, "and in the past seven days of relative inactivity has been five, the August total may be 5,000, as heavy fighting is in store for 2 Corps."[9] Yet his proposal, vigorous remustering, strenuous conversion training, and a shortening of conversion training to about four weeks, was no advance on Stuart's. However, he then advised:

> In view distinct possibility that operations of next four weeks may prove turning point remustering policy should be based on short view. It is vital that our offensive power be maintained and long term futures must be risked to produce early results. Suggest use specialised facilities possibly 13 Cdn Inf Bde for conversion trg. I consider that personnel must be trained to minimum acceptable standards on which subject separate cable follows.[10]

The idea that the war was about to come to an end was commonly held at the end of the month and for about ten days into September, but Crerar was taking an unwarranted risk in encouraging Stuart to take a short view and cut training time and standards as early as this. The moment for Crerar to behave like a commander had arrived, and he ought to have written firmly to the minister, even if nothing could be done to alleviate the immediate shortage. Crerar did not do that, and Stuart sent Murchie a flabby signal on August 26, telling him that he would have the reinforcement situation in shape in three weeks to a month when the remustered men would flow. Until then he could not replace the deficiency, which was then three thousand infantry, although it would help if Murchie gave him the authority to continue to allow the tradesmen and specialists he was sending over to France as general duty (GD) men to receive trade pay:

> The present situation is not a manpower problem in the true sense. We have the men. It is not a problem of general supply. It is a problem of detailed distribution. We have taken British FFC [field force conspectus] rates as a guide. Experience of particular conditions of war in France has shown that FFC rates for infantry are too low and for practically all other arms are too high. In addition, we did not anticipate that practically all inf[antry] cas[ualties] would be in GD personnel. We are now going through a period of adjustment. In three weeks to a month we shall be alright. I need assistance to bridge this intervening period. My recommendations [regarding paying tradesmen] *represents [sic] the only way you can help me to bridge this gap.*[11]

On August 31 Crerar signalled Stuart: "Action taken by you should soon produce amelioration existing situation but would emphasize its urgency. Infantry battalions 2 Inf Div yesterday averaged close to 300 ORs below WE [wastage estimate]. As this deficiency mainly due to cas[ualties] in rifle companies it will be appreciated that battle worthiness of units seriously affected." On September 18, when the Second Corps was fighting for the Channel Ports and on the Leopold Canal, he signalled: "Reinforcement situation as regards GD infantry shows no general improvement over that which obtained a month ago. Matter concerns me greatly and requires your personal and urgent investigation."[12] The struggle to open the Scheldt was about to begin, and heavy casualties could be expected.

Time had run out for Crerar, who ought to have admitted to Ralston much earlier that CMHQ/First Army reinforcement policy had been faulty and asked him to increase the flow of Canada-trained men. On that same day the cat was let out of the bag in Canada, as we shall see shortly: the whole country heard of the shortage of trained men and the government was forced to take some action. Consequently, to look ahead, by early December there appeared to be light at the end of the tunnel, for the government was forced at last to order NRMA men overseas. About sixteen thousand of the approximately seventy thousand nominally available were expected to arrive in units after special training in the new year. However, the light proved to be an illusion. Not until March did NRMA men appear in units, by which time hard and prolonged fighting was at an end. Until then infantry battalions fought gravely understrength during the intense combat of September, October, part of November, all of February, and early March. Fortunately the German Ardennes offensive in December caused the Battle of the Rhineland to be postponed from December to February, and the lull in the fighting allowed the reinforcement pool to build. In February heavy casualties in the Rhineland depleted units again and morale fell once more.

As the supply of reinforcements was clearly inadequate from July 1944 until the end of the heavy fighting in early March 1945, some concluding remarks on the part played by Crerar and Stuart are required. Clearly Crerar never intervened directly with the minister or even with the CGS but was content to urge Stuart to make adjustments within the Canadian domain in Europe. Why did he not report the situation to Ralston firmly and formally as well as personally? First, because he knew that Mackenzie King's policy was to avoid directing NRMA men into the CASF, and political animal that he was, he avoided rocking the boat. That meant taking a line of least resistance. So he continued to comb and remuster, to rely on the wounded returning to combat, the officers and NCOs to lead, and the willing and courageous to die setting an example. All the time he hoped that the war was nearly over and that he would be saved from the consequences of his inaction. So he never impressed on the politicians the rising feeling among combat troops that what was happening was not only unfair and inefficient but was immoral and costing lives. At the same time he took the hard line with his soldiers over discipline. Having volunteered for service, every man must do his duty; malingerers, stragglers, and absentees must be punished according to military law. There could be no sympathy for them.

Crerar maintained his silence on this subject even after the war, never apologizing, never explaining. When the affair came to a political head in October, he was sick in the United Kingdom but allowed his staff officer, Major General Stuart, to be recalled to Ottawa and to take the blame. Indeed, Stuart should have predicted the August shortage of reinforcements and the need to remuster some of the arms, as had been done in Italy earlier. High infantry casualties had been a fact in the British army since the end of 1942. The autumn and winter of 1943-44 and the Liri Valley campaign in spring 1944 had rubbed in the point for the Canadians. The demand for more infantry in the armoured divisions in the early summer of 1944, which Crerar had opposed, was a reminder that more infantry rather than armour was required. Stuart had no excuse for pleading that he had been led astray by British FFC rates, and his remark that the staff was surprised that the rifle companies had suffered so heavily in the infantry is incredible. The last chance for action to avoid the August crisis was April. Clearly, in Ottawa, Murchie was aware of the state of affairs at that time, so Ralston cannot have been surprised by it, either.

On September 27, when Crerar fell sick and handed the First Army over to Simonds, the storm in Canada was brewing, and Simonds was left to handle its effects in the First Army. Indeed he had had to handle the direct and indirect effects of inferior equipment, high casualties, and insufficiently trained reinforcements on inexperienced units since July.

We have seen that the Third Canadian Division was tired and that its morale had suffered by the time it was briefly rested after Operation Spring on July 25, while the Second Division had been handled roughly in Atlantic and Spring. Furthermore, the commanders of both divisions were under a cloud. The Fourth Armoured, in its first battle, along with the infantry divisions, had battled forward in Totalize and Tractable, reached the Seine, and crossed it, while the Second Army had embarked on a rapid and glamorous advance to Brussels and beyond in the first week of September. Just as the Fourth Armoured began its fighting advance to the Seine, after helping the beleaguered Poles, Simonds removed George Kitching from command. Newly promoted from the Ninth Brigade, Major General Harry Foster's opening remarks when he arrived to take over were: "What the hell's gone wrong, George? You and Guy Simonds were so close?"

Robustness is one of the essential qualities of a good commander. In different ways Kitching and Simonds were both robust. Suddenly Kitching's major field command had been removed from him — unfairly, he felt. Nevertheless, he bore Simonds no grudge, and the two men remained friends. Simonds was visibly upset by the sacking. Kitching went on to serve Foulkes as chief of staff in the First Corps in Italy and Holland and had a distinguished postwar career. He was not ruthless, as Simonds has been described, but he could be detached and objective, particularly when judging his own actions. When it came to his friends, including his subordinates, he was sometimes too trusting, perhaps because at this time he was inexperienced as an armoured commander. Simonds, though, had hardened his heart and demanded that men under his command should drive their subordinates in his own impersonal, objective manner. Unwilling to remove divisional commanders because of their performance in Atlantic and Spring, he was surer of his requirements after two more battles. Although he had chosen Kitching and knew him well, he sacked him because he felt the man lacked this quality, and he gave him no second chance.

In Normandy Simonds demonstrated not so much lack of sympathy as intolerance for weakness in his subordinates and their units whether because of heavy casualties, inexperience, fatigue, bad weather, or unforeseen and changing orders. In *Mud and Green Fields* Kitching informed his readers of some of the strains and stresses in his units:

When one reads in Professor Roy's book, *1944: The Canadians in Normandy*, about the number of tanks that were destroyed each day, imagine the impact this must have had on the squadrons and troops to which they belonged. When a tank was hit perhaps two of the crew of four or five escaped unhurt. When a replacement tank came forward with a replacement crew, no one, perhaps, would know much about that crew and yet they were supposed to be able to go straight into action as if they were as good and as well versed in the squadron's procedures as the tank crew that had been knocked out.[13]

If one extends the effect of casualties from troops and squadrons to regiments and from platoons and companies to battalions, the bursting of a few shells may mean regiments commanded by squadron second-in-commands and battalions by captains. And, as we saw, the Fourth Armoured Brigade ran through three commanders before Brigadier Moncel arrived from corps headquarters to take over. Without sufficient trained replacements, efficiency will fall off drastically even after moderate casualties.

Corps and divisional commanders cannot afford the indulgence of emotional involvement with their subordinates' hardships. Simonds's sacking of Kitching showed his capacity to be a "good butcher," a quality lacking in some senior officers who are, in consequence, badly served by their "friends." In time the growth of a commander's confidence in himself and his units and his staff will bring some mellowing so that stories about him circulate to the effect that "despite his bark, master has a soft spot. He really cares." That time had not arrived for Simonds in August 1944. If it was in his nature at all, he kept that sentiment under wraps from all, including his closest staff, who were at pains in the mess to make him relax and smile by introducing nonmilitary subjects into the conversation. Even there, among his military family, he was tense. Where else may one expect to find stories of his humanity? The impression that he gave was of a cold man with little but theoretical sympathy for the hardships that his men were suffering. His reactions today may seem unlikable; back then, in battle, they were militarily correct. What mattered was winning, not being loved.

Terry Copp and William McAndrew, the historians of *Battle Exhaustion: Soldiers and Psychiatrists in the Canadian Army, 1939-45*, found that Simonds had no trace of sympathy for their stressed subjects during "the battle exhaustion crisis of July 1944" and would no doubt disagree with my assertion that Simonds's handling of battle exhaustion and its symptoms — malingering, straggling, and absence without leave — was militarily correct. They tell us that Simonds failed to grasp the psychological implications of the technical inferiority of British armour and antitank weapons. "This ignorance," they write, "had a profound effect on the fortunes of the [Second] Division in its first weeks of battle." And the authors further state: "The senior officers of the Corps and the 2nd Canadian Division had decided that psychiatric casualties were largely the creation of psychiatrists and had refused to integrate such services into the corps or divisional medical system."[14]

On weapon inferiority everyone in the chain of command, starting with Montgomery himself, recognized the ill effects of inferior tanks and antitank weapons. However, they were wary of allowing the inferiority of the Sherman, and all that followed from it, to become an excuse first for timid tactics and then for demoralization. In a memorandum that he signed himself Montgomery pointed out the weaknesses in British armour and what should be done about them. However, he concluded: "Provided our tactics are good we can defeat them [Panthers and Tigers] without difficulty."[15] Nevertheless, the New Zealander Brigadier Hargest was scathing about the timidity of British armoured units in supporting infantry attacks and in dealing with enemy tanks and puts much of the blame for the failures of the infantry on bad tank tactics.[16] The handful of veterans in the Fourth Armoured Division had met neither Panthers nor Tigers in Italy. Their range and hitting power in Normandy was a shock and threw Canadian tactics into disarray. Some armoured units were demoralized, which had an adverse effect on the infantry they should have supported.

As to the corrective action, removing the basic cause of low morale — failures on the battlefield — would have obviously taken time. Other measures would have been only palliative. Copp and McAndrew, quoting medical officers, stretch their evidence to assert that tea, rest, and sympathy in the forward area, the standard treatment for stress cases before returning them quickly to their units, was not Simonds's policy. I prefer to be less critical. With the experience of Italy, where nearly a quarter of battlefield casualties had been stress cases, the Second Corps staff expected the same *average* ratio in Normandy. That insufficient medical resources were provided in the forward area to treat the flood of stress casualties in Atlantic and Spring, so that many were evacuated with other battle casualties instead of being treated and returned to their units, showed that the size of that drain on manpower was miscalculated, not that the need for treatment was denied.

Simonds's attitude to the matrix of morale problems, of which the statistics of "battle exhaustion" cases, straggling, and absence were an indication, was shared by most other senior commanders. A prime cause of the epidemic in Normandy was the impression that the enemy's performance on the battlefield was superior. Only success would remove that cause of battle exhaustion. His proper course was to ensure success by every means within his power, even if it meant cautious plans and the use of overwhelming air and artillery support.

It also meant removing any officers whose performance did not contribute to success. In the meantime it was essential to take a hard line with those who would not stick it out unless they were men who had had a very long spell in infantry companies or armoured squadrons and needed rest. But at this early stage in the war in France few could justify an escape from fear on those grounds. Simonds expected a percentage of battle exhaustion cases and also that numbers would rise and fall with conditions in the field. He did not tolerate its symptoms, particularly straggling and absence. It was over this necessarily hard line that some psychiatrists disagreed with their commanders. The commanders disagreed with the psychiatrists whose prime responsibility, they argued, must be to the army rather than the patient.

Success in battle was lessened when units went over the start line understrength and the number of men that reached the objective was further reduced by straggling, as much as by casualties. Morale was weakened when the unit failed in consequence. Obviously the aim was to maintain both morale and force strength, for stress increased in understrength units. There was a syndrome linking these factors in Normandy. Crerar emphasized discipline and punishment to deter straggling and condemned the natural tendency of leaders at all levels to want only sound apples and to get rid of the rotten ones in the barrel with the least fuss. Court-martial action had to be taken as a deterrent to absence, cowardice, and desertion, he insisted. Simonds's letters on the subject in July, August, and October, when he was temporarily commanding the First Army in the Scheldt, laid more emphasis on teamwork: the proper use of rare periods of rest to absorb reinforcements, the retraining of subunits, and the briefing of men on the last battle, including visiting the ground on which it was fought. On August 29, after the closing of the Falaise Gap, he referred to battle exhaustion and straggling at a time when the reinforcement shortage was acute:

> Medical officers may be inclined to take a lenient view of so-termed "battle exhaustion" cases. It requires the close attention of commanders to see that malingering is not only discouraged, but made a disgraceful offence and disciplinary action taken to counter it. Battle exhaustion may be an acute problem under the most adverse fighting conditions — winter, bad living conditions and bad feeding resulting from small parties of troops having to fend for themselves — the drabness of static warfare with its inevitable drain on morale. It is quite inexcusable under the conditions in which we have been fighting in the last few weeks. . . . I appreciate the problem which faces

unit commanders who have a high proportion of reinforcement officers, short of regimental experience and with little opportunity to get to know their men before they are actively engaged with the enemy. . . . The reinforcement situation being what it is, every serving soldier must be made to pull his weight whether or not he may feel temporarily disinclined to do so.[17]

In September and October the inadequate training of reinforcements caused an outcry among battalion commanders over time wasted in training reinforcements in the United Kingdom, particularly on remustering courses. Conditions in reinforcement units on the lines of communication were also bad so that men arrived disgruntled in their units. Reforms were begun in October, but battalion commanders reported in November that men were arriving who had scant training on the PIAT and had thrown no more than three grenades. They had had no organized range practice and no instruction on fire orders or target recognition. Neither field craft nor night fighting was taught. One group arrived in the training unit on a Saturday morning and did not attend a training parade until the following Friday. The daily hours were 0745 to 1730, with an hour and a quarter for lunch — hardly emergency hours of work. After taking nine days' leave, nearly half of the month allotted had been wasted.[18]

To send men into battle with so little training was a death sentence. The most scathing account of this situation in October is given by Denis Whitaker, the battalion commander of the Royal Hamilton Light Infantry, the battalion that had taken and held Verrières in Operation Spring.[19] Many infantrymen arriving in the field had left Canada only the week before, providing no time for any kind of course on European conditions.

At this time in October Simonds was calling on his unit commanders to take better care of the reinforcement on his first arrival in the unit. "When the reinforcement officer or soldier joins the unit with which he is going to fight, it is one of the great moments of his life — comparable with birth, marriage or death. . . . He comes as a stranger. Regardless of how thorough his preliminary training may be, in the stress of his first battle, he may react in a way contrary to his training unless steps have been taken to win his confidence." Simonds had previously laid it down that battalions should have a strong "left out of battle" party to preserve a cadre of experienced men and to give them a rest, and, in the German fashion, they should manage a school to hold reinforcements for at least twenty-four hours before they went into battle.[20]

The promulgation of this instruction was virtually impossible in October when new men had to go straight into the line. Companies were often down to forty men. However, it was written in the expectation that the reinforcement logjam was breaking, thanks to the angry remarks of hockey hero Major Conn Smythe, M.C., on his arrival in Halifax on a stretcher. The *Globe and Mail* had headlined the story on September 18. In a signed statement Major Smythe said that "large numbers of unnecessary casualties" had resulted from the fact that "reinforcements received now are green, inexperienced, and poorly trained." Smythe's remarks caused an outcry from all parts of the country, and Ralston announced hastily that he would visit Europe, Italy first and then the First Army, to find out the truth.[21]

Ralston had declared several times that the moment the voluntary system failed to produce the required number of men for overseas service he would speak out in the Cabinet for conscription. On July 11 he declared in Parliament: "If we cannot maintain the army overseas with volunteers and it is necessary to send NRMA men, there can be no alternative for me but to recommend action under the act, and I shall do so."[22] It is stretching belief that with his own CGS hunting for more volunteers in April, and Stuart struggling to reshuffle men from one category to another in August, and still short of men in the infantry divisions in September, Ralston can have remained ignorant of the situation until Smythe spoke out.

Predictably those who had tolerated a failed policy in London, Italy, or Ottawa were already compromised. They could hardly complain to Ralston that the reinforcement flow and the standard of their training had been inadequate since July. Ralston let them off the hook by looking at the training of the men as though it were a separate matter from the supply. The training, he wanted to believe, was an internal matter for the army. However, it was the embarrassing inadequacy of the supply that he wanted to conceal because it exposed Mackenzie King's policy on the NRMA as a fraud.

On October 11 Brigadier E. G. Weeks, the officer in charge of the Canadian Section in GHQ First Echelon at Alexander's AAI headquarters, reported to Stuart on the completion of Ralston's visit to Italy: "From the military point of view I am not unduly concerned regarding the reinforcement situation in this theatre." He went on to say that Ralston was told by General Leese that his British divisions were habitually understrength and that it did not worry him. It was more important for political reasons, Leese had suggested according to Ralston, to keep up the *number* of divisions. But when Ralston suggested that to save infantry the First Division should be reduced to two infantry brigades which, with the addition of the First Canadian Armoured Brigade, would make it identical to the Fifth Armoured Division, Leese "strongly deprecated the suggestion."

Ralston tended, when he found commanders in Italy who complained about standards of training, to put it down to the phenomenon of bad workmen blaming their tools. In Italy there had been a system of retraining in the field that worked fairly well during the period of low casualties ending in late August. Until then there was time to train reinforcements before they were called for. So if Ralston asked about the standard of training in general, he received reassuring replies. However, at the end of August a month of hard fighting and heavy casualties began in the Gothic Line. So when the minister visited the veteran First Division, which had been in the thick of it, officers, warrant officers, and NCOs brought him down to earth by emphasizing that the training and the supply of infantrymen were inseparable, and he was being misled if he thought otherwise. Unless there was a good supply of men, well ahead of the need for them, there was no time to train them. *That had been the problem all along.* The army had been made to live from hand to mouth.

Having received an earful from outspoken First Division officers in the absence of their commander, Major General Christopher Vokes, who was enjoying a short leave in Rome, Ralston spoke to Vokes there before he left Italy. He was told, certainly in blunter words than he had heard so far, that what his division had told Ralston was true. Sending untrained men into action was murder. Trained men had a seventy-five percent chance of survival; untrained men had none. If Ralston had gathered from Weeks, as he might have judging by Weeks's correspondence with Stuart in London, that the solution lay in administrative steps within the theatre, Vokes's emphatic reaction would have disillusioned him.[23]

Ralston told Vokes that if Simonds, who was still commanding the First Army in the Scheldt while Crerar was sick in Britain, corroborated what he had learned in Italy, he would advise the Cabinet to release the trained NRMA men for service in Europe. The Second Corps was then in the thick of the nastiest battles of the whole campaign — the polder fighting of the Scheldt. Infantry, and trained infantrymen at that, were essential, and neither the Second nor Third Division had sufficient numbers. When Simonds spoke to Ralston in Antwerp, he confirmed the situation that his divisional commanders had already made clear. After the war, Simonds was angry that Stacey made it appear that he had supported Stuart and Crerar in covering up the deficiencies. He insisted that one reason

THE PRICE OF COMMAND

why Crerar had opposed his appointment as CGS in 1945 was that he had told Ralston the truth, putting Crerar in a bad light. Unfortunately Simonds did not keep a diary and kept his own counsel at the time, as was his habit. After the war, when he was disturbed over the way Stacey was handling the reinforcement question in the official history, he wrote his thoughts to Marshal Stearns, and we can be confident that it was the truth. His comrades, Elliot Rodger, for instance, bear that out. "I know that Guy Simonds would not play up to any politician," he told Denis Whitaker.[24]

Circumstantial evidence supports this interpretation, for when Ralston returned to Ottawa Mackenzie King deftly accepted a previous letter of resignation tendered by him and appointed McNaughton in his place. Stuart was sent for and admitted that he had miscalculated casualty forecasts by seventy percent from July to September inclusive, so McNaughton removed him. The case was presented as a mere failure of communication over numbers between London and Ottawa, for which Stuart was to blame, whereas the gross error had been the failure to provide enough trained men to replace casualties from June 6 onwards. Indeed, the training of reserves should and could have been accomplished in the six wasted months before D-day had the men been made available from Canada.

To blame Stuart for conspiring to keep Ottawa in ignorance of the situation, as was done, was dishonest. C. P. Stacey was quite wrong to follow the same line in his account, which was what so annoyed Simonds. Staff officers do not command and do not make policy, and commanders who allow them to do so are themselves culpable. The minister, the CGS, and General Crerar, as the commander of the First Army, were equally responsible for what happened. Their responsibility was twofold. First, to face up to the fact that infantry casualties since Alamein had been increasing and that the British were running out of infantry by October 1943. Second, when the men were not being made available in sufficient numbers to train as replacements *before* D-day, to make Mackenzie King face up to the consequences of his policy *before* it cost men's lives. The need for more men was recognized by General Murchie in April 1944. C. P. Stacey makes much of shortages in the German and British armies, too, as though that excused the Canadians, but their situations were different. The Germans were using the halt, the blind, and foreigners. Fit Canadian men *were* available.

McNaughton, Ralston's replacement, attempted to have the NRMA men volunteer, but sufficient numbers failed to do so. Why, many asked, should they excuse the Cabinet from doing its duty, which was to order them overseas? Only then did the Cabinet authorize fifteen thousand to be posted to Europe. They were ordered to sail in January, but owing to desertions less than half served overseas. Only about twenty-five hundred reached operational units — too late, in March, to remove the nasty taste in the mouth of the CASF when the name Mackenzie King was mentioned.[25]

12

Battles in the Polders

....

THE BATTLE OF THE FALAISE GAP, regarded at the time as a decisive victory that destroyed the German armies in Normandy, was the subject of historical controversy later. The controversy arose because the German armies recovered from their defeat, blocked the First U.S. Army's drive through the Aachen Gap to Cologne and the Ruhr, and denied the Second British Army a crossing of the Lower Rhine at Arnhem in Operation Market Garden. The German recovery suggested two lines of argument to latter-day controversialists. One was the proposition that the battle of the Falaise Gap had been bungled and that the Germans did not suffer a decisive defeat west of the Seine at all. Kurt Meyer's evidence on Totalize and Tractable had that as its theme. The other is that the bungling occurred after Falaise when Eisenhower permitted his armies to advance on the broadest possible front instead of mounting a single thrust aimed at Antwerp and the Ruhr. As a result, the armies ran short of gasoline and, when they attacked the Germans across the whole line of the German frontier, they ran out of munitions and then men. They were not strong enough anywhere. Exhausted by their efforts to break the German front in October and November, the Americans laid themselves open to the German counterstroke in the Ardennes in December. The second proposition fits the facts; the other, whatever may be thought of Bradley's decisions at the time of the Falaise Gap or the "slowness" of the First Canadian Army in closing it from the north, does not.

Both interpretations are tinged with hindsight to the extent that the Germans recovered to fight on. However, the proposition concerning the broad front and single thrust rests on the logistical imbalance of the armies on the German frontier, which the SHAEF and Twenty-first Army Group staffs both foretold at the time when they advised that the heaviest thrusts should be north of the Ardennes and not south of it. Defenders of Eisenhower's broad front argue that instead of careering northwards to Arnhem in Operation Market Garden between September 17 and 27 Montgomery should have opened up the great port of Antwerp to bring in the supplies required to continue the offensive. Like the Falaise Gap argument, this one is also fuelled by hindsight, as we shall see in this chapter.

Simonds argued that Eisenhower's cry, after Falaise, of *tout le monde à la bataille*, lost the First U.S. and Second British Armies an opportunity to combine to destroy the German armies north of the Ardennes. Moreover, he believed that the First Canadian Army missed the boat in allowing the Fifteenth German Army, which had been guarding the Pas de Calais and had not been involved in Normandy, to escape to defend both banks of the Scheldt and deny the Allies the use of Antwerp until late November. When the Second Army, spearheaded by the Thirtieth Corps, advanced rapidly to take Brussels and Antwerp in the first days of September, the Second Canadian and the First British Corps, both under Crerar, were directed to clear the Channel Ports from Le Havre northeastwards. Antwerp, the largest port on the Continent, fell to the Eleventh Armoured Division in the Thirtieth Corps on September 4. However, in order to open Antwerp to shipping, the estuary of the Scheldt had to be cleared of mines and its shores of guns. The Second Army did not have the resources to advance along the Beveland shore of the Scheldt to Flushing at its mouth on Walcheren Island. This task eventually fell to the Canadians, but Simonds was convinced that had Crerar been content to mask the German garrisons in the lesser Channel Ports the Second Corps could have raced the Germans to Breskens and cleared the south shore of the Scheldt. With Breskens in their hands they would have had a base for an assault on Walcheren and, moreover, would have caught the Germans in a pocket against the Channel coast.

Crerar, Simonds informed Stacey after the war, could have ordered the Second Corps to take this course:

Crerar, on the Canadian side, always took a leading part in defending the Dieppe raid. This had its aftermath during the campaign of 1944, and led to his row with Monty. Crerar was hypnotised by Dieppe. He kept on instructing me to mount a great assault on Dieppe, supported by heavy bombers, when all our intelligence from captured German commanders and staff officers, was to the effect that the Germans had withdrawn, the post would not be defended, and I had told Crerar I would walk into Dieppe with a recce patrol. [Dieppe was cleared on the sixth, and on the ninth four hundred tons of gasoline left by train for the Second Army.] I pointed out that we should be giving attention to operations further north. Then his insistence on himself supervising the preparations for the Dieppe parade and staying to take the salute and missing Monty's conference which led to a row between them. Crerar was just not minding the shop at this time. In consequence we delayed to capture the channel ports when we should have masked them, pushed on north to Breskens and dealt with the channel ports later.[1]

It must be remembered that at this time it was believed the war was virtually over. Crerar's attitude to the reinforcement problem was coloured by that belief, which might also have been a motive for him to mask the Channel Ports. The urgent pursuit of a beaten enemy was more important than supplies. Indeed, Montgomery and Eisenhower both thought so, although their conclusions about the strategy of pursuit differed. Antwerp was important but less urgent than the destruction of the Fifteenth Army on Crerar's front, which would have led to substantial economies. Eisenhower's directives until mid-October spoke of Antwerp as necessary for the offensive *beyond* the Rhine. In September maintaining the momentum of the advance was in everyone's mind. Simonds believed that Crerar was simply not paying attention to the way the battle was flowing, that he was obeying his orders to take the Channel Ports literally and looking no further.

On September 1 Crerar gave orders for the Fourth Armoured Division to reorganize near Abbeville and told the Second Infantry Division to muster in the Dieppe area, but was quickly questioned by Montgomery on the second directive. "*It is very* necessary that your two Arm[oured] Div[ision]s should push forward with all speed towards St-Omer and beyond. NOT repeat NOT consider this the time for any div[ision] to halt for maintenance. Push on quickly."[2] To which Crerar replied that the Second Division had to halt to absorb about a thousand reinforcements and that the objective of the advance was a single crossing over the Somme for which only one armoured division was required. He kept the Second Division at Dieppe until the sixth.

Simonds was unfair to Crerar in that, as late as September 9, Montgomery appeared to think the Channel Ports were more important than opening the Scheldt, perhaps even a greater priority than destroying the Fifteenth Army. He needed the ports to supply his advance, since the Americans would have most imports coming through Le Havre. Market Garden, though, increased his logistical demands so that he needed Antwerp, too. Consequently on September 12 Montgomery signalled to Crerar: "The early opening of the port of Antwerp is daily becoming of increasing importance and this cannot repeat cannot take place until Walcheren has been captured and the mouth of the river opened for navigation. Before you can do this you will obviously have to remove all enemy from the mainland in that part where they are holding up northeast of Bruges."[3] On that day Maczec's Poles were at Ghent and Foster's Fourth Armoured Division had reached the Leopold Canal. With an extra infantry division he would probably have reached Breskens.

The next day Montgomery told Crerar that he had ordered heavy bombers to destroy the forts on Walcheren. When Crerar attacked Walcheren, Montgomery told him, he would lay on the whole weight of the strategic bombers to support him. He suggested that Crerar should give up the projected operations against Calais and Dunkirk in order to accelerate the clearing of the estuary. Of Crerar's two tasks Antwerp was now "probably" the most important, Montgomery observed. "I am very anxious" that both go on simultaneously "if you can possibly arrange it, as time is of the utmost importance."[4] And he suggested that Crerar might use one corps for the Channel Ports and the other for the opening of Antwerp.

If Simonds had a case against Crerar, it was that he reacted too slowly to this change in focus; indeed, that he had not anticipated Montgomery. The row between Montgomery and Crerar, to which Simonds referred, was really about Crerar resting the Second Infantry Division at Dieppe, against Simonds's desires, when there was an urgent need for them on the Scheldt. Crerar had shown no initiative. A plodding man who had not been given a positive order, his response to Montgomery's call to mask the lesser ports and to get on with the Scheldt was not dynamic. He could have quickly answered in the negative the question whether he could take the ports and seize the Scheldt simultaneously. The conclusion made by Simonds then followed. But by the time Crerar had laboriously examined the question he had lost the chance to tackle the Scheldt and chose the Channel Ports instead. On the fourteenth he held a conference to consider Montgomery's idea, but the Royal Navy, seldom adventurous or even interested where land operations were concerned, told him that Boulogne could not be used until the heavy guns of Calais were silenced. The die was cast then against going for the Scheldt immediately.

On the nineteenth Crerar's First Army General Plans Staff produced an appreciation and outline of operations "to serve as a basis for further discussion." On the twenty-first Crerar consulted with Admiral Ramsay, the senior SHAEF naval officer, about combined operations across the Scheldt, and on the twenty-third he held a major conference of all concerned, including Simonds. Only then was it officially decided to take Calais before concentrating against the Scheldt. Boulogne had fallen on the twenty-second, but Calais did not surrender until the thirtieth. Until Calais fell the Third Division could not join the Fourth Armoured on the Breskens shore.[5]

In the meantime Operation Market Garden had begun on the seventeenth. Two of its aims were to cross the two branches of the Rhine at Nijmegen and Arnhem and to throw another loop around the beleaguered Fifteenth Army in Belgium and southwest Holland. At the same time the First U.S. Army was to resume its drive on Aachen and reach the Rhine at Cologne. These operations offered three sequels if they were successful. First, an advance beyond the Rhine eastwards to surround the Ruhr, with the Second Army on the north and the First U.S. on the south. Second, a drive between the Rhine and the Maas, southeastwards from Nijmegen and northeastwards from the Roer Valley, to clear the west bank of the Rhine and to outflank all the remaining German forces holding the Siegfried Line farther south. The third development was to advance down the lower Rhine from Arnhem to capture the great port of Rotterdam, more accessible from the sea than Antwerp. It was the prospect of these operations and the logistical demands of their developments that had influenced Montgomery's call for Crerar to clear the Scheldt speedily. Le Havre was to be mainly an American port and Antwerp was required by the British and the Americans to supply operations beyond the Rhine. In the event, since operations west of the Rhine proved so intense, the demand for Antwerp grew urgent earlier than expected. We shall return to this motive for the Canadian operations on the Scheldt shortly.

Crerar had started planning for what was to be called Operation Infatuate, the seaborne assault on Walcheren, with an appreciation on September 19. Simonds returned his comments in a memorandum dated the twenty-first, and pencilled other remarks on his own copy.[6] Opposite Crerar's paragraph "Assumption: That the First Canadian Army has cleared the mainland up to the south shore of the Scheldt from Antwerp to the sea," he wrote: "A very unsound assumption to begin with. . . . It is apparent that the enemy intend to base their defence of Scheldt approaches on their present forward positions along the Leopold Canal. Taking into account the difficulties of ground and the fact that these positions can be supported from guns on Walcheren and Beveland, the clearing of the area north of the Leopold Canal will be a preliminary and a most important part of the whole operation." Under "Courses Open" Crerar had written: "It is reasonable to discard at the outset the possibility of mounting a successful combined operation to capture Walcheren Island by assaulting the only possible suitable beaches, which are on the northwest and southwest coasts because this could only be done after considerable time spent on combined training and preparation." Simonds disputed this, adding at the foot of four pages of argument a pencilled remark: "After further study, it occurred to me that if the dykes at West Cappelle could be widely breached by bombing it might provide an approach by which a seaborne assault could reach the dunes on either side — very difficult to assault otherwise. I put forward this proposal at the conference on the 23rd September."

At the big conference on the twenty-third Brigadier Geoffrey Walsh, now chief engineer, First Army, was instructed to look into Simonds's proposal. The next day Lieutenant Colonel Love, an officer on Walsh's staff, signed and handed in a report on it. His main points were that breaching the dykes might flood Walcheren Island but to an insufficient depth to allow assault craft to operate, and that the channel would not be deep and clear enough at the breach to allow the passage of amphibians. Crerar commented on these findings on the twenty-fifth:

I am strongly of opinion that the flooding of Walcheren is *NOT* a practical proposition in the conditions which face us. Show Comd 2 Cdn Corps this appreciation and unless he has other convincing arguments, then obtain his agreement to proceeding with Hy Bomber assistance on [that] assumption. . . .

On this Simonds later pencilled an observation:

This letter, annotated by General Crerar, was brought to me by Col (now brig) Beament in the evening of 25 September. I insisted that the attempt ought to be made. If it failed we had lost nothing — if it succeeded we stood much to gain. Its practicality was a matter of opinion. From a study of heavy bombing patterns and plans and photographs of the dykes and Walcheren I could not agree that it was impossible until a serious attempt had been made.[7]

Crerar submitted a request through the Eighty-fourth Group, RAF, as Simonds had asked on the twenty-sixth.

The next day Crerar told Simonds that although he thought he had been suffering from dysentery, the local doctors now told him he had a blood disorder. He had decided to go back to Britain for treatment. Simonds was to become acting army commander forthwith and Foulkes was to command the Second Corps. Simonds would handle the Scheldt operation in Crerar's absence.[8]

On October 2 Simonds issued an operation order to his two corps commanders, Lieutenant General Sir John Crocker and Major General Charles Foulkes. In it he explained that the First U.S. and Second British Army were going to attack between the Maas and the Rhine. They would have priority for supplies, and their demands as they advanced would grow, not diminish. Consequently the need for Antwerp to be opened had become pressing. The First Canadian Army had another task besides opening the Scheldt with the Second Corps. The First Corps would clear the Second Army's rear or western flank by thrusting north from Antwerp. There would be a conflict between the First Army's two tasks. Clearing the Scheldt was urgent, but it was important that the large force required for it should be released for operations farther north in western Holland as early as possible. "Unless engaged offensively [the Second Corps] constituted an uneconomic" detachment. It must be speedily engaged.

During the Scheldt battle, Simonds's headquarters was in Antwerp at the Château den Brandt, an estate on the south side of the city. Châteaux were chosen as headquarters because they were well-treed and provided excellent cover from the air for the trailers and marquees used by Simonds's staff, as well as his own office and sleeping trailers. King George VI visited the château to appoint Simonds a Companion of the Bath and to have lunch with the staff. Rumours had been circulating at that time that the Germans had poisoned the wine stocks they had left behind, so when Simonds offered the king a glass of red wine His Majesty asked to see the label. When he saw that it did not bear the notice *Réservé pour le Wehrmacht*, he made a wry face and said to Simonds, "That rather takes the fun out of it, doesn't it?" He accepted a Scotch and soda instead. Soon after the Allies arrived in Antwerp, the V1s and V2s started landing in the town and the dock areas. One exploded close enough to suck the maps on the table out of the window.[9]

The Scheldt was a more demanding command task than Normandy. One of a handful of officers commanding armies, Simonds was now dealing with the most senior commanders of the three services. He saw or spoke to Admiral Ramsay, the senior SHAEF naval officer, Air Chief Marshal Tedder, and the Allied Expeditionary Force (AEF) chief airman Trafford Leigh-Mallory almost daily. Montgomery was close at hand, ever helpful as in the past. Dutch political authorities, supported by Prince Bernhard, who did not want their countrymen bombed nor their farmland flooded, tried to make him modify his plans. They were referred to Eisenhower and Churchill, who assured the Dutch that their view would be presented to Montgomery and Ramsay, but that the decision whether or not to flood Walcheren had to be left to the operational leaders.

The First Army staff benefited immediately from Simonds's positive approach to his tasks. Conferences did not drag on; his orders were clear and concise, as usual. Oscar Lange, a chief clerk who had served with Simonds on earlier occasions, as well, remembers him at that time: "A strict disciplinarian, he expected no less than excellence from everyone under his command. He looked like a soldier; he acted like a soldier. He was stern and he was clever. He stood for no nonsense."[10]

Planning with the navy went forward apace as soon as Simonds took over. The Navy's Force T, under Captain Pugsley, assigned to the Walcheren landings, issued its combined plan for Operation Infatuate on the tenth. The assault force was the Fourth Special Service Brigade, Marine Commandos, with a follow-up brigade of the Fifty-second Lowland Division. Weather was as serious an obstacle as the ten-thousand-strong garrison and their formidable coastal defence guns, most of them protected by concrete. In October major landing craft could operate off the western tip of the island for only two days in the week on average; LCAs and amphibious craft for only one day. Heavy bombing to break the huge, compressed clay dyke just south of Westkapelle and near Flushing had begun. The idea was to bring the assault force to the breach in daylight in LCTs as soon after low tide as possible. Parties would land to seize the flanks of the breach to allow amphibious craft, LVTs (Landing Vehicles Tracked — Terrapins and Buffaloes), to sail through to unload on beaches in the flooded interior. Earlier, "Tarbrush" parties would have landed to inspect the damage to the forts and test the defence. The assault force would gather at Ostend, or possibly at Zeebrugge, on D minus 7. The progress of operations on the Breskens (south) shore and the Beveland (north) shore might have prevented Simonds from naming a date for the assault but, taking a calculated risk, he gave Ramsay November 1 as the target date.

By the twelfth the drive of the Second Army between the Maas and the Rhine had been cancelled, largely because the First Army was unable to fulfill its part of the plan. A grave shortage of ammunition in the Twelfth U.S. Army Group, caused by Bradley's obstinate refusal to concentrate force and supplies behind the First Army effort, was the reason. Eisenhower then seized on Antwerp as a panacea for his problems, although the proper cure would have been to persuade Bradley to cease attacking everywhere on his front and to order Lieutenant General J. C. H. (Jesus Christ Himself) Lee, the European Theatre of Operations (ETO) commander of his lines of communication, to sort out the chaos in his logistics. A logistics mission from Washington was soon on its way for that purpose, but to little avail, for things were still in a muddle when the Germans attacked in the Ardennes in December. As a result of the cancellation of its eastern operation and the urging of Eisenhower to open the Scheldt, the Twenty-first Army Group was able to pay a little more attention to clearing the Scheldt and the Second Army's western flank.

Simonds issued the First Army plan on October 19. The Second Division was to tackle the Beveland, or north shore, and the Third Division the Breskens, or south shore of the Scheldt. The Fifty-second Division would be available to make a ferry assault from Terneuzen on the south shore against South Beveland Island beyond the Beveland Canal at the western end of the Beveland Isthmus, and a landing at Flushing on Walcheren Island. The First Corps would push the enemy northwards, away from the eastern entrance to the Beveland Isthmus, part of its task to clear the Second Army flank before the Second Division began its drive westwards (Vitality 1). The Breskens attack (Switchback) was the first step of the Second Corps operation because gun positions and ferry sites for the assaults against Flushing (Infatuate 1) and South Beveland (Vitality 2) could not be prepared until the south shore was cleared. The second step, coincident with the first, was for the Second Division to push the enemy behind the Beveland Canal (Vitality 1) when the Fifty-second Division assault across the Scheldt against South Beveland could take place. The start of the Second Division's attack depended only on the release of one of its brigades by the First Corps and the latter's clearance of the area north of the line Woensdrecht-Bergen Op Zoom. Its target date was October 23.

The third step was the assault on Walcheren (Infatuate 1 and 2). It did not have to await the completion of the second step, provided the Second Corps had a firm grip on South Beveland and enemy forces there were fully engaged: "Whilst preparations should still proceed for a setpiece assault on the western tip [of Walcheren, Infatuate 2], the practicability of a direct assault into Flushing, covered by heavy bombers and guns massed on the south shore of the Scheldt, seems more promising. This will become an even better prospect when the Breskens bridgehead has been cleared and we have fully engaged the enemy forces in Zuid Beveland."[11] They had to accept the disadvantage of not having specially trained people to handle underwater obstacles and inundations and having to work to a flexible plan, Simonds stated, "for time is such a vital element that the troops first available must be used at each stage if time will thereby be saved . . . this is a disadvantage which must be accepted in view of the importance of the time factor."[12]

Receiving confirmation of the dates of the army plan from Simonds on the twenty-second that the bombing against the shore batteries would take place on the twenty-ninth, thirtieth, and thirty-first and that he intended to take Walcheren and Beveland by November 1, Admiral Ramsay signalled, "Red Hot. Best of luck."[13] It was he who had been badgering Eisenhower to have the Scheldt opened as soon as possible, for he knew that clearing the mines and the shore guns would be time-consuming.

On the ground Simonds felt the hardship of his three divisions of Canadians, now shamefully short of men and very tired by the end of the struggle in wet and cold conditions. From the actual fighting on the ground he was further removed, as army commander, although he was able to influence the fighting. The assault across the Braakman, or Savojaard Plaat, west of Terneuzen to get behind the obstinate German positions on the Leopold Canal was his idea. On October 3 the bombing of the Walcheren dykes was carried out by 243 heavy bombers carrying 1,263 tons of bombs, thanks to his persistence with the Eighty-fourth Group, who were responsible for tactical support and communications with Bomber Command. The results were precisely as he had supposed. A seventy-five-yard gap was made and the sea flowed in. By the time of the invasion the island was like a saucer filled with water. Beaches were formed by the flooding in the breach and inside the island, causing German communications and ammunition supply to fail. The bombing was declared by Montgomery to have been an operation of truly magnificent accuracy.

All was not, by any means, plain sailing. Montgomery's prestige had been shaken by the relative failure of Market Garden, and he was a less powerful ally than before. As army commander, Simonds's planning was affected by interservice and international politics, and it was a harsh fact that opening the port of Antwerp, however essential it was said to be, did not have complete priority. It was not as important to the air forces as their own concerns. Eisenhower had recently lost the control of the air forces for ground operations that he had had in Normandy. Against the opposition of Tedder, Eisenhower's chief airman, and Leigh-Mallory, who was about to be removed from his anomalous position in command of the AEF air forces, even Eisenhower and Montgomery seemed unwilling or unable to make a stand in Simonds's support.

As in Normandy, the RAF would not allow a direct link between Bomber Command and army headquarters. It would have been invaluable for reporting progress in bombing the dykes and the coastal forts. The RAF reserved the right to judge when a target was suitable for them, when it was not, and when it was adequately hit. They decided what kind and how many aircraft to use and how many and what kind of bombs they should drop. Eisenhower's promise that all the resources of the strategic air force would be used to destroy the coastal guns was meaningless when priority went to the oil targets of German industry after the dykes were breached.

Air Commodore T. N. McEvoy, commander of the Eighty-fourth Group, RAF, told Simonds that the policy of Bomber Command was to offer support only when ground troops would attack the target area immediately.[14] That ruled out preparatory heavy bombing over a period to destroy the coastal guns, which Simonds requested. Instead, he was promised three days of heavy bombing just before the assault, but Tedder put his foot down on October 24 on the grounds that the guns were a proper target for the tactical not the strategic air force. Handed the task of destroying the guns, the Eighty-fourth Group pointed out that it did not have the weight of bombs to do the job on the last three days. Simonds had to shame the Eighty-fourth Group into taking on the guns by saying that the casualties would otherwise be on its conscience.

In the end Bomber Command tackled the targets requested, but with a fraction of the aircraft that it devoted to Germany each night, and on October 31, the night before the assault on Walcheren, weather prevented any significant bombing. Tedder's view was that the Canadians were "hooked" on heavy bombers. His casual disregard for the courage of assaulting commandos, naval support forces, and the humble infantryman was unattractive, and the Canadians did not forgive him.[15] It appeared that Tedder, Leigh-Mallory, and Air Vice-Marshal Arthur Coningham were carrying on their Normandy feud against Montgomery at the expense of the Royal Navy and the Royal Marine Commandos. After the operation, Ramsay was furious about the casualties his ships suffered from the shore batteries.

Earlier, at the conference on September 29, Simonds had to announce his failure to obtain an airborne brigade to seize the eastern end of the causeway between South Beveland and Walcheren. Eisenhower had promised airborne support, but the commander of the Airborne Army, Lieutenant General Lewis Brereton, declared the task unsuitable because ground troops might not be able to reach the dropping zone quickly enough. It appeared to Simonds that Brereton was uninformed about his plan when he gave his decision, but Brereton did not alter it when he was briefed in detail. When the rhetoric of Eisenhower was tested, his declaration that the Scheldt had priority proved empty.[16]

The assault of the Fourth Special Service Brigade and the Royal Navy against Westkapelle on November 1 was dramatic and courageous, but the long struggle of the Second Corps's understrength battalions towards Breskens and the Beveland causeway demands our admiration as a demonstration of guts during great difficulty. The Seventh Brigade of the Third Division opened the operation on the Leopold Canal on October 6. They were held up until the Ninth Brigade took the enemy by surprise with a seaborne assault across an arm of the Scheldt called the Braakman, which brought them on to the enemy's flank on the ninth. The Eighth Brigade followed them over and attacked on October 11. The enemy then fell back to a line covering Breskens. The final attack went in on the twenty-first, but the operation was not completed until November 3 when the operations log of the division showed the entry: "Op Switchback now complete." Someone wrote beside it: "Thank God!"[17]

Vitality started on October 24, and the Second Division reached the Beveland Canal on the twenty-seventh. On the twenty-ninth it joined up with the Fifty-second Division near Gravenpolder. By the thirtieth a battalion was within half a mile of the narrow, cratered twelve-hundred-yard-long causeway, but the western end was stoutly defended. A small bridgehead was eventually held, but it could not be reinforced until the Fifty-second Division was shown a way across the Slooe on the south side and the German defences crumbled.[18]

The success of the Walcheren assault seemed to hinge on the weather and on Bomber Command knocking out the concrete-encased coastal guns, particularly W13, 15, and 17 near Westkapelle, which the Eighty-fourth Group's bombs could not penetrate. At first Ramsay and Simonds agreed that the decision to proceed or not with the assault once the force had sailed would be made by Captain Pugsley only on naval considerations. At Bruges, with the weather deteriorating on the thirty-first, Ramsay, Simonds, and Foulkes agreed that the convoy should sail if the weather got no worse. The question remained whether to leave the decision to assault with Pugsley alone. Then, late in the afternoon on board the headquarters frigate HMS *Kingsmill* at Ostend, Simonds and Ramsay made Pugsley and Leicester jointly responsible for cancelling the assault if, in their opinion, "on all available information (with particular reference to the probabilities of air support, air smoke, and spotting aircraft for bombardment ships) at the time of taking such decision the assault is unlikely to succeed." At 9:15 p.m. on the thirty-first Ramsay and Simonds agreed on the phone that the force should sail and confirmed these conditions.[19]

At 6:00 a.m. a message reached the *Kingsmill* at sea that owing to bad weather at British airfields the preparatory bombing was most unlikely to occur. Indeed, it was cancelled, and there were no spotter aircraft for the naval guns or air smoke, either. By this time the sea was calm, a rare event. Furthermore, the sky appeared to be clearing, which made air support from rocket-firing Typhoon aircraft possible later. Although there had been no bombing attacks on the guns, Pugsley and Leicester decided to proceed, signalling back to Second Corps headquarters at Ijzendijke the appropriate code word, Nelson.

The landing craft and their close-support squadron under Commander K. A. Sellar went in, although the coastal guns had opened up a smart fire largely unaffected by the big ships, which had to shoot blind without their spotting aircraft. Among the support squadron two large and two medium Landing Craft Guns (LCGs), two LC Flak, and three support craft were sunk. Seven more craft were damaged and put out of action and four were damaged but still able to continue. When the squadron withdrew, they carried 126 badly wounded and 172 dead. The fact that the defenders concentrated their fire on the assault squadron and not the Royal Marine craft, and that Battery W 13, which covered the breach, ran out of ammunition, may have enabled the attackers to get ashore at 10:10 a.m. with few casualties. As well, signalled Commander Sellar, "Timely and well-instituted support by RP Typhoons undoubtedly vital factor in turning scale to our advantage at a time when eighty percent support craft out of action due to enemy fire."[20]

The success of the assaults at Walcheren and Flushing, which was covered by an enormous force of guns from the Breskens shore, enabled a minesweeper to reach Antwerp on the fourth. She was the first fruits of Operation Calendar, an intricate sweeping operation already under way. Calendar enabled the first three coasters to reach the port on the twenty-sixth, and on the twenty-eighth a convoy of eighteen ships was safely in Antwerp. On November 4 Simonds issued a congratulatory note to all those who had fought in the Scheldt battle. After explaining the importance of their achievement in the campaign, he went on:

> The fighting has had to be conducted under the most appalling conditions of ground and weather. Every soldier serving in this army — whether he has fought along the banks of the Scheldt or in driving the enemy from the northeastern approaches to Antwerp — and every sailor and every airman who has supported us — can take a just and lasting pride in a great and decisive victory.[21]

Twenty-two thousand prisoners were taken, and it was estimated that the Germans had suffered thirty thousand other casualties.

Montgomery wrote a congratulatory letter on November 3. In his message he included the following passage: "It has been a fine performance and one that could have been carried out only by first-class troops. The Canadian Army is composed of troops from many different nations and countries. But the way in which you have all pulled together, and operated as one fighting machine, has been an inspiration to us all. I congratulate you personally."[22]

Crerar had been asked to delay his return to command the First Army until Simonds had completed the operation. He sent a friendly signal from the United Kingdom: "My sincere congratulations to you on the great ability and drive with which you have carried through your recent very difficult responsibilities to most successful conclusion. As a result, the reputation of [the] First Canadian Army has never stood higher."[23]

On the sixth Simonds gave a lunch to all those who had helped the First Army in the operation. One of the guests was Major General Sir Percy Hobart, commander of the famous Seventy-ninth Armoured Division, armed with a variety of curious armoured vehicles that had been invaluable in minesweeping, crossing boggy ground and water, filling ditches, and demolishing obstacles. Hobart wrote to thank Simonds:

> I would like to say myself how much I enjoyed working with you. You are always ready to discuss ideas: you have provided a whole series of new techniques and methods and have succeeded in surprising the enemy on many occasions; and it has been a great relief to be able to get firm decisions from you and to feel sure they would remain firm. I hope very much that I shall have the satisfaction of working with you again.[24]

This was praise from a soldier with long experience who was not known for soft-soaping either younger or older colleagues.

Sometime after Crerar was back in the saddle Admiral Ramsay sent a report to him complaining about the performance of the Royal Air Force and saying that First Army headquarters had not pressed the air force hard enough to obtain air support for Infatuate. A joint plan might have tied down the air force, he believed, and saved the navy casualties. In sending Ramsay's report to Simonds for his comments, Churchill Mann, Crerar's chief of staff, commented on the air planning: "The RN can only share our views as they never expressed different ones and received copies of the material always. They sometimes seem not to have read it clearly — as it was delivered after 'gin-time' on occasions. They always wanted a Joint Plan on the Neptune pattern, and if they were to have it, the op would still be pending!"[25]

Simonds's reply covered five pages.[26] He pointed out that on D-1 all concerned were warned that the weather forecast made air support doubtful, which was why he and Ramsay had left the decision to land to the joint commanders. After he signalled them in the morning that air support was "most unlikely," their subsequent decision to continue was "a courageous and correct one."

On the structure of command, on the question of a joint command, and on air support, I quote extensively from Simonds's paper, not only because he makes points of general interest but because the paper gives the reader an impression of the size of the operation that Simonds had managed. It also supports the opinion expressed by several of his colleagues that Simonds grew with his rank. He was a better army commander than corps commander and a better corps commander than he had been a division commander. The Scheldt marked Simonds as an international soldier to be trusted with British, Polish, Czech, and American troops as well as Canadians. After it he and Lieutenant General Sir Brian Horrocks were Montgomery's preferred corps commanders:

> The complications in planning arose from the fact that "Infatuate" was a subsidiary part of a much larger Army operation with which it had to be timed and coordinated. The number of army commanders with whom Commander Force "T" [Captain Pugsley] had to deal arose directly from the fact that in operational matters he worked back through naval channels of command which were not represented by an officer empowered to make decisions at the corresponding army headquarters. In my opinion, in such circumstances, the naval

force required should have been placed directly under the command of the army with the right of access to higher naval authorities in technical naval matters . . . once the operation has been decided upon at the higher level. . . .

Simonds listed the points that had to be decided at the highest level, including "Nomination of the naval forces and their commander and agreement in outline for combined training and planning." Then he expanded the latter point:

It is true that training the naval forces in England increased the difficulties of detailed planning at the lower levels since army and naval commanders were not able to work together from the outset. This was a condition imposed by naval considerations affecting the use of Ostend as a training port and one only accepted by the army on naval representation that training from a continental base was impracticable. . . . Though no joint plan was submitted in writing to the Supreme Allied Command, I do not accept the statement that "No proper joint plan was ever produced." A joint naval and army plan, based upon the tasks and outline which had been given to them, was produced by the force commanders responsible for the execution of the operation. In my opinion this is a correct procedure.

Simonds's report continued:

From the outset, it was made clear to the two force commanders that the plan must be flexible. Its final form depended upon the success of the attempt to breach the dykes, the extent of flooding and enemy reactions to the attacks in the Breskens bridgehead and South Beveland. It is my opinion that a tendency has grown up to make combined planning too rigid and inflexible. As a result of early failures because of *No* proper combined plan we now veer to the other extreme and attempt to legislate in detail for events which will depend upon the sway of battle. Three other amphibious assaults were mounted during the Scheldt operation (crossing the Savojaards Plaat, the assault on South Beveland and the assault on Flushing). All three were mounted at short notice and all three were most successful because they were timed with the "run of the battle." Had the "full dress" procedure been adopted they could never have been mounted in time to take advantage of favourable situations.

Simonds ended his report with three pages of analysis of the RAF effort, which had been the bone of contention for Admiral Ramsay. His main target was the way air support was practised, not the staff procedure for selecting targets, which Ramsay criticized. In particular he disliked RAF insistence that it should be the sole judge of both the means to be employed against a target and the effect of its bombs on that objective. Also, he was annoyed that the agreed heavy bomber support had been whittled down without consultation, which had certainly caused naval casualties. The risks of bad weather interrupting the fire support for the assault were evident from the meteorological records. Therefore, more than ever, it was necessary to deliver all the support promised and not to reduce it.

When all was said and done, Simonds had no wish to wage a vendetta against the RAF and advised Crerar that he should not take Ramsay's criticisms any further, as the admiral desired. With such a recommendation Simonds demonstrated a sense of proportion as well as an awareness that he would have to continue working with the Eighty-fourth Group, RAF, with whom his relations were good.

13

The Tide's In

THROUGHOUT *Rhineland: The Battle to End the War*
Denis and Shelagh Whitaker are quite critical of how
that conflict was conducted. At various points they quote participants in
the battle to bolster their personal exasperation and anger at the mistakes of senior officers and their pride at the courage and endurance of
the fighting men of the Second Corps. A selection of comments by the
Whitakers and some of the men they interviewed is quite graphic:

> Two hours later the flood level [of the breached Rhine winter dyke]
> had reached 30 inches and [was] rising at the rate of one foot per
> hour. . . . [T]he roads were slowly sinking. Half of his [Crerar's] battlefield now lay under five feet of water. The rest had been transformed by the thaw into a morass of mud.

> [I]t was as if a dozen men on a playing field were trying to score a
> goal without any one of them having the slightest idea of what the
> others were doing.

> "[R]eminiscent of the muddy fields of Passchendaele and the shell-
> torn slopes of Vimy Ridge, a struggle to the death between Canadians
> and Germans of equal valour, attack and counter-attack. . . ." A total
> of 3,638 Canadians were killed or wounded opening up Blockbuster's
> 16-mile corridor to the Rhine.

> Both Horrocks and Simonds must have realized that the terrain they
> faced — low, soggy, and traversed by numerous small waterways —

promised monumental difficulties for their armoured units. Yet both apparently felt that tanks would be indispensable in dealing with the enemy defences.

"I must have a road through which the momentum of the advance can be fully maintained to its conclusion," Lieutenant General Simonds insisted at the start of Blockbuster. Getting Simonds his road was to be an exercise in frustration and futility, costing many more hundreds of casualties than the possession of that two-mile passage seemed to warrant.[1]

Denis Whitaker himself commanded the Royal Hamilton Light Infantry in the Second Division, and it must be stated that more than forty years later the memories of soldiers are no more reliable than those of any other actors in exciting events. Their memories, apparently so vivid and precise, have been fused with published accounts they have read, and like Humpty Dumpty's dictum that "what I say three times is true," with their own oft-repeated versions of the truth. The Battle of the Rhineland was indeed unexpectedly tough, the weather was foul, and the shelling worse than it had been in Normandy. For those reasons it was a shock, and being the last in the war of a series of ugly battles stretching back to the bridgehead, it made an indelible impression on all who fought in it.

Yet, at the level of the junior regimental soldier, the confusion of the Battle of the Rhineland was typical of battles in general. No soldier ever glimpsed more than a shifting, partial view of the battle in which his infantry company or his armoured squadron was fighting. His attention riveted to his own small part of the battlefield, he had the impression that his unit was fighting alone. In a sense it was fighting alone as, across the front, his battle became disconnected from that of his neighbours. Looking over his shoulder for support that never came, weakened by casualties and exhaustion by the second or third day of a great battle, he and his friends were unwilling or impotent to obey a fresh offensive order and felt like cursing the officer who gave it. Despite that, corps and division commanders who retained in their minds the shape of the battle they had planned to fight ordered their subordinates to press on with whatever means remained to them so that a break in one small corner might restore momentum to the rest. Experience taught that that was often the case for, however bad the state of their own units, that of the enemy's was worse. With that in mind they had to be tough with their brigade and battalion commanders, who often wanted more time and resources before acting — time and resources being opposite sides of the same coin.

The opinion of Major Radley-Walters, a thoughtful, experienced, and analytical tank leader with a distinguished fighting career, that from division level upwards commanders did not know "what the hell was going on," was a common impression of battles in the Second World War from the Desert Campaign onwards.[2] It leads us to suppose that senior commanders made errors, neglected opportunities, and were ill-informed which, of course, was true some of the time. Still, even if we grant that that was probably true of Blockbuster, the real villains were the Germans who, for political rather than military reasons, fought their last great battle west of the Rhine and not behind it. That was a strategic surprise. Tactically it was not a surprise that they used the ground with their usual ability and made the Allies pay a high price for taking it, as they had all the way from the Normandy beachhead. However, the Germans' task in the Rhineland was eased by the behaviour of a few American senior commanders who, delaying the entry of American divisions into battle on the Roer River, enabled the Germans to concentrate against the First Canadian Army for the first fifteen days of Veritable.

In Normandy Montgomery made the overall plan that guided the Allies. From the time that Eisenhower took a hand at the Falaise Gap, Allied strategy drifted. Although the plan for the Rhineland battle was Montgomery's, and Crerar's First Army and Lieutenant General William Simpson's Ninth U.S. Army fought the battle under Montgomery's Twenty-first Army Group, Montgomery could not choose its starting date. It will be remembered that Veritable, the British part, and Grenade, the American, were originally planned for early October when the Second Army was to advance from Nijmegen southeastwards between the Rhine and the Maas while the First U.S. Army moved northeast from the Roer. The pincer movement was intended to force the German right flank back across the Rhine. German armies south of the Roer would have to withdraw from the Siegfried Line when their flank was opened.

In October the ground was moderately dry and armoured units could use a network of farm tracks to open the German flank on the Maas and swing it back against the Rhine from Wesel to Düsseldorf. The plan had to be postponed because the First Army lacked the ammunition and the divisions to undertake its part in Grenade while simultaneously fighting for the Aachen Gap and on the Moselle, where Patton was allowed to continue his private war. The First U.S. Army's struggle in the Huertgen Forest continued through

November until the Germans struck their counterblow in the Ardennes in December. After the Germans were stopped in the Ardennes and withdrew, General Bradley persisted through January in an ineffectual and expensive offensive to turn the German gamble into a great American victory that would wipe out the evil memory of the Ardennes debacle.

Bradley's offensive in the Ardennes prevented the transfer of his divisions to Lieutenant General Simpson's Ninth Army for Grenade. Eisenhower aided and abetted Bradley by withholding his directive for Veritable/Grenade until February 1. To cap it all off, Bradley was supposed to have seized the Schwammenaul Dam on the Roer with his First Army to prevent the Germans from opening the sluices and bringing the river to flood levels. He ordered Hodges to take the dams only on February 4. By the time that was achieved on the ninth, only the day before Simpson was due to attack, the German engineers had fixed the water release valves so that a steady discharge of water made it impossible for Simpson to attack for thirteen days. Instead of starting two days after the First Canadian Army launched Veritable, Grenade was delayed by the flood until February 23, fifteen days later. In consequence the Germans were free to transfer divisions north to face the Canadian attack, satisfied that Simpson could not cross the Roer to attack their flank and rear.

Here, at the very start, was a setback for Veritable. Bradley was also indirectly responsible for a second one. Montgomery and Crerar expected their armoured units to advance over frozen ground, but the delay to wait for Bradley brought a thaw, and when the Germans broke the Rhine dykes, they flooded the ground between the Reichswald Forest and the Rhine. Roads disappeared underwater and the whole nature of the operation changed. Armour lost much of its potency, and the approaches to enemy positions, already narrow, were constricted further.

A central factor in the Germans' defence of the Rhineland was their determination to defend the bridge leading from Wesel on the east bank of the Rhine to a naturally defensible bridgehead surrounded on three sides by the river. The northern Rhineland was a narrow salient running from the suburbs of Nijmegen, at its point, southeastwards between the Maas and the Rhine and Waal. Since the Wesel Bridge was to be the last German escape route across the Rhine, a successful delaying action in the northern and narrowest part of the peninsula was the key to the battle as long as the Americans could be pinned by flooding behind the Roer in the south.

From the First Canadian Army positions on high ground just east of Nijmegen an observer looks across lower ground to the dark mass of the Reichswald, which was the crux of the Germans' forward position. From it a spur higher than the Maas and Rhine floodplains on either side runs, with interruptions, southeastwards to the Wesel bridgehead. There is a gap in this spur at the end of the Reichswald and south of Bedburg. Passing through the gap runs the road and railway from Cleve to Goch and the road from Bedburg to Udem. Beyond it a convex swelling that rises just south of Calcar leads south, narrows, and ends in important features above Udem. A wet valley east of this feature is overlooked by the prominent, wooded ridge called the Hochwald, which forms the handle of a sickle, the blade curving from north-south to east-west as it wraps itself around Xanten. Just southeast of Xanten a swelling guards the northeastern entry to the Wesel bridgehead. The southern entry is covered by the Bonninghardt feature.

This ridged country was a better approach to Wesel than the terrain between it and the Maas, which was low-lying with a few small rises and many woods. The latter's main features were the large town of Goch, which was well defended, and the smaller towns of Weeze and Kevelaer. The Niers River flowed north past these places and then west on its way to join the Maas. The countryside was wet and generally unsuitable for tanks in February. A good road and a railway followed the general line of the Niers and passed through the towns. Apart from one along the Maas it was the only road west of the Niers suitable as an axis of advance southeastwards.

As Crerar viewed the battlefield from Nijmegen, the mass of the Reichswald Forest blocked its centre. His routes to the southeast around the Reichswald passed through narrow gaps between it and the Maas River on the west and the Rhine on the east. The latter blocked his chosen thrust line to Wesel. Crerar planned to divide the operation into three phases. In the first there would be an advance along the north face of the forest to seize Cleve and the gap between the end of the Reichswald and the Rhine. At the same time other divisions would fight through the Reichswald and broaden the gap south of Mook on the east side of the Maas.

The seizure of these three objectives would be the responsibility of the Thirtieth Corps under Lieutenant General Sir Brian Horrocks. The Second Canadian Corps would then enter the battle on the left, taking over the narrow front from about Bedburg to the Rhine to fight the second and third phases. By then the Thirtieth Corps, on the Second Corps's right, would face southeast as it emerged from the Reichswald with its right on the Maas and its left on Goch and the Niers River. In phase two of Operation Veritable the enemy's second defensive position east and southeast of the Reichswald, roughly on the line Weeze-Udem-Calcar, would be breached and the communications between these places secured. Phase three would be a breakthrough of the Hochwald lay-back defence line and an advance to secure the general line Geldern-Xanten.[3]

The main thrust line of the First Canadian Army in the second and third phases would be made by the Second Corps towards the ridge from Calcar to Udem, then the Hochwald Ridge from Marienbaum to Sonsbeck and, finally, to Xanten and the Wesel bridgehead. The Thirtieth Corps would move south from Goch to take the important towns of Weeze and Kevelaer and drive southeast to join the advancing Americans before swinging east towards Wesel. Its role was secondary to that of the Second Corps after the first phase of Veritable.

Roads, transport, and "going" were central subjects in the planning and in the operations themselves. Much of the early stages of the battle north of the Reichswald depended on amphibians to carry infantry and supplies through the floods. Submerged fence lines and buildings snagged vehicles, and ground that was covered by only a couple of feet of water was impassable except by wading infantry. Gun positions were on islands of higher ground served by DUKWs.[4]

The bombing of Cleve by heavy aircraft, which cratered roads and blocked them with debris, proved an expensive mistake, for it strengthened rather than weakened the enemy position blocking the Bedburg Gap. Farther south the Fifty-third Welsh Division and the Fifty-first Highlanders fought through the thick, dark pines of the Reichswald and suffered heavily. It was slow going and, in consequence, when Simonds was ordered to take over in the gap east of the Reichswald, the first phase of Veritable was incomplete. Goch had not fallen, and the Bedburg Gap was not cleared. In particular Germans in the Moyland Woods on the left of the Bedburg Gap prevented Simonds from deploying his divisions for the next phase of Veritable, which he named Blockbuster.

Simonds's Second Corps was large. Not only did he have the Second and Third Canadian Infantry Divisions, the Fourth Armoured Division, and the Second Armoured Brigade, but at the beginning he also had a brigade of the Fifteenth Scottish Infantry on the Rhine flank and the Forty-third Wessex in the Bedburg Gap. The Canadian divisions and the Eleventh British Armoured Division, which was to fight on Simonds's right flank, had yet to concentrate. The Second Division came from Nijmegen and the Third was extracted from its flooded phase one battleground along the Rhine where they had aptly called themselves the "water rats." The armoured divisions had not yet been engaged and had to come through the Reichswald to positions behind the infantry divisions.

In winter weather, and after a thaw, the farmland over which Simonds had to fight was atrocious tank country, but tanks had to play an important role nevertheless. Although the infantry would do most of the work, tanks and antitank weapons were essential to protect them from German tanks and to help them muscle their way into hamlets and farms and the towns like Udem and Calcar. The effectiveness of tanks depended on the ability of troop commanders and drivers to avoid getting bogged down in the excitement of making contact with the enemy, and on their staying with their infantry throughout twenty-four hours of battle. Supplies for them had to be brought forward on wheels, which meant roads and dry tracks.

So Simonds's first consideration was the choice of a good road or roads as centre lines. An obvious one was the main road that followed the Rhine from Cleve through Calcar to Marienbaum and Xanten. Intelligence reported that it was badly cratered and that its culverts had been blown. Furthermore, the area around Calcar and the flats between the road and the Rhine were flooded. On the right flank the road from Bedburg to Udem was good, but through Kervenheim and Sonsbeck it followed the intercorps boundary and had to be shared between the Thirtieth Corps's Third Division and the Eleventh Armoured Division. The third possibility was the railway line running from Goch to Xanten, which crossed the Udem-Kervenheim road on the southern outskirts of Udem and then ran over the Hochwald to Xanten. After Simonds's engineers told him the line could be torn up and the bed used for wheeled transport, he chose it as the axis of his advance from Udem to Xanten and on to Wesel. However, it was not his intention that the rail line should necessarily be used tactically.[5]

One of the more difficult operations in war is advancing from a bottleneck into a wider front. Much depends on the speed with which the bottleneck can be cleared of the enemy and then on the efficiency of the movement through it. Operation Goodwood had suffered from the difficulty of passing three armoured divisions through the Caen suburbs and over the Orne. When Simonds's Second Corps took over on the left of the front, the Moyland Gap was such a bottleneck. A brigade of the Fifteenth Scottish Infantry was still fighting in the Moyland Woods and along the Cleve-Calcar road near Hasselt. Moyland and the woods southwest of it not only dominated the Cleve-Calcar road but flanked the German defences southeast of Bedburg along the Bedburg-Udem road on which the Forty-third Wessex was fighting. The Moyland Woods had to be cleared before Simonds could move his Canadian infantry through to the start line for Blockbuster.

On February 16, after the Fifteenth Scottish had fought in the woods for three days without clearing them, Simonds ordered Major General Dan Spry's Third Division to do the job. Spry offered the Whitakers his impressions of Simonds at that moment:

> Steaming down the Bedburg-Louisendorf road in his armoured Scout car — having administered a blistering dressing-down to his commanders — Simonds was stopped by a near-miss from a German anti-tank gun. A traffic jam on his way back, even more extensive than usual, did nothing to improve his disposition. Later that morning, Simonds chaired a hot meeting of his senior commanders. "Clear those woods!" he repeated.

> "Simonds was pushing me and I was pushing the brigadiers and battalion commanders," Spry recalls. "He was very determined. Just by the glint in his eye and the set of his jaw you knew what he wanted. When he was angry, he became icy."

The Simonds "cold front" quickly found its way to the sharp end. The Regina Rifles reported bitterly: "By now Brigade HQ were screaming that the Wood 'should have been cleared by now and what were we going to do about it?' The huge casualties list was a mute answer."[6]

Spry further commented:

> "These personnel, logistical, geographic, and weather problems were being partially ignored by the senior commanders . . . They really didn't understand the sharp end of battle. They had a mental block; they'd never been there. If we had taken a little more time, even another two or three hours of preparation, of reconnaissance, of plotting and planning at various levels (perhaps even my own), we would have done better, without the staggering and unnecessary losses. We rushed our fences."[7]

Rushing his fences was a criticism levelled against Simonds more than once. Seldom does the critic suggest a better course than the one Simonds took, then or afterwards. On this occasion, before Blockbuster could begin, there had to be a major regrouping of First

Army forces in which the Fifteenth Scottish moved across to the Thirtieth Corps and the Forty-third Wessex took their place on the Cleve-Calcar road. That part of the regrouping could not begin nor could the deployment of the Canadian divisions. So the Third Division had to clear the Moyland Woods, and do it quickly. How they did it was Spry's responsibility. He was complaining, as commanders usually do, that he had not been given enough time for reconnaissance. He would have had a point had he shown Simonds that the time would not have been wasted. Time was always at a premium, and on this occasion Simonds wanted Spry to work quickly.

The enemy strength in Moyland, continually reinforced from Calcar, was underestimated, and it was not until February 21 that Spry cleared the wood. He had enabled the Second Division to move past on the western side of the wood and reach the important Goch-Calcar road, which was to be the start line for Blockbuster, but then the tired Forty-third Wessex had to be shifted and the rest of the Fifteenth Scottish returned to the Thirtieth Corps, and both were replaced by fresh Canadian divisions before the twenty-sixth.

Spry's remarks may be interpreted further. He had not expected to be caught up in a nasty little battle at Moyland between his naval engagement in Veritable 1 and Blockbuster. An experienced soldier who had fought in Sicily and Italy, he liked the measure of independence he had enjoyed in the Eighth Army where orders could be the basis for discussion. With Simonds orders were orders unless you could explain your contrary position clearly and concisely. In a later stage of this battle, having decided that an order he had received was unlikely to lead anywhere except to more casualties, he and his CRA went to bed where they were found by Simonds, angry at Spry's inactivity. The result was his reassignment to command the Canadian Reinforcement Unit (CRU), armed with good references and the assurance that the reinforcement system needed to be drastically reformed by a senior veteran.[8]

While Spry was busy with Moyland, the Fourth Brigade of the Second Division fought forward to the Goch-Calcar road by the nineteenth. As it was to be the springboard for Simonds's part in Blockbuster, the division had to cover it by getting a foothold on the rising ground of the Calcar-Udem feature beyond. There the brigade ran into resistance. The Whitakers criticize the four-day pause for regrouping that followed Moyland. Denis Whitaker's own division had been resting on the "island" between Nijmegen and Arnhem since the Scheldt and were fresh. He was impatient to get on with it, to be sure. However, there were reasons for the delay besides the complicated regrouping. General Simpson's Americans were watching the level of the Roer River impatiently, but it was not until February 23 that they could start their assault across it. Once they started, Crerar hoped their rapid advance might draw German reserves to their front and away from his.

On his own front Crerar wanted the Thirtieth Corps to take Goch and to make good progress towards Weeze before Simonds began Blockbuster. Goch was not cleared until the twenty-first, and it was not until the twenty-third that the Fifty-third Welsh Division made much progress towards Weeze. They did not take it until March 2. The Fifteenth Scottish and parts of the Forty-third had to debouch from the Bedburg Gap before reaching Bucholt and Halvenboom respectively on February 20. Their advance eased the progress of the Second Division beyond the Goch-Calcar road before the Third Canadian Division took over from the Fifteenth Scottish and the rest of the Second Division took over from the Forty-third Division. The pause was not wasted.

On February 25, the day before Blockbuster was to open, General Crerar drew the attention of his corps commanders to the need for reconsidering the general plan because of the enemy's determined resistance in front of Weeze. He was concerned that the delay in clearing the lateral road from Weeze to the Maas River at Welt would prevent early construction of the Wanssum-Welt bridge, which was important for the maintenance of the Thirtieth Corps. (The road was not captured by the Fifty-second Division until March 3-4, and the bridge was completed only on the sixth.) If by D plus 1 it was apparent that extensive regrouping was needed for a further deliberate attack, he pointed to the possibility of accepting a "partial" operation, which would end with the securing of the Calcar-Udem Ridge (i.e., phase two of Blockbuster). In any case, whether Blockbuster was partial or complete, the Thirtieth Corps was to keep its "left shoulder well up and to exploit any favourable situations."[9]

This passage draws attention to the Thirtieth Corps's supply problem. Its only main road ran south from the bottleneck of Cleve, around the end of the Reichswald, and through the crowded Bedburg area to Goch, which had only recently been cleared and was a shambles. The alternative ran from Hekkens through Asperden to Goch. South of Goch there was but one road. The road crossing the Maas at Welt, to which Crerar referred, ran northeast to Weeze, where it joined the Goch centre line, and over the Second Corps boundary to Udem. If the Second Corps failed, the Thirtieth Corps could not take over the battle until the Welt bridge was built and the road to Weeze cleared of the enemy. Until then it did not have the roads and its country was wet and unsuitable, hence the need for some regrouping in that event.

The deduction Simonds made from Crerar's statement was that the Second Corps would have to carry the ball through to Xanten, and that the Thirtieth Corps would have to take Weeze, not only for its own administrative comfort but to help the Second Corps forward. It is curious, though, that Crerar did not alter the intercorps boundary to the Niers River to give the Eleventh Armoured Division a wider front and the assistance of the Third British Infantry Division, which had been directed on Kervenheim. It was unlikely, otherwise, that the Third British would strain every nerve when the Thirtieth Corps's role was only to provide a defensive flank for the Second Corps.

Simonds's operational plan, as usual clearly expressed and requiring no written confirmation, gave the decisive roles to the Second Infantry and the Fourth Armoured Divisions, which were responsible for getting astride the broad northern half of the Calcar-Udem Ridge. On their right the Third Division would take Keppeln and move down the road from Bedburg to Udem, which was their main objective. The Fourth Armoured, working in two groups, had the most dangerous and exciting tasks. Brigadier Moncel's Tiger Group would move between the two infantry divisions and, seizing Todtenhugel, sweep south along the ridge to its high features. Lion Group under Brigadier Jefferson would then establish itself north of Udem and, still under cover of the darkness of the early morning of February 27, attack across the valley to seize the gap between the Hochwald feature and its continuation, the Tuschen and Balberger Wälder. By then the Third Division would be fighting in the town of Udem and should have cleared it by daylight on the twenty-seventh.

Simonds hoped that the direction of the initial attack would give the Germans the impression that he was aiming at Marienbaum and the northern part of the Hochwald. The Forty-third Division, by attacking along the main road to Marienbaum and Xanten, would reinforce the deception. Then a sudden switch of the Fourth Armoured Division down the ridge and its thrust at the Hochwald Gap might catch the enemy unawares. The Eleventh Armoured Division was to follow the Third Canadian and pass around the southern tip of Udem during the battle for the town, lending valuable support to Lion Group's right flank by advancing south of the Balberger Wald on the morning of the twenty-seventh.

Defrocked Priests, now called Kangaroos, had become a permanent part of the Second Corps's tactical drill and were to be used in the attacks to bring infantry through fire-swept areas. Simonds's dominating idea for the battle was to keep the attack moving day and night at least until he had occupied the Hochwald feature and launched a force down the railway line to Xanten.

Refighting battles is intellectually entertaining but seldom results in conclusions that are based on more than conjecture. At best we can be certain of the course chosen by one side and the countermeasure of the other. Soon after the battle is over the opportunity to analyze it objectively is lost. As Sir Ian Hamilton wrote in his observations on the Russo-Japanese war: "On the actual day of battle naked truths may be picked up for the asking; but the following morning they have already begun to get into their uniforms." Battles, like other historical events, are untidy, and narratives that make them appear otherwise are usually based on the right explanations for actions rather than the real ones. Blockbuster illustrates this tendency.

As far as battles ever go according to plan, Blockbuster did so, notwithstanding the impressions of the participants whose views I have offered. In the small hours of February 27 Lion Group's Algonquin Regiment, less one platoon that had not rejoined from Tiger Group, and a squadron of South Alberta tanks, were poised to advance from the ridge above Kirsel, down through or around the wet, wooded area in the valley, and through the lines of trenches blocking the entrance to the gap between the Hochwald and the Tuschenwald. Behind them the Third Division was fighting in Udem. Nothing was known about the progress of the Eleventh Armoured Division south of the railway except that there were no sounds of battle in the darkness. However, the Fourth Armoured Division was still a pioneer in the use of tanks at night, although not always to the satisfaction of its armoured regiments. On this occasion they had been ordered to remain with their infantry at night, and not depart to rear-rally, as had once been the unpopular fashion.

The foray to the Hochwald Gap was risky, since the going in the valley was boggy and the enemy had not been systematically cleared from the ridge above Kirsel. The hope was that the enemy would be astounded and confused as the tanks ground and clanked noisily by in the dark, the infantry on their backs. As a precaution, lest the main attack run into trouble with the enemy or the boggy ground, a squadron of Albertas and the carriers of the Algonquins were sent across the railway south of Udem to accomplish a right hook to the vicinity of Udemerbruch. By the time they found their way to the railway, it was light and the column had misread its maps in confusing country. They were caught on the railway by antitank guns from in front and behind and were virtually destroyed. The main force was successful in negotiating the valley, and soon after first light a company of the Algonquins drove the enemy from their positions below the gap and the rest of the battalion moved up on the flanks. Later in the day a second battalion of Lion Group, the Argyll and Sutherland Highlanders of Canada, were committed to force the gap and to seize the top of the ridge at Point 73. They got no farther than a few hundred yards short of their objective, where they dug in. What was required now was a flood of armour and Kangaroo-borne infantry to burst through the gap.

That evening Major General Vokes gave orders to restore the momentum of the attack. Starting in the early morning darkness, Brigadier Jefferson was ordered to take Point 73 and press through the gap to the lateral road. He was also to take the wooded ridge of the Tuschenwald on the right of the railway cutting. In the meantime the rail line between Udem and the Tuschenwald was to be secured so that the engineers might get to work on it. When these objectives were secured, the tanks of the Grenadier Guards and the Lake Superior Motor Battalion would burst through the gap and seize the wooded area on the far bank of the Hohe Ley.[10]

A turning point had been reached. The Germans had been forced to send troops to the American front where they were being driven back rapidly as they were caught in flank and rear. They knew they had to hold the northern part of the front on the Hochwald front until their divisions opposite the Americans could withdraw to the Wesel bridgehead, otherwise German forces west of the Rhine would be encircled. Simonds was equally clear that he had to prevent the German combat divisions from withdrawing across the Rhine where they would fight the Allies once more. It was the moment to take out the whips, and he insisted on offensive action across the front.

From February 28 until the front began to break on March 3 the scene was set for a bitter fight all along the Hochwald, particularly around the gap. A feature of it was the German artillery defence, which fired every round it could lay its hands on, knowing there was no point in carting ammunition back across the Rhine. The defence was strengthened from guns east of the Rhine. Disconcertingly their shells often arrived over the left shoulder of the attackers, giving them the impression that friendly fire was dropping short.

On the twenty-eighth Vokes's plan of the previous evening for renewing the assault on the gap was put into force. Critical questions about the conduct of the battle from then onwards have been voiced, and even if they cannot be answered, at least an attempt must be made. First, though, it must be accepted that the battle had reached a point at which a supreme effort was required by the Second Corps. The defenders, too, were on a knife edge. General von Luettwitz, who commanded the Forty-seventh Panzer Corps, "looked forward to the twenty-eighth with great anxiety," although in his circumstances the ground favoured him.[11]

The railway climbed the ridge in a deep and narrow cutting that divided the Hochwald from the Tuschenwald feature. The cutting could not be used as an approach, since it was a trap. It also divided the attackers. As long as defenders held one side of the cutting, they could enfilade the attackers on the other. Beyond the crest of the hill the railway remained in a cutting until it emerged at a road running across the front on which there was a farm. From the farm, which was on a forward slope for the attackers, another road led down a valley parallel to the railway to a small hamlet and the Hohe Ley Brook. Beyond the brook was the wood, which was the objective of the Lake Superiors and the Grenadier Guards. The road and the valley were overlooked from the high ground of the Balbergerwald on the right and from the Hochwald in the left rear. Any force that tried to advance straight through the gap and down the valley was in a shooting gallery and was unlikely to succeed.

Simonds has been variously criticized for obstinately pressing the assault on the gap and for not attacking the enemy's flank.[12] It has been said that he was ill-informed and that ambition motivated him lest the battle be taken out of his hands and handed to Horrocks. In *Rhineland: The Battle to End the War* the Whitakers write: "Nevertheless, under pressure from this threat of Crerar's to denude his operation and give the main thrust to Horrocks, Simonds urged Major-General Vokes to strike eastward through the gap with his 4th Canadian Armoured Division, seize its rail line, and continue on to Xanten. At the same time, he instructed 2nd and 3rd Canadian Infantry Divisions to clear out the enemy strongpoints in the two flanking woods."[13] Germans have suggested, on the other hand, that the way to Xanten was still open on the evening of the twenty-eighth,[14] and they asked why Simonds attacked across the front instead of concentrating on the gap.[15]

Simonds's movements during the battle were as energetic as usual. With Marshal Stearns, his signaller/driver Corporal Jarvis, who had been with him since Italy, and Corporal Speer, who had joined him in England and drove the Staghound or the jeep, he spent all the hours of each day at divisional and brigade headquarters, or looking at the ground. Stearns, on the radio, kept him in touch with his own staff. The weakness in the communications system continued to be within battalions where the Number 18 set with infantry companies frequently failed. There, artillery communications were a help to Simonds. Battery commanders at battalions sent their COs at brigade headquarters information that was quickly passed to the CRA at divisional headquarters. Consequently Simonds was as well informed as battalion COs.

The possibility of outflanking the Hochwald-Balberger-Hammerbruch feature was removed by the slow progress of the Eleventh British Armoured and the Third British on the right. Reports on the two British divisions' progress are vaguely worded in C. P. Stacey's *The Victory Campaign*. The Third Division took Kervenheim on March 1, and the armoured brigade of the Eleventh Division dropped out of the battle on the second.[16] Neither was much use to Simonds. In consequence the Third Canadian Division was responsible for the flanking movement that affected fighting in the gap on March 1 and subsequent days. That action started when Vokes's operations on February 28 saw the weakened Argyll and Sutherland Highlanders holding the farm beyond the gap with the help of a few tanks, but the Lincoln and Welland Regiment failing on the right of the railway cutting. Because of boggy ground, heavy shelling, and the narrowness of the salient to the Argylls, the sally of the Lake Superiors and the Grenadiers was postponed.

There was one more attempt to force the gap before the effect of the progress of the Third Division on the right of the railway cutting and of the Second on the left in the Hochwald forced the Germans to relinquish their hold on the feature. The Lake Superior Regiment in Kangaroos and the Grenadiers made their gallant thrust forward to the Hohe Ley, followed by the Algonquins, in predawn darkness. They were late in passing through the gap at Point 73 and reached a location well short of the woods beyond the Hohe Ley. It was a gallant attempt in which Algonquins and Superiors, both with half-strength companies, fought with skill and bravery. The tanks and Kangaroos found the deadly shooting of tanks and antitank guns from the higher ground on their right beyond the railway too much for them. When the light of day exposed them, their losses rose and they had to withdraw, leaving the infantry to manage as best they could. Three companies of the Superiors and one of the Algonquins had about 140 casualties, exceedingly heavy losses considering that the companies of the former were only about fifty strong at the start.

This last effort ended with the Second Division taking over the Fourth Armoured Division's positions west of the Hohe Ley early on March 3, and that night the effects of fighting on the left and right of the gap made the German commanders decide to pull back. Early the next morning Simonds appeared in his Staghound in a fury over the "stickiness" of the Second Division infantry. He drove forward alone, and when no one fired at him, he could see that the enemy had gone. Returning, he shouted at the forward company to follow him: "Come on, you bastards, there's no one there." Indeed, the German positions were empty but for their dead and a mess of abandoned equipment. But the Second Division infantry were exhausted and that part of the front had ceased to be decisive. By the end of March 4 the Second Corps was less than two miles from Xanten. The front on the right had broken open as the Thirtieth and Sixteenth Corps of the Ninth U.S. Army made contact at Geldern on the third and swung in towards Wesel. On March 8 Simonds took command of the Thirtieth Corps's divisions, giving him nine, the total of an average army. On March 11 the Germans evacuated the Wesel bridgehead, bringing to an end the campaign west of the Rhine.

By way of contrast, before Operation Plunder, the crossing of the Rhine on March 23, a number of social events proved memorable. On March 4 Winston Churchill, Sir Alan Brooke, and Bernard Montgomery met Simonds, accompanied by Elliot Rodger and Darrel Laing, in the Reichswald. The party went to a vantage point where Simonds pointed out some of the main features. Winston Churchill took the opportunity, now that he was on German soil, to have "an unscheduled leak" in a ditch. He was in an expansive mood at lunch, consuming brandy and waving his cigar around as he gave his views on the future Polish boundary, capital ships, tank construction, looting, permitted or otherwise, and any other subject that crossed his mind. Salmon had been sent for the luncheon by Lieutenant Colonel Anderson from his Scottish river. Unfortunately the mess sergeant served red wine with it. Churchill made no comment, but after the meal he sensitively presented the embarrassed man with his cigar box and thanked him for an excellent meal and an enterprising choice of wine. Afterwards they went outside for photographs.

According to Charles Lynch, Churchill had started the day too early for his liking and had been denied alcohol by Montgomery, all of which had put him in a surly mood by the time he joined the Second Corps officers:

Dieppe, the invasion that went wrong. A captured German photograph records the devastation on the beach, August 19, 1942. (Department of National Defence)

Operation Overlord, success at last! The Canadians arrive on the beaches near Bernières-sur-Mer, June 6, 1944. (Department of National Defence)

Nursing Sisters O'Donnell *(left)*, Woolsey, and Mackenzie pause for a cup of coffee in France, July 1944. (NATIONAL ARCHIVES OF CANADA)

Canadian soldiers, one of them a dispatch rider, fire into a house in Caen, July 1944. (NATIONAL ARCHIVES OF CANADA)

Pursuing the enemy across the Seine River: General Simonds and his ADC, Marshal Stearns, in a Staghound. (DEPARTMENT OF NATIONAL DEFENCE)

Three generals in front of a Dakota: Miles Dempsey *(left)*, Bernard Montgomery, and Guy Simonds. (Department of National Defence)

Admiral Sir Bertram Ramsay pays a visit to Simonds at Canadian army headquarters in Belgium on the eve of the Walcheren decision, November 1944.

Infantrymen in a French City, Boulonge, France. The Highland Light Infantry hunts for snipers in the ruins of Boulonge, September 1944. (O. N. Fisher/Canadian War Museum)

Nijmegen Salient, December 1944. A soldier of the North Shore Regiment strips his Bren gun during a pause in the action. (Alex Colville/ Canadian War Museum)

Senior officers in the First Canadian Army. Front *(left to right):* Major General Maczec, unknown, Lieutenant General Simonds, General Crerar, Lieutenant General Foulkes, Major General Hoffmeister, unknown. Rear *(left to right):* Brigadiers Gilbride, Mann, Lister, Kitching, Keefler, Matthews, Burns, Foster, Moncel, Rodger, and Laing.
(DEPARTMENT OF NATIONAL DEFENCE)

The Canadian army liberates a Dutch town. (NATIONAL ARCHIVES OF CANADA)

The surrender: German General Stroube, the Emden-Wilhelmshaven commander, with Simonds's ADC, Captain Marshal Stearns, just before the enemy's official capitulation in May 1945.

(Department of National Defence)

The legacy: Private Grant of Edmonton gazes down on the bodies of dead Russians in a liberated POW camp north of Meppen in Germany. (National Archives of Canada)

The war in Korea: Brigadier "Rocky" Rockingham *(left)*, commander of the Canadian Brigade, and CGS Simonds. (DEPARTMENT OF NATIONAL DEFENCE)

Chief of the General Staff Simonds visits the Seventy-ninth Field Regiment in Hohne, Germany, 1952. (DEPARTMENT OF NATIONAL DEFENCE)

Guy Granville Simonds: a civilian, but not fading away. (ASHLEY AND CRIPPEN)

The funeral procession for Lieutenant General Guy Simonds in Toronto in May 1974.
(DEPARTMENT OF NATIONAL DEFENCE)

The general's grave in Toronto's Mount Pleasant Cemetery.
(DEPARTMENT OF NATIONAL DEFENCE)

The Simonds family unveils the inaugural plaque of the Simonds Auditorium, Canadian Forces College, Armour Heights, Toronto, October 16, 1989. Mrs. and Colonel Charles Simonds *(left)*, Dorothy Sinclair Simonds (General Simonds's widow), and Major Christopher Simonds (the general's grandson).
(CANADIAN FORCES COLLEGE)

It was not for nothing that Simonds was regarded as the keenest of the Canadian general officers. Quickly perceiving Churchill's mood, he told one of his junior officers to take one of the big tin tea mugs, fill it with whisky and place it in front of Churchill without comment.

This was done and when Churchill took a sip of what looked like tea, his eyes brightened on the spot and he took two more long draughts. The effect was that of the sun breaking through dark clouds and there was a magic change in the mood, with Churchill becoming more and more ebullient as the lunch proceeded.

He granted us a press conference, and when Montgomery tried to cut in, Churchill waved him off. Then the motorcade proceeded in the direction of the Rhine, with cheering troops lining the roadsides and Churchill giving them the V-sign. That's not all he gave them, though. Having had so much to drink, the great man had to have a leak. In fact, he had to have one every 20 minutes . . .[17]

In the last days of the Wesel bridgehead the First Canadian Corps headquarters arrived, with Charles Foulkes as commander and George Kitching as his chief of staff. On March 15 A Mess of First Corps HQ held a dinner for senior Canadians to celebrate the reunion of the two corps under General Crerar's First Canadian Army. Operation Plunder was to be a Second Army operation. A few Third Division Canadians were to fight on the left of Horrocks's Thirtieth Corps in its early stages to provide a bridgehead for the Second Corps's crossing. The First Canadian Army would then be responsible for the liberation of Holland. Thus were to begin the ties between the two countries, which Simonds cemented further when he became GOC in Holland after the armistice.

The two Canadian corps, one from the Eighth Army and the other from the Twenty-first Army Group, and the two corps commanders, Foulkes and Simonds, were interesting to compare. Foulkes consulted his divisional commanders before making a plan and his chief of staff was involved in the planning. That suited the Eighth Army's informal way of doing things but may have started in the First Corps only after E. L. M. Burns took over from Crerar two experienced and self-willed divisional commanders, Chris Vokes and Bert Hoffmeister, the latter having commanded a company, battalion, and brigade. Later, Major General Harry Foster, who exchanged divisions with Vokes, taking the First Division when Vokes took the Fourth Armoured Division, was also a strong commander.

In contrast to Foulkes Simonds made his own plans and Elliot Rodger carried out the required staff work. Rodger was in awe of Simonds but not afraid of him, because he was competent in the role he filled. Their spheres did not clash. Simonds trusted him and relied on him. He was the perfect staff officer in all respects but one: he could not, indeed had no desire to, tell Simonds when he was wrong. But there have been few staff officers who were perfect. What matters is that they form a marriage with their commander. After that, confidence may go further: the commander may come to trust his chief staff officer to the point of accepting objective criticism from him, while the staff officer may come to know his man well enough to be able to offer criticism in an acceptable manner.

It could not be said that Foulkes was the better staff officer, for Simonds had proved to be a superb one, but when Simonds became a commander he took charge in a more positive manner than Foulkes. Simonds's divisional commanders were not allowed to form a soviet as were Foulkes's in the First Corps. Foulkes's more malleable management style proved to be more appealing to strong subordinate commanders like Dan Spry and Bert Hoffmeister. Politicians, too, preferred him when they came to choose a chief of the General Staff in the postwar years.

14

Postwar Frustration

....

THE THIRTIETH CORPS CROSSED the Rhine near Rees on March 23 with the Highland Division on its left. The Ninth Brigade of the Third Canadian Infantry joined the Highlanders the next day to expand the bridgehead northwards towards Emmerich. The rest of the Third Division entered the bridgehead as it was expanded and took Emmerich. The Second Corps built a bridge there and entered the battle under the First Canadian Army's command, its task being to advance northwards into Holland and northwest Germany. The First Corps crossed the Lower Rhine from the island, took Arnhem, and advanced into western Holland.

Since the Battle of the Rhineland had broken the back of the German army, the Allied senior staffs shifted their main attention from planning major battles to the pressing need to administer refugees, process hordes of prisoners, and feed the population of Holland. Although Simonds himself was as busy as ever guiding the actions of his divisions, the fluid operations were mainly the concern of brigades and battalions.

Psychologically the final days were difficult. Men continued to die and suffer wounds in bitter battalion battles for features like the Hoch Elten that overlooked the Rhine outside Emmerich. Until the very end artillery batteries were caught on the roads by *Nebelwerfers* and snipers, and tanks and wheeled vehicles and their crews were blown up by mines, sometimes sea mines, which utterly destroyed their victims. It was a dangerous time for liaison officers travelling at speed on deserted roads, for staff officers moving between headquarters, and for reconnaissance parties and those taking the surrender of German troops whose comrades continued shooting. Colin Anderson, the son of Ian and Mona, was killed in April while serving as ADC to Simonds. In the back of everyone's mind was the fear that at the eleventh hour they would be killed or severely wounded.

When General Crerar signalled to all ranks on May 4 that no more offensive action was to be taken after midnight, stiff fighting was still occurring on the Third and Fourth Division fronts. Crerar's message ended with the sentence: "In rejoicing at this supreme accomplishment we shall remember the friends who have paid the full price for the belief they also held that no sacrifice in the interests of the principles for which we fought could be too great." Since the Rhine crossing, 1,482 Canadians had been killed and 6,298 wounded. The total cost since the beaches was 11,336 killed and 33,003 wounded.

When hostilities ceased on May 5, the Second Corps was spread over a wide area of low-lying country that included Oldenburg and the western parts of Bremen in the east and Emden in the west. The attractive little town of Bad Zwischenahn, in the centre, became Simonds's headquarters. Brigadier Elliot Rodger's diary recalls the "strange feeling of restlessness and wonder" at the Second Corps headquarters during the last few days of the war:

> The long-awaited end is at hand and instead of a celebrating and exciting atmosphere developing it is almost the reverse. The battle becomes slower, less fighting but lots of craters and blown bridges. The troops become more careful; rumours of demobilization start, officers wonder what job they will get on return and when. Who is going to do occupation — Corps or Army . . . ? Also the realization of what a grand bunch of people we live and work with. A mess is a happy and comfortable family group. The "workers" in the offices all excellent lads who are faithful and loyal and have a real sense of proportion and humour. The break-up of such a gang will have its drawbacks. 2230: Radio announces "Hitler is dead." Doenitz takes over.[1]

Simonds took the surrender of German forces under General Straube at Zwischenahn on May 5. He was coldly correct with the Germans and brushed off their attempt to behave as though they were merely handing over a bankrupt business before retiring on pension. Simonds read the terms of the surrender document aloud and then, handing it to Straube, told him to read it carefully to satisfy himself that he was physically able to fulfill its terms. The next day the German staff group responsible for marching all German troops off Dutch soil and back to Germany for dispersal appeared, were briefed by Brigadier Rodger, and then closeted with their opposite numbers on the Second Corps staff. That evening Canadian troops started to round up German soldiers, disarm them, and place them in controlled areas.

There was much to-and-fro, but Rodger found dealings with the German army straightforward once he gave its officers clear and workable orders. The Germans were glad to be going home, and when Rodger passed their columns marching on the roads, there were no surly looks. He commented: "Everyone seems much busier than during the days of the 'war!'" On May 9 blackout was abolished, but not censorship of letters. Fraternization was not only forbidden but, for the moment, was unnatural to men who were only slowly emerging from the penumbra of war. The message was: "Don't lose the peace for the sake of a piece."

There was dancing in the streets of London, New York, Paris, and Ottawa when the armistice was declared. It seemed that the rejoicing crowds expected a return to prewar normality the next day. Certainly most of "the boys" would soon come home. Families would be reunited and husbands would return. But the war was not over, for some of those "boys" still faced the Japanese enemy. But all the individuals, families, villages, and towns that made up whole nations faced a huge adjustment for which they were not as well prepared as they thought. The men in the field were probably more aware and apprehensive of this than civilians in the streets, for when they arose from holes in the ground on the fifth, as usual before dawn, the change from war to peace was not striking. Only slowly, as the first day wore on to be followed by new dawns and sunsets, did each realize the remarkable fact that he had survived. Survival sealed the fraternity of those who had shared a great adventure. They looked at one another with new eyes as they considered its consequences.

Many in the CASF had not been home since December 1939, and they would return to meet a son or a daughter for the first time. Others had married British girls or were about to marry Dutch ones, and the young wives would soon travel to Canada, probably alone, to meet their husbands' families. The majority would not take that step but had come to think of England as their home during the war that had occupied so much of their young lives by 1945. Since they had left Canada, they had fought beside foreigners who had become friends, had been adopted first by Britain and later by Holland, and had joined a fraternity of survivors that was truly international. Membership in it would give them a sense of separateness for the rest of their lives.

Simonds well understood these sentiments. He was not going to find adjustment to a humdrum life easy when the music stopped. He had commanded a corps, and for a time an army at the age of forty-one. It was a matter of pace. He was not able to slow down. Everything still had to be done right and done quickly. But would the people of Canada and their political representatives want to jump on his moving bus and travel with him to his chosen destination? The shape of the coming conflict was soon evident in his expressed determination that never again should his country be so totally unprepared for war as it had been in 1939. Nor did he want it to sink back into self-indulgence. Quite the contrary, he wanted to retain the idealism that had driven the young army he had gathered around him. He dreaded being forced into a pedestrian life every day of which was identical and in which ideals were luxuries you could not afford. Crusader that he was, he said amen to the following prayer:

> Je crois que dans l'Armée canadienne outremer, nous avons trouvé un esprit vraiment canadien dans lequel le service pour le Canada a pris la première place. Si nous pouvons ramener avec nous, au Canada, cet esprit, nous aurons, alors, remporté une double victoire en Europe.[2]

Sentiments like the above had raised storm warnings in political communities after every war.

The end of the fighting brought the very difficult problem of repatriating the army fairly and expeditiously. So many armies had mutinied and turned sour during that exercise. It had to be done in an orderly fashion, though, and that conflicted with everyone's desire for speed and equity, as well as efficiency. Some of the very people who were most deserving of rapid repatriation were required to administer the scheme, to stay behind to feed the army until they, too, folded their tents and stole away. A Canadian army of occupation was also required to stay behind in Germany for perhaps a year or more. Volunteers would not fill its ranks completely. And then there was the Japanese war, for which a division of volunteers was going to be consigned to the Pacific.

Experience warned that "military" administrators, some of whom were civilians in uniform, in countries that were emerging from enemy occupation would have plenty of opportunity illegally to take home with them their "just reward" for wartime labours. Vehicles, food, art treasures, and contracts were in demand and would be within their grasp and control. The field army had grown accustomed to loose accounting, or none, amid the wholesale destruction of property around them and the profligate expenditure of national treasure to achieve it. The expenditure of comparatively small sums to ensure the comfort of the troops after the armistice was a natural extension of the habit, during the fighting, of requisitioning comfortable houses, vehicles, wine cellars, and anything that had belonged, whether by right or not, to the enemy or his collaborators.

The different standards and procedures demanded by peacetime administrators were sometimes ignored by natural right. This was particularly the case in Germany where an occupying power could justifiably enjoy its victory, as the Germans had done in the immediate past. In this matter there seemed to be two rules: one for Allied countries like Holland, and the other for Germany. The proceedings of courts of inquiry and courts-martial in Canada and overseas showed that the army took years to adjust to peace in this respect and chafed at the meanness of the financial regulations that prevented it from looking after its soldiers using public funds.

Simonds left for England for Colin Anderson's memorial service on May 7, and Ian Anderson returned with him to see his son's grave on the tenth. On the thirteenth the whole staff of the Second Corps headquarters paraded for a memorial and thanksgiving service. The last service had been at Dover eleven and a half months earlier when Simonds told them he had complete confidence in every member of his staff from top to bottom. This time, when he told them that no other corps had a record equal to theirs, "he had a tough time finishing his sentences." The series of dinners and last parades and the gradual disappearance of friends to retirement, to civilian jobs, or to take up appointments — Elliot Rodger in Washington, Charles Foulkes in Ottawa as CGS, General Bert Hoffmeister to prepare his division for Japan in Vancouver — was a roller coaster for Guy Simonds's emotions.

Amid the departures Simonds continued his regime of visits, interspersed with pleasures such as sailing on the lake at Bad Zwischenahn and a period of leave in Britain. The corps headquarters was finally dispersed on June 25. The First Corps followed it on July 17 and the First Army on July 30 when General Crerar sailed for Canada on the *Ile de France,* bound for retirement. Simonds assumed command of Canadian forces in the Netherlands.

By early September Simonds was engaged in repatriating Canadian troops in Europe. It was difficult to ensure equity. The original scheme in early May was designed to repatriate divisions in their order of seniority and to return their units to the regions in which they had been raised. When he was shown the first draft by Crerar, Simonds urged that long-service men receive more consideration, for the order in which divisions moved overseas bore no relation to the average length of service of the soldiers serving in them at the armistice. As a result of his intervention, though, only the longest serving men were separately catered for; the rest were to be repatriated with their divisions. In August, still dissatisfied, Simonds modified the scheme when the reposting of other long-service soldiers to the First and Second Divisions, to ensure their prompt repatriation, had reached almost a state of chaos.

The modified scheme that Simonds directed in early September gave men two parallel paths to repatriation. Priority was given to individuals with the most repatriation points, three being awarded for every month overseas and two for every month in Canada, with bonuses for married men and divorced men with children. As well, complete divisions were repatriated in order of seniority. By September 6 drafts of men with scores of 150 points or more had been repatriated and the First Division was moving from the United Kingdom back to Canada. Men who could be spared from the Third, Fourth, and Fifth Divisions with 130 points or more would follow. Then went the Second Division and individuals having 110 points, Third Division and men with ninety points, Fifth Division, Fourth Division, and finally drafts to liquidate army troops and CMHQ in that order.

Further complications surrounded the Third Division, which was chosen as the basis of the Canadian Army of Occupation Force (CAOF), known as the Third Canadian Infantry Division CAOF, to distinguish it from the Third Division proper (CASF). It consisted of volunteers, nonvolunteers with fewer points than fifty, and nonvolunteers with scores of more than fifty. The last group was to be phased out as replacements volunteered or could be trained as they were released from other units being disbanded:

> There is no workable plan which will suit the wishes of every individual. That is because this very big problem of moving an army home cannot be solved from an individual and restricted point of view. The picture must be looked at as a whole and a balance kept between making the greatest possible concession to the individual and maintaining a proper standard of living for those who have to wait. I consider that the plan I have outlined above is a good plan and makes reasonable concessions to long service men whilst meeting the requirements of returning Divisions and units to Canada as such.[3]

Simonds's final sentence anticipated the case of men who had come to Britain with the First or Second Divisions and found themselves at the end of the war with CMHQ, for example, which had the lowest priority. At the same time luckier men with more than fifty points who found themselves in a high-priority division might be repatriated after only a few months overseas. This was particularly the case with NRMA men who might have compiled seventy-two points for three years of service in Canada and another six for only two months overseas, perhaps spent in the United Kingdom. Every effort had been made to move ex-members of a division with high point totals back to their original divisions, but it had not been possible if the individual was in a reserved occupation. Hence, there was much bitterness when some NRMA men were repatriated before volunteers with between fifty and ninety points from combat service overseas.

The spokesman for the disgruntled was Major J. D. MacFarlane, the managing editor of the *Maple Leaf*, the army newspaper. He wrote two strongly opinionated editorials on September 19 and 20, condemning the repatriation of NRMA men, and hence the scheme in general, on the grounds that some NRMA men had joined the First Division after the armistice and were repatriated because they happened to have more than fifty points. His remarks disregarded a decision made in 1944 not to differentiate between NRMA men and the volunteers, apart from denying them the volunteer medal. As could be expected, the correspondence columns of the *Maple Leaf* were full of letters in support of the editor's point of view, which stirred up the long-standing grievance against the so-called Zombies.

Simonds, who was not the designer of the general principles of the repatriation scheme but had amended it in favour of longer-service soldiers, removed MacFarlane from his office and packed him off to Canada. His grounds were perfectly sound. The long-standing agreement with the *Maple Leaf* was that provided it published news and facts that were not of benefit to the enemy the Canadian commanders would not interfere with it. In turn the first editor of the newspaper, Lieutenant Colonel Dick Malone, undertook not to publish editorials about domestic political issues in Canada likely to cause friction within the army and between the troops overseas and people at home, or to injure army morale. Neither would he enter any internal military question likely to cause antagonism and set one group, formation, or service within the army against another.

In response to the two editorials Simonds asked MacFarlane to publish, editorially, the other side of the controversial question he had raised in his own editorials, namely that it was DND policy not to differentiate between NRMA men and volunteers. MacFarlane refused to accede to this request and to the principle that editorials should present a balanced view of the subject. In consequence Simonds removed MacFarlane and published a statement of the facts himself.

Part of the problem was that the planning rate of repatriation in the first scheme — thirty thousand men a month starting in June — had been too optimistic. Simonds had determined that to be the case before Crerar retired, after he inquired into the shipping available during trips to England in the latter half of June and in mid-July. He calculated that the Fourth Division, the last to leave, could not be embarked until June 1946. Subsequent to Crerar's departure, Simonds had had to modify the scheme, as we have seen. He explained that point in a report to the CGS:

> Whilst length of service of individuals would not, I believe, have been a contentious point had the return of the army to Canada been quicker, as matters stood, with a spread of nearly a year between the first and the last troops to be repatriated, it assumed marked and urgent importance. As a corollary, if the plan was followed of repatriation by formed units and Divisions subsequent to the move of Canada drafts withdrawing soldiers with 150 points and over, the Division to which a soldier happened to be posted made a very great difference to the probable time of his return to Canada.[4]

In July discontent over the scheme was fanned by the speed of demobilization of the Americans and of the Home Service troops in Canada, by clerical errors within the army that overlooked about six thousand men with point totals over 150 who were not repatriated before the First Division, and by the number of men with totals of between 130 and 149 who would have to wait for their formed division before being repatriated. It was to attend to these matters that Simonds brought in his two-handed scheme in early September, which allowed men with high points to be repatriated regardless of the division to which they belonged.

Consequently, having attended to the inequities in the original scheme and speeded it up to the extent that the shipping would allow, he was disinclined to treat MacFarlane leniently in September. The Canadian press, not having studied the details, at first gave Simonds a hammering. As far as it was concerned, Simonds had removed the freedom of the press and turned on a man who was doing his job of protecting the soldiery and exposing inequities. Although the members of the press agreed that Simonds had the right to discipline MacFarlane, they felt he was unwise to do so. The *Globe and Mail* argued that although MacFarlane had refused to write an editorial representing views that were not his own, he did not deny Simonds himself space in its columns to reply. MacFarlane had drawn attention to a situation created by the government's adherence to the two-army system:

> The editor acknowledged its existence and took the stand that it must not continue to work against the volunteers who made the Canadian Army, and who, in fact, carried the load to the limit that the Government was able to perpetuate its policy to the very end of the war.[5]

Dick Malone wrote to Simonds on September 26 to support him:

> Dear Guy,
>
> I feel I can once more revert to your Christian name as within another few days I shall be "mistered" out of the army. As you can imagine, I have been following the reports very closely in respect to your action re MacFarlane and the *Maple Leaf*. It was too bad after such a good record for the various editions of the paper that it had to happen. But you certainly had no alternative. Mac was undoubtedly wrong in his stand. He contravened the paper's editorial policy — a policy which was not originated by the higher command or the government — was in fact self-imposed. When I founded the paper, I drew up the policy — and "for information" sent it to both Monty, Crerar and NDHQ. On our voluntary adoption of the policy these three authorities agreed to non-intervention. It is a stupid error for Mac to jump the rails on it. Being a tricky matter to deal with, your action was very courageous and your statement on the subject extremely good. In fact the government here couldn't think of any improvement to add in comment. Certainly it was all to the good that the army on its own took the action in the field rather than have the matter enter political levels in Ottawa. . . .[6]

The minister responsible, Douglas Abbott, tabled Simonds's report and used parts of it in his speech in the debate in the House of Commons on September 24. He prefaced his remarks by saying:

> [T]he action which General Simonds took in removing the editor of the *Maple Leaf,* and the statement which he issued giving reasons for that action, were entirely on his own initiative, and without any question or request from Ottawa to do so, but both action and statement have my entire approval.[7]

Abbott went on to read or place on the record all the communications between Simonds, Murchie (by then chief of staff CMHQ), and

Foulkes in Ottawa. He emphatically dismissed MacFarlane's argument that a scheme that had been altered once to allow more flexibility and to benefit long-service men could be altered again to exclude NRMA men from being considered on an equal footing with volunteers. That, said Abbott, was unacceptable. And he read some passages from Simonds's paper on the subject of the NRMA:

> When we were hard-pressed last autumn and spring and the NRMA were sent over as reinforcements, I believed the feeling of the whole army was that if they "did their stuff" they would be accepted as equal members of this army. They did "do their stuff" and it would be morally wrong at this time when the fighting is over to say that they should be treated differently from other soldiers. If the criterion is taken as to whether or not a soldier served in an operational theatre, what about volunteers who never served in an operational theatre? A comparison of risks is not valid at this stage, for those of us who are awaiting repatriation have in fact survived. We are here alive and well regardless of comparative risks to which individuals might have been exposed. There are both volunteers and NRMA men who have fought in battle. Some of both have been killed. Some of both have been wounded. Some of both have come through the battle unscathed. There are both volunteers and NRMA men who have never served outside Canada. There are both volunteers and NRMA men who have never served in an operational theatre. Length of service and length of service abroad are the only proper individual yardsticks at this time. . . .[8]

The government should have been obliged to Simonds in particular, and the army in general, for allowing Abbott to say that the repatriation scheme had been designed by General Crerar and his officers overseas, and not by the government. Yet it was obvious that the dispute over NRMA men was of the government's making. Abbott handed a measure of blame to the army for allowing NRMA men who arrived after the armistice to be posted to the First Division and to be repatriated immediately if they had fifty points or more. It should be asked where else they might have been posted. The Second Division, scheduled to be repatriated next? The only logical place for them to go would have been the Third Division CAOF. And had that been done when they had more than fifty points it would have constituted discrimination.

Handed the unpleasant and burdensome task of disbanding the army with which he had fought since Normandy, Simonds had accomplished it with good judgement. He had done it despite the great disappointment of seeing Charles Foulkes appointed CGS in Ottawa instead of himself. The grounds on which Foulkes was preferred can be conjectured from living witnesses who argue that the Cabinet believed he would be easier to handle when wholesale economies for the services were in store. Simonds was of two minds whether he wanted to serve with the Canadian army under those conditions. Earlier he wrote to Montgomery for help and advice about his career after the war. Montgomery replied:

> I would say myself that the appointment of CGS Canada is in your pocket: if you want it. Harry Crerar agrees with me in this. I would say that politically you stand well, and Mackenzie King (who looks like coming back in a strong position) knows my high regard for your abilities. If, however, Canada has no use for your services, I am sure that the British Army would be glad to have you. I would personally do all I could to get you on our books. The next few months will show us all how we stand; and during that time you will be usefully employed in Europe.[9]

Montgomery was not the most astute politician, and politics were going to determine Simonds's career in the postwar years. The British army had to absorb officers from the Indian army and also find a use for many capable officers of its own. It might offer Simonds a single engagement but was unlikely to admit him to the British service. The Canadians wanted to keep him out of Canada, for there was no appointment they could offer him that would keep him so busy that he would be disinclined to disrupt the government's dismantling of the armed forces and also persuade him to remain in the army.

In October Simonds wrote objecting to the appointment of the recently promoted Lieutenant General Murchie to be chief of staff CMHQ, to whom he was virtually subordinated, although Simonds was the senior, as he had also been senior to Foulkes. The deputy minister wrote to explain that his instruction that Simonds communicate "on all questions including matters of general policy" to the chief of the General Staff through the chief of staff at Canadian Military Headquarters, London, had also been the instruction given to Crerar in May 1944. However, Simonds had never believed that that was how Crerar understood his relationship to the CGS and the minister in Ottawa. Nor was he mollified by the deputy minister's concluding remark that he wanted to "emphasize again the great appreciation of the Government of Canada for the outstanding services which you have rendered and its confidence in your ability to continue your present task to completion."[10]

Marshal Stearns had returned to Toronto, and Simonds corresponded with him during the next difficult years, telling him what he could not tell others. Stearns was notably closemouthed and became the recipient of a number of postwar analyses from Simonds, who was equally "secure." On November 24, 1945, he told Stearns that he hoped to return to Canada with the Fourth Division near the end of January 1946. It did not look as though the Canadian army was going to employ him, he said, in which case he intended to retire. He was young enough to change to some other occupation whereas, if he hung about doing inconsequential jobs in the army for another four or five years, he would be wasting his life.

On December 3 he wrote that repatriation was now going well and he expected to return around the first week of February 1946. Still bent on retirement, he commented that any post he might usefully have filled had been filled, adding: "It looks as though the government [is] manoeuvring me into a position where I have no honest alternative."[11] He regretted that the excitement, companionship, and glamour of the past few years was coming to an end in typical Canadian style — without heroes. The other side of that coin was that the politicians who had served Canada so poorly were back in charge. He was sanguine and arrogant enough to imagine that he could have done something about that as CGS. That was now out of the question, and he wondered whether he could earn a good salary and continue to fight for the army and Canada as a civilian. In that role influential businessmen like Bruce Matthews, younger rising men with whom he had served like Stearns, and the fighting politicians who had served under him might join him in preventing another war.

These mixed thoughts were stirring in his mind when he sent Stearns copies of the maps on which were marked the travels and travails of the Second Corps. "They are a small memento of the time we spent together and go with my real expressions of gratitude and appreciation for all the invaluable help you gave me. I cannot thank you enough for your efficient work and your loyal companionship."[12]

Retirement was not, after all, immediately ahead. Soon after, negotiations between Douglas Abbott and the CIGS, still Sir Alan Brooke, reached a point at which the British were willing to accept Simonds as an instructor or student at the Imperial Defence College or as commandant at the Staff College, Camberley. Shortly afterwards he was allotted a place as a student at the IDC for the 1946 course. In exchange Major General Jock Whiteley became commandant of the new National Defence College at Kingston. Whiteley had been a deputy chief of staff at SHAEF throughout the campaign in northwest Europe and was an excellent choice, for he knew all the senior Allied officers.

At once Simonds found that the work at the IDC engaged his alert intelligence. He met and talked to leading politicians, industrialists, and servicemen of the Western Alliance. He still thought that "the politicians," among whom he numbered Charles Foulkes, were deliberately keeping him out of the country. In fact, that was true. The reason was not far to seek: they had no post to offer him that he would accept. Indeed, there was only one that he wanted, and it was not vacant.

In April 1946, during a vacation from the IDC course at Seaford House, Simonds returned to Canada. He consulted with officials at NDHQ and publicly nailed his own colours to the mast on the Canadian role in the defence of the West. He also met his family for the first time since 1939.

15

His Colours
to the Mast

....

O N APRIL 4, 1946, Simonds was honoured by the
Ontario legislature. He was introduced by
Premier George Drew, who described him as "one of the war's
most brilliant leaders." The theme of Simonds's address was that
the efficiency claimed for a totalitarian state could be achieved by a
democracy when people recognized that rights and freedom were
only possible if they accepted their responsibilities, as well.
Through accepting the duty to serve in peacetime they made it
possible for the whole strength of the nation "to be put into the
pool for victory," if war occurred.

Now that victory had been won it was easy to forget how perilous-
ly close to defeat Canada had been at the beginning because of her
failure to prepare herself. She was fortunate that she had almost four
years to raise and train her army from scratch before it had to fight
in 1943. The public, ignorant of the army's condition in 1939, had
been impatient to see Canadians engage in battle. Had they fought at
once, as their fathers had in 1914-18, they would have been defeated
like the British in 1940. Who could doubt that great though the
Canadian contribution had been the outcome of the war had been
decided by the Russians and the Americans. That, and the lesson of
the 1930s, should teach them not to depend on a United Nations
without teeth, or even on Great Britain and the United States, to
defend democracy on their behalf. They must provide their share of
the teeth in future. For this reason Simonds declared:

I am a believer in a system of universal military training. I think in a democracy we must recognize the principle that, with equal rights must go equal, shared responsibility, and that when the nation is engaged in a life-and-death struggle, the whole effort of the nation must be put into the pool for victory.[1]

This address was not likely to endear Simonds to the Liberal Party, which had avoided conscription and was dismantling the armed services. The Liberals would not want an ardent advocate of universal military service (UMS) as chief of the General Staff in peacetime. The Canadian Army Active Force, on the other hand, and most Conservatives and citizens of Ontario, welcomed it. However, although Simonds's sentiments were shared by many across the country, he could have passed his message to the country without mentioning UMS specifically. In making UMS his conclusion Simonds showed lack of political sense, for there was no likelihood that any party would introduce it.

But the press did not let the matter lie there, and reporters interviewed Simonds before he addressed a meeting of the Canadian Club in Winnipeg. He told them that the world would expect much more of Canada now than before the war. He repeated that if the United Nations was to have sufficient strength, Canada would have to contribute its share. He envisaged a flexible call-up for UMS: training would be given in periods when trade was slack and few would be called when the economy was active. He pointed out that it was quite wrong not to have made use of this principle in the late 1930s when Canada and Britain had great numbers of unemployed. An insurance policy then might have saved them from the most expensive and destructive war in history.

K had met Guy when he disembarked from the *Mauretania* at Halifax on March 27, 1946, and accompanied him to Toronto. They travelled on to Winnipeg by train together, where they stayed for a few days until Simonds went to Vancouver and over to Victoria to see his father. Cecil was still a fine-looking man and had followed his son's wartime career with pride. As usual, the gatherings in Vancouver and Victoria where Simonds spoke were impressed by the content of his address and the manner in which it was delivered. He had always been at home with small groups; now he seemed to be able to project his message and personality to large ones, too.

In Toronto he and K had stayed briefly with Helen and Marshal Stearns and saw Bruce Matthews. Writing to thank Marsh on May 18, 1946, Simonds mentioned that he had had to return to Holland to give evidence in the court-martial of Brigadier J. F. A. Lister, who had been his chief of staff as GOC Canadian Forces in Holland. It was an uncomfortable affair that had begun when Simonds believed Lister was involved in black market dealings in liquor, cars, and paintings. Coupled with the charge was the accusation that Lister had acquired an apartment in Amsterdam, a considerable distance from the headquarters at Apeldoorn, which he was suspected of using as a meeting place with dealers.

Lister argued that the service chiefs who were his subordinates were based in Amsterdam and that he preferred to have his headquarters there. Simonds felt he could not allow a senior officer to escape retribution when juniors were being punished and extravagant living was no longer acceptable. He had taken the advice of Charles Foulkes when he was in Ottawa, and the minister agreed that Lister ought to be court-martialled:

> I found the same difficulty over the removal of the editor of the *Maple Leaf*. I was only supported over that when it became apparent that most reasonable people realised I could do nothing else, in spite of the fact that I was adhering to the official directive laid down by the Minister. Marsh, it is the *moral cowardice* of our politicians which I cannot bear — and I am sure it cannot pay in the long run. It *has* paid in the past and I am very afraid that our "younger generation" of statesmen may draw the wrong lesson that it will pay in the future. I am sure that it will not. I think our own and younger people have realised the disastrous results of the political cowardice that concealed the true situation from the people and led to the outbreak of war in '39. . . . Tell old friends to look me up if they come over . . . will pass on your message to the Andersons.[2]

A court of inquiry under Lieutenant General Price Montague at CMHQ found Lister not responsible for dealing in the black market, but that he had neglected his duties in allowing it to be conducted. For that he was sent home but, although the court recommended that he should be reemployed and not court-martialled, the minister decided to proceed. Simonds had initiated proceedings against Lister on verbal evidence from a customs officer and a member of the Canadian embassy, which proved either false or not proven. Lister's successor was similarly suspended from duty and sent to England under arrest, although charges against him were also dropped for lack of evidence. Subsequently the court-martial charge was that Lister misused requisitioned property in that it was used for recreation, not military business. It was a charge that, in the inquiry, Simonds had stated to be trivial if committed by a junior officer.

The trial appeared to be exemplary, although it was uncomfortable for Simonds to be cross-examined as a prosecution witness for an hour and twenty minutes and to have it revealed that he had himself reserved a set of rooms in the Anstel Hotel in Amsterdam from December 1945 until March 1946. He explained that they were used only for official entertainment. The defence also made it appear that he lived in some splendour in a house in Apeldoorn, although he was required to maintain it to entertain a continuous flow of distinguished guests. The newspaper reports did not bring out the fact that the minister, with the advice of the adjutant general, had initiated the court-martial, not Simonds himself.[3]

The whole family came over to London with Simonds and lived in a very expensive flat until June 1946 when the Andersons offered them the "Barn," adjoining their own house, Old Surrey Hall, East Grinstead, until the Simondses could find something less expensive in London. Guy Simonds commuted daily to his IDC course.[4] In accepting the "Barn" Guy was playing with fire. K was bound to fathom his relationship with Mona. Ruth, Simonds's daughter, was the first to suspect, and K learned the truth at a party in the main house when she and other guests powdered their noses in Mona's bedroom and found photographs of Guy displayed on Mona's dressing table. She insisted on their moving to London, and a year of tension ensued between K and Guy, which K finally found impossible to endure:

Dear Guy,

I hope I have time to write this letter before you come home as there are things I must say to you that seem quite impossible to speak. We don't seem to be able to talk things over and both have realised that we cannot carry on a marriage in silence. I have just finished ironing your shirts etc. and have tried to leave things as easy for you as I can. The last few days I have hated and I often felt that if you came to me and put your arms around me and asked me to stay I would. However, this way will give us back a chance to relax our private tensions and find the results. You will never probably know how unhappy and hurt and miserable I have been. I never get any sign of love or encouragement from you that any wife needs and I saw you lavish those attentions on Mona in front of me and in front of other people. I don't want to go and I don't want to break up our family but it has not been all my choosing as I have no alternative. It cannot be a happy family this way. I find my love turning to contempt for you but every now and then I get a glimpse of the old Guy and I get sort of hopeful again. It is up to you and you entirely if we can try again. It has to be without Mona, and I have to know I can trust and respect you as a husband and not just be proud of the soldier and ashamed of the man.

This is not "spite and bitterness" entering but any divorce proceedings, if they come, *must* be the obvious one and I will insist on naming Mona as co-respondent. Any cooked up one won't do your career any good. In fact, it would show you up in an even lesser light than the other way. If Monty ever hears of any scandal in your life he will probably not make you his successor, as it seems he plans to do, and although you blame me on [sic] ruining your career, when I tried to show you where you were heading six or eight months ago, you laughed it off and said you didn't care. I think you do really care, and if she really cared she should see that she is the one who is ruining your career.[5]

Shortly after her return to Winnipeg K became seriously ill with cancer. At first Guy believed it to be psychosomatic, but it was not, and she had a hysterectomy that she ought to have had in England. X-ray treatment and various drugs did not cure her, and for weeks she was in danger. There followed some reconciliation, but whether it was brought about by shock at K's illness or fear that rumours were being circulated in Ottawa about his affair with Mona, he reached an agreement with K after a leave spent in Winnipeg in the summer of 1948. They would try to live together again.

In 1949 Guy returned to Canada to take command of the National Defence and Staff Colleges, a joint command in Kingston, Ontario. K had agreed to live with him through his tour of command there and afterwards as chief of the General Staff in Ottawa. Visitors to their house noticed nothing wrong with their relationship; K was a charming hostess. She was fun to talk to and a noted Charleston performer. However, family members in whom K confided found her paying Guy back in kind for his infidelity. She was unfriendly and made Guy as unhappy as she herself had been in England. It was an unpleasant situation for both of them. In the meantime, whenever Guy was in Britain or Germany, and occasionally on transatlantic ships, he met the Andersons. It seemed that nothing had changed in that direction and that his own marriage was over.

In 1950 Simonds's mother had an accident in Virginia and, by declaring herself destitute, obtained free hospital treatment in Washington, D.C. At the same time she wrote to Cecil Simonds, telling him not to tell Guy about her situation "so as to protect his career." Apparently she had started to subscribe to Blue Cross before the treatment started but after her accident, and had concealed that from the hospital authorities. Of course, she was not destitute, and the Canadian consul investigating the matter just ahead of the American hospital warned Peter and Cecil that she would have to either pay or be deported from the United States. In an exchange of letters between Peter, his father, and Guy, this fresh drama in Nellie's life was revealed. It became obvious that Guy, and perhaps his father, would have to provide the funds once more to extricate his mother, and that Guy would have to travel to Washington to bail her out. As Peter explained:

The most casual investigation, either through the U.S. Immigration, the Canadian Embassy, the Bank of Montreal, or even the British Embassy, with which she is in full contact, will reveal who she is and who her relatives in Canada are. Guy is not only not being protected by her folly, but he is in danger of being semi-publicly made to appear a perfect heel who holds a high position in the Canadian Army while he lets his poor old mother lie in a public ward, destitute, in a hospital. He simply cannot afford to let such a situation develop behind his back. It is not the first time, and probably won't be the last, that Mummy has tried to pose as a great heroine to a group of strangers, with results that have proven disastrous to some innocent bystander. In one instance, you were the innocent bystander. In this instance, I'm afraid it looks like Guy is being fattened for the kill. . . .

I was half tempted to sit back and see this thing run its course to Guy's discomfort, as, despite his great qualities and splendid uphill fight to success, he has never shown himself in any great sweat to help me and, on the one occasion he did so, accomplished the feat with just about the maximum of groaning recrimination and unctuous complacency that he could muster. But I realised, on calmer reflection, that it would be a crime to sit back; as the thing would prove to be much worse than a slight set-back to his vanity and self-respect. At the critical stage of present Canadian Army politics, of which I hear a great deal here in Ottawa, it could easily ruin his career; and through no fault of his own.[6]

Guy answered Peter by reminding him that his mother had not done quite as much for him as Peter often suggested. At fourteen he had left school to work. He had worked every summer at the RMC and, when his funds ran out in the last year, it was the commandant, Archie Macdonnell, who had arranged with one of the scholarship funds to advance him the money on the understanding that he pay it back after he gained his commission. Referring to Peter's remarks about himself, he reminded Peter that when asking anyone's help, particularly your own brother, it was wise to tell him the truth and the whole truth and not fly into a frenzy when it was pointed out that you had not done so. And he advised Peter that his own finances, in relation to his commitments and the pleasure he obtained from his life, were probably no better than Peter's. He had satisfied himself that his mother would be well looked after and assumed she was telling the truth about her insurance.[7]

Guy and Peter had never been on good terms, largely because Peter, like Nellie, could never screw himself up to face reality. They both "made pictures" for themselves, as Napoleon used to say of those who lost battles against him. Guy, the complete soldier, prided himself in always facing the facts. In his career it seemed that he had always done so, and with success. It made him rather a cold man, or appear to be cold. In some ways his career had indeed been an uphill struggle. But he had made the road tougher for himself by pushing aside K's love, which he had for the asking, and by reaching out for Mona's, which was practically unattainable.

Ambition for the lifestyle that Mona enjoyed, which K did not envy, persuaded him that he had left K behind and that she could never be the contented wife of a successful public man. For himself he yearned for the tranquillity he had never imbibed at home. With Eric he had found contentment on fishing and hunting expeditions in the Vancouver Island bush. But Eric was dead. Ambition had been his driving force from the beginning. He never saw that his absolute and self-centred determination to succeed might cost him a devoted wife and ensure him a lonely middle age.

At the end of his course at the IDC in 1946 Simonds was told that Montgomery, who became CIGS in June 1946, had agreed that he should be on loan to the British army for two years from January 1947 to fill the appointment of chief instructor at the IDC, of which Field Marshal William Slim was the distinguished commandant. He was confirmed in the rank of lieutenant general on the active list while at the IDC and until his retirement. Allowances to cover the high cost of living in London were turned down by the Treasury Board, although supported by the minister. As Foulkes pointed out, drastic economies were being applied in Canada. The air force was reduced to less than four squadrons and left with only one aircraft that could fly across the Atlantic. A trip for the IDC across Canada, as part of the 1947 course that Simonds arranged, was out of the question in these circumstances. The estimates for all three services in 1947 were less than the army's budget the previous year.[8]

Simonds had no more luck when he wrote to Lester B. Pearson, the under secretary of state for External Affairs, to ask for a Canadian Civil Service candidate to attend the IDC. He would have liked to send one, Pearson replied, but could not spare the money. Perhaps another year it might be possible.

The correspondence with Marshal Stearns continued while Simonds was in England. On March 12, 1947, Simonds observed that he envied Marsh seeing the Andersons in New York and asked him to send "Mrs. A some flowers for me when they sail." The Simondses had a flat in Hampstead then, which made it easier to get to and from work, although Guy missed the country on weekends. But the weather had been "so hellish" it did not matter where you were. "This is a good place to be to keep up-to-date," he told Stearns. Truman's action in regard to Greece and Turkey was "initiated of course by Marshall and Ike — I expect they actually wrote Truman's words for him!" Simonds welcomed the step and hoped Congress realized it was "more than money now but policy and commitment later." It was the most important step taken since the war. The world situation, he observed, was predictable after such an economic effort as was required to win the war. Instead, everyone blamed everyone else for what was unavoidable and needed cooperation and team-work to be overcome. Only inspired leadership could exploit the greater degree of class cooperation that now existed. He was going to tour British industry at the end of the month and then head for the Middle East and Africa. Both were "a bit of a blank" in his educa-tion. He had not seen Monty since his last talk but would have a quiet tea with him next week and then attend Monty's Camberley conference in the first week of May.[9]

On September 8, 1947, he wrote Marsh:

You mention the difficulty of compromising with politicians (or "statesmen" in the case of those who deserve the name!). Every soldier must be prepared to compromise on matters of national importance which are not at variance with vital principles. But our politicians (or most of them) expect their soldiers to play up to domestic *party* poli-tics, which is a totally different matter. Without mentioning names, it is the reason for many of the difficulties and much grief that resulted in connection with the fate of senior officers of the Canadian Army. Some came a crasher by compromising vital principles in order to retain good will of party politicians and some escaped — or were res-cued by the politicians in their (the latter's) own interests.[10]

Ten days later he told Stearns:

I took a group to the Middle East in the summer break and then to
Kenya, Eritrea and back to Egypt. Saw Monty and he has accepted the
three main points which I considered important as regards future
strategy in the ME Theatre. I saw many old friends in the ME. John
Crocker now C-in-C and "Babe" McMillan commanding in Palestine.
You will remember him as GOC 49 Div.

K and the children went back to Canada in the summer while I was
away. I think I will have the children there at least until the spring,
though K, I hope, will be able to "park" them and fly back to join me
for the Xmas break. I was thinking of flying home then myself but as
nearly all the staff at the IDC, except yours truly, changes this year I
will probably have to stay here to assist the reorganization of next
year's work.

As regards my future I just have to wait and see. Charles Foulkes tells
me that the minister would welcome my voluntary retirement from
the Army. I believe Crerar has done me much damage in a quiet way,
ably assisted I am told by the ex-editor of the *Maple Leaf* who is the
energetic promoter of a whispering campaign. As I saw Crerar's
handiwork in undermining McNaughton, I appreciate how subtle it
can be!

Naturally, my heart is with the Canadian Army, but after I have done
the next year here I intend to return to Canada whether still with the
Army or not. I have got to establish roots somewhere for the sake of
the children who are reaching an age where they have got to settle
into a school before going on with their education.

IDC has been fun and interesting but after another year I will become
stale and cease to contribute. If K cannot get over at Xmas I will try to
get a trip to the Far East, India, Australia and New Zealand to establish contacts there.[11]

Simonds's remarks about K showed that he was concealing the
separation, or that he hoped it would not be permanent. Stearns
telegraphed Simonds to advise him to hold his hand over retirement
and suggested that he might be able to take action on his behalf.

Concerned about his future, Simonds wrote to Montgomery for
help and advice in September. He proposed leaving the army if the
Canadians had nothing to offer when his tour ended in 1948.
Montgomery replied that he had written to Charles Foulkes to ask
Brooke Claxton, who became defence minister in 1946, to give him a

firm answer "so that I can then decide what we should do [at] this end. I have been into the question of a transfer to the British army; in view of our present situation and run-down, that is not now possible. . . . I could always extend your time at the IDC up to the end of 1949."[12] Foulkes replied that Simonds's case was to be discussed by the Cabinet shortly. A month later Simonds learned that he was to replace Whiteley as commandant of the NDC, Kingston, at the end of 1948. After that the plan was for him to succeed Foulkes as CGS in August 1949. A spell at the NDC would give Simonds time to adjust to Canadian problems and give Claxton a chance to see him at work. "As you may be aware," Foulkes wrote, "the appointment of CGS is done by the Cabinet on recommendation of the Cabinet Defence Committee by the Minister of National Defence."[13]

On December 21, 1947, Simonds advised that the rumour Stearns had heard about his return to Canada in August and subsequent retirement was only a rumour. He had another year to serve at the IDC. However, he would not play musical chairs, although he did feel he was the most qualified man, the one with the most experience in both war and peace:

I have the handicap that I do not know personalities in the "political racket" in Ottawa but I am perfectly confident I can contend with them. McNaughton and Crerar do not worry me in the least, if *only* I have the opportunity to make my contacts personally and not through their jaundiced reports and descriptions. I am quite satisfied I can "see them off" provided we meet on the same field — in fact, both of them have already pretty well "seen themselves off," I gather. Certainly they are "busted flushes" as far as most people who knew them here are concerned and from what people tell me in Canada too, they have both tried to be "great men" a little hard to succeed.

I believe I have some contribution to make to Canada and, though this is *absolutely personal* to you alone, Marsh, may at the end of my military service, turn to the political racket myself. I would feel I could do so more readily and usefully, except that as far as I can see from here, none of our present political groupings seem to be facing the real issues that must be faced in the not very distant future.[14]

The issue that Simonds thought important at this stage was resolute psychological, economic, and military resistance to the Soviet Union by the West. In this resistance Canada must play a significant part in view of her experience in the late 1930s, her relative wealth in comparison with a bankrupt Europe, and her performance in the recent liberation of Europe. The temptation to look for union with the United States rather than continuing the British Commonwealth connection had to be resisted:

> I do not believe anything could be more fatal to our future. Personally I believe that we as *Canadians* have a great future ahead of us if only we keep our heads during these next difficult years. I am not in the least unrealistic in not appreciating the difficulties vis-à-vis our great neighbour to the south or the importance of maintaining the very best relations with them. There is every reason why we should do so both in our own and the world interest. But we can still do that and maintain our independence and I strongly suspect some of those who have complained so much at nonexistent "dictation from Whitehall" have been too ready to sell us out to dictation from the White House. Further, those who dangle the advantages of union are ready to close their eyes to the fact that those advantages would disappear in a flash the moment such a union became a "fait accompli." Our economy is *NOT* complementary to the U.S. at all. It may appear to be in the light of immediate circumstances of present world shortages. That gives the impression that the U.S. could easily absorb our agricultural surpluses merely because at the moment, with existing world food shortages, she can pass on in the Marshall Plan, or some later equivalent, anything she cannot herself absorb. But that is a very temporary condition.[15]

His views on the relationship of Britain to the U.S. are interesting. With a Labour government in power British industrial leaders were grinding an axe in emphasizing the success of American methods. Labour in Britain was not as lazy as had been made out. The real problem was that war industry was efficient but peace industries were run-down. Businesses in the U.S. would consider the success of socialism in the United Kingdom as a disaster. What was going on in Britain was a world problem. Capital rehabilitation was what Europe wanted, not the provision of consumer goods. U.S. and Canadian trade barriers had to come down, otherwise European debts could not be paid in goods and services. If the U.S. then blocked imports, there would be another world depression and Russia would say it was the capitalist system at work. Finally he suggested that unless price controls were imposed in the U.S. the Marshall Plan would lose twenty percent of its value through inflation. There was a school of thought against controls, but the intentions of the U.S./U.K. loans were being wrecked on that point.

Simonds had become acting commandant of the IDC because Bill Slim had left to work with the Transportation Board and Air Marshal Slessor, his successor, was in hospital. He was so busy that he could not get home for Christmas, he told Stearns disingenuously. On January 17, 1948, he told Marsh that K had been ill and had had to have an operation but had recovered by Christmas. He was able to speak to the family on the telephone: "It was good to hear all their voices. I am definitely going to have the children in Canada. Life in general and schooling in particular, at their age, is too difficult here. If K can arrange to park them for the summer months, she is going to join me here, otherwise we shall have to wait until next December before joining up again."[16]

On the political and economic scene he was prepared to predict *"as a certainty"* that if they failed to win the cold war, a shooting war was inevitable and much sooner than most people seemed to realize. And the cold war would not be won without very great effort and some considerable material sacrifice. Nevertheless, if only people could be persuaded of the fact that the cold war would be infinitely less costly than another shooting war. However, it was useless for service people to talk about such things because they would be charged with having a special interest.

In February 1948 Simonds was told that his tour at the IDC was to be extended in order to give Jock Whiteley longer to establish the NDC in Kingston and, as his second course there was to be extended from six to nine months, it would not end until August 1949. That meant that Simonds would not now take over from Foulkes until August 1950 at the beginning of budget planning for 1951. Foulkes went on to say that the deterioration in the international situation had helped improve funding, to a small extent, but recruiting was slow. "We have only just passed the fifteen-thousand mark and we still have a long way to go before we reach our ceiling." He hoped to have the army at its full strength of twenty-six thousand before handing over in 1950.[17]

Simonds might have been expected to accept this arrangement, but the estrangement from K in July and her illness in Winnipeg had changed the situation. His sharp reaction was partly explained by a cable that preceded the letter. It simply read: "Minister of Defence has approved extension of the exchange arrangements Simonds/Whiteley to Sep 49 and your appointment as commandant national defence college effective Sep 49. Letter follows." Instead of waiting for the letter Simonds sent a long telegram to Foulkes on February 11, with instructions to pass it on to Claxton:

In Dec 48 I will have served overseas continuously for nine years during which I have spent one month in Canada. At the end of the war I suggested attendance at IDC and exchange for further two years to save you and the govt embarrassment. I now consider I have earned the privilege given every cdn soldier who served overseas in the late war to return to cda long enough to establish a home for my family. I cannot usefully contribute to a further year at IDC and I know that such similar employment as commandant at cdn national war college except for purely nominal period will benefit neither that institution nor myself. Nor will I contribute to the vicious practice which existed pre-war whereby senior offrs retained appointments beyond period of their usefulness merely to increase their pension for I know its vitiating and demoralising effect upon the service. If the cdn government does not now intend to offer me employment in cda in Dec 48 appropriate to my rank seniority and experience I request recall then so that I may tender my resignation and ask leave to seek other employment pending retirement. If Minister wishes to discuss I am available to visit cda on his instructions between 25 Mar and 28 Apr or between 31 Jul and 15 Sept. This is in answer to your cable passed to me by Graham. [Graham was head of the Liaison Staff.] I have not yet received your letter.[18]

Foulkes's letter, explaining that Simonds was not being "put off" by Claxton, arrived the next day. Simonds replied:

I have no comments except request you will remind Minister that at the end of 48 I will have served abroad continuously for nine years during which I have been allowed one month in Canada. This new extension will make nearly ten years. I would therefore appreciate official recall to visit Canada during this coming summer break from 31 Jul to 21 Sept for consultation or to refresh myself on Canadian scene or what have you. Cannot arrange such visit from this end because of dollar difficulties.[19]

Shortly after Simonds had arranged to sail on the *Queen Elizabeth* to New York on July 30, 1948, and return on September 16, Montgomery wrote to say that Charles Foulkes had agreed to Simonds's relief at the IDC in April 1949 and that he should return to Canada by way of India, Singapore, Hong Kong, Japan, Australia, and New Zealand, for a fact-finding tour. Claxton had agreed to recall Simonds for consultations in August 1948.[20]

At much the same time the conception of a "super chief of staff" or a chief of the Defence Staff to match the defence minister was being discussed in Ottawa. It was to become the general practice in the West and had been mooted in England in the Salisbury Committee recommendations in the 1920s. The measure eventually took effect when Simonds became CGS, with Foulkes filling the post of chairman of the Chiefs of Staff Committee.

In the spring of 1948 there was a flood of semisocial occasions for Simonds to attend in England: a Silver Jubilee service in Saint Paul's; a big gunner rally in the Albert Hall at which Lord Alanbrooke, now master gunner of Saint James's Park, spoke superbly; and an air exercise held by Air Marshal Tedder at Old Sarum. On May 21 Sir Winston Churchill unveiled the Memorial Window to the Commandos in Westminster Abbey, and on the twenty-fourth Viscount Montgomery held his CIGS conference at Camberley. Then there was a three-day land/air warfare exercise at Old Sarum. In August Simonds returned, after a briefing in Ottawa and discussions with Brooke Claxton, to join his family at Tennis House, Winnipeg Beach. "A really good holiday with K and the kids swimming and playing a bit of golf," he told Marsh. He was to be godfather to Marsh's son and returned via Toronto for the christening. He also saw Bruce Matthews and many other friends.

On the way back to England Mackenzie King was on the boat, and they had a number of talks together. He struck Simonds as having aged considerably and was not very fit.

> He constantly tended to look back (going at great length and detail into what amounted to an apologia for his actions in the Ralston-McNaughton reinforcement question, rather than looking forward). He spoke with obvious and genuine enjoyment of his forthcoming retirement from active politics. I certainly felt then that he was feeling and showing signs of strain and I am not surprised by his illness here. However I hope he makes a good and speedy recovery, because whether one admires all his actions and methods or not, he has certainly done great service for Canada, according to his lights, and fully deserves honoured recognition of his services. I think it a great pity that he has been prevented from attending the present conference of Commonwealth P.M.'s because he is not only a great smoother of difficulties on such occasions but has great experience of Commonwealth affairs and personalities.[21]

In January 1949 Arthur Meighen and others demanded to see the drafts of the official history prepared by C. P. Stacey and circulated to many senior officers for their comments. They wanted to investigate Stacey's treatment of the reinforcement and conscription questions, which they suspected was a whitewash. Simonds told Stearns that the matter was set out very clearly, and since the drafts were "restricted" and not secret, he imagined Meighen could have access to them if he asked. Simonds had refused to comment on any of the drafts:

> . . . as they were so obviously marked by special pleading and it was quite apparent that the early publication of an official account was to be largely a whitewashing process. Notable examples being the space and exaggerated importance given to Dieppe and Hong Kong (failures in which both the government and Crerar were involved up to their necks) in relation to other actions. But you are quite right, Marsh, I certainly have no desire to become involved in any controversy now, which must obviously be provoked for purely party political reasons.

> As the records show, I did all I could to impress on others the urgency of the reinforcement problem, *when the war was on and it was vital that we should get the reinforcements.* In fact, I think I did more than anyone else to impress on Ralston the plight we were getting into over failure of a proper reinforcement flow, but I did my best then to avoid making it a political party issue, and I certainly have no wish to have it so used now when it can do no good.[22]

Simonds went on to discuss Stacey's treatment of the reinforcement question in his *The Canadian Army, 1939-45: An Official Historical Summary.* He told, at best, only part of the truth and omitted facts of major importance, Simonds wrote. It would have been better to have written the truth and withheld publication for twenty years, if necessary. But he did not like the way Meighen was making party capital:

> You can tell Meighen that all my military diaries and records — i.e. official operational and other records — were handed in (exactly as they were at the close of hostilities) to the Historical Section General Staff, without omissions or deletions. I have a few entirely *personal* documents — personal letters from Monty, Dempsey and others but there is nothing in them which would in any way affect the validity of the records in the possession of the historical section. Anyone seeking information should therefore address their enquiries to Stacey.[23]

Simonds started his round-the-world tour, bound for South Africa, on April 21. He returned to Vancouver in July, saw his father, and went on to Winnipeg. In August, accompanied by his family, he relieved Whiteley and took up residence at Roselawn, the official residence of the commandant of the NDC. He was also to be commandant of the Staff College, an unusual double appointment. Just before he left London he sat for the National Portrait Gallery.

16

Chief of the General Staff

....

SIMONDS'S QUERULOUS LETTERS from Britain about his army career seemed to belie the cold, imperturbable Simonds familiar to his contemporaries. Yet his energy and enthusiasm, natural hot temper and impetuosity, had always lain just beneath the surface, schooled by an iron self-control that kept his mask of command in place. Frustrated at being kept waiting in the wings at the IDC and NDC while great events proceeded without him, the mask had slipped. It had done so in Italy when Crerar's intervention seemed to threaten his progress and independence. As in Italy, the advice of Montgomery, whom he so greatly admired, and of Stearns and other friends, rallied him this time. They made him realize that the prize of chief of the General Staff must be his if he waited; his thirst for action did the rest. He was appointed CGS in January 1951.

Simonds revealed another side of his personality in his U.K. years. He enjoyed writing and made his points and expressed his feelings best in writing. He preferred a written communication on an emotive subject because it shielded the recipient from the warmth of the writer's delivery, the expression in his eyes, and the impact of his personality. These psychological effects intervened between the listener and the speaker and coloured the argument. Simonds sensed the effect of his personality on his senior critics when they attacked his manner, the way he did things, rather than his achievements. Crerar's behaviour towards him showed that he feared Simonds and recognized him as a threat. Unable to challenge him face-to-face on professional grounds Crerar resorted to innuendo and intrigue.

Simonds put little stress on theatre and loathed intrigue, preferring to persuade by reason; he was not a bully like Crerar and Foulkes. Instead, he resorted to writing whenever he felt strongly that Canada's and the army's future demanded the honest and necessary decisions he was urging. From Britain his written papers had to be a substitute and a preparation for action. Monologues with an invisible audience of critics, they relieved his tension when he feared that those in charge were unwilling, for political reasons, to accept the course demanded by the logic of events.

Brooke Claxton had been defence minister since December 1946. A forceful, bulldozing extrovert, he handled Simonds very well. Guy was in a tense state in the postwar period, one that recalled Crerar's impression of him in December 1943, and Claxton knew what he was taking on. Fortunately for their relationship the men respected each other. Strong, obstinate characters who spoke up for what they considered right, both were devoted to the army, and Claxton, a veteran of the CEF with a D.C.M., was still a marksman with the rifle. Unlike Foulkes, who trimmed his sails and his course to the current winds, Claxton and Simonds were partisans in action. They were bound to clash in the office; unfortunately they had little to say to each other out of it. That was Simonds's fault, for he did not relax, like Foulkes, when Claxton broke out the inevitable bottle of Scotch on plane and train and transatlantic liner. Guy Simonds was still not a social animal, and he could not, nor would he have desired to emulate Claxton, who could drink until 2:00 a.m., pop a few pills into his mouth, finish a book in his bunk, and be up as bright as paint the next morning.

Simonds's arrival in his office in A Building on the corner of Elgin and Laurier was timely. The year 1950 was one of great activity, culminating in an announcement in the Throne Speech on January 31, 1951, that Canada would return to Europe under the NATO treaty. Expenditure on defence had risen from $384.9 million in 1949-50 to $782.5 million in 1950-51, and in 1951-52 the figure doubled again to $1,415.5 million. It peaked at $1,971.2 million in 1952-53. The NATO buildup and the Korean War in 1950 reversed the postwar dismantling of the forces, which were partially mobilized and reconstructed under Simonds, who rode this breaking wave with the support of the army and with a style and enthusiasm that Foulkes could never match. Apart from the energy, ideas, and reputation that he had banked in the previous years, his ruthlessly clear mind prepared him for the tumultuous action in Western defence into which he was pitched. That clarity and objectivity had its adverse side, for it made compromise more difficult.

Claxton had acquired the right horse for the course but was slightly apprehensive that Simonds still resented the way the Liberals had delayed his appointment. In his diary Claxton noted that the press had made a fuss when Canada's leading soldier was sidelined in Holland, handling repatriation instead of being appointed CGS in 1945. He excused the choice of Foulkes by his predecessor, Douglas Abbott, on the grounds that Foulkes was the senior man, which was nonsense, of course. Foulkes had been a year junior at the Camberley Staff College before the war, and he was appointed BGS, divisional commander, and corps commander after Simonds. However, soldiers with outstanding records in war are often difficult to handle in peace, although they may be better servants of their country than more biddable men. So the Cabinet chose Foulkes on the reasonable grounds that the government intended to dismantle the army and Simonds would have fought that policy at every step. All this, of which he had complained a short time before, was water under the bridge to Simonds when he became CGS. Claxton's problem proved to be Simonds's annoyance that Foulkes became the first chairman of the Chiefs of Staff Committee coincident with his own appointment as CGS. His was a more powerful political position than Simonds's as professional head of the army alone, and he held opposed views on most things.

Simonds had made his opinions on politics, defence, and international relations perfectly clear, perhaps too clear, since the war. His antipathy for political soldiers like McNaughton and Crerar, who had matured under an earlier regime, was well-known. Simonds placed Foulkes in the same camp. He had never liked Foulkes, who had been protected by Crerar when Simonds wanted to sack him as the Second Division commander in Normandy. When Whiteley's tour at the NDC was extended, causing Simonds's return to Canada to be delayed for a year, he suspected Foulkes's hand in the arrangement. After an immediate explosion of wrath, he complained no further when the arrangement was sweetened by a proposal that he become CGS in January 1950, although Foulkes pointed out that August 1950, by which time the budget negotiations would have been completed, gave Simonds a year as commandant of the NDC after taking over from Whiteley in August 1949 and a clear start in a new financial year as CGS. That was the plan after Montgomery and Foulkes arranged that Simonds should be usefully employed from

April until August 1949 in a tour of Africa and Asia on his way back to Canada before taking over the NDC for a year.

In the early winter of 1949-50 rumours circulated that Simonds, by then commandant at the NDC, was not to be CGS in August 1950, after all. Simonds's imminent voluntary retirement in disgust was a plausible rider to this story. It was not until Foulkes telephoned Simonds in January 1950 to tell him that Claxton had decided to extend his own tour as CGS for a year so that Simonds would not take over until 1951 and then under Foulkes's chairmanship that part of the rumour was confirmed. Since NATO negotiations over Western defence were taking place in 1950, Simonds quite understood Claxton's wish not to make a change at that moment. What riled him was that the minister did not have the common courtesy to communicate both decisions personally, although he had the opportunity on several occasions. Writing to Foulkes about the way he had been informed of the new arrangements, Simonds raised his old grudge against Crerar:

> I despise *intrigue* and am very well aware that certain senior officers in Ottawa have intrigued against me in a manner not very creditable to them. They were "passengers" in the posts they held during the war, are well aware that I know it, and therefore try to discredit me, but their efforts have turned what sympathy I had for them to nothing but contempt.[1]

Foulkes indignantly denied that he had personally intrigued against Simonds, explaining that in 1945 he had tried to refuse the post of CGS on grounds that Simonds was better qualified.[2] He inquired who were the "passengers" to whom Simonds referred, saying that no retired officers had any influence over him. He had always stood up for Simonds and was most embarrassed to have to telephone him at the NDC to pass on the decision because the minister omitted to do so himself. He explained that the decisions still awaited the agreement of the Cabinet, a veiled hint that Simonds should not make another fuss. Taking the hint, Simonds assured Foulkes that he had not accused him of intrigue, but wrote that he was upset that Foulkes had not taken him sufficiently into his confidence to brief him on current events and policies in the way he would have expected as his successor. For instance, it would have been appropriate to have invited him to join the recent defence negotiations in Paris, particularly as he was well informed on the subject from his tenure at the IDC and NDC and was in Britain with an NDC course at the time.

After assuming the post of CGS in 1951, fundamental differences between the two men continued over procedure and policy. The role of a chairman or chief of the Defence Staff was to serve the minister of defence, in Britain a post proposed by the Salisbury Committee after the First World War but not created until Winston Churchill filled it in the Second War. Foulkes's function as chairman was to iron out differences between the chiefs of the services and to present to the minister a workable compromise when they could not agree. He also had to represent a unified Canadian view abroad in military negotiations concerning the country's international defence obligations.

Simonds was responsible for presenting to the Chiefs of Staff Committee the army's preferred courses of action and for pressing for their adoption when he believed the defence of Canada or Canada's part in an international force would be adversely affected otherwise. He objected, on occasion, to the way Foulkes interacted with the other service chiefs, and to the way Foulkes involved C. M. "Bud" Drury, the civilian deputy minister of defence, in military decision-making. He found that Foulkes and Drury often made decisions after reaching an arrangement behind closed doors with one or more chiefs of staff, or with the minister. Obviously compromises were necessary when an examination of the detailed papers supporting each service's case did not yield a decision in open committee. Simonds had almost an obsession, though, that the resulting "political" decision was second best militarily.

Essentially Simonds disliked the CDS/chairman of the Chiefs of Staff Committee approach to making defence policy. In practice he believed it gave the chairman too much influence, allowing him to meet privately with the minister or the Cabinet and save the minister from reaching a decision openly in the presence of all the service chiefs. Simonds's experience made him prefer the traditional British army staff system in which advice reached the commander or minister directly from his staff heads and was not filtered through a chief of staff. The staff chiefs, that is the quartermaster general, adjutant general, and chief of the General Staff, had equal right of access to the commander, although the latter was first among equals. Had Simonds held Foulkes's post he would probably have argued that like a commander in the field, with an interservice staff to advise him, he would make the decisions, not they. But Foulkes, when he was a field commander, had not operated in so positive a fashion as had Simonds.

Making defence policy in peacetime Ottawa was not the logical process Simonds would have wished, and he had a low tolerance for the personal and political influences that were evident in making it.

He could never accept that it was impracticable to expect the wartime teamwork he was used to at the corps level in a peacetime capital. Furthermore, the system in which he worked was new; it had not yet been adopted in either the U.S. or the U.K. His premise that the army was at the centre of defence policy, as if it were still in the field, was not accepted by the other two services or the chairman of the Defence Research Board, Dr. Solandt, the fourth member of the committee. When a subject was clearly of central interest to the army and only peripherally concerned the others, Simonds was often thwarted by the chief of the Air Staff and occasionally Solandt, although the chief of the Naval Staff, Admiral Mainguy, who objected to "outside interference" as much as Simonds, usually supported him.

Wrongly Simonds was averse to talking his opponents round before the meetings, not only because he was not good at what he called "buttering them up," but because his papers were usually so clear and logical that he felt there was no more to be said. He often used his deputy, Major General Sparling, for these head-to-head encounters. Sparling was not renowned for diplomacy, either, and while Simonds's submissions were better written and more persuasive than those of the other chiefs, his assumption that the action they called for was self-evident seemed arrogant. Air Marshal Slemon, chief of the Air Staff for most of Simonds's time in the chair, was seldom known to smile, although Simonds, Solandt, and Mainguy were friends.

Foulkes and Simonds disagreed on some fundamentals of policy as well as over procedure. Simonds thought it essential to maintain the Commonwealth and British connection; Foulkes considered that it was more realistic to rebuild the forces on American lines with American equipment and was not dismayed at the prospect of falling deeper into the American sphere. The two agreed that Lester Pearson's bridging position between Canada's powerful allies and his support of the smaller powers in upholding their rights was wise and just. Simonds argued that, in practice, without power to influence the main protagonists, and with the Soviet threat hanging over all of them, the policy was not credible and weakened the alliance, although, like Talleyrand's France after the Congress of Vienna, it gave Canada a position of importance as leader of the lesser powers. He expected Canada to join wholeheartedly in the struggle against Soviet communism and blamed Foulkes for allowing Canadian politicians to backslide, as they had in the 1930s, by suggesting compromises, such as nominal brigades that were actually under-strength, and agreeing to defence arrangements in principle but not when it came to the detail.

Simonds's relations with the RCAF were not smooth. He opposed the estrangement of the RCAF and the RAF because it led the RCAF into the American camp. (The origins of the rift lay in the overbearing treatment of the RCAF by the RAF in the war and in Western defence after it.) Foulkes wanted the RCAF to join the Air Division in Europe, which required it to migrate from the British sphere of influence into the American one. He favoured the adoption of American aircraft, as he did army equipment, on the grounds that American equipment was better and more readily available. In turn that required the RCAF in NATO to be based in the French zone of Germany. The Canadian army had gotten on very well with the British, followed the same staff procedures and doctrines, and was not impressed with the U.S. Army's performance in the Second World War. It was disinclined to "go American." The departure of the RCAF made the Canadian army choose between fighting in the British zone without Canadian air support and joining the U.S. Army zone of Germany to fight with RCAF support.

The government decided that since Canada had left the occupation force in Germany in 1946, unlike the British and the Americans, it was not consistent with the bridging position to reclaim former status. As a result, the presence of the Twenty-seventh Brigade as a paying guest in Germany caused some friction with the British, increased the charge to the Canadian taxpayer, and caused a prolonged and irritating disagreement between the Department of External Affairs, the Canadian ambassador to the Federal Republic of Germany, the high commissioner in London, and the British army over who should pay for Canadian accommodation, what was the legal status of Canadian soldiers in Germany, and what were their passport rights outside it.

This controversy went on long after military questions, such as the location of the brigade, had been resolved. Foulkes argued that a base in France for the RCAF and one in southwest Germany for the army would be best, although training areas were inferior to those available to the British in the north. Fortunately General Eisenhower, the Supreme Allied Commander Europe (SACEUR), made it clear that while he preferred the RCAF to be in the U.S. zone he wanted the Canadian army to be with the British on several grounds, including the Supreme Headquarters Allied Powers Europe (SHAPE) tactical scheme and availability of accommodation. Simonds held that military efficiency, not politics, should be the criterion in these and other controversial questions, and General Gruenther, Eisenhower's chief of staff at SHAPE, agreed with him and passed on the word to Eisenhower. The army went to the British zone as a result.[3]

The role of RCAF aircraft and their location and control could not be separated from one another. In wartime the Allied air forces had given their independent strategic role precedence over their interdiction role and the latter precedence over tactical ground support. To some extent Simonds's problems with the chief of the Air Staff stemmed from the extension of that policy by the RCAF and of the long-running wartime dispute between Tedder and Montgomery into the peace; in the memory of the army the Second Canadian Corps had not been satisfied with staff arrangements for air support and blamed Tedder for it.

Simonds always urged the case for tactical air forces, particularly for transport support for the field army. The political drive of the RAF before 1939 towards an autonomous role in policing the empire and the Middle East was in his mind when he insisted that the air forces could not have the main role in defending Europe, whatever new weapons were available to them. When nuclear bombs and then warheads carried in ballistic missiles became the agents of deterrence in the 1950s, Simonds continued to oppose Western dependence on them. He had regarded it as false policy while at the IDC, where he foretold that the advent of small-yield tactical nuclear weapons was inevitable and that progressive escalation through tactical to strategic nuclear weapons would occur if effective conventional forces were not maintained. The credibility of such weapons would soon be undermined when their possession by the Soviets led to mutually assured destruction through nuclear escalation. The consequence would be that the West would have to rely, once more, on conventional forces, only to find that the will to maintain them had ebbed.

Foulkes's views on these matters was that they were the responsibility not of the military but of the political community; his task was to offer the evidence to the politicians and theirs to make the decisions. Simonds, on the other hand, had never been one to shirk responsibility nor to consider problems in isolation. He did not take as detached a view of his responsibilities as Foulkes, nor did he rely on politicians to make the right decisions on the basis of facts alone. They had to be persuaded to do "the right thing" by the cogent and broad arguments of their military advisers. Obviously Simonds accepted that politicians made decisions but not before the military had made clear what course they preferred, and pressed it until it served no further purpose. Simonds treated defence as an international responsibility. Understandably Foulkes and the Cabinet were inclined to be more parochial when a minister of defence had to convince Cabinet and Parliament that his actions in defence matters were in the national interest.

Claxton's own observations add perspective to the relations between Foulkes and Simonds. Claxton's cooperation with Foulkes was unequalled. On every occasion, Claxton wrote, Foulkes fought to protect Canadian interests; something that had to be done all the time because, as Canada was independent and wealthy, other allies, including the British, would "take the shirt off our backs if we let them and insinuate that we were disloyal if we did not hand it over." As for the Americans, he only succeeded in getting them to spend more in Canada than Canada spent in the U.S. in one fiscal year. The other chiefs did not always act in Canada's best interests. Sometimes they encouraged allies to ask for or expect more from Canada with the hope that they would get a bigger share of the defence dollar for their service.[4]

Whether Claxton had Simonds in mind on this particular question or not, he went on to discuss the political inexperience of senior officers after a war in which they had received astonishingly rapid promotion. Simonds, Claxton wrongly stated, had been only a captain in 1939 and was quite inexperienced in handling political questions on a national or international level. Of course, while that was true of all Simonds's contemporaries, including Foulkes in 1945, Simonds had had several years of absorbing the politics of defence at defence colleges. Besides, there had to be a trade-off between years of peacetime experience in National Defence Headquarters, which no officer had in 1951, and a relatively long and intense experience of command in the field like Simonds's. Simonds knew and was respected by all the senior international military in 1951, and a few, notably Generals Lemnitzer, Ridgway, Slim, Slessor, and Harding, were close friends. After a war a minister could not expect to have both kinds of experience in his senior officers, and he probably considered Foulkes's comparatively slight reputation in such circles as an advantage. Claxton was really saying that Simonds's experience had made him not only self-willed and opinionated but very convincing when expressing his case. He did not want to have to spend time justifying himself to Simonds and preferred a more amenable man like Foulkes.

Claxton described his first meeting with Simonds when the latter returned home for a spell in the summer of 1948:

> In August he was in Canada on leave, and he came up to spend a day with me at our summer place. It happened to be Labour Day and we were closing the cottage so it was not very convenient. I expect the impression I made on him as I was working around the place in a pair of paint-covered shorts was equally as unprepossessing as the

one he made on me. However there was no doubt of his intelligence and his keenness. I could see that almost certainly he would be a success at the Defence College; he had the experience and attributes necessary to fill this post with distinction. There was one proviso: he must not go on making speeches. I am all for silent soldiers as well as sailors. I had more doubts about his having the generalized qualifications of good judgment, ability to get along with people, and the knack, the wisdom, the instinct, whatever it is, to keep out of trouble. As I recall it I voiced these views pretty frankly that day at Wonish and said his posting to the Staff College would be a time when he could acclimatize himself in Canada and win the confidence of those with whom he would continue to have to work should he become chief of staff. As to this I could make no promise. I would let him know what I thought about it just as soon as I could after his appointment at Kingston. That would be twelve to eighteen months.

As I expected, General Simonds was a success at Kingston and from my several visits there I got to know him well and like him a good deal more than I had. There was no doubt about his great professional qualities. After he had been there about six months I felt satisfied that he could be made chief of the general staff, though I must say that quite a few people, including some high-ranking military personalities from all three services, took it on themselves to state the contrary view. None gainsaid his qualifications as a soldier but they seemed to think he was so ruthless and self-seeking that he could not help but prove embarrassing and even disloyal to his minister. However, I put my judgment against theirs and I must say I was generally happy about the result.[5]

Between early 1948 and October 1950 when the Standing Group of NATO was established, the main achievement of Claxton and Foulkes, in the former's opinion, was to shape the NATO military structure and the responsibilities of its committees so as to ensure that they were subordinated to the political element and that the three major powers — the United States, Britain, and France — were not so overbearing that they left the smaller powers with hardly so much as a "toe in the door."[6] Canada's position was unique in that it had taken a major part in the war, had worked closely with Britain and the United States, with whom it had special ties, and had continued planning with them after the war. Furthermore, Canada had a French and British background, had large amounts of arms to supply to the lesser powers in NATO, and had an enviable reputation for honesty and efficiency. In sharing this NATO adventure the cooperation between Claxton and Foulkes blossomed into friendship. That could never be said of Claxton's relations with Simonds. In comparing the two men, Claxton observed that Foulkes always worked in Canada's interests whereas Simonds "would not know what her interests were."

This harsh comment in an interesting memoir that is, nevertheless, self-satisfied and even smug deserves a reply. Simonds's formative years had been years of appeasement that ended in a war that could have been avoided had the powers cooperated and faced reality. Events since 1945, the civil war in Greece, the Berlin airlift, the taking over of Czechoslovakia by the Communist Party, the struggle in Malaya, and the recent invasion of South Korea, were campaigns in a new war. In the cold war in Europe the will of the West to resist pressure from the Soviet Union and its allies was being tested continually.

Unlike Foulkes, Simonds was at one with the international military, largely Americans, who sought to create a military barrier in Europe that would make an opportunistic attack by the Soviets a foolish risk. On the other hand, after his time at the IDC and NDC, he quite understood that a strong economy was the best defence and that there was a trade-off between keeping men in arms and industrial growth. Claxton knew that NATO, as a political alliance, could only be sold to the Canadian public if it gave Canada influence at relatively low cost — an insurance policy with a low premium. Therefore, his aim was to gain political influence in NATO in return for Canadian military expenditure. Simonds sought military effectiveness, without which Canadian money was wasted and Western defence illusory, and feared that the political structure and manoeuvring for political position would frustrate the defence of Europe and make joint military action impossible if hostilities occurred.

Believing that Foulkes was helping Claxton towards his political goals rather than presenting the military view and that he was playing off one service against another to that end, Simonds took on the onus of filling the gap and restoring the balance. This aspect of Simonds's actions as CGS seems to have been in the forefront of Claxton's criticism. His remark that Simonds was uninformed about or uninterested in Canada's special interests was superficial. On reflection the different aims of Claxton and Simonds were complementary and remained so as long as each stood firm.

There were two sides to the NATO coin in the 1950s, as there are today. Simonds stood for one, Claxton mainly for the other. What counted politically was not the North Atlantic Treaty Organization but the North Atlantic Alliance. While NATO was its military manifestation, the political substance resided in the alliance itself.

Simonds would have agreed with Sir Michael Howard, who was to write in 1992: "Though the real value of NATO may be sacramental, the outward and military sign of an inward and political grace," the grace could not be preserved if its manifestation had no practical utility. Indeed, its value was twofold. It not only melded together the countries of Western Europe in a common defence, but it also threw the armies of those countries into an international force with a convergent military doctrine. Canada, as in the past, sought to merge with a larger organization in order to protect itself against its powerful neighbour and, in some views, against the Old Country, as well.[7]

When Canada had to provide brigades for NATO and Korea, too, raising manpower was obviously crucial and posed many questions. What was the appropriate kind of enlistment? Should they create reserve brigades for rotation and training? What should be the relationship between the mobile striking force in Canada, the Korea brigade, and the NATO integrated force? The most controversial subjects in the papers of the CGS were concerned with answering these questions. The struggle between advocates of British and American equipment and methods was always a factor, and underlay divisions between the chiefs of staff. Disagreements between the services about manpower naturally came to a head when funds were being allocated in the budgets. On those occasions two closely related subjects were in dispute. First, the role of the Canadian forces as a whole and the particular part to be played by each service. Second, the comparison of the army's manpower and equipment needs to the others; the army, it has been said, equips the man whereas the others man the equipment. Equipment was central and visible to the air force, manpower to the army; given adequate manpower, the latter, although with protest, could subsist in the 1950s on wartime and immediate postwar stocks of equipment.

A particularly operational difference between the air force and the army emerged in planning Canadian contributions to NATO. The RCAF operated from airfields that were wartime and peacetime bases from which their frontline aircraft operated. Furthermore, their repair facilities, supplies, and spare aircraft were found on these airfields, as were their families. On the contrary, the army moved out from a barracks, a nonoperational base, to fight in the field. They had to bring their logistics with them. Peacetime administration, efficient enough in peace, was largely shared, static, noncombative, and inappropriate in the field. Operational logistical support was in cadre only; the rest of it could not be improvised and had to be mobilized, for which the army required a huge reserve commitment that was slow to move overseas.

At the end of Simonds's tenure, when the unification of the services was just around the corner, RCAF officers were often unconcerned about the significance of this fundamental difference between the modes of operation of the services, tending to advocate functional organizations rather than linear ones with functional units under command as in the field army. The air force conception was suitable for an industrial process but not an army in the field. It centralized functions on grounds of efficiency in controlled conditions but removed from units the flexibility necessary for army field units and formations that had to operate in fluid conditions. Paul Hellyer, the minister responsible for integration and unification in the 1960s, strengthened the staff with air force officers who thought in terms of function rather than command.

Simonds was adamant that the Canadian army should be capable of going to war without an extended period of mobilization to call up and train reserves as in 1939. It was essential that NATO units be ready to fight, with trained reserves available. He did not believe that they could stop the Soviets east of the Rhine if the Soviets were sufficiently determined to penetrate that far. But he was acutely conscious of the moral ill effects of resting Western defence on nuclear weapons as a substitute for a force at readiness, and of the possible impracticality of moving equipment and men across the Atlantic to the operational zone after a brief emergency period had given way to active operations. Therefore it was essential to incorporate trained reserves of men and matériel in the active force, which had to be enlarged accordingly, and to store equipment in Europe in peacetime. His experience of the situation in Europe in 1944 was fresh in his mind.

The policy about mobilization, the readiness of the armed forces for war, affected the distribution of senior appointments in Ottawa and in overseas missions in peacetime. In turn that affected the balance of power between the services. In other words, national strategy was not only a political question for the Cabinet, but it had its political implications within the forces. In this matter Simonds held the unpopular opinion that the professional functions of the other services did not train their senior officers to make global decisions. Korea and other conflicts in the 1950s were primarily army affairs in which the navy and air forces were in support. For the defence of Canada alone the reverse was the case. Withdrawal from Canadian interests overseas meant the rise in influence of the other services.

It was inevitable that Simonds would raise his potentially explosive belief in universal service in one form or another when he was CGS. He did so during Claxton's tenure and in that of Claxton's successor, Ralph Campney, just before his own retirement. There were two sides to Simonds's case. The first was that the opportunity to serve a cause, a benefit that his generation had received in the war, could be given young people in a variety of services in peacetime. This idea was hardly a radical conception and was to be given form in the Canadian University Services Overseas (CUSO) and its equivalents in Britain and the United States. Simonds did not believe that the military should be responsible for correcting the character faults of young people, as though one of its functions were analogous to water purification. However, well-conducted military training, particularly overseas, did strengthen the character and broaden the education. Simonds did not believe in conscription as opposed to voluntary enlistment in principle, nor in conscription with no reserve commitment, but in military service that provided a reserve and a reservoir from which to feed the Nonpermanent Militia in times when its recruitment lagged.

This matter arose indirectly when the Twenty-seventh Infantry Brigade Group under Brigadier Geoffrey Walsh was raised as Canada's initial contribution to European defence. At first its discipline and morale gave some cause for concern in Canada where churchmen criticized both and asserted that the army was responsible. In NATO its appearance and performance were praised. Simonds and Claxton were both incensed at the criticism. The former pointed out that the low education standards of many men and the rough social milieu from which they came were to blame. Perhaps the church and local school boards should have attended to their formative years, he suggested, instead of blaming the army when the men had already reached maturity. The army had improved their educational standard by giving them courses and had transformed their characters for the better. He pointed out that a system of service might have helped them to be better citizens.

The Korean Brigade was raised as a Special Force nominally consisting of second battalions of the three active service infantry regiments, the RCR, the Princess Patricia's Canadian Light Infantry (PPCLI) and Royal Twenty-second, and the Second Regiment of the Royal Canadian Horse Artillery. All told, nine battalions served in Korea in rotation, three battalions at a time, in three brigades. The decision to raise the first brigade was made quickly in July 1950. The order to start mobilizing was issued on July 28, and the operation began on August 8. Because of this hasty procedure, there was no time to prepare the recruiting organization for action. It had almost enlisted the authorized grand total of fifty thousand men for the three permanent services by July and had been virtually stood down when it was ordered to raise the Special Force for Korea.

The process has been described as a shambles. Volunteers waited in large numbers while the careful screening to which they had to submit dragged on. The decision to enlist active service volunteers, civilian veterans, and untrained men on different terms of service added to the administrative difficulties. The newspapers counted the applicants and assumed they had already been enlisted, giving the impression that the recruiting target had been reached quickly. To conceal the mistake and speed up the operation so that men were attested and posted within thirty-six hours of applying, Claxton intervened and ordered the recruiting officers to cut their interviews from one hour to five minutes.

By March 20, 1951, after Simonds terminated recruiting for the Special Force, 10,308 men had been enlisted. A price for Claxton's helter-skelter proceeding, against the advice of the adjutant general, was paid when reinforcements with ailments and incapacities were discovered, much like those of whom Wellington complained during his campaign in the Netherlands at the end of the eighteenth century:

> "I'm told we even enlisted a couple of hunchbacks," one recruiting officer told another with a grin.
>
> "I doubt that," the other replied, "but we came pretty close. When the political heat is on, you can't reject anybody who's able to walk."[8]

A seventy-two-year-old and a man with one leg were enrolled. The sorriest-looking lot he had ever seen in uniform, one officer described his first parade. When a brigade draft reached Japan, it was found to include men suffering from ailments such as "chronic bronchitis, flatfeet, atrophy of leg muscles, cardiac palpitation, perforated eardrums, traumatic arthritis of the spine, hernia, and hypertension," all of which indicated to Simonds that a proper mobilization plan was needed.[9] A system of national service would have been a fairer way of providing for an emergency, but most serving officers thought training conscripts was an extravagant use of regular manpower.

The future of the RMC as the main source for officers for the Permanent Force and the Nonpermanent Militia was an issue on which Simonds had strong views. He had not wanted the RMC to close down in 1942, and he had not been happy with the products of the officer training school at Brockville that replaced it. On the other hand, the prewar course, in his opinion, wasted time on inessentials and the curriculum could have been covered in three instead of four years. After the war, the civilian staff pressed for the nonmilitary part of the curriculum to be extended and for the educational standard of the faculty teaching it to be raised to university standards. The same idea was advanced in Britain and Australia; the latter opted for a university standard course of four years, the former, despite the urging of General Sir John Hackett, for the eighteen-month course offered in 1939.

Simonds was afraid that the civilians in the RMC, having longer tenure than military instructors, would be too influential and would emphasize academic rather than military virtues, making the college a more expensive institution. He preferred a two-year course. The battle continued after his retirement when the degree courses were introduced and the RMC became an educational institution catering, with Saint-Jean and Royal Roads, for the three services and the reserve of officers.

Simonds was regarded by the Canadian press and by senior officers of the other services as a stormy petrel, a thorn in the flesh of politicians, and someone who was liable to self-destruct. According to them, he did not have the sense to realize that the Second World War was over and that military matters had to give way to more important ones like the Canadian economy. That is not at all the way he was regarded in the Canadian army, nor is it a historically correct view. Towards the end of the 1950s, after his retirement, conventional forces were reinstated as the cutting edge of Western defence. At much the same time the unification of the Canadian forces reared its head. As the commander who had effectively rebuilt the army, stood up for his service, and fought for it throughout his career and after his retirement in 1955, he took a leading part in resisting the measure.

17

Refusing to Fade Away

....

ON JUNE **9, 1955,** Montreal's *Gazette* blared out the news in big headlines: "Rift on Defence Policy Behind Shakeup: Army Chief Simonds' Retirement at 52 Biggest Surprise." The article went on to report:

> Lt Gen Guy Simonds, chief of the Canadian Army General Staff, has been relegated to the retired list because of a series of disagreements with Defence Minister Campney and the Cabinet over defence policy, it was reported tonight. . . . But dwarfing all of the other [changes] in importance was the Government's announced decision to dispense with the services of the man whom Field Marshal Montgomery rated — and the opinion was widely shared — the most brilliant army field commander Canada produced during the Second World War.

The *Vancouver Province* had this to say:

> The retirement of Lt Gen Guy Simonds . . . is a serious loss to the Canadian military effort to maintain the peace and secure the defence of Canada.
>
> He was this country's ablest senior field commander in World War Two. Canada was fortunate in retaining his services following that conflict, for the British Army would have welcomed him — and in fact tried to persuade him to change over.
>
> For the past four years as CGS, he has demonstrated initiative and drive such as the defence department has not seen in a long time in

providing army forces for our commitments in Korea, Europe and at home.

And now he goes on the shelf at an age when he is in his prime.

There must be many Canadians who are wondering why. The official explanation from Ottawa so far provides no satisfactory answer.

Could it be that General Simonds has come to the conclusion: That it is utterly impossible to try to build up the regular and reserve armies under the present voluntary system of recruiting? Has he applied his keen judgment to the enormous problems he knows face us in continental defence and in various tasks abroad and simply said: "We can't do it this way; but the government won't budge on compulsory training until the shooting starts. I cannot honestly stay as CGS under these circumstances?"

This conclusion might not be far off the mark.

In the House of Commons debate in the following days, General Pearkes, V.C., George Drew, and others were told by Ralph Campney, the minister of defence, that Simonds was retiring in the normal course of events. However, speculation about defence policy and recent articles in the press suggested to them that Simonds was going because he disagreed with the new initiatives that the minister was taking following his 1954 Defence White Paper. A manpower shortage, it was alleged, prevented Canada from manning its own northern defences. The courses open to the minister were to withdraw Canadian troops from Europe, to permit U.S. or NATO troops to move into the Canadian northland on a large scale, or to invoke a type of compulsory service to provide the men. In the House of Commons it was widely believed that the *Vancouver Province* was right about Simonds's views.

Ralph Campney was promoted from associate minister of defence to succeed Claxton in the summer of 1954.[1] He did not get on well with Simonds and never earned the latter's respect as Claxton had done. By allowing Foulkes more scope, he exacerbated relations in the Chiefs of Staff Committee. In particular Campney was persuaded by Foulkes that since strategy was the chairman's business, Simonds was poaching on political reserves by expressing his opinion on it and by demanding that the government's strategic plan be examined by the chiefs of staff before its defence policy was changed.

In June 1954 Simonds told a gathering of Nonpermanent Militia officers in Saint John that he advocated a period of conscription to establish a reserve for the militia, and in January 1955 he unwisely repeated this opinion to the Canadian Club of Montreal. The first address was to a closed military audience on militia matters, and Claxton accepted Simonds's explanation when the press reported it; the second was treated by Campney as a criticism of government policy and settled Simonds's fate.[2] In his Canadian Club address Simonds repeated some of the points he had made when summing up the annual CGS Exercise Broadsword at the end of 1954. Naturally, on that occasion, he compared the army's capabilities with its commitments. Simonds had circulated the exercise conclusions widely to his American and British colleagues, all of whom agreed with his recommendations.[3] In April Campney told him that his services were no longer required.

In the House of Commons opposition members pointed out that it had sometimes suited ministers to allow soldiers to explain how government policy was affecting them rather than grasp a prickly subject themselves. However, since lying to their subordinates was not in their nature, soldiers found it difficult to draw the line between the truth and the half-truth that their political masters demanded from them on such occasions. Perhaps this was an example of that difficulty, the opposition suggested. Other examples during Simonds's career were the disturbance over repatriation in 1945 and the complaint about the discipline of the Twenty-seventh Brigade in Germany. Pearkes and Drew also had in mind the manner in which the soldiers, deservedly or not, had taken the blame for the reinforcement crisis in 1944. Now they pointed out that Simonds had not given offence in this respect since the beginning of 1955, so they argued that it could hardly be his well-known outspokenness that had caused his retirement.

In his memoirs Claxton denied that Simonds was dismissed. He had made it clear to Simonds in 1951 that his tour was to be for four years; by August 1955 Guy would have served four and a half years. This convenient explanation is at variance with the circumstances in 1950 when Claxton was anything but specific over Simonds's appointment. On the other hand, Simonds himself had often argued against senior officers blocking the promotion of younger men by retaining their appointments beyond their usefulness. However, his successor, Howard Graham, was five years older than he, and Foulkes, who was the same age, stayed on as chairman until 1960, although he had served as CGS since 1946.

Simonds resigned because he realized that after four years of army development, which he had managed superbly, defence policy was returning to the doldrums. Unsuited to the inevitable frustrations ahead, he decided that he could do more for his country's defences outside than inside the service. To appear to be forced to resign at the height of his powers by the incompetent Campney was a positive factor in the campaign he intended to wage as a retired officer. Of course, he had disagreed with government defence policy since Claxton had left office and he had always been outspoken. On this issue he knew that he, not Foulkes and the other "political soldiers," spoke for the army and his profession. As the overwhelming majority of the army shared his views, he was determined to make them heard.

Nevertheless, Simonds had been ambivalent about his retirement until the last minute, just as the *Vancouver Province* suggested. At various times in his career he entertained the idea of entering the international defence field in which he might have played a hand in changing the attitude of governments towards defence. He was well qualified for a number of posts in Europe. In 1955 Campney and Foulkes had suggested to Montgomery that Simonds might be employed in Europe in some capacity after his retirement, perhaps to ensure that he did not remain in Canada to harass the government. The commandant of the NATO Staff College, deputy commander at SHAPE in succession to Montgomery, and commander of the northern NATO front in Oslo were suggested by incumbents but turned down one after the other by the British or the Americans, who wanted the posts for themselves. These rebuffs made Simonds decide to stay in Canada.

From time to time he had been dissatisfied with the government's attitude to its NATO commitments, and after Claxton's departure it was clear that its policy was shifting towards American continental defence in which the RCAF and the RCN were to play the major roles. For the first time army manpower and expenditures were to take second place. Cuts could no longer be avoided, and the First Canadian Division that he addressed on the Gagetown Ranges on July 19, 1955, shortly after the debate in the House of Commons, was broken up a few months after he retired, its headquarters scattered, and one brigade disbanded. As Major General J. M. Rockingham, the divisional commander, told the ten thousand men on parade that day, the division was the creation of the CGS. Three battalions of Canadian Guards, arguably one of Simonds's less happy initiatives, testified to Rockingham's remark.

Rockingham's formation was the Canadian response to the NATO call for a division to be at readiness in Germany immediately after M-day (NATO mobilization). The division had to be organized in peacetime and not created on mobilization. Simonds had raised two of its brigades in 1951 as support or rotation brigades, stationing them in Canada to match the brigades in Korea and Germany, to handle the training of reinforcements, and to provide a base for men and families on their return from overseas. It had been hard to persuade the Defence Committee to raise these brigades. Discarding the division as a force at readiness was to backslide on a NATO commitment and was unacceptable to Simonds.

Events in the Soviet Union had been an important motivation for this and other changes in Canadian defence policy. Indeed, the defence stance of the West started to shift in 1954, the year after the Soviets detonated their first hydrogen bomb and were making strides in rocketry that led to the launching of Sputnik in 1957. It seemed to Simonds that the politicians had lost their heads, even if the senior officers in NATO, the U.S., and the U.K. had retained theirs. The politicians embraced the idea that conventional forces of the size previously envisaged for the defence of Europe, that is about forty-six divisions at readiness and ninety within a month of mobilization, were no longer required urgently, if at all. If the Soviets invaded Europe, they would be massively struck by nuclear weapons, it was asserted. Nuclear deterrence had replaced conventional forces as the basis of NATO defence rather than its last resort.

Never very serious about European defence beyond the provision of a brigade presence for political advantage, the Canadian government set its sails to the new wind. Reserves had always been a problem and now nuclear deterrence downgraded their relevance. The Canadian government embraced the idea as a retreat from forward defence to North American continental defence, and from the U.K. and Commonwealth connection to closer American ties. It gave priority to surface-to-air guided weapons to defend its airspace against intruding aircraft and to the purchase and development of aircraft.

The Korean commitment had ceased in 1954. As an indication of the change, Air Vice-Marshal Plant caused a stir by asking in a light-hearted fashion whether the active army was necessary at all when civil defence was its only role — and that could be accomplished by the militia. His address achieved headlines and caused an angry stir in the army. The idea was echoed by the ignorant, who started to talk about push-button warfare and to say that infantry, tanks, and artillery of the old style were obsolescent. They would be obliterated by nuclear weapons as soon as they concentrated to attack. The air forces were the dominant arm, it was widely stated. In 1954 and 1955 the NATO armies experimented frantically with new divisional organizations, and the great guru, Sir Basil Henry Liddell Hart, preached mobility and small divisions. Even the levelheaded Brooke Claxton was attracted by these ideas, not least because they appeared to save manpower and even money. A division, even a small one, was still a division in the NATO political circles concerned with national contributions; and it was commonly stated that nuclear defence was very economical, for it made large conventional forces unnecessary.

Obviously, it was said, the Soviets had stolen a scientific march on the West, and money was poured into scientific education to enable the West to catch up. Wishfully it was thought that science, not manpower, was going to defend the West. At the same time a Soviet peace offensive, emphasizing peaceful coexistence, soothed the nerves of Western politicians unversed in the Soviet technique of "blow hot, blow cold." It seemed that time was no longer so important. In short, the resolve and vision of the political and military community, unstable even in secure times, was shaken.

Simonds was frustrated by this talk of reliance on nuclear weapons. He argued that surface-to-surface missiles would soon replace aircraft carrying bombs and there was no defence against them. So the fuss over bombers invading northland airspace was ephemeral nonsense. Money spent on building fighter aircraft such as the new Arrow to intercept them would prove to be wasted. He had rehearsed the argument about nuclear weapons some years earlier and agreed wholeheartedly with the SHAPE commander, Lauris Norstad, when Norstad answered the question "What are you going to do?" with "Nothing. We shall carry on as before."

Two extracts from presentations at Exercise Gold Brick sum up what the army thought about it all:

Fission-Fusion-and flux
It's no longer safe riding in trucks
Reduce the battle to mathematics
And don't be bothered with normal tactics.

So use all the weapons known to man
And dig in your troops as best you can
All the principles remain the same
A bigger bang, but the same old game.[4]

In the 1940s at the IDC Simonds foretold that tactical nuclear weapons would have no future even before they had appeared. Although on his retirement they were being hailed as both the cause of and the answer to current battlefield problems, they had proved a cul-de-sac by the end of the 1950s. One nuclear cannon could do the work of the artillery of an army, it was said. But small-yield weapons were expensive in fissionable material and as vulnerable to higher-yield, blunter weapons as the soldiers they supported. What was more, they escalated the nuclear exchange. Simonds visualized the end result when the American Sixth Fleet in the Mediterranean acted as a nuclear platform using small-yield weapons to take out key targets without creating destruction over a wide field. The Soviets, he argued, would have no compunction in using large-yield weapons to destroy the whole of the fleet that carried American tactical weapons.

In the real world, in Korea, for example, nuclear weapons had not been used for sound reasons. Fighting had been conventional except for the introduction of helicopters and a good deal of airlift. The humble French infantrymen had borne the burden in Indochina until Dien Bien Phu in 1954 and were still doing so in Algeria. The same had been true in Malaya. In the work against the Soviets and their proxies outside Europe, basic soldiering was the rule. In Europe neither side would use nuclear weapons, and they would return to the hard fact that there was no deterrent as effective as well-equipped and trained conventional divisions.

The composition of a division had been at the centre of Simonds's Broadsword exercise at the end of 1954. It found that the armoured division in NATO lacked stamina because of its weakness in infantry and should be replaced by a standard infantry division with integral armour. The aim of all thinking was to reduce the divisional tail — an expression used to describe its considerable technical and supply backup — and staff without affecting the division's hitting power. Trials showed that a small division required a larger proportion of administrative troops than the conventional one. Simonds proposed to reduce the tail and thus the vulnerability of the division to nuclear action by using either short-takeoff or vertical-lift aircraft for divisional, although not unit, supply. Experiments with the Twin Otter and Buffalo showed that they were even more effective in that role than helicopters, and Simonds tried hard to persuade the RCAF to support the idea. But like the RAF before 1939, the RCAF did not heed the army's desire for air support in general or Simonds's "flying truck" idea for replenishment.

Simonds had a reputation among his colleagues in other armies, and his peers in his own, for his ability to foresee the future and to describe it in clear prose. He read prodigiously and fast and derived conclusions from the historical record that later became commonplace. Canadians of a later generation have been rather less discerning about his capacity in this respect. Indeed, he performed better with every promotion, and in that sense he was a big man who would have performed well in a bigger scene had he had the opportunity. Unhappily for him his ideas were unlikely to be adopted on the Canadian stage.

Economy of military effort had concerned him at the IDC, he told his audience at Broadsword:

> I set a group of Air Force officers a problem on the "economics of strategic bombardment." German and Allied detailed records and statistics were available in the Air Ministry. The terms of reference were "Ignoring range and accuracy, which was the most economical Allied or German bomber in terms of man-hours required to design, test, produce, launch and deliver a ton of explosive into the *target area* and how did the best bomber compare in efficiency, expressed in these terms, with the V-1 and V-2?" Within these terms of reference the "Mosquito" proved the most efficient bomber: the V-1 was twice as efficient and the V-2 five times as efficient as the best bomber. You will notice that the factors of range and accuracy were to be ignored, and that was because in the history of scientific development, once a vehicle is in being, these two characteristics are susceptible to rapid improvement. At the end of the First World War, the best British bomber (a Handley-Page IV) had a maximum radius of 320 miles with a bomb load of 1568 pounds and the best German bomber (Gotha IV) a radius of 125 miles with a bomb load of 1100 pounds. These bomb-loads were for night bombing and either range or bomb-load had to be sharply reduced to gain the additional height needed in daylight operations. The V weapons at the end of the Second World War were better in performance than the bomber was at the end of the First . . .[5]

Simonds went on to say that the modern missile designer faced the same problems as the Germans who designed the V weapons. It was not beyond the power of scientific brains to extend the range of those weapons to enable them to be intercontinental in the not-too-distant future. The Western powers had neglected that field, he told his audience, but on the Russian side there were indications that they were giving much attention to it. They must realize that airpower was not only airplanes fighting airplanes, but the ability to use airspace for offensive and transport operations while denying that use to the enemy. Rocket missiles by attacking fixed airfield runways could quickly deny aircraft their function while being invulnerable themselves.

Planners can always see through windows of opportunity, or expect that their opponents can. Simonds shared the SHAPE view that the years 1954 to 1956 were crucial because during them the Soviets had attained a superiority in missile capability and still had superior conventional forces. By 1957 German conventional capacity would be added to NATO strength and, they expected, the Americans would have responded to the Soviet surge forward in missiles. Nineteen fifty-four was no time to swallow the Soviet talk of peaceful coexistence and to surrender the initiative by retreating to Fortress America. The militia was still required as a reserve for NATO and ought to be trained for that purpose and not for civil defence. Besides, civil defence would not attract men to the colours at a time when recruitment for the active force was lagging. Compulsory military service was needed to swell the ranks of the militia with trained men.

One of Simonds's enduring contributions was the Camp Gagetown training area and establishment at Oromocto. It was there that Rockingham's division trained in 1955 before the camp itself had been opened. The choice of the area was made in 1952, and in 1954 it was announced as sixth among New Brunswick industries in importance. The nation had packed its soldiers off to four hot wars and one cold war since 1867 but had never given its army enough room to train even the smallest major formation — an infantry brigade — wrote David MacDonald in *Maclean's* on September 15, 1954. The units of the Twenty-fifth Brigade and its successors in Korea had been trained in separate camps all over the country but had had to go to Fort Lewis in Washington State to train as a brigade. The Twenty-seventh Brigade had had to train in Germany.

The army was delighted to have a good training area at last. Now it could train two divisions at Gagetown and make money by bringing in American National Guard and European NATO troops to use it. Almost any possible battlefield could be replicated somewhere in the area from mountain through prairie to jungle; and there were ghost villages connected by dirt roads through the dark woods. In 1957 the camp itself opened, a monument not only to Simonds but also to the premier of New Brunswick, Hugh John Flemming, and to Brigadier Milton Gregg, V.C., who was a minister in the Liberal governments from 1950 to 1957.

By the end of 1959, four years after Simonds retired, the Kennedy era was at hand and the temporary eclipse of conventional army forces by bombers and ballistic missiles was about to end. Hermann Kahn's views on escalation, which restored the importance of conventional forces and economic factors, were accepted, and the focus of the cold war overtly shifted to the Far East. In

Canada Simonds was already engaged in fighting the movement towards the unification of the Canadian Armed Forces. It was an experiment eventually carried through in 1966 by the then minister of defence, Paul Hellyer. In the meantime preliminary measures, described as integration, were begun, initially with considerable support within the services.

Simonds had always believed in the integration of the combat arms and of the three services, and Gagetown was designed as a place where the arms' schools would work out combined doctrines at a combat arms centre, something the British and Americans lacked. One of the reasons for his scepticism about "massive retaliation" by the air forces was that it was the offspring of the wartime air force policy of winning the war by strategic bombing, in its extreme form without the armies' assistance. When the separate naval, army, and air force headquarters in Ottawa were abolished and replaced by an integrated national defence headquarters under one defence chief, Simonds considered it a long overdue reform. The second step in integration was more controversial. Six integrated functional commands were created: Maritime, Mobile, Air Defence, Air Transport, Training, and Maintenance. Simonds's initial misgivings were that no titular head of each service was created and that, consequently, it might not measure up under the strain of mobilization. Services often had to operate separately and might have to be reintegrated along service lines under a commander for each.

The real conflict occurred when the second step was followed by a third one, termed "unification," before integration was completed and had been analyzed. As Denis Healey advised in similar circumstances, it was unwise of the government "to operate on a man's appendix when he was lifting a piano." The aim of it all was economy and greater efficiency, measured statistically and with mainly administration rather than operations in mind. At the same time the White Paper of April 1964 alleged that the commitments of the three services and Canadian commitments to NATO and North American defence were going to be honoured more effectively. By 1966 Paul Hellyer was claiming that integration had been a success, although errors had been made and it was apparent that the new organization was not capable of taking the country into war. Nor had it created the economies which, he promised, would finance the reequipping of the armed forces on a reduced budget. The minister, wrote Simonds in 1966, had not produced the military efficiency, the manpower, nor the financial savings that he had promised. More of the same medicine, namely unification, would be disastrous.

As far as manpower was concerned, the minister's intended reduction of the strength of the forces from 120,000 to 110,000 men had slid into wastage of about 7,000 a year so that the probable strength of the forces would be about 92,500 by 1971. That was far too small a figure for Canadian commitments. Indeed, the services could not meet their commitment with 110,000 men; they needed 125,000, which indicated that either the initial calculation of need was wrong or the estimation of the savings through integration. In practice an infantry battalion, the Second Battalion of the Canadian Guards, had needed a large draft of men from the First Battalion before beginning a six-month tour in Cyprus and still required an artillery battery to act as one of its companies. The Second PPCLI, scheduled for Germany in the fall of 1966, was taking drafts from three other regiments, including artillery, to bring it up to strength. Maritime Command was down to twenty-four operational ships, and six modern destroyers were laid up without crews. The air division in Germany had been reduced in the previous five years from twelve to six squadrons. The RCAF pilot shortage continued to be severe, and the fifteen Buffalo aircraft bought recently could not be manned, although the minister was talking of expanding the transport force with American C-141 Starlifters.

The 1964-65 defence budget was $1.65 billion, and the minister assured the House of Commons that since savings would amount to $100 million, he would be able to spend twenty-five percent of the budget on new equipment. The promise proved empty, and in 1966 the Department of National Defence was about $100 million short to cover essential purchases and only thirteen percent of the budget was spent on equipment.

Much of the problem, Simonds observed, was the way the minister ran the department. Decisions were made in the Defence Council in which sat the chief and vice-chief of the Defence Staff, the minister and associate minister, and the three civilians representing the civil service:

> Every direction that is taken is, in the final analysis, taken between the Minister and the Chief of Defence Staff, "eyeball to eyeball": and it has been demonstrated fully in the last two years that service advice based on decades of professional experience is thus only too easy to overrule.[6]

Examples were the dismissal of five hundred experienced pilots in 1964 against the advice of the chief of the Air Staff. The drain of pilots to the airlines was such that the RCAF could not man its own aircraft and the minister had to raise the pay of pilots in the spring of 1966 with special pension provisions to bring them back. The minister changed the technical study that had recommended the purchase of the A-7 Corsair tactical aircraft so that the less expensive CF-5 was bought against the advice of the chief of the Air Staff. The CF-5 was proving inadequate whereas the U.S. Air Force had ordered well over fifteen hundred A-7 aircraft. Canadair and other Canadian subcontractors were the losers.

To ensure that unification would be acceptable the minister had fired objectors, taking little or no service advice, and promoted amenable officers in their places. There had been no protection against the minister's fancy or displeasure, wrote Simonds. He went on to report that the former "general staffs" of the three services had been reorganized at least four times in the previous two years and that none was now capable of carrying through a reform the scope and object of which were still obscure. Unification was the equivalent of merging, without proper preparation, Canadair, Sorel Industries, and General Motors of Canada. You could hardly expect the new organization to be "completely merged, its accounting, sales and production programmes re-drawn, and reorganized right down to its overseas sales offices and its last plant, and at the same time to be turning out an economic and efficient series of new products in two years. For this is indeed what the minister would have Parliament and the Public believe."[7]

At that stage integration had not reached a point where unification, whether desirable or not, could possibly proceed. Mobile Command, for example, was at twenty-five percent strength and had only just moved to its new location at Saint-Hubert in July 1966. HQ Air Defence Command was still moving from Saint-Hubert to North Bay and would not be ready until spring 1967. Training Command would not be reorganized until at least 1969. All this had not saved money, nor did it promise to make the Canadian Armed Forces better prepared for their tasks.

Earlier Simonds and Chris Vokes had written a paper for public consumption on the effects of unification on army units. In it they commented:

The Army is unified in the true sense of the word *only* because it has a unified chain of command. It is divided into a number of compartments known as corps — artillery, armoured, infantry, engineers, signals and those dealing with maintenance and supply. In each corps, the soldiers of which it is composed are taught a set of military skills necessary for the function of their corps in battle. A commander in the field does not employ his gunners as infantry, nor his infantry as gunners. Nor does he employ any corps on tasks for which its men have not been trained. (It has been done as a last resort, but by then the battle has been lost.)[8]

The art of command was to coordinate the tasks of each corps to meet any tactical situation and produce the best results. Officers were trained from the outset to obtain this result and, as they rose through the ranks, controlled arms other than their own and coordinated other services. However, even as senior officers they could not be expected to serve as naval officers or airmen, or to command directly a unit of another service. Unification meant nothing less than that they should, and it was a horse of a very different colour from integration, which had yet to prove itself. Unification was change for the sake of change.

Simonds, and those who resigned rather than carry through a process that would destroy the morale of services that had provided superb fighting men in two world wars and in Korea, were right. That is now generally recognized. Integration, in the sense of training the artillery, say, to fight on their feet as infantry, was correct. German divisional engineers, for instance, did so with excellent results in the Second World War, and the Royal Artillery has done so in Northern Ireland. As we have seen, rebadging provided infantry for the Canadian army in Europe in 1944. That is not to say that uniforms and traditions and the skills of the arm in question should be discarded. They remain the primary consideration.

In truth Hellyer's reforms were thought to be headstrong, ignorant, and politically motivated. They were unprofessional and as such were opposed by professionals, not only within the Canadian forces but elsewhere.

The impression Simonds left behind in the army was of a highly professional man. It did not, of necessity, imply that he was simply a military man, but that he was professional about everything he did. By the time he was fighting unification he was demonstrating his professionalism to new colleagues in business and the arts and in activities as diverse as the Royal Life Saving Society and the Canadian Corps of Commissionaires. In civil life he continued to fight the good fight with all his might, just as he had done all his life. But with more time to laugh and, occasionally, to be laughed at, he enjoyed it more.

18

A Man of Integrity

ONE VERDICT on Guy Granville Simonds was that he was "a brilliant man but a cold fish." Those closest to him, however, disagree. Mike Kearney, Simonds's ADC when he was CGS, remembers one early-morning meeting in the office at the start of their relationship. Simonds said, "I see you've opened this letter. Who told you to do that?"

"My predecessor told me that that was the practice," Kearney replied.

"That is why he is your predecessor."[1]

A wintery smile on Simonds's face was brightened by the twinkle in blue eyes that could be like ice. Kearney lasted the course, but there were occasions when he could have strangled his master. On their way back from Winnipeg he went ahead to the train station with the baggage and, when the train came in, loaded it. He waited, but there was no sign of Guy Simonds. As the train began to move, he pulled the baggage onto the platform. Obviously Master had missed the train. Not so, an official told him. He had handed Guy into the front coach a few minutes earlier. Panic! A young woman with a taxi was commandeered, and Kearney got her to chase the train, a pursuit that terrified the driver. They missed the train at the first stop, but telephoned ahead and halted it at the next one. Kearney paid off the taxi driver and, panting with the cases, struggled up into the train, where he found Guy Simonds, cool as a cucumber and smiling mischievously. "Missed the train, did you, Mike?"[2]

There was much travelling in their life together, and ADCs had to ensure that the right brand of cigarettes and whisky were at hand, money available, accounts maintained, cabins and sleepers reserved. Simonds travelled first class when on a transatlantic ship but saw to it that Mike had plenty of opportunity to dance and meet pretty women, which he did. Guy, too, enjoyed the company of women. Noticing that Mike was dining and dancing with an attractive blonde, he beckoned him over to his table. "Introduce me please, Mike." Guy danced with her for the rest of the evening.

The opportunity to meet important men was one of the advantages and rewards of the otherwise harrowing duties of an ADC. "I want you to meet the future president of the United States," Guy informed him at a function hosted by General Eisenhower, pushing Mike to the front of a group of generals.

The announcer introduced them loudly as they came to the front. "Generals Kearney, Simonds, and Clark."

Dwight Eisenhower knew the other two well and had a great laugh about Kearney's instant promotion.[3]

The RCAF had stolen a march on the army since it had family accommodation on its stations in Germany. When Brigadier Bill Anderson took the second relief brigade to Germany, there was much doubt about whether and on what conditions families were to be allowed to join their menfolk. Claxton was in favour of it and the Cabinet had agreed, but Simonds's view was that Germany was an operational station and families were a grave handicap. It was, he insisted, a one-year tour that might become operational, not a two-year peacetime posting. Simonds was not sensitive to the advantage that husbands would at least be kept out of trouble and that the presence of women added tone to the proceedings. At the time the brigade embarked from Canada under the command of Brigadier Anderson it was generally but not officially accepted that once there, if the husbands could find accommodation and the Q staff inspected it and found it acceptable, the wife could come out, but live "on the economy" in Soest.[4]

In the event, almost forty percent of married men found accommodation, which left more room in barracks for schools and recreation. Bill Anderson intended to have a place called Hilltop, overlooking the Mohnesee, as his "married quarters." With Bob Moncel, then senior officer on the U.K. Liaison Staff, and Jack Pangman, who had served in Italy in the First Division, they were enjoying a drink together at Hilltop with Guy Simonds on the evening after the takeover of the brigade. Bill's family was already on its way to Germany, although Guy had not intended that his brigade commander should have his wife, Jane, with him.

Moncel wondered how they were going to "pop the question to Master." "You know, CGS, the brigade commander will have to have his family here. And this is the place for them to live and show the flag," he began.

There was the longest two-minute silence, then Simonds simply said, "Oh, I suppose you're right."[5]

On the way back to Düsseldorf from which Guy was to fly back to Canada, Bill said, "I'm glad Bob raised the subject. I suppose it will be okay for me to use Hilltop?"

"Yes," Guy replied, saying nothing more.[6]

As soon as he had seen Guy off, Anderson drove to meet Jane at The Hague.

There was a real comradeship between these younger members of the fraternity and Guy Simonds, who had been the Young Turk himself for so long. They had learned how to handle him, and he was used to trusting them never to go too far. Now, at only fifty-two, he was about to retire. In some ways they were sorry for him, for he was a lonely man and about to be even more alone without a wife. He was far too young to retire.

On Dominion Day, 1955, a couple of months before Guy Simonds retired, Anderson's brigade gave him a splendid farewell at Soest — a march-past for Guy and all the trappings of a county fair for the children. After enjoying mixing at the booths, all majors and above were entertained at Hilltop to lunch. Anderson was conscious that in the Canadian fashion his country would give Guy Simonds nothing. An unemotional man, Guy was very moved by the end of the day.[7]

Louis St. Laurent wrote a letter of appreciation in which he said:

> I feel I should be remiss if on this occasion I did not express to you something of the admiration and regard with which we all look back over your long and distinguished career, including your brilliant and courageous military leadership during the last war. Your great contribution to the defence of our native land and the preservation of the principles for which it stands will long be remembered.[8]

Simonds liked and respected the prime minister, as did most who served him. In his reply of thanks he observed: "I am sure that you will appreciate that my retirement at this time does not signify any unwillingness on my part to render further military service to Canada as long as I remain fit to do so."[9]

In retirement Simonds did, indeed, throw himself into defence questions, speaking at gatherings across the country. Soon after he left the Department of National Defence, he was invited to attend the Law Society's annual meeting in Calgary at which there were many veterans who hailed him with friendly cries of "Guy!" Dressed impeccably in a pinstripe suit, as perfect a fit as his uniforms, he found it an effort to relax. He could do that with the group of war comrades whom he knew intimately and trusted, but not with a crowd, even of men who had fought somewhere with him on the ground, above him in the air, or had taken him to war over the water. He was essentially a respecter of position. It took him a few minutes to realize he was just one of the boys and was expected to behave as such. Then he started to grin, finally joined in the fun, and enjoyed himself.[10]

Very different was the reverse situation in the war when Douglas Harkness commanded the antitank battery supporting the First Brigade and greeted Guy on his arrival to command, "Guy! Well, I'm glad you've got the brigade."

"Harkness, you'll call me 'sir'" was Simonds's chilling response.

Guy had been the IG at Harkness's practice camps before the war. Harkness earned the George Medal for his bravery and leadership when his slow convoy ship bound for Husky was sunk. This story had a sequel. Some years after Guy retired, Harkness was minister of defence. Guy wanted help with a regimental band for the Royal Regiment of Canada. He made an appointment, and was shown into Harkness's office, and introduced himself with a slight smirk. "General Simonds, sir!"[11]

Shortly before his retirement Guy met Dorothy "Do" Sinclair, the elegant widow of Graham "Gus" Sinclair, who had been killed at Dieppe. She was the sister of Malim Harding, who succeeded George Kitching as GSO I of the First Canadian Division in Italy. Do had met Gus Sinclair at the University of Toronto and married him in April 1937. When the war came, his regiment was sent first to Iceland and then to England. In order to be with him there Do joined the (British) Mechanized Transport Corps (MTC) and through the corps succeeded in reaching England in April 1942. Gus was killed that August. Not wanting to return to Canada, Do stayed on in various capacities until December 1945.[12]

Although there had been fun in those war years, they were not easy for Do. Through a vaccination infection she almost lost her leg. The doctors saved it using penicillin, a drug that had only recently been introduced. A Canadian friend, Mary Mitchell, looked after her with infinite care in her own house until she recovered and could return to work.

During her convalescence, Colonel Agnes Neill, head of the Canadian Nurses Service, asked her to run a London club for the nurses. Remonstrating that she had never run even a house in her life, Do was silenced by Agnes. "Well, you're not stupid, are you?" So with an excellent housekeeper, and a traditional English butler who was also an alcoholic, she got on with the job.

Mary Plow and Louise Beveridge, who joined the MTC at the same time as Do, became close and lasting friends and were a wonderful help to her. Mary was married to Johnny Plow, a senior gunner, and it was through the Plows that Do eventually met Guy.

The club at 59 Cromwell Road was sponsored by Garfield Weston, but he became disillusioned because the club accepted men friends and served alcohol. When he handed it over to the Red Cross, the tone of the place changed, for it became a hostel not a club. Its life was finished by a flying bomb, and there was looting and much ironic handing over of keys and sweeping out of rubble-strewn rooms.

Do was a success in London and was asked to run a club in Brussels under the aegis of the Knights of Columbus, although she was an Anglican herself. Bruce Matthews remembered her in those years. He first described her as "stern," then reconsidered the word and suggested "no-nonsense" was better.[13]

As a member of the relatively small expatriate Canadian community, Do had seen Guy at a distance at functions in England. She accepted the view that he was self-centred and entirely devoted to fighting the war. She was attractive, but not in any mood for affairs of the heart, although she met talented, even remarkable Canadians frequently. These Canadians, men and women alike, were to be bonded for life, separated from those who had not gone overseas to take part in an extraordinary adventure.

After the war, Do remained at home to look after her mother. Besides her brother, Malim, she had three sisters. It was at this time, when Guy was still CGS, that Do's mother invited Guy to dinner. Do thought him a bit of a pill and rather cold and self-centred. It was his usual accursed shyness. Later Guy went to inspect Johnny Plow's Eastern Command. Do, still a close friend of the Plows, was staying with them, and they all had a very happy time together. It was at the Plows that Guy, in his disconcertingly direct manner, asked Do, "Why do you dislike me so?"

"Because of what I have heard about you," she replied.[14]

Back in Toronto, he phoned her and a courtship began that limped along for a time. He was still married to K, and Do had no intention of living with him, although he suggested it. On a later occasion, after his retirement, she asked him whether his marriage was reparable. Guy told her that it had been finished for years. It was then that she told him he must get a divorce if their affair were to mature. K had no interest in her marriage to Guy, for the past had hurt her deeply, but she was a spirited woman and insisted that Guy ensure that his pension would remain with her when he died. His only recourse was to obtain a Reno separation, the terms of which the government would not recognize as a legal divorce. This was done. The Anglicans did not permit a church ceremony for divorced persons, but through the good offices of an uncle of Do's they were introduced to Ralph Sockman, rector of Christ Church, New York, a well-known minister, preacher, broadcaster, and writer who married them on January 16, 1960. The family and a few close friends joined them for the service and a reception, following which Guy and Do set out for Nassau.[15]

At that time, before the permissive society, the marriage of young people was usually at the beginning, not the end of a voyage of discovery. Do loved Guy, warts and all, and under her care he became what he longed to be — accepted socially for himself and not because of what he had done or because of his position. He threw out new shoots, and people laughed with him and enjoyed his company; they agreed that Do and he were right for each other.

Indeed, Do stood for no nonsense, which Guy liked. As a matter of fact, he had always recognized competence and warmed to those who were independent, secure, and natural. These were traits he had long recognized as being necessary for a happy life, but they remained just out of reach while he was obsessed with duties, service, and efficiency. Marriage to Do gave him the key, and to the extent that any of us can unlock a door to a new life and easily pass back and forth between old and new, he did so. Do, who had never been on time for any appointment, had to learn from Guy's attention to detail. She dreaded public appearances but learned the lines of her speeches by heart like an actress, walking up and down in their apartment at Benvenuto Place in Toronto.[16]

A great bonus for Charles Simonds and Ruth Smith was that they got to know their father. Do was the bridge between them. In Guy's last years they began to understand what had gone wrong between K and Guy and to sympathize with both of them. Charles had been lucky with his wife, Barbara, and they had four sons. Ruth had had rough passages in her first marriage but was happy in her second one.[17]

Simonds's new life included his work as deputy director to Tony Griffin of the Halifax Insurance Company. The firm was part of a group, Netherlands Investors, owned by the Roell family, who had befriended Guy when he was commanding Canadian forces in Holland. Griffin had been a naval student at the NDC under Guy. J. E. MacNelly, another executive in the group and an official in the Insurance Agents' Association, remembered, as a tour de force, Guy's address on personnel deployment in the attack on Holland in 1945, which he gave to the group when he was CGS.

These contacts led to Guy handling particular personnel problems and contributing his wisdom to deliberations on the board. He was not employed in an executive capacity so much as in setting up procedures and in the management of people, at which he was a brilliant success. It seemed remarkable to Griffin that Simonds easily threw off the stiff general officer that he had taken him to be, accepting the pecking order that placed him below himself. He was an easy colleague with the milk of kindness in him when he dealt with people he had the unpleasant duty of sacking. One of these told MacNelly, "I was treated like a gentleman," and it seemed to MacNelly that Guy was an excellent advertisement for army methods of handling personnel and work methods.

As a member of the board, Guy was always the best-informed and prepared, although most of the subjects must have been quite new to him. The same had been said of him on the Chiefs of Staff Committee to which his colleagues so often came unprepared, despite their being provided with briefs written by their staffs. At the Halifax Insurance Company Guy had to prepare his own briefs.[18]

His work as managing director of Toronto Brick and Associates, a German group, was less happy, for the parent company tried to run everything from Germany without considering the conditions in Canada. He turned business around nevertheless before retiring with a pension that he had to negotiate with the somewhat Byzantine management. Business was not his forte. It was not that he had no ability in that direction, simply that making money did not interest him except as an indication that a firm was efficient. He enjoyed the perquisites of money, as he always had, and power. But he had never abused power himself and was disgusted at the abuses he found in business. Most of all he was angered at the unfair treatment of employees who were relatively helpless in the face of it. His reaction illuminated his integrity as an officer and showed that his ambition, so often held against him, was rooted in professional standards. He had been consistently rigorous in his treatment of officers but always caring when it came to the men they were supposed to lead.[19]

Simonds's association with the Royal Life Saving Society of Canada was of another kind altogether. Lord Louis Mountbatten parachuted him in to take over the direction of the Canadian Society, and he completely turned it around by organizing it along military lines. Some of the people in this biography reappeared as regional organizers — Bill Anderson, Elliot Rodger, and Rocky Rockingham, for example. He was again associated with Tony Griffin when he took over from him as chairman of the National Ballet, a surprising role for him to play perhaps, but the arts had always interested him, and this became one of his most loved activities, not least because it associated him with the men and women who gave their time to it. Celia Franca, the artistic director, and Lyman Henderson, an ex-chairman, were but two of these.[20]

For Guy, growing old was a time when he began to knit together the strands of his life, a time when all things seemed to be related to the rest. Linda Stearns was a ballet dancer and a choreographer and became artistic director of Les Grands Ballets Canadiens. The Stearnses and Simondses took holidays together, and the younger Stearnses, Linda, Nora, and Marshal, were friends of the Anderson daughter. Sadly there was another connection. Guy had always been particularly attached to Helen, Marsh's wife. She had cancer and was an example of courage to him, for she was fighting it successfully. Guy had always been a heavy smoker, but his excellent physique seemed to be unaffected by the habit until Do noticed how thin he had become. Cancer was diagnosed in him, too. He stopped smoking and, like Helen, fought the disease. He had always admired Helen's courage, but when she died, it was as if he said to himself, "Well, if she can't beat it, I know that I can't. It's all up with me, too."[21]

That was still in the future as he immersed himself in the Gurkha Appeal, which was close to his heart, for not only did he admire those inimitable mountain soldiers, but his great-grandfather and grandfather had soldiered in India in the time of the East India Company and in Queen Victoria's army after the Mutiny. During the Canadian flag debate in the mid-sixties, he wrote to Prime Minister Lester Pearson on behalf of the many who wanted to retain in it the record of the provenance of the Canadian people in Britain and France: "The Union Jack, as its name implies, is a symbol of unity — the combining together of old symbols, not their relegation to the discard in favour of a new revolutionary design." Those who deny their past have no future, he advised, and he called the new flag a bland symbol and its choice to represent the country a limp surrender to what he hoped was a passing phase in his country's history.[22]

His visits to the Normandy battlefields and to Holland and Belgium again reminded him of the spirit that seemed so lacking in the country's leadership. In Normandy there were few national memorials of the sacrifice and achievements of Canadians in 1944. What there were had been raised by regiments. The British Graves Commission looked after the cemeteries as well as ever, and local people and their children, particularly in Holland, placed flowers on the graves. But there was no national rallying centre such as had been set up on Vimy Ridge in 1936.

Simonds was not given to bitterness, but it was saddening that a street was named after him in Antwerp, whereas only the army and veterans remembered him in Canada. A piece in the Belgian *Le Matin* on June 7, 1968, had this to say:

> Antwerp has recently been visited by a tourist of whom the least that can be said is that "he was not a visitor like others" who rush past the cathedral, museums, glance at the Escaut canal and its installations and spend a moment in the zoological gardens.
>
> No! The visit we wish to talk about was more like a reverent pilgrimage and the visitor who came incognito to Antwerp was none other than Lieutenant-General Simonds who, leading a Canadian regiment *[sic]*, participated in 1945 in the battles that resulted in the liberation of Antwerp.
>
> Discreetly — too discreetly, in our opinion — this great soldier to whom the citizens of Antwerp owe so much, first went to the Luchtbal district for a short walk along the street named after him, between Havanastraat and Quebecstraat.
>
> Next, still discreetly, the general went to Middelheim Park, where he meditated a moment in front of the Plaque commemorating the liberators of Antwerp, where is engraved, among others, his name, already forgotten by the younger generation.
>
> But do not worry, General. The not so young remember you, the heroism of your soldiers and the important part you played in their liberation.
>
> The only regret they have is not to have been told of your coming, and so not being able to show proof of their gratefulness and express the admiration they feel towards you.
>
> General Simonds left Antwerp the way he came: discreetly. It's a pity.[23]

While Guy was CGS, and after his retirement, he continued to enjoy hunting. He loved his shotguns, for he had been an excellent shot since boyhood. One of his companions was that same lieutenant colonel whom we remember snipping amendments and pasting them into his manuals at Ford Manor in 1941. John Bennett, the only lieutenant colonel on the course, had pointed out to Simonds, on behalf of other students, that the time spent amending manuals was better employed on course exercises. Wisely he did not press the point and, when push came to shove, for a small consideration he hired a clerk at CMHQ to do the job for him.

Back in Canada Bennett was a noted wildfowler and ran a shoot on Pelee Island in Lake Erie to which Guy was invited. It was on one of these shoots that a hunter fired down the line at Guy's bird and peppered Guy instead. When Guy remonstrated, the miscreant picked up the bird — "my bird, I think," Guy recalled later — and disappeared, leaving Guy at a loss for words. In Saskatchewan they shot sharp-tail grouse, Hungarian partridge, ruffed grouse, and many kinds of duck and goose, in company with several wartime friends, including Elliot Rodger, then GOC Prairie Command. Bennett recalled:

> I felt I got to know Simonds quite well over this period. He was a brilliant conversationalist, witty and good-natured. However, he was always reserved and had difficulty in being completely relaxed . . . I found Guy an excellent hunting companion from whom one never failed to learn some valuable lessons on every shooting trip.[24]

Fishing was not his métier, although he enjoyed fishing trips with army friends. At a camp on Georgian Bay he arrived impressively equipped with all the right gear, including a huge tackle box of flies and other lures. He rose an hour before everyone else in order to get himself ready. Just as the party was about to move off, including Do, whom he was courting and hoping to impress, he dropped the box. Half its contents disappeared between the slats of the cabin porch. There was much laughter, and Bill Anderson exclaimed, "Guy!" It was the first time he had ever addressed Simonds by his first name. The others who had been in the habit of doing so for years applauded ironically.[25]

The RMC invited him to accept an honorary degree. He wrote a letter thanking them but declined the honour. For so long an opponent of the degree course, he could not now accept one himself. He was honorary colonel of the Royal Regiment of Canada at the time of the regiment's hundredth anniversary in October 1962. Although never a colonel commandant of the Royal Canadian Artillery, he was elected an honorary life member of the Royal Canadian Artillery Association: "In recognition of his outstanding service to the Royal Regiment of Canadian Artillery." On Friday, October 29, 1971, he was made a Companion of the Order of Canada. Now he was properly addressed as Lieutenant General Guy Granville Simonds, C.C., C.B., C.B.E., D.S.O., C.D.

But Guy's last battle was soon upon him. In February 1974 Sparky Sparling, who had been his CRA briefly in the Fifth Armoured Division and then his deputy chief at army headquarters in Ottawa, where he had fought many battles on the army's behalf, sent him the message of encouragement from all the gunners of Canada that appears at the beginning of this book in the prologue. Simonds replied: "Would you please kindly convey, by means which you find most convenient, my very real and deep appreciation of the message sent to me on the occasion of the recent meeting of the Conference of Defence Associations. With the many important items which I am sure they had to deal with on their agenda, I was indeed moved to receive such a very kindly remembrance." Guy had addressed the association annually when he was CGS and had found its advice and support invaluable.[26]

A visitor to Guy's room in his last days, when he was in pajamas and a dressing gown, was "Uncle" Stanley Todd. The two men — Stan Todd was a decade older than Guy — had much to say to each other. Stan had passed out of the RMC in 1916 and joined the British army. Returning to Canada, he had joined the Nonpermanent Militia and remembered the practice camps at which Guy had been an instructor. They were hard times, for out of twenty-four gun detachments only four had Permanent Force "numbers one." Leylands had replaced the horses in 1932 as gun towers in the Permanent Force, but the Nonpermanent Militia had nothing and did foot drill on their eighteen-pounders. They had eight nights of training a year and camp for eight days. On mobilization Stan commanded a regiment in Ottawa and combed the streets for three hundred unemployed to make up their strength. It was amazing that from this low level the Royal Canadian Artillery grew to fifteen field regiments in divisions, ten field, medium, or heavy regiments in Army Groups Royal Artillery, five antitank and five antiaircraft regiments, and a heavy antiaircraft brigade. It was particularly extraordinary that the original men were usually unemployed and uninterested in the war, or office workers who had given up their jobs to join.[27]

Todd was CRA of the Third Canadian Division in the Normandy landings and was there when Keller was so shaky. He was Guy's CCRA in the Second Corps when Dan Spry was "sacked." Recollections of Normandy started Guy talking, particularly about sacking Ben Cunningham and the Keller and Foulkes decisions. He still worried whether he ought to have sacked Keller and saved Cunningham. He was concerned that he had prosecuted the war with his whole soul and personality and without regard for persons. Anything that did not fit into his scheme of things he had taken as a personal challenge. But beneath the confident exterior Guy was ever a worrier. After the war in Holland, he confided in "Uncle Stanley": "Let's go for a walk . . . I'm a very lonely man. As you know, I've sent a lot of prominent men home. I've made enemies. But I leave one thought with you. I've never committed a soldier to battle under an officer in whom I did not have full confidence."[28]

That was the argument he had used with Crerar when they quarrelled in the caravan in Italy. On his deathbed he was still concerned with the price he had had to pay for maintaining his principles. It was the price of command, but in paying it he remained, to the bitter end, a man of integrity.

19

Simonds the Soldier

....

"**W**ITHIN THE CANADIAN MILITARY SYSTEM,** Simonds was, and remains, *sui generis* . . . the best of the lot," wrote John English in *The Canadian Army and the Normandy Campaign: A Study of Failure in High Command.* "The trouble is," Brereton Greenhous commented in a favourable review, "Simonds was not very good either — in fact, he was poor by any objective standards. . . ." Earlier Greenhous had conceded that "Generalship, at whatever level, is among the most difficult of all the arts — perhaps the most difficult. Every general will make mistakes but the good ones will learn from those mistakes. Simonds never learned any more than Montgomery did." And Greenhous criticized British doctrine, which he identified with Montgomery and his protégé Simonds, for its emphasis on firepower at the expense of manoeuvre and, in the Canadian army, the "unholy alliance" between the doctrine and "the artillery generals" — McNaughton, Crerar, and Simonds.[1]

Brian and Terence McKenna, who expounded in their CBC/NFB docudrama *The Valour and the Horror* the Marxist view that all Western military leaders were butchers and the men they led heroes, naturally condemn Simonds. Canadian war historians of the younger school who dislike Simonds, perhaps for being more British than the British and, like Greenhous, judge him by "objective standards," which are presumably universal, must be treated more seriously. However, their critical method must also comply with "objective standards."

Although they are not so formidable as those of the practising general officer, the methodological difficulties of historical criticism are considerable. For example, critics are expected to offer alternatives to the course of action to which they object. That leads them into a cul-de-sac, for the outcome of a military alternative of any moment can only be conjectured. If the opinion of a veteran is invoked to buttress the argument against the general, his evidence is, at best, that of an expert witness, and is no better than the questions he is asked. The critics' general principles, Greenhous's "objective standards," usually turn out to be subjective preferences — manoeuvre over mass and firepower, or an indirect rather than a direct approach to the enemy, for example. Critics offered such panaceas between the major wars of the twentieth century when revulsion from war and peacetime economy combined to overwhelm recorded war experience. A critical method that begins by judging actions in light of doctrine and theory, criticizing either the doctrine itself or the way it has been applied, is starting at the wrong end. The proper method is inseparable from the art of generalship itself. Consciously or not, commanders analyze their problem using detailed case experience, not doctrine and theory.

This was the method Carl von Clausewitz recommended.[2] In explaining the proper way to extract truth from historical examples he admonished his readers to start with the lower levels of combat where results can be identified and causes are relatively certain and concrete. He should then trace results back to causes in the shape of orders, methods, weapons, training, and so on, as far as that is possible. Doctrine and theory were the outcome of much practice and were always in the process of change in its light. They were not sound starting places for analysis or criticism.

Like most commanders, Simonds followed Clausewitz's method in his after-action analyses. The disaster experienced by the Black Watch in Operation Spring led him from the actions of battalions to brigades and finally to divisions. Not surprisingly he found errors at each level. Eventually he examined his own part in the action and decided that he could find a better way, in future, of setting up the battles his units had to fight. Consequently he used defrocked Priests, a night attack, and a mass assault in Operation Totalize. However, learning is continuous at every level. Although Totalize did not succeed to the extent that he hoped, the Second Corps learned from it and Tractable and performed better in the next phases of the campaign.

In assessing Simonds's decision not to cancel the bombing in the second phase of Totalize we enter the realm of conjecture. Could

Simonds be assured that all the bombers would be stopped, and if not, would some drop their bombs and give his troops the worst of both worlds? Experience was discouraging in this respect, for communications with Bomber Command were slow and cumbersome and bombing accuracy faulty. Intelligence about the strength of the German second line was ambiguous. Simonds's decision was not a doctrine-inspired call for a massive strike but a judgemental one in which he may have been wrong. However, whether he was right or not will remain conjecture, except to those who condemn the use of heavy bombers in all circumstances.

To recapture the mood and assumptions of a past occasion is difficult for a historian. The participant may have been overimpressed by some facts and ignored others at the time, and the order in which information reached him may still be unclear even after a review of the documents. The enemy's capability and intentions were, at best, partially obscured at the time, which inclines us, years later, to accept as true what an opponent says he was doing and thinking — Kurt Meyer, for instance, on Totalize and Tractable. The ex-enemy is by no means an impartial witness. He has critics, too, and certainly has an axe to grind. Nor is his memory better than ours. We seldom subject him to a hostile cross-examination, which is essential if the truth is to be reached. We do not know how often an experienced general like Meyer beats the odds because his mistakes are concealed under a landslide of later events. Armed with a pitiless pile of paper and all the time in the world to read it, and never having commanded in battle ourselves, we latter-day Canadian critics set our leaders "standards" that are anything but "objective."

In August 1944 Simonds's subordinate generals were inexperienced. His own experience at the divisional level made him inclined to fight his divisional commanders' battles for them, a tendency encouraged by Keller and Foulkes, who were poor performers, and Kitching, who was fighting his first battle with untried armour and using untried methods and equipment. Across the Allied front no corps commander springs to mind who imposed his will on the Germans in Normandy at the tactical level until Lieutenant General Joe Collins broke through with his Seventh Corps on the Saint-Lô front at considerable cost and after two massive air strikes. Neither the American nor the British/Canadian armies were well trained or, on balance, experienced. It was not to be expected that Simonds would produce electrifying results from a relatively poorly equipped and trained force in circumstances in which the Germans had a decisive technical advantage in everything but the air and the artillery and were fighting on ground of their own choosing. Nevertheless, we are right to ask why Western performance, so late in the war, was inferior. Should Simonds not take his share of the blame if the Second Corps was ill-trained?[3]

Simonds was certainly not satisfied with the standard of his divisions. He took over only two of them in January 1944; the Third Canadian Infantry Division and the Second Armoured Brigade were not under his command before D-day. Although the Sherman had been available in gradually increasing numbers since the Americans generously gave the few they had to the Eighth Army in the fall of 1942, the reequipping of the Canadian armoured regiments with 75 mm Shermans was delayed until May because of misplaced national pride in the useless six-pounder Rams. It was too late, in May 1944, to rebuild drills for tank-infantry support around the new tanks, particularly the seventeen-pounder Fireflies, which had technical problems in the field. It needed very experienced troops to master both the open conditions in the rolling Caen countryside and the closer wooded country farther south. Furthermore, much of the training in Britain had been specifically task-oriented. The assault force had concentrated on the landings and the movement inland, while the Second Corps had focused on Axehead and the Seine crossing. It was believed that if the first phase of the invasion went well, July and August would see a reduction in casualties and a change in the style of the fighting. That did not happen. Instead, the Twenty-first Army Group suffered its heaviest casualties in July and August. If the standard of training for the dogfight inland was poor to start with, it was made worse by heavy casualties to the first team and declining morale among survivors.

In Britain Simonds improved staff procedures and the communications of his own headquarters. Second Corps HQ functioned well in Normandy and his own command procedures were impeccable. When he relieved Crerar for the Scheldt, his influence at First Army headquarters was felt immediately. He coordinated the actions of three services, made the decision to bomb the dykes, and twisted the arm of the air force to make them carry out the operation. With Admiral Ramsay he made the decision to assault Walcheren. Everyone with whom he worked respected him and praised his performance. His criticism of Crerar in the phase of clearing the ports was overstated, bearing in mind the changing priorities of Montgomery at the time and the indefinite actions of Eisenhower in respect to the opening of the port of Antwerp.[4]

By the end of the year, when Simonds and Horrocks fought Operation Veritable together, they were acknowledged to be the two leading corps commanders in the Twenty-first Army Group. Simonds had proved a worthy successor to Arthur Currie, the Canadian army was proud of him, and he was enormously proud of the men he had led. Whatever historians might say of him later, those who were in the Second Corps were convinced that Simonds was a fine leader as well as a commander respected by the British and the Americans. The sting in the tail may be that the men in the ranks, when asked who were their leaders, would have been hard-pressed to name anyone else but "Monty."

Simonds had prepared himself all his life to lead Canadians in war. He had also expected to become the professional head of the Canadian army. After the story of his part in the major episodes in his tenure as CGS, NATO and Korea, has been told, it must be asked what he achieved for the postwar army. Between 1939 and 1951 the army's prewar pomp and colour had been bleached to a utilitarian grey. Foulkes was not, at heart, a regimental soldier; Simonds, on the other hand, understood the importance of smart uniforms, efficiently run and colourful messes, bands, protocol, good food, physical exercise, and recreation. He looked like an advertisement for his own policies. He restored regimental spirit and the morale of a drab and run-down army. The fear of losing all that had been gained was a prime reason why he fought unification after his retirement.

Simonds's second contribution was to break the prewar mould of an army that was a militia with a small permanent cadre to train it. He changed the prewar idea that there would be time to mobilize and train for war after it started and that there was no need for the army to be always on its toes, ready to go into the field. Instead, he called the army a regular army in the British fashion. Following the Cardwell idea of the nineteenth century, he established six regiments of infantry, each with three battalions and regimental depots and training bases. He established the Gagetown training base where the regular army and militia could train in realistic conditions, and where British, American, and other troops could rub shoulders with Canadians. When watching a march-past at Camp Wainwright, and having seen the British Army Physical Training School in Germany, he realized the need for a Canadian Physical Training Corps and established one. Colonels of regiments who received expenses but no pay were appointed to look after historical and regimental matters and provide a link between the scattered battalions of the regiments. The boy apprentice scheme was started, and he laid the foundation for training officers to fly helicopters and for the Army Service Corps to operate a helicopter service.

The fact remained that Canada's army was by tradition and function a militia army, sprung from the people and close to it in sentiment. A professional force, of necessity, was one remove from this tradition. Before the war, and during it, Simonds seemed to embody the British tradition of a standing army, an alien idea. It flourished under his care in the special conditions that existed while he was CGS. But he had less success in preparing the militia reserve for that army. He knew that the fighting record of militias was not good, despite the glowing North American myth, French and English, of people successfully taking up arms to defend their homes and families. Hence his struggle to have the militia provide a ready and efficient reserve for the regular army, reinforced with some kind of compulsory service, was one that he could not win. It seems obvious today that that measure would be unacceptable in peacetime even during Simonds's tenure as CGS, which was abnormal. It was early in the cold war and Canadians and other Westerners were not used to the idea that the struggle with the Soviet Union was going to last at least a generation and that peace, in the usual sense, was not going to return.

We shall not cease from exploration
And the end of our exploring
Will be to arrive where we started
And know the place for the first time.

T. S. ELIOT, *Little Gidding*

Epilogue

....

IN PREPARING HIMSELF for military command so single-mindedly Guy Simonds paid the price of loneliness. As a professional, he learned that some traits that made him a success were unattractive, but being a shy man he could not soften them. Throughout the war he focused his burning energy on fighting it. When it ended, he suppressed his hunger for social acceptance and family love by fighting for peace as assiduously as he had for victory. He continued to discipline himself and his life and his unassuaged thirst for perfection made him an uncomfortable associate. That few could satisfy his demands raised a barrier that was difficult for him or others to penetrate.

When he was laid to rest in Mount Pleasant Cemetery, the fourteen happy years of his second marriage had taught him that his desire for control was incompatible with his own happiness. He had learned to reach out, not only to his erstwhile comrades, but to his own family and acquaintances, as well.

The funeral is the opening and closing scene of our story. The veterans who lined the route and marched behind the coffin had played their part in making a tiny prewar army grow and attain in battle as much respect in the eyes of the world as the Canadian Expeditionary Force of 1914-18. They gave Guy Simonds much of the credit for that and the funeral was their acknowledgement of it. It was also a celebration, not only of the exciting and memorable years that many present had shared as comrades-in-arms, but also of a life that had been fulfilled.

Appendix 1:
The Dieppe Raid

GUY SIMONDS'S LETTER TO C. P. STACEY, FEBRUARY 10, 1969

[The circumstances in which the Dieppe raid was mounted in August 1942, despite its cancellation in July, have still not been completely explained. Neither the British chiefs of staff nor Winston Churchill appear to have authorized it, although Lord Louis Mountbatten insisted they had. C. P. Stacey, in his official volumes, denied Canadian responsibility. The plan for the assault has been criticized in respect to the bombing of the town, the direct assault across the town beaches, and the attacks designed to enter the town from the flanks. However, Stacey argued that the Canadians had not been involved in these tactical details.

Brian Villa, in *Unauthorized Action: Mountbatten and the Dieppe Raid* (London: Oxford University Press, 1990) and "Mountbatten, the British Chiefs of Staff, and Approval of the Dieppe Raid" in *The Journal of Military History* 54 (April 1990): 201-226, wrote twenty-one years after Simonds's correspondence with Stacey, Mountbatten, and the others mentioned in this appendix. Richard Hough's *Mountbatten, Hero of Our Time,* in 1980, and Philip Ziegler's *Mountbatten,* in 1985, preceded Villa's book. Only John Terraine's *The Life and Times of Lord Mountbatten,* in 1968, which was not concerned with the controversial question of responsibility, had been published when Simonds wrote to Stacey.

In 1969 Stacey was justifiably confident in his work, for it had proved accurate. He attributed Simonds's letter to his continuing feud with Crerar. However, in trying to be loyal to his country, the army, and his profession, Stacey may have allowed the first two of these loyalties to obstruct the third — as had James Edmonds, the chief historian of the British army official series on the campaigns of the First World War. But Stacey realized that official history was not the place to resolve conflicts between Mackenzie King, whom he disliked, the Liberal Party, and the country's interest; between the army and party and country; between the good of the field army and its leading figures and the British army and leadership. In the 1940s Simonds was of the same mind. By 1969, however, it seemed to Simonds that twenty-four years after the war those responsible for the Canadian part in Dieppe should no longer be shielded by an account that made it appear that Canadians had been herded like cattle to the slaughter. He felt the same about the reinforcement crisis, for which responsibility had not been placed on those in authority.

Two conclusions about Simonds may be drawn from this episode. First, that he put his finger on the question that was to concern Villa, namely, who was responsible for the August raid, which Stacey shirked. He did not himself entertain the idea that Mountbatten alone could have authorized it, nor did he accept that the chiefs or Winston Churchill could have done so without Canadian agreement. Neither did Simonds suggest that Crerar could have authorized Canadian participation, not only because it was uncharacteristic but because he did not have the power to do so. However, Simonds knew that the operation could not have gone forward without Crerar's agreement, nor could the details of the plan have been foisted on the Canadians without it. Second, Simonds felt that in telling the story as he had, Stacey was concealing the character of Crerar, which was an important factor in the story of the Canadians in the Second World War, and distorting the relationship between the British and Canadian armies. In Simonds's opinion McNaughton, Stuart, Murchie, Ralston, and King were representatives of a political network which, by diffusing responsibility whenever possible, made the Dieppe disaster and the reinforcement crisis possible.]

When Crerar relinquished the post of CGS in Canada and took over 1 Canadian Corps in England (I was Chief of Staff and had been "continuity man" [after] McNaughton went sick and during Pearkes' period of temporary command) he [Crerar] told me he intended to assert his right as a "national contingent commander" to have direct conversations with Brooke and the Chiefs of Staff in regard to getting Canadian troops into action, and specifically cross-channel raiding operations. Later, in succession, he called on Monty (S.E. Army) and Paget (C-in-C Home Forces) and explained to them that he was not in a position of just a British Corps Commander, but was Commander of the Canadian Army overseas, and as head of a national contingent, had the right of direct access to the CIGS in matters of special interest to Canadians as such. No one quarrelled with this stand.

After a meeting with Brooke, Crerar was authorized to have direct conversations with Mountbatten on the subject of cross-channel raids.

It was at the meeting on the morning of 6 March 1942 that Mountbatten mentioned Dieppe as the major target area on COHQ list of potential operations. The project had been considered in outline. Crerar urged that the operation should be proceeded with, and that Canadian troops should carry it out.

I might add here, that earlier that winter, as Chief of Staff, Canadian Corps, I had attended a special study, directed by COHQ on cross-channel target areas for raiding. The Normandy beaches, even as early as that, were regarded as "out" because they offered the best site for a major invasion operation, and it was undesirable to attract attention to them, or encourage strengthening of defences. The west coast of the Cherbourg peninsula was difficult because of the rugged coast, difficult tidal conditions, exposure to westerly gales, and at the extreme limit of fighter cover. This left the area between Le Havre and the Pas-de-Calais, and Dieppe had been mentioned then as a possible target.

From conversations with Crerar, following the meeting of 6 March, I have every reason to believe that he "lobbied" the British Chiefs of Staff, and even with Winston himself (through Eden — Crerar took me with him to lunch with the Edens at their country place at this time, and whilst alone with Eden, Crerar mentioned the paramount importance from the Canadian point of view, of getting Canadian troops into battle) to get approval for the Dieppe raid as a Canadian operation.

Now for planning. Brooke having agreed: (a) to the Dieppe operation [and] (b) to it being a Canadian operation. Crerar insisted upon Canadians being brought into the planning, on the principle that militarily, planning and responsibility for execution of an operation are inseparable. The Staff of 2 Canadian Division was included, in fact took a leading part in all the detailed planning. Two or three times a week throughout the planning stage, Roberts, sometimes with Church Mann, would call on Crerar at Corps HQ and review the planning to date. *There was every opportunity at every stage of planning for Canadian objection to any aspect of the plan.*

There has been some controversy over the decision to cancel the heavy bomber attack originally planned to precede the landing. The cancellation of the bombing was a direct result of the decision to make a frontal assault with armour on the Dieppe beaches *and this was a Canadian decision* (see Mann's appreciation). If the town of Dieppe had been heavily bombed, it would have sealed, with rubble, all exits from the Dieppe beach front and tanks would have been trapped on the open beach. (See Monte Cassino. In all my own attacks with armour supported by heavy bombers, I picked bomber targets *on the flanks* or away from the armoured channels of advance so as not to create anti-tank obstacles in their path.)

Though Monty, as Commander South Eastern Army, was given a place in the chain of command, he too, took the stand that primarily *[sic]* planning and responsibility for execution are inseparable and in the main acted as "chairman" and backed the planning decisions of Roberts and 2 Canadian Div Staff. However, in one respect, his responsibility was quite specific — insofar as the army was concerned, the final decision as to whether the raid was to be launched or not rested with him. When the necessary weather conditions failed to materialize between 3-8 July — the dates for the original "Rutter" Dieppe Raid — he said "no" and finally recommended cancellation of the raid and that it should not be revived. Had he still been in Command of S.E. Army in August, I do not think he would have changed his view, and I consider it derogatory to suggest he was "just lucky" in being transferred to 8 Army in the meantime. However, whether he could have overridden Canadian pressures to carry out the operation is a matter for speculation.

The outline I have given above of the inception of the original "Rutter" raid, and regarding its planning, I know first hand.

Of what subsequently happened in the revival of the raid as actually carried out — Jubilee — I have to depend to some extent on deduction from conversations with McNaughton, Crerar and others. I was then engaged on the appreciation for operation Jupiter. [Jupiter was the operation against Norway favoured by Churchill but opposed by the chiefs of staff.] Crerar was not on the coded "need to know" list for Jupiter. (As you will recall, those actually engaged in planning an operation were given a card with the code name on it. If anyone asked a question, or a leading question inferring he knew about it, you immediately asked him to produce his card. If he did not have one, you had no discussion of the operation with him.) Crerar knew I was engaged on a special planning task, and when I would see him in London, at meetings dealing with other subjects, he remarked several times, "If it's going to get Canadian troops into action, for God's sake recommend in favour of it, whatever it may be."

Whilst the Jupiter planning staff was working in the War Office underground planning HQ, McNaughton would visit me once and usually twice a day and I would brief him on our progress. On one of these visits McNaughton said to me: "They want to revive Dieppe" and asked what I thought of it. I asked him who "they" were and he said the "Chiefs of Staff."

This very much surprised me. Churchill and the Chiefs of Staff were urging McNaughton to come up with the appreciation on Jupiter. I knew that by that time TORCH was under very active consideraton and the Americans were coming around to it. Why would they, at this stage, revive Dieppe except under Canadian pressure? I asked McNaughton if he had asked for a revival of the operation, and he said he had not.

He said that if there should be a decision to launch JUPITER, Canadian troops would be heavily involved. I told McNaughton that I was completely absorbed in the JUPITER appreciation; it had to be very thorough, and carefully presented and I was very much under pressure to produce it quickly. I recoiled from offering irresponsible advice, and was in no position to know the arguments for a Dieppe revival, but I had never liked the concept as originally planned.

You will note in Hughes-Hallett's letter [January 31, 1969, to Lord Louis Mountbatten] that "the effective decision to remount Dieppe . . . was taken on the evening of July 11 at a *private* meeting at which I think the only people present were yourself (Mountbatten) and myself, Leigh Mallory, General Crerar and Roberts."

There has never been any doubt in my own mind that Crerar was primarily responsible for the revival of Dieppe as a Canadian operation, as he had been in the original initiation.

Among other remarks that Crerar made to me in conversation at this time, as TORCH moved more and more towards Anglo-U.S. acceptance, are to the effect "It will be a tragic humiliation if American troops get into action on this side of the Atlantic, before Canadians, who have been waiting in England for three years."

When I reported to Crerar on my return from Washington and Ottawa (where I was when the raid took place) [delivering the results of the Jupiter appreciation to the Combined Chiefs of Staff], he told me that when the results of Dieppe were first known, McNaughton's reaction had been "This is a disaster, I am responsible for it, and I must tender my resignation." Crerar advised him strongly to make no such admission and do no such thing, but to take the positive line, and in concert with Mountbatten and COHQ take the stand that though the raid had been tragically costly, it had been well worthwhile because of what had been learned from it.

An important point relevant to all of this, and of which I know nothing, is whether Crerar acted entirely on his own initiative, or whether, when he gave up as CGS and came to England to take over 1 Cdn Corps, he had a directive from the Canadian government, verbal or written, to get Canadians into action at almost any cost. Heeney or perhaps Pickersgill are the only two I know of, still alive, who might be able to throw some light on this.[1] Crerar, on the Canadian side, always took a leading part in defending the Dieppe raid. This had its aftermath during the campaign of 1944, and led to his row with Monty. Crerar was hypnotised by Dieppe. . . .[2]

Appendix 2: Guy Simonds — Mona Anderson Letters

EXTRACTS FROM LETTERS OF GUY SIMONDS TO MONA ANDERSON, 1943-44

June 27, 1943

By the time you get this you will have heard of our great adventure and will understand why you have not heard from me. I may now explain, too, what must have seemed to you crazy and inconsiderate activities between the time I came back from Tunisia and the last few days I spent with you and Ian. Then the afternoon of Fiona's party Harry Salmon was killed as he was leaving for Cairo and at very short notice I had to take over 1 Div and the planning and staging of this operation. With less than a day to pick up the threads and find what it was all about I left for Cairo by air the morning after you and Ian had dinner with me at the Savoy. Vian too had replaced Mack only the day before so during our flight out we had our first chance of discussing joint plans. . . . I got home on Tuesday 11 May when we dined together that night.

You will understand what all this means to me — this will be the Canadians' first real operation apart from the Dieppe raid and I will bear a very heavy responsibility. I do not care about myself but it is terribly important that it should go well for so many reasons — the reputation of Canadian soldiers which stood so high in the last war — the fact that so many friends are with me and above all the great importance to the future of the war that we should do our share in this particular operation — I am confident I have prepared myself as well for this task as I am able and if I fail I shall be finished and rightly so, for it will mean I am not really fitted for the responsibilities which have been placed upon me. I do not feel I shall fail — I have lived my whole life for just such an opportunity.

June 29, 1944, Normandy

[After describing the pretty countryside and the detachment of the people who show neither enthusiasm nor enmity, Simonds writes about the fate of civilians in battle zones.]

I have learned to be genuinely sorry for the civilian inhabitants of a country through which a modern battle passes — more especially the children who always look frightened-eyed and wan. I do not believe that such emotions should be allowed to influence our judgment in matters of practical politics but I promise you that the people of an occupied or liberated country will never receive anything but sympathy and courtesy from me. So you need not worry that because I regard them as potential trouble to us in the future, I will give any sign of it in my attitude towards them now.

August 23, 1944

I think the magnitude of our victory is only now beginning to be revealed. . . . It was against us that the Boche SS and Panzer troops made a desperate attempt to break out two days ago — it was desperate madness — the battle was terrific and awful (in a literal sense) whilst it lasted — the slaughter and destruction we administered simply appalling. You could not believe it without seeing it. . . .

September 4, 1944

I wonder if you realise how *terrifying* responsibility can be at times in war. Thousands of men's lives at stake and great issues and you decide on your own deep convictions which convention — and those of great experience — consider difficult and risky. It is all very well when it turns out successfully — everyone cheers — but someday I will try to tell you of the feelings which you have to hide right away inside yourself and outwardly "radiate confidence" as zero hour arrives and passes and the first battle reports start to come in. . . .

I hate the way the French are treating their own people who have shown the slightest friendship towards the Germans — the French at their worst and a reason why I can never respect them the way I would like taking into consideration their many fine qualities. . . . I hate to see them being cruel to their own kind merely because of personal friendships. How on earth is the world ever going to settle down unless these fanatical hatreds are quenched?

December 22, 1944

I send you a letter from our MA in Washington passed on to me by Church Mann. I send it because I was thrilled to see that my mother even at her age is still attractive. She is a very wonderful woman and any success I have ever had I owed to her. Even during the hardest times she always insisted that our schooling should never be interfered with. It is many years since I have seen her and I expect I would be almost a stranger to her now. . . .

During the bad weather I have had plenty of time to visit all troops of all arms and services and it has been very refreshing. I have spent some time with the field ambulances going into questions of "shell-shock" as they used to call it but "battle exhaustion" or various neuroses now. I became very interested as all doctors were unanimous in stating that it is a mixture of physical and emotional exhaustion working together — another proof positive of the inter-relation of the physical and the spiritual. Both have to be cured together as they are closely inter-related — physical improvement parallels emotional recovery and vice versa. . . .

Maps

....

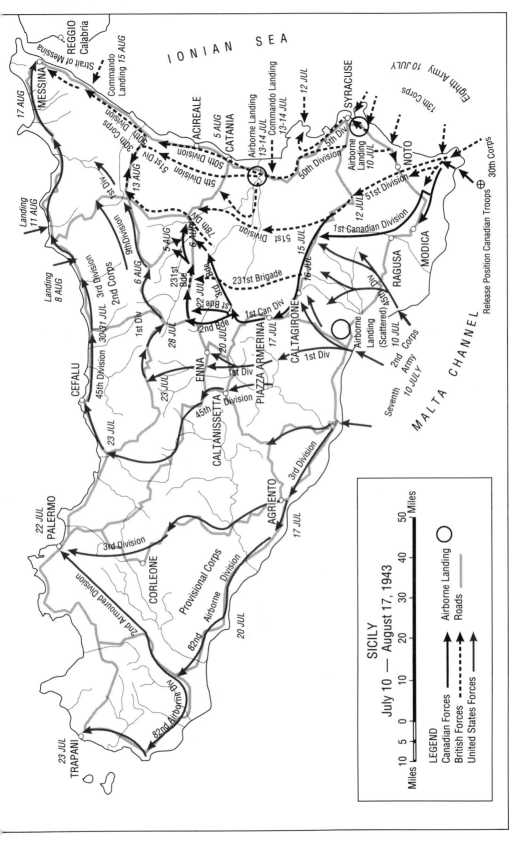

IONIAN SEA

MALTA CHANNEL

REGGIO Calabria

Strait of Messina

Commando Landing 15 AUG

17 AUG

MESSINA

Landing 11 AUG

1st DIV

9th Division

3rd Division

Landing 8 AUG

2nd Corps

30-31 JUL

1st Div

45th Division

CEFALU

23 JUL

ENNA

23 JUL

45th Division

CALTANISSETTA

Division

PIAZZA ARMERINA

45th Division

AGRIENTO

17 JUL

3rd Division

PALERMO

22 JUL

3rd Division

CORLEONE

Provisional Corps

Airborne Division

82nd

20 JUL

2nd Armoured Division

23 JUL

TRAPANI

82nd Airborne DIV

ACIREALE

5 AUG

CATANIA

3rd Corps

30th Corps

50th Division

13 AUG

51st DIV

5th Division

Airborne Landing 13-14 JUL

Commando Landing 13-14 JUL

5th Division

50th Division

5 AUG

6 AUG

78th DIV

6 AUG

5 AUG

231st Bde

231st Brigade

3rd Bde

22 JUL

1st Bde

2nd Bde

20 JUL

28 JUL

1st Div

17 JUL

1st Can Div

12 JUL

SYRACUSE

13th Corps

Eighth Army 10 JULY

Airborne Landing 10 JUL

NOTO

51st Division

1st Canadian Division

12 JUL

15 JUL

16 JUL

RAGUSA

45th DIV

MODICA

Release Position Canadian Troops

30th Corps

CALTAGIRONE

1st Div

Airborne Landing (Scattered) 10 JUL

2nd Army 10 JULY

Seventh Army 10 JULY

2nd Corps

LEGEND

SICILY
July 10 — August 17, 1943

Airborne Landing ◯
Roads
Canadian Forces ▬▬
British Forces ┅┅
United States Forces ▬▬

Miles
10 5 0   10   20   30   40   50
                              Miles

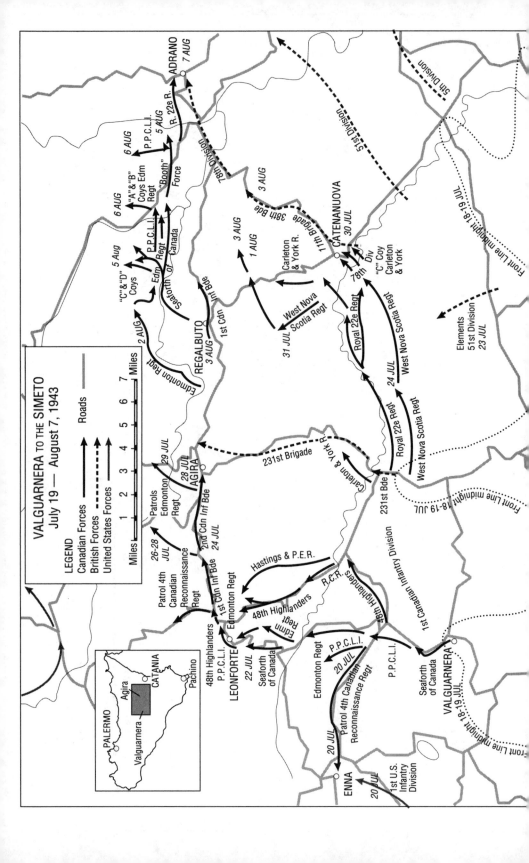

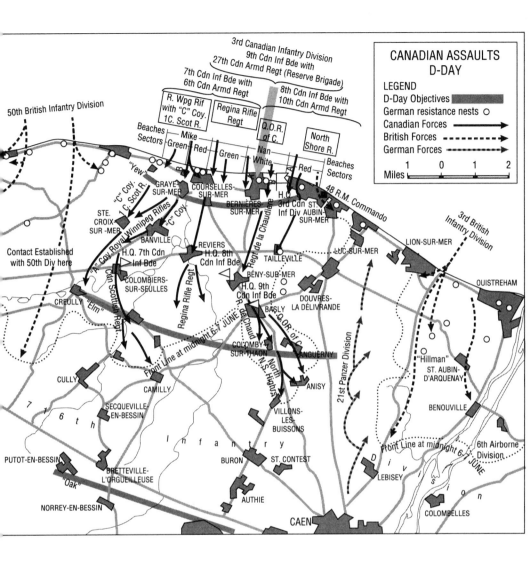

CANADIAN ASSAULTS
D-DAY

LEGEND
D-Day Objectives
German resistance nests ○
Canadian Forces →
British Forces ---→
German Forces ···→

1   0   1   2
Miles

3rd Canadian Infantry Division
9th Cdn Inf Bde with
27th Cdn Armd Regt (Reserve Brigade)

7th Cdn Inf Bde with
6th Cdn Armd Regt

8th Cdn Inf Bde with
10th Cdn Armd Regt

R. Wpg Rif
with "C" Coy.
1C. Scot R.

Regina Rifle
Regt

Q.O.R.
of C.

North
Shore R.

50th British Infantry Division

Beaches
Sectors

Mike
Green   Red   Green

Nan
White   Red

Beaches
Sectors

"Yew"

"C" Coy.   1C. Scot R.

GRAYE-
SUR-MER

COURSELLES-
SUR-MER

BERNIÈRES-
SUR-MER

H.Q.
3rd Cdn
Inf Div

ST.
AUBIN-
SUR-MER

48 R.M. Commando

3rd British
Infantry Division

STE.
CROIX
SUR -MER

"A" Coy Royal Winnipeg Rifles

"C" Coy.

BANVILLE

REVIERS

Regt de la Chaudiere

TAILLEVILLE

LUC-SUR-MER

LION-SUR-MER

OUISTREHAM

Contact Established
with 50th Div here

Cdn Scottish Regt

H.Q. 7th Cdn
Inf Bde

COLOMBIERS-
SUR-SEULLES

H.Q. 8th
Cdn Inf Bde

BÉNY-SUR-MER

H.Q. 9th
Cdn Inf Bde

DOUVRES-
LA DÉLIVRANDE

"Hillman"
ST. AUBIN-
D'ARQUENAY

CREULLY   "Elm"

Regina Rifle Regt

BASLY

Q.O.R. of C.

BENOUVILLE

CULLY

Front Line at midnight 6-7 JUNE

CAMILLY

R. de Chaud

COLOMBY-
SUR-THAON

North
N.S. Higlhs

LANGUERNY

ANISY

21st Panzer Division

Front Line at midnight 6-7 JUNE

6th Airborne
Division

7   6   t   h

SECQUEVILLE-
EN-BESSIN

VILLONS-
LES-
BUISSONS

I   n   f   a   n   t   r   y

D   i   v   i   s   i   o   n

LEBISEY

COLOMBELLES

PUTOT-EN-BESSIN

BRETTEVILLE-
L'ORGUEILLEUSE

"Oak"

BURON

ST. CONTEST

NORREY-EN-BESSIN

AUTHIE

CAEN

THE BATTLE FRONT IN NORMANDY 1 JUL 44

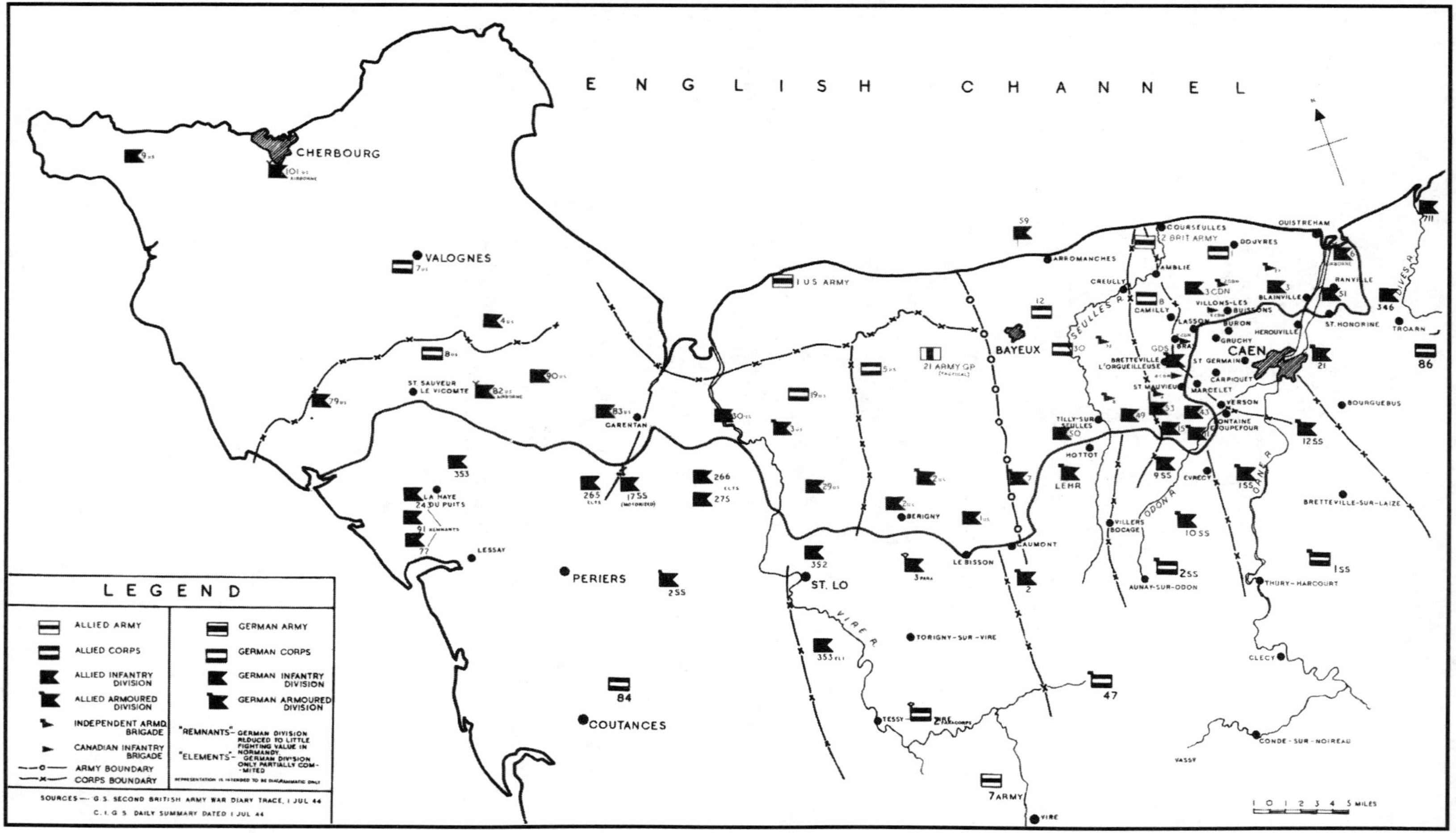

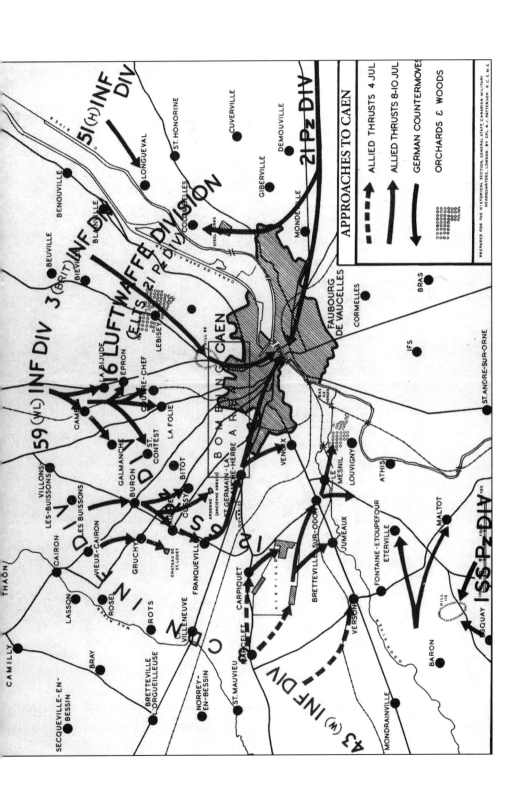

APPROACHES TO CAEN

ALLIED THRUSTS 4 JUL
ALLIED THRUSTS 8-10 JUL
GERMAN COUNTERMOVES
ORCHARDS & WOODS

PREPARED FOR THE HISTORICAL SECTION, GENERAL STAFF, CANADIAN MILITARY
HEADQUARTERS, LONDON. BY CPL. W. J. PATTERSON, R.C.M.C.

THE THREAT TO FALAISE

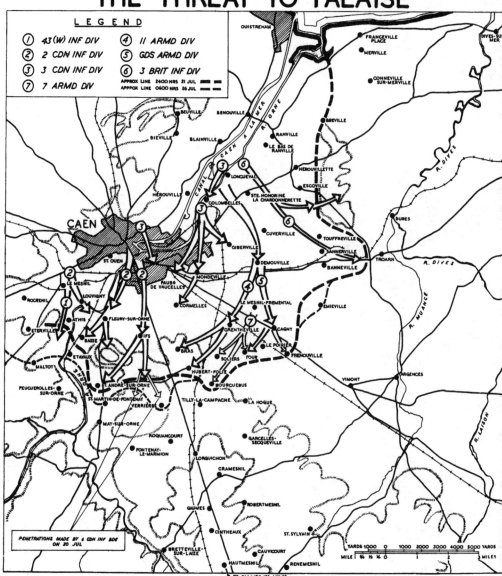

OPERATION "GOODWOOD"
18 - 21 JUL 44

OPERATION "SPRING"
HOLDING ATTACK BY 2 CDN CORPS 25 JUL 44

3 CDN INF DIV

2 CDN INF DIV

BASSE
IFS
ETAVAUX
BRAS
SOLIERS
HUBERT-FOLIE
BOURGUEBUS
BEAUVOIR FARM
T. ANDRÉ-UR-ORNE
CHURCH
ST. MARTIN-DE-FONTENAY
TROTEVAL FARM
TILLY-LA-CAMPAGNE
VERRIÈRES
R. ORNE
MAY-SUR-ORNE
ROQUANCOURT
GARCELLES-SECQUEVILLE
FONTENAY-LE-MARMION
LORGUICHON

DS 1000 500 0 1000 2000 3000 4000 YARDS

— L E G E N D —

NUMBERS INDICATE ATTACKS AS FOLLOWS:—
① FUS MR   ② CAMERONS OF C
③ CALG HIGHRS, 6 CDN ARMD REGT (MORNING 25 JUL)
    AND R DE MAIS (1900 HRS 25 JUL)
④ RHC   ⑤ RHLI   ⑥ R REGT C

⑦ 7 ARMD DIV TANKS   ⑧ NTH NS HIGHRS

APPROX LINE 0600 HRS 26 JUL........... ■■■ ■■■ ■■■

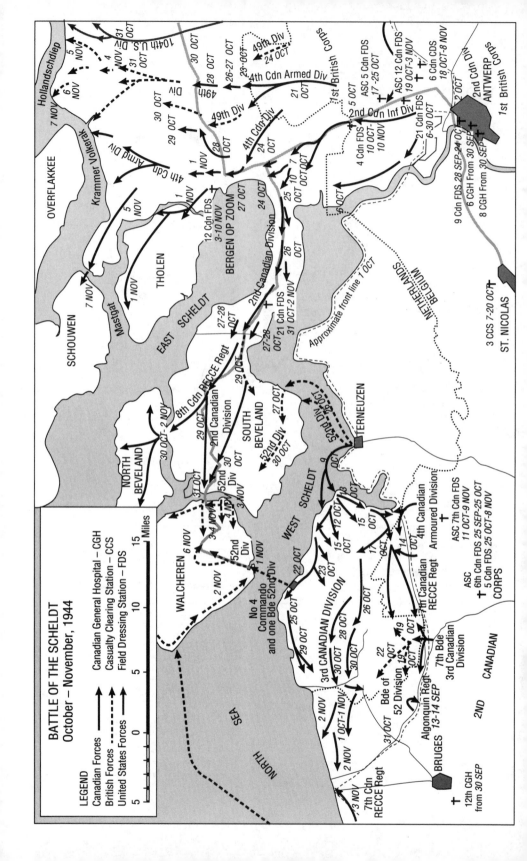

BATTLE OF THE SCHELDT
October – November, 1944

LEGEND

Canadian Forces ⟶
British Forces ⟵ ⟶ (dashed)
United States Forces ⟶ (dashed)

Canadian General Hospital – CGH
Casualty Clearing Station – CCS
Field Dressing Station – FDS

Miles
5 0 5 10 15

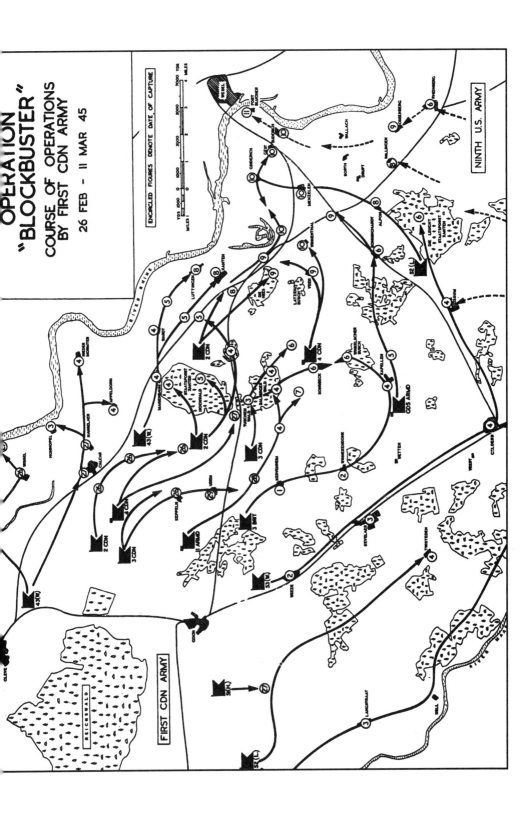

OPERATION
"BLOCKBUSTER"

COURSE OF OPERATIONS
BY FIRST CDN ARMY

26 FEB – 11 MAR 45

ENCIRCLED FIGURES DENOTE DATE OF CAPTURE

NINTH U.S. ARMY

FIRST CDN ARMY

Notes

PROLOGUE

1. Simonds Papers, 1960-74 Box.

CHAPTER 1: FAMILY AFFAIRS

1. Cecil Simonds, in his autobiography in the Simonds Papers (which are still in family hands), wrote: "In taking this fateful step which meant such a change in my career, I was governed by many considerations: the first, of course, being the economic situations then, too, the unsettled state of the Army's future under the handling of the existing Government as to whether my being to some extent considered a lame duck would be balanced by the fact that I was the youngest of my rank and standing: but against that was the stagnant condition of regimental promotion, with the Government cutting down expenses to the prejudice of the Army. Against all these uncertainties I felt that if war were to come, it would be on some big scale, when everyone would be needed, and that, being posted to the Reserve of Officers, I should still have some chance of being employed, whether serving, or on half-pay, or retired."

2. The main source of information about Guy Simonds's early life is the draft of his autobiography in his papers, which he completed to the outbreak of the Second World War. Lieutenant Colonel William E. Hutchinson's excellent unpublished master's degree thesis for the University of Victoria, "Test of a Corps Commander: Lieutenant General Guy Granville Simonds in Normandy, 1944," relied heavily on this draft for his early life. Hutchinson takes Simonds's life forward to the end of the Normandy campaign. Christopher Hull's more recent unpublished M.A. thesis for Purdue University, "A Case Study of Professionalism in the Canadian Army in the 1930s and 1940s: Lieutenant General G. G. Simonds," includes additional interview material and analyzes his methods as a commander but casts no fresh light on his earlier life. J. S. McMahon, a fellow cadet at the RMC, published a small biography of Simonds, *Professional Soldier* (Winnipeg: McMahon Investments, 1985), and it remains the only published work on the subject.

I took a different approach to Simonds's early life because I intended to write a full biography and not just a military one. I thought it necessary, in consequence, to analyze his background more thoroughly, even if I did not enter into as much detail about his ancestry as had Simonds himself. His relations with his mother, father, siblings, and first wife, Katherine (K), are central to the story, but were not likely to be handled by Simonds himself, and had not been by the writers above with candour. Fortunately letters in the Simonds Papers shed more light on these relationships.

Mr. Justice John Matheson, who at one time intended to write a biography of Simonds, kindly gave me the tapes of his interviews with Peter Simonds. As one of the central characters in a family drama, Peter Simonds is important. His testimony was useful in explaining Nellie Simonds's relations with her children and husband.

For the professional circumstances of the British army between 1906 and 1914 the reader is referred to Shelford Bidwell and Dominick Graham, *Fire-Power: British Army Weapons and Theories of War, 1906-1914* (London: Allen and Unwin, 1982).

3. Grierson, as Lieutenant General Sir James, led the Second Corps to France but died of a heart attack on a train before action.
4. Guy Granville Simonds, Unpublished Autobiography, chapter 2, 38, Simonds Papers.

CHAPTER 2: BUILDING A REPUTATION

1. Simonds Autobiography, chapter 3, 38.
2. Simonds, chapter 3, 72.
3. Simonds, chapter 3, 77.
4. Burns's articles were: "A Division That Can Attack" and "Where Do the Tanks Belong?" in *Canadian Defence Quarterly* 15 (April 1938): 282-98 and 16 (October 1938): 28-31. Simonds's articles were "The Attack," "An Army That Can Attack, a Division That Can Defend," and "What Price Assault without Support?" in *Canadian Defence Quarterly* 15 (July 1938): 413-17; 16 (January 1939): 142-47; and 16 (July 1939): 379-90.

CHAPTER 3: ON AN INSECURE FOUNDATION

1. Peter Simonds, letter to Cecil Simonds, 1950, Simonds Papers, Prewar Box.
2. Katherine Taylor, letter to Guy Simonds, January 5, 1931, Simonds Papers, Prewar Box.
3. Katherine Simonds, letter to Guy Simonds, June 1933, Simonds Papers, Prewar Box.
4. The *Courageous* was to be torpedoed in the English Channel on September 17, 1940, with the loss of five hundred men, including her captain.
5. Eleanor Simonds, letter to Guy Simonds, 1937, Simonds Papers, Leather Case.
6. Vincent Massey, telegram to Guy Simonds, 1938, Simonds Papers, Prewar Box.
7. Taped interview by Mr. Justice John Matheson with Peter Simonds.
8. Katherine Simonds, letter to Guy Simonds, July 31, 1943, Simonds Papers, Prewar and 1940-45 Boxes.

CHAPTER 4: THE PERFECT STAFF OFFICER

1. Guy Simonds, letter to Cecil Simonds, December 7, 1939, Simonds Papers, Prewar and 1940-45 Boxes.
2. Guy Simonds, "Preliminary Narrative: The History of the Canadian Military Forces Overseas, 1939-1940," chapter 4, 8-12, Simonds Papers.
3. An account of these events can be found in Simonds's unpublished "Preliminary Narrative: The History of the Canadian Military Forces Overseas, 1939-1940," chapter 5, 1-24 and 34-61. This document is one of the drafts that served the official histories. A copy is in the Simonds Papers and was sent to senior officers for their comments. I was offered an entertaining verbal account by Lieutenant General Robert Moncel, then carrier officer of the First RCR.
4. Simonds Papers, Prewar and 1940-45 Boxes.
5. General Andrew McNaughton, letter to Guy Simonds, April 1941, Simonds Papers, 1940-45 Box.
6. Guy Simonds, letter to Trumbull Warren, 1969. Author's collection.
7. Guy Simonds-Marshal Stearns Letters. Courtesy Miss Stearns, Toronto. The author has seen no evidence that this was actually the case.
8. Brian Villa, *Unauthorized Action: Mountbatten and the Dieppe Raid* (London: Oxford University Press, 1990).
9. Directorate of History, Ottawa. Historical Section Reports, numbers 100, 128, 130, 142, 153, and 159. Simonds Papers Box 2, Memoirs and Postwar, contains

Simonds's correspondence with C. P. Stacey, Admiral Hughes-Hallett, and Lord Louis Mountbatten. There is correspondence between C. P. Stacey and Crerar on June 10 and 11, 1944, in Report 128.

10. Lord Mountbatten, letter to Guy Simonds, February 4, 1969, Simonds Papers. Mountbatten says COHQ had not wanted a frontal assault, and he is right. According to Stacey, he is wrong when he says the Canadians wanted it, for the COHQ documents suggest the Canadians only came into the planning after the decision to mount a frontal attack was made on April 25, 1942, when Montgomery was in the chair. Guy Simonds pointed out that it was a Canadian decision to use tanks on the town beaches. That necessarily prevented the use of bombers on the beach defences, because they would have created obstacles. On the other hand, a decisive flanking operation would have taken too long. Hence a frontal attack without heavy bombing but with tanks was mounted. The point that Simonds wanted Stacey to admit was that Crerar did have a hand in the tactical plan before the decision on the twenty-fifth because he attended the planning meetings and he could not believe that the Second Infantry divisional commander, J. H. (Ham) Roberts, would have been excluded until that time by Crerar. That would have been against a principle followed in such cases that the commander should be brought into the plan at the earliest stage. However, extant documents show only that Crerar was responsible for encouraging the participation of Canadians in raiding operations. Yet one of the specific raids considered from the beginning was Dieppe. It can be argued that out of Crerar's persistence over raiding and his determined pressure to have the Canadians involved in full-scale operations came the Dieppe raid.

11. Brian Villa, "Mountbatten, the British Chief of Staff, and Approval of the Dieppe Raid," *The Journal of Military History* 54: (April 1990) 201-226; Philip Ziegler, *Mountbatten* (New York: Collins, 1985).

12. C. P. Stacey, letters to Guy Simonds, December 1 and 22, 1968, February 25 and April 22, 1969, Simonds Papers. In January 1969 Stacey wrote to Major General Elliot Rodger, Simonds's brigadier chief of staff in the Second Corps: "I have been having some dealings with Guy Simonds about it [his final volume of the history]. Guy is still, unfortunately, carrying on the feud with Harry Crerar and is anxious to stick Harry with the responsibility for the Dieppe raid."

13. Simonds Papers, 1940-45 Box.

CHAPTER 5: IN COMMAND OF THE OLD RED PATCH

1. Hutchinson 103-05.

2. Gregory Clark, *The Standard*, February 10, 1951.

3. Field Marshal Bernard Montgomery, letter to General H. D. G. Crerar, Simonds Papers, 1940-45 Box.

4. Lieutenant General Howard Graham, *Citizen and Soldier* (Toronto: McClelland and Stewart, 1987).

5. G. W. L. Nicholson, *The Canadians in Italy, 1943-45* (Ottawa: Queen's Printer, 1956) 29-32.

6. Cicely Simonds, letter to Cecil Simonds, April 20, 1943, Simonds Papers, 1940-45 Box.

7. Cecil Simonds's files of newspaper clippings about his son, Simonds Papers, 1940-45 Box.

8. *Winnipeg Free Press*, May 19, 1943. Clipping found in Simonds Papers, 1940-45 Box.

9. Information about the trip to Cairo is from Brigadier A. F. B. Knight.

10. The mobilization of the First Canadian Division for Husky illustrates the insuperable difficulties in the way of invading northwest Europe in 1943 as the Americans desired. There were simply insufficiently trained and equipped divisions in the United Kingdom at that time. The six-pounder was first employed by the artillery in the desert.

11. A. T. Sesia Diary, Directorate of History, Ottawa.

12. Michael Howard, *British Intelligence in the Second World War,* vol. 5 (London: HMSO, 1990) 86-91.

13. A. T. Sesia Diary.

14. A. T. Sesia Diary.

CHAPTER 6: THE OLD RED PATCH GOES TO WAR

1. Major General George Kitching, *Mud and Green Fields: The Memoirs of Major General George Kitching* (Langley, B.C.: Battleline Books, 1986) 158-59.

2. A. T. Sesia Diary.

3. A. T. Sesia Diary.

4. Graham 154.

CHAPTER 7: THE GERMANS AND THE MOUNTAINS

1. Graham 158-64.

2. Interview with Stuart Graham, April 1990.

3. Interview with Robert Kingstone, November 1990.

4. Kitching 169-70.

5. Carlo D'Este's *Bitter Victory: The Battle for Sicily* (London: Collins, 1988) is the most scholarly account to date of the campaign and of this incident, which is mentioned in the chapter "The Great Boundary Dispute," 321-33.

6. General Oliver Leese, letter to Guy Simonds, July 15, 1943, Simonds Papers, Sicily and Italy Box. The Americans had not reached Caltagirone. The cooperation and exchange of information between the Allies continued to be faulty. There appear to be almost endless pieces in the puzzle concerning the sacking of Graham. Perhaps the most reliable additional information comes from Montgomery's Tac HQ. Montgomery sided with Graham but ensured that he received a rocket and that Simonds was admonished, as well. The object was to teach each a lesson and to heal the relationship. Montgomery was very experienced in handling quarrels between his lieutenants.

7. Field Marshal Bernard Montgomery, letter to Guy Simonds, July 17, 1943, Simonds Papers, Sicily and Italy Box.

8. William J. McAndrew, "Fire or Movement? Canadian Tactical Doctrine, Sicily — 1943," *Military Affairs* 51 (July 1987).

9. Major General George Kitching, letters to author, 1991-92.

10. Kitching, letters to author.

11. Nicholson 121.

12. Simonds Papers, Sicily and Italy Box.

13. A. T. Sesia Diary.

14. A. T. Sesia Diary.

15. A. T. Sesia Diary.

16. Guy Simonds, letter to General Andrew McNaughton, 1943, Simonds Papers, Sicily and Italy Box.

17. General H. D. G. Crerar, letter to Guy Simonds, August 10, 1943, Simonds Papers, Sicily and Italy Box.

18. General Miles Dempsey, letter to Guy Simonds, September 22, 1943, Simonds Papers, Sicily and Italy Box.

19. General Miles Dempsey, letter to Guy Simonds, October 12, 1943, Simonds Papers, Sicily and Italy Box.

CHAPTER 8: CANADIAN ARMY POLITICS

1. The logistical and operational units required to maintain and support each division in an army, over and above its divisional establishment, are called a divisional

"slice." The sum total of the slices in an army increases as the size of the army increases. The Canadian field force in the Second War was not double that of the First. Four infantry divisions were maintained in the field in the First War, three infantry and two armoured divsons plus two independent tank brigades without infantry in the Second. However, logistical and command overheads were relatively heavier in the Second, and more Canadians served with the RCN, the RCAF, and the British forces of three services.

2. In 1917 General Pershing commanded the First U. S. Division, but he was authorized to represent American military interests as well as to manage the expansion of the American forces.

3. Nicholson 340.

4. Precisely how much Montgomery knew about the arrangements for Timberwolf is unclear. I suspect that only the code name was unknown to him.

5. The Fifth Division's route from Naples to the Adriatic has been described as littered with broken-down tanks and wheeled vehicles. Some had no brakes worth the name, and a considerable number had to be towed at the start of the journey. It was clear that the Seventh Armoured Division had let its friends pick over the best runners.

6. It will be remembered that Simonds and Burns had exchanged ideas in the *Canadian Defence Quarterly* before the war. Burns was to be a distinguished commander of peace-keeping forces after it.

7. Anecdote from Professor Reginald Roy, Pearkes's biographer. See *Most Conspicuous Bravery: A Biography of Major General George R. Pearkes, V.C., Through Two World Wars* (Vancouver: University of British Columbia Press, 1977).

8. Crerar Papers, MG30 E157, vols. 4 and 7 (files on the Burns affair), National Archives of Canada.

9. General Richard McCreery, letter to H. D. G. Crerar, October 31, 1944, Crerar Papers, vol. 4, 958C.009 (D178).

10. Field Marshal Harold Alexander, letter to the War Office, June 3, 1944, Crerar Papers, vol. 4, 958C.009 (D178).

11. Crerar Papers, vol. 4, 958C.009 (D83), June 3 and 4; July 3 and 15. In the end the First Corps found its infantry by remustering whole units of artillery, reconnaissance, and motorized infantry. Ironically, later, remustering was the solution to infantry shortages in the First Army but not by units, as the Eighth Army had done, which was a more economical process, but by individuals.

12. Professor Reginald Roy, author of *1944: The Canadians in Normandy* (Toronto: Macmillan, 1984), has remarked that when the First Division went overseas not one officer, from McNaughton down, had had the opportunity to exercise a full battalion of infantry in the field for twenty years.

13. Field Marshal Harold Alexander, letter to H. D. G. Crerar, June 29, 1944, Crerar Papers, vol. 3, 958C.009 (D178).

14. H. D. G. Crerar, letter to Lieutenant General Kenneth Stuart, July 2, 1944, Crerar Papers, vol. 3, MG30 E157, 958C.009 (D178).

15. The ensuing exchanges between Crerar, Simonds, and Montgomery are in Crerar Papers, MG30 E157, vol. 7, 958C.001 (D180) various dates in December 1943 and January 1944. Also in Simonds Papers, Prewar and 1940-45 Boxes.

16. Crerar Papers, December 10, 1943.

17. Crerar Papers, December 8, 1943.

18. Crerar Papers, December 15, 1943.

19. Crerar Papers, December 11 and 18, 1943.

20. Crerar was to take precisely the same step in trying to have Crocker transferred from command of the First British Corps in Normandy.

21. Crerar Papers, December 17, 1943.

22. Crerar Papers, December 21, 1943. Shortly afterwards Montgomery left for the United Kingdom and the matter was discussed no further.

23. Field Marshal Bernard Montgomery, letter to Guy Simonds, November 18, 1943, Simonds Papers, Box 1.
24. Crerar Papers, January 2, 1944.
25. Crerar Papers, December 21, 1943, and January 13, 1944.

CHAPTER 9: THE ALLIED CAMPAIGN IN NORMANDY

1. *Overlord: D-day and the Battle for Normandy 1944* (London: Michael Joseph, 1984) by Max Hastings is an excellent general account of the tactical shortcomings of the Allies. Carlo D'Este's *Decision in Normandy: The Unwritten Story of Montgomery and the Allied Campaign* (London: Pan, 1984) is the standard work on the planning and conduct of the battle. Reginald Roy's *1944: The Canadians in Normandy* (Toronto: Macmillan, 1984) serves the purpose for the Canadians. On the training and performance of the Canadians in the field see John A. English's *The Canadian Army and the Normandy Campaign: A Study of Failure in High Command* (New York: Praeger, 1991).
2. Some of the works that are unfavourable to Montgomery when discussing his conduct of the battle in Normandy are: Walter Bedell Smith, *Eisenhower's Six Great Decisions: Europe 1944-45* (New York: Longmans, Green, 1956); H. C. Butcher, *My Three Years with Eisenhower* (New York: Simon and Schuster, 1946); and Arthur Tedder, *With Prejudice* (Boston: Little, Brown, 1966). Books favourable to Air Marshal Tedder rather than Montgomery include John Terraine, *The Right of the Line: The Royal Air Force in the European War 1939-45* (London: Hodder and Stoughton, 1985) and Omar N. Bradley and Clay Blair, *A General's Life* (New York: Simon and Schuster, 1983).
3. The airfield at Carpiquet, overlooking Caen on the west, and taken before Caen fell, was the chief capture. Otherwise fields were used in the very crowded bridgehead. The feeling between Tedder and Arthur Coningham, commanding the Second TAF, and Montgomery had been strained since the Desert Campaign when the airmen believed that Montgomery hogged the glory for the Eighth Army's successes.
4. Brooke was one of the few senior officers to whom Montgomery paid attention. He had little respect for Eisenhower's capacity as a field commander but realized that Montgomery would get nowhere unless he treated Eisenhower with great care and took the trouble to explain what he was trying to do. On the German frontier in October the relations between Eisenhower and Montgomery came to a head and Brooke had to step in again.
5. General Elliot Rodger, manuscript diary in the general's personal papers.
6. *Winnipeg Free Press,* August 14, 1944, clipping in Simonds Papers, Second Corps Box.

CHAPTER 10: A MAMMOTH CANVAS

1. Notes on conference held by the commander-in-chief of the Twenty-first Army Group on June 22, 1944, Simonds Papers, Second Corps Box.
2. H. D. G. Crerar, letter to Guy Simonds, June 23, 1944, Simonds Papers, Second Corps Box.
3. Minutes of a special conference held by the chief of staff, First Canadian Army, June 27, 1944.
4. General Elliot Rodger, private diary.
5. The published sources for this chapter are: Carlo d'Este, *Decision in Normandy: The Unwritten Story of Montgomery and the Allied Campaign* (London: Pan, 1984); John A. English, *The Canadian Army and the Normandy Campaign: A Study of Failure in High Command* (New York: Praeger, 1991); and Reginald Roy, *1944: The Canadians in Normandy* (Toronto: Macmillan, 1984). The latter is the standard text on the Canadian campaign. I have used some of the reports concerning these operations prepared by members of Colonel Stacey's historical team in the field, found in the

Simonds Papers. Where that source has failed me I have used copies of National Archives documents, to some of which my attention was drawn by William McAndrew and Jack English, in particular.

6. A description is in Report No. 162, Historical Section, CMHQ, November 8, 1946, 50, Simonds Papers.

7. CMHQ Report No. 162, 57-59, Simonds Papers.

8. Draft statement, n.d. Reply from Guy Simonds to chief of staff CMHQ, January 31, 1946.

9. RG24 vol. 12, 745, National Archives of Canada.

10. Simonds Papers, Second Corps Box.

11. Crerar Papers MG30 E157, vol. 3, Simonds to Dempsey, July 27, 1944; Crocker to Dempsey, July 5; Dempsey to Montgomery, July 6; and Montgomery to Crerar, n.d., in which Montgomery wrote: "the Canadian soldier is such a magnificent chap that he deserves, and should be given, really good generals."

12. John English, Thesis, "The Casting of an Army" (basis for his book *The Canadian Army and the Normandy Campaign*) 424. The sacking of Ben Cunningham worried Simonds for the rest of his life. He felt that he ought to have sacked Keller instead. It seems that the division was run by the GSO I, Lieutenant Colonel Mingay, and the CRA, Stan Todd. Cunningham and he remained friends.

13. Simonds Papers, Second Corps Box.

14. Simonds Papers, "GOC's Activities," Second Corps Box.

15. English, "The Casting of an Army" 422.

16. General Dempsey's expansion (March 18, 1952) of the notes he wrote down in brief form on February 21, 1952. Checked and revised on March 28, 1952, and titled "The Aims of Operation 'Goodwood.'" Sent to C. P. Stacey by Captain Liddell Hart on September 7, 1954, RG24, Box 10800, National Archives, Ottawa.

17. Appreciation and Outline Plan for Operation Totalize, August 2, 1944. Presented orally to GOC-in-C First Canadian Army on July 31. The original was handed to Crerar on August 3. RG24, vol. 10799, National Archives.

18. Immediate Report on Totalize, August 7 and 9, RG24, vol. 10799, National Archives.

19. English, "The Casting of an Army" 447.

20. Remarks to Senior Officers by GOC-in-C, 051100, August 1944, RG24, vol. 10799, National Archives.

21. English, "The Casting of an Army" 451.

22. General Elliot Rodger, letter to author.

23. Guy Simonds, letter to H. D. G. Crerar, August 6, 1944, RG24, vol. 10799, National Archives. The author was told that Simonds was indoctrinated into Ultra. Whether that is true or not he does not know. It appears to have been of little use to him on this occasion. The plan for this operation was captured by the Germans but, again, whether they were able to use it to anticipate the Canadians is not clear. Battlefield information depends largely on the efficiency of radio. British radios at the unit level were poor and frequently failed, even when the signallers carrying sets were not singled out by snipers.

24. English, "The Casting of an Army" 465.

25. Major General George Kitching, letter to author, 1992.

26. Document given to author by William McAndrew, Directorate of History, Ottawa.

27. Notes of Kurt Meyer, interview with Major James R. Millar, September 3, 1950, Directorate of History, Ottawa.

28. Brigadier Churchill Mann, letter to H. D. G. Crerar, August 11, 1944, Simonds Papers, Second Corps Box.

CHAPTER 11: MORALE AND FORCE STRENGTH

1. MG30 E157, vol. 7, National Archives, Ottawa.

2. MG30 E157, vol. 3, National Archives. Also Simonds Papers, Box 1, J. L. Ralston, letter to Guy Simonds, November 14, 1945, when Simonds was GOC Canadian Forces in the Netherlands and objecting to his subordination to Major General Murchie, then appointed chief of staff CMHQ.

3. RG24, Box 10650, National Archives.

4. CMHQ Historical Report No. 183, August 8, 1944, Simonds Papers, Second Corps Box.

5. CMHQ Historical Report, Simonds Papers.

6. CMHQ Historical Report.

7. CMHQ Historical Report.

8. RG24, Box 10650.

9. RG24, Box 10650.

10. RG24, Box 10650.

11. RG24, Box 10650. Author's emphasis.

12. RG24, Box 10650.

13. Kitching 218.

14. Terry Copp and William McAndrew, *Battle Exhaustion: Soldiers and Psychiatrists in the Canadian Army, 1939-45* (Montreal: McGill-Queen's University Press, 1990) 121. My comments should not contradict my admiration for the authors' chapter on the army in Normandy.

15. Memorandum on British armour, Twenty-first Army Group, July 6, 1944, Simonds Papers, Second Corps Box.

16. Cabinet 106, 1060, Public Record Office, London, England.

17. Simonds Papers, Second Corps Box.

18. RG24, Box 10650, folder 215C1.b19 (D4), November 12, 1944, National Archives, Ottawa.

19. W. Denis Whitaker and Shelagh Whitaker, *Tug of War* (Toronto: Stoddart, 1984) 212-35.

20. Simonds Papers, Second Corps Box.

21. Whitaker and Whitaker, *Tug of War* 226.

22. J. L. Ralston, *Hansard,* House of Commons, Ottawa, July 11, 1944.

23. Whitaker and Whitaker, *Tug of War* 228. Also "General Observations on the Visit to Italy of Colonel the Honourable J. L. Ralston, Minister of National Defence" and other papers dated October 1, 10, and 11, 1944, Simonds Papers, Second Corps Box.

24. Whitaker and Whitaker, *Tug of War* 232.

25. The formula by which casualty wastage rates were estimated was reassessed in 1942-43. In 1942 the War Office's Research Committee under the chair of Major General Jack Evetts examined field force conspectus (FFC) rates and issued various reports of which the Tenth Interim Report was approved by the Executive Committee of the Army Council in April 1943. At that time the monthly casualty rate was tentatively set at twenty percent in infantry of the line. The European theatre was to be the standard, not North Africa, although the fighting in Tunisia was noted as instructive.

The Twenty-first Army Group casualty estimates were drawn up in February 1944 when extremely heavy casualties were projected for the first month of the campaign at a new "double intense" rate, which proved too pessimistic. The estimate of infantry casualties in the next two months at half the double intense rates proved to be optimistic because of heavy fighting caused by the German decision to stand and fight instead of withdrawing to the Seine. The estimate that the infantry would bear forty-five percent of casualties in the first month, thirty-eight percent in the second, and thirty-five percent in the third month were underestimates in aggregate. (War Office 163/89-90 and 205/152, quoted in correspondence from John Peaty, Army Historical Section, March and April 1992, to the author.)

Canadian staff could hardly have been so naive as to accept statistical figures of

April 1943 before the heavy infantry casualties from July 1943 to June 1944 had forced further British reassessment for conditions from Italy to Normandy. Nor would they have overlooked the point that the figures had to be applied as averages over a long period that included inactive operations. Either a good reserve of trained men was required to cover intense fighting or a plan made to disband divisions to provide the men. The latter was the British plan before D-day. With a large army that was a practicable solution, although undesirable. The Canadians had no such reserve of divisions to disband.

Furthermore, the cutting edge of the infantry, sixteen percent of the total force, was the rifle company, and an average of even twenty percent casualties in infantry as a whole was likely to fall on it, not on the support units. Heavy casualties in rifle companies rendered a battalion ineffective.

As we have seen from Simonds's visit to the Eighth Army in April 1943, and the correspondence over the shortage of infantry in the armoured divisions in Italy in June 1944, remustering to infantry was essential. The British remustered thirty-five thousand men to infantry before Normandy and called on the Canadians to provide infantry officers, who joined British units before D-day under a special training scheme called CANLOAN. Officer casualties were markedly higher than the FFC rates for other ranks.

CHAPTER 12: BATTLES IN THE POLDERS

1. Guy Simonds, letter to C. P. Stacey, February 10, 1969, Simonds Papers, Second Corps Box.
2. Historical Report No. 154, Simonds Papers, Second Corps Box.
3. Historical Report No. 154.
4. Historical Report No. 154.
5. Historical Report No. 183, Directorate of History, Ottawa.
6. RG24, Box 10799, National Archives, Ottawa.
7. Simonds Papers, Second Corps Box.
8. Folder P, Part 2, Items 59 and 60, University of New Brunswick. Taken from Simonds Box, GOC Second Corps.
9. David Carmichael, *The Canadian Magazine,* October 12, 1968.
10. Oscar Lange, letter to author.
11. "First Army Plan," Simonds Papers, Second Corps Box.
12. Simonds Papers, Second Corps Box. An exchange with the Poles at this time amused Simonds. The Tenth Polish Armoured Reconnaissance Regiment had captured an armed enemy patrol vessel and raided other German naval vessels in the Scheldt. They asked for the definition of eligibility for saltwater pay and allowances. Simonds replied that he would approve an application for the certificate PSW, which stood for Passed Saltwater.
13. Simonds Papers, Second Corps Box.
14. Air Commodore T. N. McEvoy, letter to Elliot Rodger, cited in C. P. Stacey, *The Victory Campaign: The Operations in Northwest Europe 1944-45* (Ottawa: Queen's Printer, 1960 and 1966) 378.
15. Stacey, *The Victory Campaign* 407-09. Oral evidence given by General Walsh.
16. Quoting Brigadier Churchill Mann, Operation Infatuate, conference on September 29, 1944, WD Plans Section, First Army headquarters, September 30, 1944.
17. Stacey, *The Victory Campaign* 392-400.
18. Stacey, *The Victory Campaign* 400-06.
19. Stacey, *The Victory Campaign* 413-14.
20. Stacey, *The Victory Campaign* 416-22.
21. Simonds Papers, Second Corps Box.

22. Field Marshal Montgomery, letter to Guy Simonds, November 3, 1944, Simonds Papers, Second Corps Box.
23. H. D. G. Crerar, letter to Guy Simonds, Simonds Papers, Second Corps Box.
24. Major General Percy Hobart, letter to Guy Simonds, November 6, 1944, Simonds Papers, Second Corps Box.
25. Churchill Mann, letter to Guy Simonds, Simonds Papers, Second Corps Box.
26. Simonds Papers, Second Corps Box, January 1, 1945. Copies to Admiral Sir Bertram Ramsay and Field Marshal Sir Bernard Montgomery.

CHAPTER 13: THE TIDE'S IN

1. W. Denis Whitaker and Shelagh Whitaker, *Rhineland: The Battle to End the War* (Toronto: Stoddart, 1989) 43; 193; 194; 220; 219.
2. Whitaker and Whitaker, *Rhineland* 228. Brigadier Sidney Radley-Walters, then a major and an armoured squadron commander, was not present in Blockbuster.
3. Operation Directive, General Crerar, January 25, 1945, CMHQ Report 186, Simonds Papers.
4. CMHQ Report 185, page 57, Simonds Papers.
5. Interview with Major P. A. Mayer, December 17, 1947, Simonds Papers.
6. Whitaker and Whitaker, *Rhineland* 144-45.
7. Whitaker and Whitaker, *Rhineland* 144-45.
8. H. D. G. Crerar, letter to Price Montague, March 4, 1945, concerning the appointment of Spry, but there is no mention of the reason for it.
9. H. D. G. Crerar's directive to Corps commanders on February 25, 1945, Crerar's Diary. Quoting Stacey, *The Victory Campaign* 494 and CMHQ Report No. 186, page 12.
10. Stacey, *The Victory Campaign* 505.
11. Stacey, *The Victory Campaign* 507.
12. Whitaker and Whitaker, *Rhineland* 226.
13. Whitaker and Whitaker, *Rhineland* 221.
14. Stacey, *The Victory Campaign* 507n.
15. Whitaker and Whitaker, *Rhineland* 228. "No one was more surprised at Simonds's tactics than the Germans themselves," a comment that does not support the Whitakers.
16. Stacey, *The Victory Campaign* 513.
17. Charles Lynch, *Montreal Gazette,* October 5, 1983.

CHAPTER 14: POSTWAR FRUSTRATION

1. General Elliot Rodger, manuscript diary in the general's personal papers.
2. Simonds Papers, Second Corps Box.
3. Simonds Papers, Repatriation Directive, Holland Box.
4. Simonds Papers, Holland Box.
5. Editorial, *Globe and Mail,* September 25, 1945.
6. Richard Malone, letter to Guy Simonds, September 26, 1945, Simonds Papers, Box 1, 1945-49.
7. *House of Commons Debates,* September 24, 1945.
8. *House of Commons Debates.*
9. Field Marshal Montgomery, letter to Guy Simonds, Simonds Papers.
10. Deputy minister of defence to Lieutenant General Simonds, November 14, 1945, Simonds Papers, Postwar Box.
11. Guy Simonds, letter to Marshal Stearns, December 3, 1945, Stearns family papers.
12. Guy Simonds, letter to Marshal Stearns, December 11, 1945, Stearns family papers.

CHAPTER 15: HIS COLOURS TO THE MAST

1. Simonds Papers, 1946-49 Box.
2. Guy Simonds, letter to Marshal Stearns, May 18, 1946, Simonds-Stearns correspondence, Stearns family papers.
3. Guy Simonds, letter to chief of staff, CMHQ, May 22, 1946, Simonds Papers, 1946-49 Box.
4. Simonds-Stearns correspondence, September 8, 1946.
5. Katherine Simonds, letter to Guy Simonds, July 4, 1947, Simonds Papers, Leather Case.
6. Peter Simonds, letter to Cecil Simonds, n.d., Simonds Papers, Leather Case.
7. Guy Simonds, letter to Peter Simonds, n.d., Simonds Papers, Leather Case.
8. Charles Foulkes, letter to Guy Simonds, March 5, 1947, Simonds Papers, Postwar Box.
9. Simonds-Stearns, March 12, 1947.
10. Simonds-Stearns, September 8, 1947.
11. Simonds-Stearns, September 18, 1947.
12. Bernard Montgomery, letter to Guy Simonds, September 30, 1947, Simonds Papers, Postwar Box.
13. Charles Foulkes, letter to Guy Simonds, October 31, 1947, Simonds Papers, Postwar Box.
14. Simonds-Stearns, December 21, 1947.
15. Simonds-Stearns, December 21, 1947.
16. Simonds-Stearns, January 17, 1948.
17. Charles Foulkes, letter to Guy Simonds, February 5, 1948, Simonds Papers, Postwar Box.
18. Guy Simonds, telegram to Charles Foulkes, February 11, 1948, Simonds Papers, Postwar Box.
19. Guy Simonds, letter to Charles Foulkes, February 12, 1948, Simonds Papers, Postwar Box.
20. Bernard Montgomery, letter to Guy Simonds, March 14, 1948, Simonds Papers, Postwar Box.
21. Simonds-Stearns, n.d.
22. Simonds-Stearns, n.d.
23. Simonds-Stearns, n.d.

CHAPTER 16: CHIEF OF THE GENERAL STAFF

1. Guy Simonds, letter to Charles Foulkes, January 24, 1950, Foulkes Papers, Raymond Collection, Directorate of History.
2. Charles Foulkes, letter to Guy Simonds, January 27, 1950, Simonds Papers.
3. Guy Simonds, letter to Brooke Claxton, July 16, 1951, Claxton Papers, vol. 108, 32 B5, National Archives, Ottawa. Also memorandum for Cabinet Defence Committee, August 24, 1951.
4. Claxton Memoirs, vol. 9, page 1519 *et seq.*, Claxton Papers, MG32 B5, vol. 222, National Archives, Ottawa.
5. Claxton Memoirs, vol. 9, Claxton Papers.
6. Claxton Memoirs, "NATO," page 1229, Claxton Papers, National Archives, Ottawa.
7. Sir Michael Howard, "Shooting at a Moving Target," *Times Literary Supplement,* March 13, 1992.
8. Cited by Lieutenant C. G. Rennie, "Mobilization for War: Canadian Army Recruiting and the Korea Conflict," *Canadian Defence Quarterly.* Article found in Simonds Papers, Postwar Box.
9. Rennie, "Mobilization for War."

CHAPTER 17: REFUSING TO FADE AWAY

1. The basic source for this chapter is James Eayrs, *In Defence of Canada: Peacemaking and Deterrence* (Toronto: University of Toronto Press, 1977).
2. Simonds made this speech after a stormy and prolonged meeting of the chiefs of staff, which he had to leave early. An aide gave him a speech, which Simonds launched into without realizing that it was identical to the one he had recently given in Saint John.
3. Simonds Papers, Broadsword File, containing letters and replies in February 1955, Postwar Box 1953-55. Also letter to and reply from Prime Minister John Diefenbaker, March 1959.
4. Simonds Papers, CGS Box.
5. Simonds Papers, CGS Box.
6. Simonds Papers, paper prepared by Simonds in cooperation with Lieutenant Colonel J. M. E. Clarkson, onetime military assistant to the CGS and in October 1966 a student at the National Defence College. 1960-74 Box.
7. Simonds-Clarkson paper, Simonds Papers, 1960-74 Box.
8. Simonds Papers, paper written with Chris Vokes, 1960-74 Box.

CHAPTER 18: A MAN OF INTEGRITY

1. Interview with Michael Kearney.
2. Kearney interview.
3. Kearney interview.
4. Interview with Lieutenant General W. A. B. Anderson.
5. Interview with Lieutenant General R. W. Moncel.
6. Anderson interview.
7. Anderson interview.
8. Prime Minister Louis St. Laurent, letter to Guy Simonds, n.d., Simonds Papers, CGS Box.
9. Guy Simonds, letter to Louis St. Laurent, n.d., Simonds Papers, CGS Box.
10. Interview with John Matheson.
11. Interview with Douglas Harkness.
12. Interview with Dorothy Sinclair Simonds.
13. Interview with Major General Bruce Matthews.
14. Interview with Mary Plow. Also interview with Dorothy Simonds.
15. Dorothy Simonds interview.
16. Dorothy Simonds interview.
17. Interviews with Charles Simonds and Ruth Smith.
18. Interviews with Anthony Griffin and J. E. MacNelly.
19. Simonds Papers, 1960-74 Box.
20. Letters to and from Lord Louis Mountbatten, n.d., Simonds Papers, 1960-74 Box.
21. Interview with Stearns family, 1990.
22. Guy Simonds, letter to Lester B. Pearson, n.d., Simonds Papers, 1960-74 Box.
23. *Le Matin*, June 7, 1968. Newspaper clipping in Simonds Papers, 1960-74 Box.
24. Colonel John Bennett, letter to Major Lieutenant General Elliot Rodger and author, 1992. Interview with General Rodger.
25. Interview with Lieutenant General W. A. B. Anderson.
26. Simonds Papers, 1960-74 Box.
27. Interview with Brigadier Stanley Todd.
28. Brigadier Stanley Todd, letter to author, 1992.

CHAPTER 19: SIMONDS THE SOLDIER

1. Brereton Greenhous, *Canadian Defence Quarterly* 21 (Autumn 1991): 50.
2. Carl von Clausewitz, *On War*, ed. and trans. Michael Howard and Peter Paret

(Princeton, NJ: Princeton University Press, 1976) 156-74.

3. John English's purpose in *The Canadian Army and the Normandy Campaign: A Study of Failure in High Command* (New York: Praeger, 1991) was to investigate that training. An example of the disadvantage under which the infantry fought is in machine gun equipment. In fighting SS divisions the British and Canadians pitted the slow-firing Bren gun against twice as many M-42s.

4. A counterview to that of Simonds is Terry Copp and Robert Vogel, "'No Lack of Rational Speed,' 1st Canadian Army Operations, September 1944," *Journal of Canadian Studies* 16 (Autumn/Winter 1981): 145-55.

APPENDIX 1: THE DIEPPE RAID

1. Of this Stacey remarked: ". . . Colonel Ralston, with General Crerar's assistance, was working in the Cabinet War Committee to obtain active employment for Canadian troops. He was largely frustrated by Mackenzie King. I have no doubt that at various times Ralston and Crerar had conversations on the question, but I would think a 'directive' very unlikely. In any case neither Heeney nor Pickersgill would have known of such exchanges. They worked for Mackenzie King and nobody else, and they reported *everything* to him; their skins depended on it."

2. In a conversation with General Kitching in 1978-79 General Pearkes told him that Crerar tried to persuade him to take on the Dieppe operation with the First Division. Pearkes told him that he would not do it because it was not "an operation of war." So Crerar gave the task to General "Ham" Roberts, a gunner who did not stand a chance since he did not know what it would take to make an infantry operation like that succeed. A month after Dieppe Pearkes was sent back to Canada.

Glossary

....

AAG and AQMG: Lieutenant colonels at the corps level responsible for A and Q functions respectively.

AAI: Allied Armies in Italy.

AA and QMG: Assistant Adjutant and Quartermaster General. Lieutenant colonel in command of the A and Q staffs of a division.

ADC: Aide-de-camp.

ADMS: Assistant Director of Medical Services. Colonel in charge of divisional medical services.

AGRA: Army Group Royal Artillery.

APC: Armoured Personnel Carrier — Kangaroo, defrocked Priest, Staghound. The latter was the armoured scout car used by Simonds in France as a command vehicle.

A Staff: Adjutant General's Staff. Responsible for morale, discipline, protocol, medivac services, and many other functions concerned with personnel.

BEF: British Expeditionary Force.

BGS: Brigadier General Staff. Senior staff officer of the G (Operations, Intelligence, and Staff Duties) Staff. At the corps and army levels.

BM: Brigade Major. The senior G staff officer at the brigade level. Staff captain, staff officer on the A or Q staff under the DAAG or DAQMG at divisional level or DAA and QMG at brigade level.

CAOF: Canadian Army of Occupation.

CAS: Chief of the Air Staff.

CASF: Canadian Active Service Force.

CCRA: Commander Corps Royal Artillery. A brigadier.

CCRE: Commander Corps Royal Engineers.

CDS: Chief of the Defence Staff. An appointment made after Guy Simonds retired as CGS. The senior officer serving on the Chiefs of Staff Committee.

CE: Chief Engineer.

CEF: Canadian Expeditionary Force (1914-18).

CGS: Chief of the General Staff.

CIGS: Chief of the Imperial General Staff.

C-in-C: Commander-in-chief.

CMHQ: Canadian Military Headquarters (London).

CO: Commanding Officer.

COHQ: Combined Operations Headquarters.

COS: Chief of Staff. Chiefs of Staff Committee.

COSSAC: Chief of Staff to the Supreme Allied Commander.

CRA: Commander Royal Artillery. Senior artillery officer in a division. A brigadier.

CRE: Commander Royal Engineers in a division. A lieutenant colonel.

CREME: Commander Royal Electrical and Mechanical Engineers. A lieutenant colonel in a division.

CRSigs: Commander Royal Signals

CRU: Canadian Reinforcement Unit.

DAA and QMG: Deputy Assistant Adjutant and Quartermaster General of a brigade. A major responsible for A and Q staff functions.

DAAG and DAQMG: Deputy Assistant Adjutant General and Deputy Assistant Quartermaster General. Majors on the divisional staff responsible for A and Q functions respectively.

DND: Department of National Defence.

DOC: District Officer Commanding.

DS: Directing Staff.

DSO: Distinguished Service Order.

DUKW: A 2.5-ton amphibious troop or supply carrier.

ETO: European Theatre of Operations.

FFC: Field Force Conspectus.

GD: General Duty.

GHQ: General Headquarters.

GOC: General Officer Commanding a division or its equivalent.

GPO: Gun Position Officer.

GS: General Staff.

GSO I, II, and III: General Staff Officer at the lieutenant colonel, major, and captain ranks on the General Staff.

HQ: Headquarters.

IDC: Imperial Defence College.

IG: Instructor Gunnery.

KOYLI: King's Own Yorkshire Light Infantry.

LCA: Landing Craft Assault.

LCG: Landing Craft Gun.

LCT: Landing Craft Tank.

LVT: Landing Vehicle Tracked.

MTB: Motor Torpedo Boat.

MTC: Mechanized Transport Corps.

NAC: National Archives of Canada. Formerly PAC or Public Archives of Canada.

NATO: North Atlantic Treaty Organization.

NCO: Noncommissioned Officer.

NDHQ: National Defence Headquarters.

NPAM: Nonpermanent Active Militia.

NRMA: National Resources Mobilization Act.

OR: Other Ranks.

PF: Permanent Force.

PIAT: Projector Infantry Antitank.

PPCLI: Princess Patricia's Canadian Light Infantry.

Q Staff: Quartermaster General's Staff.

RAF: Royal Air Force.

RCA: Royal Canadian Artillery.

RCAF: Royal Canadian Air Force.

RCASC: Royal Canadian Army Service Corps.

RCEME: Royal Canadian Electrical and Mechanical Engineers.

RCHA: Royal Canadian Horse Artillery.
RCN: Royal Canadian Navy.
RCR: Royal Canadian Regiment.
RHC: Royal Highlanders of Canada.
RHLI: Royal Hamilton Light Infantry.
RHQ: Regimental Headquarters.
RMA: Royal Military Academy.
RMC: Royal Military College.
SAC: Supreme Allied Commander. Also Strategic Air Command.
SACEUR: Supreme Allied Commander Europe.
SCAEF: Supreme Commander Allied Expeditionary Force.
SHAEF: Supreme Headquarters Allied Expeditionary Force.
SHAPE: Supreme Headquarters Allied Powers Europe.
SNLO: Senior Naval Landing Officer.
SSR: South Saskatchewan Regiment.
SUO: Senior Under Officer.
TEWT: Tactical Exercise Without Troops.
UMS: Universal Military Service.
USAAF: United States Army Air Force.
WE: Wastage Estimate.

Bibliography

....

THE MAIN SOURCE for a biography should be the subject's personal papers, but Guy Simonds discarded many that a biographer requires. His collection, which is in the possession of his family, mainly consists of official documents, a few papers on subjects that concerned him from time to time, and some exchanges with colleagues on matters of mutual concern at the time.

Runs of correspondence are interesting and ease the work of a biographer. Apart from the short two-way correspondence between Crerar and Simonds over the "caravan incident," and with Foulkes over his appointment as CGS, none exist. He retained most of Bernard Montgomery's letters but did not keep copies of his own to Montgomery. Had Marshal Stearns not retained Simonds's letters there would be no record of their important correspondence after the war, since Simonds did not retain Stearns's letters. There are no Matthews, Rodger, or McNaughton letters in the papers. Sadly, but not surprisingly, there are no copies of his letters to K nor of Mona Anderson to him.

In fact, the collection is business only. His six chapters of prewar autobiography must have been written from memory soon after the war ended, for there are no documents in the collection to support his story. Although he told friends that he was at work on the war years, there are only fragmentary drafts and chapter plans in his papers to indicate it. The arrangement of the papers is basically chronological. The contents and arrangement of the files within the boxes do not suggest that he gave much thought to future publication. Indeed, he was overscrupulous in returning papers to the army historians that might have been useful to a future biographer.

The author may have given the reader the impression that he made bricks without straw. Happily that was not the case. The RG24 series, the Crerar and the Claxton Papers at the National Archives, helped to fill the gaps. The narratives written by the army historical officers in the field during the war, some of which were in the Simonds Papers while others were seen at the Directorate of History, were useful for adding colour and detail. The author was saved by colleagues who have been working on the period, particularly William McAndrew at the Directorate of History, Jack English, and Reg Roy, who shared their knowledge, papers, and tape recordings, which are extensive and contributed enormously to the result. To an even larger extent, initial interviews with key participants and, once the first drafts were ready, second interviews and written comments from interviewees filled the remaining gaps. The edifice slowly took shape from an unpromising start and dire warnings from those who knew about the shortcomings of the Simonds Papers.

In the bibliography that follows it was difficult for the author to draw lines between reading that he had done over the years for other books and his accumulated knowledge of how the army worked and of the events of the campaigns in which Simonds played a part. It will be obvious from the notes on which sources he has leaned most heavily.

The ground on which campaigns were fought is a vital document for writers. The author never visited Sicily, but the rest of the ground over which Simonds fought is familiar to him.

Primary Sources

Blumenson, Martin. *The European Theatre of Operations: Breakout and Pursuit.* Washington, D. C.: Office of the Chief of Military History, 1961.

Ellis, L. F. *History of the Second World War.* Vol. 2, *Victory in the West.* London: Her Majesty's Stationery Office, 1962.

MacDonald, Charles B. *The European Theater of Operations: The Siegfried Line Campaign.* Washington, D.C.: Office of the Chief of Military History, 1963.

Molony, C. J. C. *The Mediterranean and the Middle East.* Vol. 5, *The Campaign in Sicily, 1943 and the Campaign in Italy 3rd September 1943 to 31st March 1944.* London: HM Stationery Office, 1973.

Nicholson, Colonel G. W. L. *Official History of the Canadian Army in the Second World War.* Vol. 2, *The Canadians in Italy, 1943-45.* Ottawa: Queen's Printer, 1956.

———. *The Gunners of Canada: The History of the Royal Regiment of Canadian Artillery.* Vol. 2, *1919-1967.* Toronto: McClelland and Stewart, 1972.

Stacey, Colonel C. P. *Official History of the Canadian Army in the Second World War.* Vol. 1, *The Army in Canada, Britain, and the Pacific.* Ottawa: Queen's Printer, 1966. Vol. 3, *The Victory Campaign: The Operations in Northwest Europe, 1944-45.* Ottawa: Queen's Printer, 1960 and 1966.

———. *Arms, Men, and Governments: The War Policies of Canda, 1939-45.* Ottawa: Information Canada, 1974.

Memoirs

Bradley, Omar N., and Clay Blair. *A General's Life: An Autobiography by General of the Army Omar N. Bradley.* New York: Simon and Schuster, 1983.

Butcher, Harry C. *My Three Years with Eisenhower.* New York: Simon and Schuster, 1946.

Eisenhower, General Dwight D. *Crusade in Europe.* London: Heinemann, 1948.

Graham, Lieutenant General Howard. *Citizen and Soldier.* Toronto: McClelland and Stewart, 1987.

Horrocks, Lieutenant General Sir Brian. *Corps Commander.* London: Magnum, 1979.

Kitching, Major General George. *Mud and Green Fields: The Memoirs of Major General George Kitching.* Langley, B.C.: Battleline, 1986.

Malone, Colonel Dick. *Missing from the Record.* Toronto: Collins, 1946.

Stacey, C. P. *A Date with History: Memoirs of a Canadian Historian.* Ottawa: Deneau, 1983.

Tedder, Air Marshal Arthur. *With Prejudice.* Boston: Little, Brown, 1966.

Vokes, Major General Christopher, with John P. MacLean. *My Story.* Ottawa: Gallery, 1985.

Selected Secondary Sources

Bidwell, Shelford, and Dominick Graham. *Fire-Power: British Army Weapons and Theories of War, 1904-1945*. London: Allen and Unwin, 1982.

Burns, E. L. M. "A Division That Can Attack" and "Where Do the Tanks Belong?" *Canadian Defence Quarterly* 15 and 16 (April and October 1938).

Clausewitz, Carl von. *On War*. Ed. and trans. Michael Howard and Peter Paret. Princeton, NJ: Princeton University Press, 1976.

Copp, Terry, and William McAndrew. *Battle Exhaustion: Soldiers and Psychiatrists in the Canadian Army, 1939-1945*. Montreal: McGill-Queen's University Press, 1990.

Copp, Terry, and Robert Vogel. "No Lack of Rational Speed: 1st Canadian Army Operations, September 1944." *Journal of Canadian Studies* 16 (Autumn/Winter 1981).

D'Este, Carlo. *Decision in Normandy: The Unwritten Story of Montgomery and the Allied Campaign*. London: Pan, 1984.

————. *Bitter Victory: The Battle for Sicily, 1943*. London: Collins, 1988.

Eayrs, James. *In Defence of Canada*. 4 vols. Toronto: University of Toronto Press, 1964-1980.

Eisenhower, David. *Eisenhower at War 1943-1945*. New York: Random House, 1986.

English, John A. *The Canadian Army and the Normandy Campaign: A Study of Failure in High Command*. New York: Praeger, 1991.

————. *A Perspective on Infantry*. New York: Praeger, 1981.

Graham, Dominick, and Shelford Bidwell. *Coalitions, Politicians, and Generals: Problems of Command in the Two World Wars*. London: Brassey's, 1993.

Hamilton, Nigel. *Monty: The Making of a General; Master of the Battlefield 1942-1944; The Field Marshal 1944-1976*. London: Hamish Hamilton, 1981, 1983, and 1986 respectively.

Hutchinson, Lieutenant Colonel William E. "Test of a Corps Commander: Lieutenant General Guy Granville Simonds in Normandy, 1944." Unpublished M.A. thesis, University of Victoria, B.C., 1982.

McAndrew, W. J. "Fire or Movement? Canadian Tactical Doctrine, Sicily — 1943." *Military Affairs* 51 (July 1987).

————. "Stress Casualties," *Canadian Defence Quarterly* 17 (1987).

Roy, Reginald H. *1944: The Canadians in Normandy*. Toronto: Macmillan, 1984.

Simonds, Guy Granville. "An Army That Can Attack — a Division That Can Defend"; "What Price Assault without Support?"; "The Attack," *Canadian Defence Quarterly* 15 (July 1938); 16 (January 1939); 16 (July 1939) respectively.

Villa, Brian Loring. *Unauthorized Action: Mountbatten and the Dieppe Raid*. Toronto: Oxford University Press, 1990.

————. "Mountbatten, the British Chiefs of Staff, and Approval of the Dieppe Raid." *The Journal of Military History* 54 (April 1990).

Whitaker, W. Denis and Shelagh. *Tug of War: The Canadian Victory That Opened Antwerp*. Toronto: Stoddart, 1984.

————. *Rhineland: The Battle to End the War*. Toronto: Stoddart, 1989.

General Bibliography

Ahrenfeldt, Robert H. *Psychiatry in the British Army in the Second World War*. London: Routledge and Kegan Paul, 1958.

Belfield, Eversley, and H. Essame. *The Battle for Normandy.* London: Pan, 1983.

Bond, Brian. *British Military Policy between the Two World Wars.* Oxford: Clarendon Press, 1980.

Burns, E. L. M. *General Mud.* Toronto: Clarke Irwin, 1970.

———. *Manpower in the Canadian Army.* Toronto: Clarke Irwin, 1956.

Crosswell, D. K. R. *The Chief of Staff: The Military Career of General Walter Bedell Smith.* New York: Greenwood Press, 1991.

Graham, Dominick, and Shelford Bidwell. *Tug of War: The Battle for Italy: 1943-45.* London: Hodder and Stoughton, 1986.

Harris, Stephen J. *Canadian Brass: The Making of a Professional Army, 1860-1939.* Toronto: University of Toronto Press, 1988.

———. "The Canadian General Staff and the Higher Organization of Defence, 1919-1939." *War and Society* 3 (May 1985).

Hastings, Max. *Overlord: D-Day and the Battle for Normandy, 1944.* London: Michael Joseph, 1984.

Higham, Robin. *Armed Forces in Peacetime: Britain, 1918-1940.* Hamden, CT: Archon, 1962.

———. *The Military Intellectuals in Britain: 1918-1939.* New Brunswick, NJ: Rutgers University Press, 1966.

Howard, Sir Michael. *British Intelligence in the Second World War.* Vol. 5. London: HMSO, 1990.

Hull, Christopher. "A Case Study of Professionalism in the Canadian Army in the 1930s and 1940s: Lieutenant General G. G. Simonds." Unpublished M.A. thesis, Purdue University, May 1989.

Kellett, A. *Combat Motivation.* Boston: Kluwer-Nijhoff Publications, 1982.

MacDonald, Charles B. *A Time for Trumpets: The Untold Story of the Battle of the Bulge.* New York: William Morrow, 1985.

Marshall, S. L. A. *Men Against Fire.* New York: William Morrow, 1947.

McMahon, J. S. *Professional Soldier: A Memoir of General Guy Simonds, C.B., C.B.E., D.S.O., C.D.* Winnipeg: McMahon Investments, 1985.

Preston, Richard Arthur. *Canada's RMC: A History of the Royal Military College.* Toronto: University of Toronto Press, 1969.

Roy, Reginald H. *For Most Conspicuous Bravery: A Biography of Major General George R. Pearkes, V.C., Through Two World Wars.* Vancouver: University of British Columbia Press, 1977.

Smith, General W. Bedell. *Eisenhower's Six Great Decisions: Europe 1944-45.* New York: Longmans Green, 1956.

Spiller, R. "S. L. A. Marshall and the Ratio of Fire." *RUSI Journal* 133 (1988).

Swettenham, John. *McNaughton.* 3 vols. Toronto: Ryerson, 1968.

Terraine, John. *The Right of the Line: The Royal Air Force in the European War, 1939-45.* London: Hodder and Stoughton, 1985.

Weigley, Russell F. *Eisenhower's Lieutenants: The Campaign of France and Germany, 1944-45.* Bloomington, IN: Indiana University Press, 1981.

General Index

Index of Military Formations